THE COMPLETE BOOK OF

PLANT
PROPAGATION

THE COMPLETE BOOK OF
PLANT
PROPAGATION

MITCHELL BEAZLEY

The Complete Book of Plant Propagation
First published in 1997 by Mitchell Beazley,
an imprint of Reed International Books Limited,
Michelin House, 81 Fulham Road, London SW3 6RB
and Auckland and Melbourne

Executive editor: Guy Croton
Executive art editor: Ruth Hope
Editor: Michèle Byam
Designers: Martin Bristow, Debbie Myatt
Production: Rachel Lynch
Artwork: Vanessa Luff and Charlotte Wess

ISBN 1 85732 753 5

A CIP catalogue record for this book is available
from the British Library

Printed in China

CONTENTS

FOREWORD

The art of propagation is one that is often shrouded in mystique. While it is undoubtedly true that some gardeners have 'green fingers' and appear to increase their garden stock effortlessly, it is more often the case that the apparently green-fingered gardener merely has a good grasp of the basic principles involved and has practised the necessary skills.

The main theme of this book is the elucidation of these basic principles and each chapter deals with the way they can be modified to suit the needs of various plant groups, whether they be the simplest of annuals grown from seed, or more horticulturally developed plants – like apples and pears – that we cultivate as grafted trees in our gardens.

One of the first principles is to identify the nature of the plant material that you wish to propagate, for this usually dictates the frequency of propagation and gives guidance regarding the sorts of techniques that may be appropriate. Plants may be short-lived and ephemeral, like annuals and biennials, thus needing annual propagation. Or they may be, to all intents and purposes, permanent garden features, as are many trees and shrubs, which need propagating only once or twice during the life of the garden. A plant may be a herbaceous clump-former that lends itself ideally to division, or it may be woody and amenable to increase by a variety of different sorts of cuttings.

Some principles are immutable and apply across the whole range of propagating techniques and material – good hygiene and appropriate environmental conditions for rooting and growth, for example, are fundamental to success. Others, such as when is the best time to take cuttings, are variable, and success relies on following expert advice and applying one's own increasing experience.

It is nearly always true that there is more than one way to achieve a successful outcome, and where one method fails, another will surely succeed. Half of the satisfaction of gardening is learning skills and applying them to the diverse plants that we grow in our gardens. It is, after all, the willingness to experiment and to learn from both successes and failures that is one of the marks of a good gardener.

◄ *Glorious mixed plantings such as this are infinitely more satisfying to gardeners who have propagated their own plants and watched them grow to healthy and free-flowering maturity.*

ANNUALS AND BIENNIALS

One of the joys of gardening with annuals and biennials is that, with such an enormous range available, their use in gardens is limited only by the imagination. Their ease of propagation and cultivation, diversity and great adaptability has, deservedly, made them established favourites. Few other types of plants provide so much colour, or give as much pleasure in the garden – one of the most rewarding activities is to grow plants that you have raised yourself from seed. Annuals and biennials need little outlay on time or materials and they can, within a matter of weeks, create glorious living tapestries.

◄ *Because annuals and biennials flower, set seed and then die, plants such as* Tagetes, Cosmos *and* Verbena *will always need to be propagated by seed.*

WHY PROPAGATE
ANNUALS AND BIENNIALS?

Although by their very nature annuals and biennials are short-lived and must be propagated each year, they compensate by possessing an intensity of colour and profusion of bloom that is unsurpassed by any other group of plants. Given the right conditions, they are also among the simplest of plant groups to propagate.

This brilliant border contains plants grown from seeds that have a variety of different needs for successful germination.

Since true annuals and biennials are propagated from seed, the gardener does not have to make a decision on a preferred method of increase. There are, however, important considerations that dictate how, when and where to sow, if success is to be guaranteed.

RAISING HEALTHY ANNUALS

True annuals complete their life cycle in a single season, flowering, setting seed and dying in a few months. Hardy annuals, like *Calendula* and *Nigella*, will withstand some frost without damage and are sown directly in their flowering site in spring, or in autumn for earlier flowers the following year.

Temperatures below 0°C (32°F) cause damage to half-hardy annuals so they are usually raised under glass in spring and hardened off in a cold frame before being planted out, when danger of frost has completely passed.

These include *Lobelia erinus* and *Tagetes*, the African and French marigolds. Fast-growing half-hardy annuals may also be sown *in situ* in mid-spring.

Frost-tender annuals, such as *Cleome* (spider flower), need warm temperatures in order to thrive. They are sown – and grown on – under glass with additional heat, usually between late winter and early spring. Once they have reached a reasonable size, they are hardened off gradually and are only planted out into their flowering positions when all danger of frost has passed and warm summer weather is well established.

PLANNING FOR BIENNIALS

In their first year, biennials produce leaves and stems and, in the second, they flower, set seed and die. Often as showy as annuals, their use demands a little more planning, since they need to be established in their flowering site in the season before blooming (usually late summer or autumn). *Bellis perennis* (daisy) and *Myosotis* (forget-me-not) are well-known examples.

PERENNIALS AS ANNUALS

Plants that are treated as annuals or biennials include some that are perennial under natural conditions. Pelargoniums, for example, are treated as annuals because they are not reliably winter hardy in frost-prone climates. Garden pansies (*Viola × wittrockiana*), though cold hardy, are naturally short-lived perennials; they bloom most abundantly in their first year, but deteriorate rapidly thereafter. A third group includes such plants as *Helichrysum petiolare*, valued for its foliage, which is most attractive on young plants.

Selecting for Double Flowers

Matthiola, or stocks, have long been valued as cut flowers, especially in their double-flowered forms. Many modern cultivars produce a high proportion of double flowers; with some the seedlings may be selected to produce almost 100 per cent doubles. In some cases, only seedlings with yellow-green or pale-coloured seed leaves give rise to double flowers. Sow the seed at 13–18°C (55–64°F) and, on emergence of the seed leaves, lower the temperature to below 10°C (50°F). The difference in colour then becomes apparent and the dark-leaved seedlings should be discarded. In other cases, double flowers arise only from seedlings with distinctively notched seed leaves, so discard un-notched seedlings.

The beautiful 'Cinderella Mauve' is a good example of a *Matthiola* cultivar with double flowers.

Perennials that are used as annuals often need a long growing season to give of their best. Raise them from seed under glass in late winter with additional heat or, with plants such as *Felicia*, propagate them by stem tip cuttings in late summer, and overwinter the young plants in frost-free conditions under glass.

Pelargonium
Pelargoniums are tender subshrubby perennials that have traditionally been raised by stem tip cuttings overwintered under glass. Modern bedding pelargoniums offer the convenience of being raised annually from seed.

Impatiens
Frost-tender perennials like *Impatiens* are also raised annually from seed for bedding. Seed needs constant warmth for germination and young plants are hardened off and set out when danger of frost has passed.

Begonia
Begonias grown as annuals include the Semperflorens types that can be increased from seed or basal cuttings, and the tuberous Tuberhybrida types that may be grown from seed, or basal or stem cuttings.

Calendula
Hardy annuals, like pot marigolds, are among the easiest of plants that are grown as annuals. Seed can be sown in spring, or in autumn, to produce earlier flowers the following season.

11

PROPAGATING TECHNIQUES
ANNUALS AND BIENNIALS

Raising annuals and biennials from seed is one of the simplest of propagating techniques, but success depends on an understanding of the various conditions required by different types of plants for germination and growth, and on the observation of a few basic ground rules – especially with regard to good hygiene.

SELECTING AND BUYING SEED

Before purchasing, check the seed packet for a 'sow-by-date' to confirm that it is the current season's stock, thus ensuring freshness and viability. Most seed begins to lose viability or degenerate after a year, especially if not stored in cool, dry conditions.

The least expensive seed is produced by open – or natural – pollination. It yields offspring that exhibit natural variation – with slight differences in colour, size and habit. For most garden uses, this gives perfectly satisfactory results, and in informal plantings such subtle variations prove a positive advantage.

F1 hybrid seeds are produced by crossing two selected, pure-breeding parents to produce vigorous, uniform and floriferous offspring that come reliably true to colour, form and habit. F2 hybrids result from crossing selected F1 parents, and are equally vigorous but slightly less uniform. Both are more expensive than ordinary seed, but are ideal where uniformity or increased vigour is required, as with bedding.

Some hybrids are offered as pelleted seed, where individual seeds are coated with a nutrient and fungicidal paste. They are also more costly, but may be space-sown and so do not need wasteful thinning later.

Sowing in containers ....

Whether sowing in trays or pots, the technique is essentially the same. Always aim to sow thinly and evenly to permit adequate room for the seedlings to grow and develop freely. Overcrowding is a primary factor in damping off, and makes separating the seedlings at the pricking-out stage very difficult without causing damage to the stems and roots.

▶ **1** Fill the container by mounding the compost loosely, slightly above the container rim. Tap the container to remove air pockets. With the back of a presser board, level off the compost so that its surface is flush with the container rim. Firm gently with the presser board, so that the finished surface is about 1cm (½in) below the rim.

▶ **2** Sow seed thinly and evenly, tapping out seed gently from a folded piece of paper held just above the compost surface to avoid bouncing.

▶ **3** Just cover the seed with a thin layer of sieved compost. To water, place the seed container in about 1cm (½in) of water in a shallow tray. Remove immediately the water is seen at the compost surface.

▶ **4** Allow the tray to drain, and cover it with a sheet of glass to conserve moisture. Place a sheet of newspaper or shade netting on top of the glass to provide shade until germination occurs. Remove both glass and newspaper as soon as germination has taken place.

WHEN AND WHERE TO SOW

The site and timing of sowing varies according to climatic conditions and the type of plant involved.

Hardy annuals are sown in spring, directly into their flowering site or in containers in an open frame. Delay sowing if the conditions are unfavourable, for example, if spring is very cold or wet. Most will germinate at temperatures of 7–12°C (45–54°F), so begin sowing once the soil temperature reaches the lower end of this range; slightly higher temperatures speed germination. Some hardy annuals may be sown in open ground in autumn and will overwinter safely in all but the most severe winters. Sown this way, they flower earlier the following year.

Half-hardy and frost-tender annuals are sown in controlled conditions under glass. Sowings are made from late winter onwards, in gentle heat. As a general guide, most half-hardy annuals germinate within the range 15–21°C (59–70°F), and frost-tender plants between 18–24°C (64–75°F). Later sowings of half-hardy annuals can also be made in a cold frame but will need additional protection if frost threatens. Insulate the frame with sacking, removing this during the day to admit light.

Biennials are raised in the greenhouse or cold frame from late spring to midsummer (depending on the individual species' speed of growth). They are grown on, in containers or a nursery bed, to be planted in their flowering site in autumn. Alternatively, sow outdoors in a prepared seedbed, and transplant later. Hardy biennials will overwinter in the open without damage but, in severe weather, protect with cloches or horticultural fleece.

CHOOSING CONTAINERS

Unless large numbers of plants are needed, small containers, such as half pots or half trays, will contain sufficient seedlings for all but the largest plot.

Biodegradable pots, whether the individual or modular type, are ideal for sowing seedlings that will not transplant easily, since they can be planted out in their pots without root disturbance. Modular plastic trays are also used for planting out without root disturbance, as well as being convenient to use for sowing and pricking out, and less extravagant with compost (*see next page*).

Sowing outdoors . . . .

Prepare a seedbed by digging over to a spade's depth and removing any large stones and all weeds. Do this a few weeks before sowing so that the soil has time to settle back again. Firm the ground lightly and evenly, but not when the soil is wet as this will cause compaction. Apply a base dressing of general fertilizer only if the soil is poor; too rich a soil will produce foliage growth at the expense of flowers. Rake over the prepared seedbed to produce a fine even tilth to a depth of 2.5–5cm (1–2in).

Sowing in drills

▶ 1 Sowing seeds in shallow drills has the benefit that rows of germinating seedlings can clearly be distinguished from weed seedlings, whose distribution is random. Mark out the drill using a garden line stretched between canes. Draw out a shallow drill with the back of a hoe. A depth of 1cm (½in) suits most seeds; sow finer seeds more shallowly. If the soil is dry, water the drill carefully before sowing. Sow seed evenly and thinly along the drill.

▶ 2 Gently cover the seeds by drawing soil over them with a rake. Firm the surface of the drill with the back of the rake and water in.

Broadcasting

▶ 1 Rake the soil to an even tilth with parallel rake lines in one direction. Scatter the seed evenly and thinly over the surface.

◀ 2 Rake in the seed in a direction at right angles to the first. Rake very gently to avoid dislodging the seed.

GROUND RULES FOR SUCCESSFUL GERMINATION

The basic requirements for successful seed germination are sufficient air and moisture, a suitable compost and temperature regime, and appropriate light levels.

Light

Light is a vital factor in the germination processes of all plants. The seeds of such annuals as *Impatiens*, *Begonia* and *Petunia* need light to initiate germination, while other annuals require darkness, and many germinate in either light or dark. Germinated seedlings must have adequate light for development, if they are not to become weak and drawn (etiolated). In the initial stages, however, they also need to be shaded from direct sun to avoid scorching the leaves.

Sowing depth

Seeds range considerably in size. Seed size gives a reliable indication of the required sowing depth. As a general rule, seeds are covered to their own depth with compost that is sieved to ensure an intimate contact – the smaller the seed, the finer the covering. Exceptions are those that need light for germination; press these gently into the compost surface. To sow dust-fine seed evenly, mix it with a small quantity of fine, dry sand before surface-sowing.

Water

Seed needs adequate moisture to begin germination, and to maintain steady growth thereafter. Seed can be watered in with a fine rose after sowing, but overhead watering can wash seed to the sides of the container,

◀ Trays and half trays are ideal for sowing and pricking out large numbers of seeds, to use in bedding, for example. They are best used for seedlings that do not resent transplanting.

◀ Modular containers are perfect for seedlings that resent disturbance to the root ball and may be used for sowing and pricking out. They also use less compost than trays or pots.

◀ Plastic pots and half pots will hold sufficient seedlings for most purposes other than bedding. Biodegradable pots (*far left*) are planted out directly and do not cause any root disturbance at all.

causing harmful overcrowding on germination. It is just as effective to water from below – before sowing for very fine seed, or after sowing for larger seed. Water is drawn up by capillary action and, when it can just be seen at the surface, the compost is sufficiently moist. After sowing and germination, keep seeds and seedlings evenly moist, but never waterlogged; if they dry out, they will not germinate or grow on successfully.

Hygiene

Containers should be new or sterilized before use, and compost must be fresh. Do not sow seeds too thickly; seedlings need room to develop properly, and overcrowding increases susceptibility to the soil-borne fungal infection known as 'damping off (botrytis), which is usually fatal. Risk of damping off is also increased by poor ventilation; maintain a flow of fresh air around the young seedlings at all times. Water with tap water rather than with rain water from a water butt, as this can be a source of fungal infection. Apply a proprietary fungicide before sowing, and when watering seedlings, as a preventive measure against damping off.

Hardening off

Plants raised under controlled and sheltered conditions under glass must be hardened off – or acclimatized – before planting out. Six weeks before planting out, when the pricked-out seedlings are growing on well, transfer them to a cooler section of the greenhouse for about seven days, then move them to a covered cold frame. Gradually increase the ventilation by opening the frame lights a little more, and for a little longer, each day. Keep an eye on the weather forecast and, if frost threatens, close the frame lights and insulate the cold frame. You sholud aim to avoid any sudden and extreme changes of temperature, as this can lead to a check in growth, or in severe cases, to the death of the young plants. After two to three weeks, the plants will be sufficiently hardened off to be ready to plant out.

Thinning

Thin the germinated seedlings to the recommended planting distances for the species concerned. Remove excess seedlings by hand, taking great care to avoid root disturbance to the remainder.

Pricking out ....

Seeds sown in containers should be transferred, or pricked out, into larger containers before they become overcrowded.

► I When seedlings are large enough to handle, prick out into a more fertile compost, to give them more space to develop. First, water the seed tray and allow to drain. Then, tap it gently on the work bench to loosen the compost. Ease individual seedlings carefully from the seed tray using a dibber or spatula, retaining as much soil around the roots as possible. Handle them only by their seed leaves, to avoid damage to roots, stem and growing tips.

◄ 2 Dibble a hole in the tray of prepared compost, and lower the seedling gently into it, so that it is at the same depth as it was in the seed tray. Firm in carefully with the dibber and water in using a fine rose.

Marking out an annual border ....

▲ To create an annual border, draw a plan on paper, arranging drifts of different varieties according to their colour and height. Mark the outlines of informal drifts on the ground using fine sand. Then, sow the seed in rows within the marked-out drift areas. Align the rows in different directions in neighbouring drifts. Seedlings are easier to weed when they are in rows, and the lines will not be apparent when the plants mature. Finally, carefully rake the soil over to cover the seeds. Firm and water in thoroughly.

DIRECTORY OF
ANNUALS AND BIENNIALS

Below are key tips on a selection of annuals and biennials that are particularly suitable for propagation. Unless otherwise specified, follow the detailed instructions given under the propagation section on pages 12–15.

Key

HA	Hardy annual
HHA	Half-hardy annual
FTA	Frost-tender annual
HB	Biennial
HHB	Half-hardy biennial
FTB	Frost-tender biennial
H	Height
S	Spread
🌱	By seed
⚥	Germination
☀	Time to flowering
⚒	By division

Amaranthus — Amaranthaceae

About 60 species of annuals or short-lived perennials with pendent tassels of flowers.
A. caudatus (Love-lies-bleeding, Tassel flower). Bushy annual with crimson tassels, to 60cm (2ft) long, from midsummer until frosts. **'Viridis'** has green tassels. Easily grown in a sunny, sheltered moist site. Water freely in dry periods. HHA.
H 60–120cm (2–4ft), S to 75cm (22ft).

PROPAGATION
🌱 under glass in early spring at 18–24°C (64–75°F).
⚥ 7–14 days. ☀ 3–4 months.

Antirrhinum (Snapdragon)
Scrophulariaceae

Up to 40 species of annuals, perennials, and semi-evergreen subshrubs with distinctive two-lipped flowers, often borne in showy spikes. *A. majus*, a short-lived perennial, is commonly grown as an annual.
A. majus. Bushy and branching with erect spikes of showy flowers from summer to autumn. Among the many cultivars available there are dwarf forms, intermediates, and tall forms. Easily grown in fertile, well-drained soil in sun. HHA.

PROPAGATION
🌱 surface-sow under glass in early spring, at 13–16°C (55–61°F).
⚥ 10–21 days. ☀ 3–4 months.

Arctotis — Compositae

About 50 species of annuals and herbaceous perennials with daisy-like, brightly coloured, often zoned flowers. The perennials are often grown as annuals.
A. venusta, syn. *A. stoechadifolia* (African blue daisy). Spreading perennial grown as an annual for its creamy white flowers, with central blue discs, from midsummer to early autumn. FTA. H 60cm (24in), S 40cm (16in).

A. **Harlequin Hybrids** (syn. *A. × hybrida*) Are similar, but with a wide colour range. Perfect for borders and cut flowers. Grow in light, well-drained soil in sun. Deadhead regularly to prolong flowering. FTA.
H 45–60cm (18–24in), S 30cm (12in).

PROPAGATION
🌱 under glass in late winter to early spring, at 16–21°C (61–70°F). Alternatively, sow in autumn and overwinter young plants under glass at a minimum of 5–7°C (41–45°F).
⚥ 10–21 days. ☀ 4 months.

Bellis (Daisy) — Compositae

Some 15 species of herbaceous perennials with rosettes of spoon-shaped leaves and daisy-like flowers; the flowers are borne singly on long stems.
B. perennis (Double daisy). Grown as a perennial. Compact plant with single, semi- or fully double flowers, from late winter to summer. **'Pomponette'** has pompon-like blooms. Deadhead to stop self-seeding. Grow in well-drained soil in sun or part-shade. HB. H to 20cm (8in), S to 20cm (8in).

PROPAGATION
🌱 under glass from spring to midsummer at 10–13°C (50–55°F), or in drills outdoors in early summer.
⚥ 7–21 days. ☀ 6–8 months.
⚒ after flowering or in spring.

Bidens — Compositae

Some 200 annuals, herbaceous perennials and deciduous shrubs with attractive flower heads on long stems. The short-lived perennials are usually grown as annuals in frost-prone areas.
B. ferulifolia. Grown as an annual for its ferny foliage and bright, star-shaped, golden yellow flowers borne from early summer to autumn. **'Golden Goddess'** has finer leaves

Antirrhinum majus

Bellis perennis 'Pomponette'

Calendula officinalis

Callistephus chinensis

Centaurea cyanus

and larger flowers. Needs moist but well-drained soil and a sunny site. HHA.
H 30cm (12in), S indefinite.

PROPAGATION
under glass in early spring at 13–18°C (55–64°F).
10–21 days. 3 months.

Bracteantha (Strawflower)   Compositae

About seven species of annuals and short-lived herbaceous perennials, usually grown as annuals, with papery, daisy-like flower heads that are good often for drying.
Bracteantha bracteata, syn. *Helichrysum bracteatum.* Upright plant bearing everlasting, glistening flower heads, from midsummer until frosts. Dwarf forms and taller cultivars are available. Easy in well-drained soil in sun. HHA. H 15–75cm (6–30in), S 30cm (12in).

PROPAGATION
in situ, in drills, in mid-spring. Alternatively, sow in trays or biodegradable pots, under glass, in early spring, at 16–18°C (61–64°F).
10–20 days. 4 months.

Calendula (Marigold)   Compositae

Up to 30 species of bushy annuals and evergreen perennials with aromatic leaves and daisy-like flower heads.
C. officinalis (Pot marigold). Annual with flower heads in shades of orange, yellow, and cream, often with dark central discs. All are free-flowering from early summer to autumn, and thrive in any well-drained soil in sun or part-shade. HA.
H 30–60cm (1–2ft), S 30–45cm (12–18in).

PROPAGATION
under glass in early spring at 13–18°C (55–64°F), or in drills *in situ* in spring or

autumn. Provide cloche protection for autumn-sown seedlings in cold areas.
7–21 days. 3–6 months.

Callistephus (China aster)   Compositae

A single, fast-growing, bushy annual species.
C. chinensis. Single to double flower heads, in shades of white, pink, crimson, and indigo, are borne from late summer until first frosts. A wide range of cultivars is offered, with compact or dwarf types and taller cultivars. They need a sheltered, sunny site in moist but well-drained soil. Provide support for tall cultivars and deadhead regularly to prolong the flowering period. China asters are susceptible to aster wilt and various other wilts; do not grow in the same site in consecutive years. HHA.
H 25–60cm (10–24in), S 25–30cm (10–12in).

PROPAGATION
under glass from early to mid-spring at 13–16°C (55–61°F).
10–14 days. 4 months.

Centaurea   Compositae

About 450 species of annuals, biennials, perennials and subshrubs bearing rounded flower heads consisting of tubular, deeply cut florets. The leaves are sometimes silver-hairy.
C. cyanus (Cornflower). Upright, slender-leaved annual with delicate florets of blue, pink, white, rose, red, or purple around darker central discs. Flowers are produced from late spring to midsummer. Dwarf and taller cultivars are available. Provide taller cultivars with light twiggy support. Grow in any well-drained soil in a sunny position. HA.
H 20cm–1.2m (8in–4ft), S 15–25cm (6–10in).

PROPAGATION
in situ, in drills or broadcast, from early to mid-spring or in autumn. Alternatively, sow in biodegradable pots; avoid root disturbance.
10–14 days. 3–6 months.

Clarkia   Onagraceae

Some 36 species of thin-stemmed annuals with satiny, papery flowers in pale shades.
C. amoena, syn. *Godetia amoena* (Satin flower). Upright annual with fluted, satin-textured flowers in shades of lilac to deep pink, throughout summer. HA. H 75cm (30in), S 30cm (12in).
C. unguiculata, syn. *C. elegans* (Godetia). Slender annual bearing masses of miniature flowers throughout summer, in shades of salmon, pink, lavender, purple, red or white. HA. H to 90cm (3ft), S 30cm (12in).
Both are easily grown in moist but well-drained, preferably slightly acid soil in sun or part-shade. Provide light, twiggy support.

PROPAGATION
sow *in situ,* in drills or broadcast, from early to mid-spring or in autumn. Provide cloche protection for autumn-sown seedlings. They do not tolerate transplanting.
10–21 days. 3–6 months.

Cleome (Spider flower)   Capparidaceae

Some 150 species of bushy annuals and evergreen shrubs. The annuals are grown for their attractive, spider-like flowers with long, prominent stamens.
C. hassleriana, syn. *C. pungens, C. spinosa.* Upright, bushy annual with spider-like flowers in delicate shades of pink, rose and white, throughout summer. Young plants are very susceptible to greenfly. Needs light,

17

Cleome hassleriana

Dianthus barbatus

Eschscholtzia californica

well-drained soil and a sheltered sunny site.
FTA. H 1–1.2m (3–4ft), S 45cm (18in).

PROPAGATION
🌱 under glass in early spring, at 18–20°C
(64–68°F).
🌱 10–21 days.   ☀ 4 months.

Cosmos   Compositae
Some 25 species of annuals and herbaceous
perennials with showy flower heads borne
on long, slender stems.
C. bipinnatus (Cosmea). Slender annual with
delicately divided foliage and single or double
flowers, some with fluted petals, in shades of
white, rose, pink, and crimson, borne from
midsummer until the first frosts. HHA.
H 90–120cm (3–4ft), S. 45cm (18in).

PROPAGATION
🌱 under glass from late winter to early
spring, at 18–20°C (64–68°F).
🌱 7–14 days.   ☀ 5 months.

Dianthus (Pink)   Caryophyllaceae
Over 300 species of annuals, biennials,
perennials and evergreen subshrubs with
linear, blue-grey leaves and rounded flowers
which are often scented.
D. chinensis (Indian pink). Compact, free-
flowering biennials or perennials grown as
annuals. They have single, fringed flowers
throughout summer in shades of pink,
crimson, scarlet, rose and white, including
bicolours with laced patterns or 'eyed'
centres. Plant in well-drained, neutral to
alkaline soil in sun. HHA.
H to 70cm (28in), S 25cm (10in).

PROPAGATION
🌱 under glass from late winter to early
spring, at 18–25°C (64–77°F).

🌱 10–25 days.   ☀ 4 months.
D. barbatus (Sweet William). Short-lived
perennial which is grown as a biennial. It
produces dense, flattened heads of small
flowers, in shades of crimson, rose, carmine,
salmon, pink, and white, including many
bicolours, from late spring to early summer,
or in mid- to late summer from early spring
sowings. Grow in well-drained, neutral to
alkaline soil in a sunny site. HB.
H 15–70cm (6–28in), S 30cm (12in).

PROPAGATION
🌱 in drills in a prepared seedbed, between
spring and midsummer or in autumn.
Alternatively, sow under glass in early spring
at 15–18°C (59–64°F), to flower in the
same year.
🌱 14–30 days.   ☀ 5–9 months.

Erysimum (Wallflower)   Cruciferae
Some 80 species of annuals and biennials
and mostly evergreen perennials with
racemes of flat flowers and lance-shaped
leaves. The flowers are often fragrant.
E. cheiri, syn. *Cheiranthus cheiri.* Short-lived,
spring-flowering perennial grown as a
biennial. The plants are compact and have
usually sweetly scented flowers in shades
of yellow, orange, scarlet, rose, pink, cream,
and white. Grow in well-drained, neutral
to alkaline soil in sun. HB.
H 25–75cm (10–30in), S 30cm (12in).

PROPAGATION
🌱 in drills in a seedbed, between late
spring and early summer. Transplant to
flowering site in autumn. Alternatively, sow
in autumn and provide cloche protection
over the winter.
🌱 14 days.   ☀ 9–10 months.

Eschscholtzia (California poppy)
Papaveraceae
Up to 10 species of annuals and perennials
with divided, light green to blue-green leaves
and poppy-like, shallow, cup-shaped flowers,
singly, often on slender stems.
E. californica. Spreading annual with finely
divided foliage and satin-textured, single
or semi-double flowers, in shades of gold,
yellow, bronze, orange, scarlet, rose, or white,
borne from midsummer until first frosts.
Easily grown in not too fertile, well-drained
soil in sun. HA. H 30cm (12in), S 15cm (6in).

PROPAGATION
🌱 in drills or broadcast, *in situ,* in mid-spring
or early autumn. Provide cloche protection
overwinter for autumn-sown seedlings. They
do not tolerate transplanting.
🌱 14–21 days.   ☀ 3–7 months.

Felicia   Compositae
Some 80 species of annuals, perennials and
evergreen subshrubs, or sometimes shrubs,
with daisy-like, mainly blue flower heads
F. amelloides (Blue daisy). Bushy subshrub,
grown as an annual for its abundant, pale to
deep blue daisies, throughout summer. FTA.
H to 60cm (2ft), S to 60cm (2ft).
F. bergeriana (Kingfisher daisy). Bushy,
spreading annual with narrow, grey-green
leaves, bearing a profusion of yellow-centred,
bright blue daisy flowers throughout summer.
It is very wind tolerant. HHA. H 20cm (8in),
S 20cm (8in). Both the above are easily
grown in any well-drained soil in sun.

PROPAGATION
🌱 under glass in early spring, at 18–20°C
(64–68°F).
🌱 14–30 days.   ☀ 4 months.

Felicia amelloides

Helianthus annuus

Lathyrus odoratus

Stem tip cuttings – for *F. amelloides* in late summer. Overwinter young plants in frost-free conditions under glass.
☀ 6–8 months.

Gypsophila (Baby's breath)
Caryophyllaceae

More than 100 species of annuals and herbacous, semi-evergreen or evergreen perennials, sometimes with a woody base, bearing small, delicate flowers, often in large, loose, cloud-like masses.
G. elegans. Graceful open, branching annual, with grey-green leaves, bearing myriad tiny white flowers in summer. Variants with pink or carmine flowers are available. Grow in sun in light, very well-drained, preferably alkaline soil. Provide light twiggy support. HA. H 60cm (2ft), S 45cm. (18in).

PROPAGATION
❦ in drills or broadcast, *in situ*, in mid-spring or early autumn. Provide cloche protection over the winter for autumn-sown seedlings. Dislikes being transplanted.
❦ 7–21 days.   ☀ 3–7 months.

Helianthus (Sunflower)
Compositae

Some 80 species of annuals and perennials. The genus is best known for its tall, rough-leaved plants that produce large showy flower heads so popular with children.
H. annuus. Rapidly growing annual bearing daisy-like flowers in mid- to late summer, each with a large central disc surrounded by golden or lemon-yellow, orange or red-bronze ray florets. They range from dwarf types to giants. Grow in well-drained, fertile soil in a sunny site. Give tall cultivars support. HA. H 45cm–3m (18in–10ft), S 60cm (30in).

PROPAGATION
❦ *in situ*, in drills or broadcast, in spring. Alternatively, sow in biodegradable pots under glass in late winter at 16–18°C (61–64°F).
❦ 7–21 days.   ☀ 3–4 months.

Helichrysum
Compositae

Some 500 species of annuals, herbaceous or evergreen perennials, and evergreen shrubs and subshrubs. Some are foliage plants, with insignificant flowers, others have pretty daisy-like or fluffy flower heads.
H. petiolare syn. *H. petiolatum.* Freely branching shrub with trailing stems and heart-shaped, woolly-hairy leaves, grown as a foliage annual. **'Limelight'** has lime-green leaves. **'Variegatum'** is cream-variegated. Grow in well-drained soil in sun. HHA. H to 50cm (20in), S 1m (3ft) or more.

PROPAGATION
Semi-ripe cuttings – in summer. Overwinter young plants in frost-free conditions under glass.   ☀ 3–4 months.

Impatiens
Balsaminaceae

Varied genus of 850 species of annuals and evergreen shrubs and subshrubs with succulent stems and leaves.
I. walleriana (Busy Lizzie). This compact, spreading perennial is grown as an annual, very commonly for its flat, bright flowers. Modern hybrids, with green or bronze leaves, bear single or double flowers in a wide colour range, including red, pink, purple, salmon, orange, and white, from summer until first frosts. Easily grown in a sheltered site in light shade or sun, in moist but well-drained soil. FTA. H and S to 60cm (24in).

PROPAGATION
❦ surface-sow under glass in late winter or early spring, at 18–21°C (64–70°F).
❦ 10–21 days.   ☀ 4 months.
Stem tip cuttings – in summer. Overwinter young plants under glass at 10°C (50°F).
☀ 6 months.

Lathyrus
Leguminosae

Some 150 species of often climbing annuals and herbaceous or evergreen perennials valued for their showy, often scented flowers.
L. odoratus (Sweet pea). Climbing annual with often highly perfumed, pea-like flowers, some with frilled petals, and in a colour range including reds, pinks, blue, lavender, salmon, cream and white. As well as the tall varieties there are also dwarf types, some of which are non-climbing, which need little or no support and can be used for making flowering hedges. Tall varieties need training on canes or other supports. Easy in fertile, humus-rich, well-drained soil. HA. H 60cm–2m (2–6ft) or more, S 30–45cm (12–18in).

PROPAGATION
❦ *in situ*, in drills, in spring or autumn. Provide cloche protection for autumn-sown seedlings in open ground, or place container-sown seedlings in a cold frame. Alternatively, sow in biodegradable pots or sweet-pea tubes under glass in late winter or early spring, at 15°C (59°F). Sweet peas have hard seed coats and benefit from chipping or abrading before sowing. They may also be soaked; do not cover with water and sow immediately the seed swells. If soaked too long they are very prone to rotting.
❦ 10–20 days.   ☀ 3–4 months.

19

Limnanthes douglasii

Limonium sinuatum

Linum grandiflorum

Limnanthes — Limnanthaceae

About 17 species of low-growing annuals, but only *L. douglasii* is usually grown.

L. douglasii (Meadow foam, Poached egg flower). Very free-flowering annual with finely divided foliage and cupped, white-edged, yellow flowers, throughout summer and autumn. Attracts bees and other beneficial insects to the garden. Grow in any soil in sun. HA. H 15cm (6in), S 15cm (6in) or more.

PROPAGATION
🌱 *in situ*, in drills or broadcast, in spring or autumn. Self-seeds freely.
🌾 10–20 days.   ☀ 3–4 months.

Limonium (Sea lavender) — Plumbaginaceae

Some 150 species of annuals, biennials, and deciduous and evergreen perennials and subshrubs with distinctive papery flowers, often carried on leafless, winged stems. Grow in sun in well-drained soil.

L. sinuatum. Upright perennial grown as an annual with rosettes of basal leaves and winged stems with flat heads of tiny, funnel-shaped, papery flowers from mid- to late summer or early autumn. HHA. H 60cm (2ft), S 30cm (12in).

PROPAGATION
🌱 under glass in early spring, at 16–18°C (61–64°F). After planting out, water in young plants thoroughly and keep moist until well established. They are fairly drought tolerant once established.
🌾 10–20 days.   ☀ 4–5 months.

Linaria (Toadflax) — Scrophulariaceae

About 100 species of annuals, biennials, and herbaceous perennials with two-lipped, spurred flowers and often grey-green leaves.

L. maroccana. Bushy, mound-forming annual bearing masses of tiny, snapdragon-like blooms in summer. Cultivars have flowers in bright shades, including many bicolours. Needs light, well-drained soil and sun. Deadhead to prolong flowering. HA. H 25–45cm (10–18in), S 15cm (6in).

PROPAGATION
🌱 *in situ*, in drills or broadcast, in spring.
🌾 14–21 days.   ☀ 2–3 months.

Linum (Flax) — Linaceae

Some 200 species of annuals, biennials, perennials, shrubs and subshrubs, some evergreen, with funnel- to saucer-shaped, five-petalled flowers.

L. grandiflorum 'Rubrum' (Scarlet flax). Erect, slender annual with grey-green leaves and red-crimson flowers from midsummer to autumn. Needs light, well-drained soil in sun. HA. H 40–45cm (16–18in), S 15cm (6in).

PROPAGATION
🌱 *in situ*, in drills or broadcast, in spring or early autumn. Dislikes root disturbance.
🌾 14–30 days.   ☀ 3 or 8 months.

Lobelia — Campanulaceae

Some 370 annuals, perennials, and shrubs with bright, two-lipped, tubular flowers. They range from trailing types to upright plants. Grow in moist soil in sun or partial shade.

L. erinus. Trailing to bushy perennial, grown as an annual with masses of small, variously coloured flowers, from summer to autumn. HHA. H 10–25cm (4–10in), S 15cm (6in).

PROPAGATION
🌱 under glass, in late winter or early spring, at 16–18°C (61–64°F).
🌾 14–21 days.   ☀ 3–4 months.

Lobularia (Sweet alyssum) — Cruciferae

Just five species of annuals or perennials with rounded clusters of tiny flowers.

L. maritima, syn. *Alyssum maritimum.* Annual forming compact mounds of grey-green foliage that are heavily studded with heads of dainty, sweetly scented, usually white flowers, in summer. Cultivars have flowers in shades of purple, lavender and rose. Needs light, well-drained soil and sun. Deadhead to encourage further flower production. HA. H 15cm (6in), S 15cm (6in).

PROPAGATION
🌱 surface-sow under glass, in late winter or early spring, at 16–18°C (61–64°F), or *in situ* in spring.
🌾 14 days.   ☀ 3–4 months.

Matthiola (Stock) — Cruciferae

Some 55 species of annuals, perennials and subshrubs with often grey-grey leaves and usually scented, pastel-coloured flowers.

M. incana (Brompton stock). Bushy, often short-lived perennial with spires of usually highly scented flowers in soft pure colours. Various cultivars are grown as annuals or biennials. Grow in moist but well-drained soil in a sheltered site in sun. HA/HB. H to 80cm (32in), S to 40cm (16in).

Brompton stocks have single or double flowers in spring and early summer. Biennials.
East Lothian stocks flower in spring or early summer, or in summer. Biennials or annuals.
10-week stocks usually have double flowers in summer, about ten weeks from sowing. There are dwarf and tall cultivars. Annuals.
Column stocks are tall, with double flowers specially bred for cutting. The best flowers are produced in a cool greenhouse.

Moluccella laevis

Nemophila menziesii

Nicotiana alata

Some strains can be selected at the seedling stage to give all double flowers. Refer to the individual seed packets for specific advice (*see also p. 11*).

PROPAGATION

Biennials

🌱 surface-sow under glass, in midsummer, at 13–18°C (55–64°F). Provide cloche or cold-frame protection over the winter.

🌱 10–14 days.   ☀ 8 months.

Annuals

🌱 under glass in early spring at 13–18°C. (55–64°F).

🌱 10–14 days.   ☀ 10–12 weeks.

Moluccella   Labiatae

Only four species of annuals and short-lived perennials with four-sided stems and unusual large, conspicuous calyces that surround tiny, tubular flowers.

M. laevis (Bells of Ireland, Shell flower). Erect annual, in late summer bearing spikes of tiny flowers with papery, pale green calyces. Grow in well-drained soil in sun. HA. H 60cm (24in), S 25cm (10in).

PROPAGATION

🌱 under glass, in early spring. After sowing, pre-chill for 2 weeks in the bottom of a domestic refrigerator, then germinate at 16–18°C (61–64°F).

🌱 14–21 days.   ☀ 4–5 months.

Myosotis (Forget-me-not)   Boraginaceae

Over 50 annuals, biennials, and perennials bearing small flowers often with paler 'eyes'.

M. sylvatica. Tufted biennial with dense clusters of tiny, yellow-eyed, clear blue flowers in spring and early summer. Several cultivars of various heights are available,

mainly in shades of blue, but there are some white- or pink-flowered variants. Needs moist but well-drained soil in a sunny or lightly shaded site. HB. H to 30cm (12in), S to 15cm (6in).

PROPAGATION

🌱 either under glass, in early summer, at 15–20°C (59–68°F), or in drills in a seedbed outdoors. Will self-seed, but cultivars may not come true.

🌱 14–30 days.   ☀ 6–7 months.

Nemesia   Scrophulariaceae

Over 50 species of annuals, perennials, and subshrubs with showy two-lipped flowers, the lower lip being the most prominent.

N. strumosa. Free-flowering, bushy annual with a profusion of flowers, from mid- to late summer, in shades of red, pink, purple, blue, yellow, orange and white. Easily grown in moist but well-drained, preferably slightly acid soil, in a sunny site. Water freely in dry weather. HHA. H 20–30cm (8–12in), S 10–15cm (4–6in).

PROPAGATION

🌱 under glass, in early to mid-spring, at 18–21°C (64–70°F).

🌱 7–21 days.   ☀ 3–4 months.

Nemophila   Hydrophyllaceae

Some 11 annual, spreading, fleshy-stemmed species, sometimes with sticky hairs, bearing saucer- to bell-shaped flowers.

N. menziesii, syn. *N. insignis* (Baby blue-eyes). Low-growing annual with finely divided leaves and saucer-shaped, white-eyed, sky-blue flowers during summer. Needs moist but well-drained soil and sun or light shade. HA. H 15–25cm (6–10in), S 30cm (12in).

PROPAGATION

🌱 *in situ*, in drills or broadcast, in spring or early autumn. Dislikes root disturbance. Self-seeds freely.

🌱 14–21 days.   ☀ 3 or 8 months.

Nicotiana (Tobacco plant)   Solanaceae

Nearly 70 species of annuals, biennials, perennial, and shrubs bearing long-tubed flowers with spreading mouths, usually opening only in the evening and at night.

N. alata, syn. *N affinis*. Rosette-forming perennial, grown as a free-flowering annual for its racemes of evening-opening, scented, funnel-shaped, pale yellow-green flowers, produced over long periods in summer. HHA. H 1.2–1.5m (4–5ft), S 30cm (12in).

N. x sanderae cultivars. Bear flowers in shades of purple, rose, crimson, lime-green, red and white. They vary from tall, open-growing types to more compact variants. Flowers remain open during the day. HHA. H 40–90cm (16–36in), 30cm (12in). Both need fertile, moist but well-drained soil, in sun or part-shade.

PROPAGATION

🌱 surface-sow under glass, late winter or early spring, at 18–21°C (64–70°F).

🌱 7–21 days.   ☀ 4–5 months.

Nigella   Ranunculaceae

Twenty species of annuals with feathery leaves and flowers often surrounded by a ruff of hair-like leaves, followed by decorative, sometimes inflated, seed pods.

N. damascena (Love-in-a-mist). Bushy annual with bright green foliage and blue, rose-pink, or white flowers in summer, followed by inflated seed pods. Easily grown in any

Petunia 'Fantasy Mixed'

Rudbeckia hirta

Salvia 'Red Arrow'

well-drained soil in a sunny position. HA.
H 45cm, S 25cm (10in).

PROPAGATION

🌱 *in situ*, in drills or broadcast, in spring or
early autumn. Self-seeds freely.

🌱 10–25 days. ☀ 3–8 months.

Pelargonium (Geranium) Geraniaceae

About 230 species of perennials, succulents,
subshrubs and shrubs, most of which are
evergreen. They have often showy clusters
of flowers and rounded to ivy-shaped,
sometimes aromatic leaves.

There are many cultivars of *Pelargonium*,
including modern bedding types which are
compact, with rounded, mid-green leaves,
often with a bronze or green-bronze, central
zone. They bear heads of single or semi-
double flowers in many shades, from spring
to first frosts. Many excellent F1 and F2
hybrids are available. These seed-raised
cultivars bloom exceptionally freely in their
first year from seed, and so do not have to
be overwintered. Older cultivars, which
cannot be guaranteed to come true from
seed, are easily raised annually from cuttings.
Protect double-flowered, old cultivar types
from rain, or grow them indoors. Grow in
fertile, well-drained soil with shelter and sun.
FTA. H to 60cm (24in), S to 30cm (12in).

PROPAGATION

🌱 under glass, in late winter, at 21–24°C
(70–75°F). Maintain a constant temperature
after sowing as temperature fluctuations
cause delayed or aborted germination.

🌱 3–21 days. ☀ 3–4 months.

Stem tip cuttings – in spring, summer or
early autumn. Overwinter well-rooted
cuttings at a minimum of 5°C (41°F).

Petunia Solanaceae

Up to 40 species of sticky-haired annuals or
herbaceous perennials with delicate, scented,
saucer- or trumpet-shaped, showy flowers.

P. x *hybrida.* Spreading, free-flowering annuals
with single or double, trumpet-shaped
flowers, in many shades, including veined,
picotée and star-marked types. Petunias
bloom throughout summer. **Grandiflora**
types have very large flowers that are easily
spoiled by rain and wind; **Multiflora types**
have smaller flowers, in greater profusion,
and are more weather-resistant. Grow in
light, well-drained soil, in a sheltered sunny
site. Deadhead to prolong the flowering
period. HHA. H 25–40cm (10–16in),
S to 90cm (36in).

PROPAGATION

🌱 surface-sow under glass, late winter, at
16–21°C (61–70°F). Do not discard the
smallest seedlings when pricking out; they
often have the most intense flower colours.

🌱 14 days. ☀ 4–5 months.

Phlox Polemoniaceae

Approximately 67 annuals, herbaceous and
evergreen perennials, and a few shrubs with
often profuse, salverform flowers.

P. drummondii (Annual phlox). Mound-
forming, free-flowering annual bearing
clusters of flowers in a range of bright
colours, many with a distinct eye. They give a
continuous display from late spring until the
first frost. Grow in any well-drained soil in
sun. HHA. H to 40cm (16in), S 25cm (10in).

PROPAGATION

🌱 under glass, in early spring, at 18–20°C
(64–68°F).

🌱 14 days. ☀ 3–4 months.

Rudbeckia Compositae

Some 20 species of annuals, biennials, and
herbaceous perennials bearing large daisy-
like flower heads with cone-shaped centres.

R. hirta, syn. *R. gloriosa* (Black-eyed Susan,
Gloriosa daisy). Short-lived perennial grown
as an annual, bearing masses of large single
or double flowers from summer to autumn.
They range from golden and lemon-yellow
to rich bronze and mahogany, including
bicolours. Needs fertile, well-drained soil
in a site with sun or part-shade. HA.
H to 90cm (36in), S 45cm (18in).

PROPAGATION

🌱 under glass, in late winter or early spring,
at 16–18°C (61–64°F).

🌱 7–21 days. ☀ 4–5 months.

Salpiglossis Solanaceae

Just two species of annuals or short-lived
perennials with sticky-haired stems and
leaves and trumpet-shaped flowers.

S. sinuata (Painted tongue). Upright annual
bearing exotically coloured, heavily veined,
trumpet-shaped flowers from summer to
autumn, in many shades. Performs best in
warm, dry summers as the flowers are easily
spoiled by rain. They are also ideal as pot
plants for growing indoors. Grow in a sunny,
sheltered site in moist but well-drained soil.
Deadhead to prolong flowering. HHA.
H 45cm (18in), S 30cm (12in).

PROPAGATION

🌱 under glass, in late winter or early spring,
at 18–24°C (64–75°F). May also be sown in
autumn or late winter for spring-flowering
houseplants. Overwinter at a minimum of
16–18°C (61–64°F).

🌱 14–25 days. ☀ 4–5 months.

Tropaeolum majus

Verbena x hybrida

Viola x wittrockiana

Salvia (Sage) — Labiatae

Some 900 species of annuals, biennials, and herbaceous and evergreen perennials and shrubs with sometimes very showy, brightly coloured, two-lipped flowers and often hairy and aromatic leaves.

S. splendens (Scarlet sage). Compact annuals with distinctive spikes of hooded, two-lipped, brilliant scarlet flowers borne well above the foliage from summer to autumn. Cultivars with purple, white, salmon and lavender flowers are also available. They are good for bedding, border edging, tubs and other containers. Grow in fertile and moist but well-drained soil in sun; provide the pastel-coloured cultivars with some shade to preserve flower colour. HHA.
H 45cm (18in), S 25–38cm (10–15in).

PROPAGATION
🌱 surface-sow under glass, from late winter to early spring, at 15–18°C (59–64°F).
🌱 7–14 days. ☀ 3–4 months.

Tagetes (Marigold) — Compositae

About 50 species of annuals and herbaceous perennials which are strongly aromatic.

T. erecta (African marigold). Upright annuals, taller in habit than the other groups, bearing mainly double, pompon-like flowers, in yellow, gold, and lemon shades, throughout summer. HHA. H 30–45cm (12–18in), S to 45cm (18in).

T. patula (French marigold). Compact annuals with single or, more usually, double flowers in shades of yellow, gold and mahogany, throughout summer. HHA.
H 15–30cm (6–12in), S to 30cm (12in).

T. tenuifolia, syn. *T. signata.* (Signet marigold, Mexican marigold). Upright, branched

annuals with dainty, single flowers in golden- or lemon-yellow and mahogany shades throughout summer. HHA. H 20–23cm (8–9in), S to 38cm (15in). All have finely divided foliage and are easily grown in well-drained soil in sun. Deadhead to prolong flowering and water freely in dry periods.

PROPAGATION
🌱 under glass, from late winter to early spring, at 18–20°C (64–68°F). Alternatively, either sow *in situ*, in drills or broadcast, in late spring.
🌱 7–21 days. ☀ 4–6 weeks.

Tropaeolum (Nasturtium) — Tropaeoleaceae

Up to 90 species of annuals and herbaceous perennials with hairless stems and leaves, and showy, spurred flowers with spreading lobes.

T. majus (Garden nasturtium). Rapidly growing annual, usually with a trailing or climbing habit. Modern cultivars, with a more bushy, non-trailing habit, are ideal for borders. The distinctively spurred flowers, produced through summer until first frosts, are in many shades of yellow, red or orange. Grow in sun or light shade in poor, well-drained soil; fertile soils encourage leaf growth at the expense of flowers. HA.
H 1–3m (3–10ft), S 1.5–5m (5–15ft).

PROPAGATION
🌱 under glass, in early spring, at 13–18°C (55–64°F). Or *in situ*, in drills or broadcast, in mid-spring.
🌱 7–14 days. ☀ 4–6 weeks.

Verbena — Verbenaceae

About 250 species of annuals, perennials, and subshrubs bearing dense terminal heads of tubular flowers with wide, spreading mouths.

V. x hybrida. Bushy perennial grown as an annual, with rounded clusters of small, salver-shaped, white-eyed flowers throughout summer in a brilliant colour range, including scarlet, blue, purple, pink, peach, and white. Easily grown in moist but well-drained soil in sun. HHA.
H 25–45cm (10–18in), S 30–50cm (12–20in).

PROPAGATION
🌱 under glass, in late winter or early spring, at 18–20°C (64–68°F).
🌱 14–25 days. ☀ 4 months.

Viola (Pansy, Violet) — Violaceae

About 500 species of annuals, biennials, and evergreen, semi-evergreen, and deciduous perennials and a few subshrubs. To a greater or lesser extent, many flowers have the characteristic 'face' of the pansy.

V. x wittrockiana (Pansy). Compact, short-lived perennials, grown as annuals or biennials, as flowering is best in young plants. Available in a wide range of colours, they flower either in winter and early spring or in late spring and summer. Grow in fertile, moist but well-drained soil, in a sunny or partially shaded site. Deadhead to prolong flowering. HA/HB.
H to 23cm (9in), S to 30cm (12in).

PROPAGATION
🌱 under glass, at 15–18°C (59–64°F) in mid- to late winter, for summer-flowering. Grow on in cool conditions at no more than 10°C (50°F). Sow in mid- to late summer for winter flowering, under glass or in a shaded cold frame. Sowing at higher temperatures than those recommended will prevent germination.
🌱 14–21 days. ☀ 4–6 months.

$\mathcal{H}$ERBACEOUS PERENNIALS

The herbaceous border in summer is one of
the glories of the garden, but as well as providing
colour, shape and texture at that time of year,
perennials make valuable contributions during
spring and autumn, too. Even winter is
brightened by plants such as hellebores and
bergenias, and dried stems and seed heads offer
continued interest in the bleaker months as well
as providing food for birds. In a mixed border,
where shrubs or small trees feature all year
round, interplantings of perennials do much to
add colour and excitement. To get the best
results from perennials, the gardener needs to
learn only a few simple propagating techniques,
for very little is required in the way of tools
and equipment.

◄ *Although many perennials
are long-lived, most rely on regular
propagation to keep them healthy
and able to give of their
free-flowering best.*

WHY PROPAGATE
HERBACEOUS PERENNIALS?

Herbaceous perennials lend themselves to a variety of propagation techniques, most of which are extremely easy. All that is required is the little forethought necessary to propagate in the year before planting and you will be able to plan the most extravagant of border schemes, secure in the knowledge that there are always plenty of plants to hand.

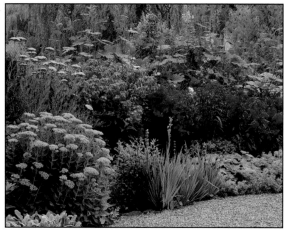

Filling a busy perennial border can be expensive, but propagating from your own plants is practical, cheap and fun.

The vast majority of perennials with fibrous roots or rhizomes, which spread from the original plant to form a clump, are perfect candidates for division. Division produces uniform offspring, and since divisions have instantly functional roots and stems or growth buds, they grow rapidly into good-sized specimens. Perennials with a tap root or a single stem are difficult to divide without

When you decide to increase your stock of perennials, there is a range of options at your disposal. Some of these techniques may be easier, or more appropriate to a certain plant group than others. All are worth mastering.

OPTING FOR SEED

The simplest way of raising perennials is by sowing seed. Using this method, large numbers of plants can be raised economically, with little effort, and a huge range of seeds are available from catalogues. However, cultivars and hybrids seldom produce identical offspring to the parent and some, particularly those with double flowers, never produce seed; these must be increased by other means.

MAINTAINING PLANT HEALTH

Division is undertaken not only to increase stock, but also to ensure that plants are maintained in good health, with maximum flowering potential. Many perennials need routine division every third or fourth year for this reason.

causing irreparable damage, so for any plant of this type alternative methods, such as stem or root cuttings, are a safer and preferable option.

PRODUCING IDENTICAL PLANTS

Cuttings produce plants that are identical to the parent and are ideal for plants that will not divide easily or which do not come true from seed. Stem tip cuttings can be taken whenever the plant is growing strongly. Basal cuttings are less often used, perhaps because they are taken in spring when so much else is happening in the garden. With such plants as *Aster × frikartii* cultivars, they are the only practical method. The best candidates for root cuttings are those plants with thick roots, whether tap-rooted, as with sea holly (*Eryngium*), or with questing roots, such as the plume poppies (*Macleaya*).

ADDITIONAL TECHNIQUES

Although layering is commonly associated with woody plants, border carnations root readily from layers. Grafting also is more often practised with woody material, the most notable exception being *Gypsophila paniculata* cultivars, which are notoriously difficult to root from cuttings.

Colourful Survivors

A small group of perennials can be sown directly in their flowering site in spring and early summer and will happily take their chances. Such attractive plants as Euphorbia, Alchemilla, Sidalcea, Aquilegia, *and* Geranium, *as well as some penstemons and veronicas, all grow well in this way, if kept clear of weeds. These same plants can be self-perpetuating by self-seeding, lending a natural charm to a border around the garden, if allowed to grow where*

they choose. Only species will come true from seed; seedlings of cultivars are likely to be inferior to their parents.

Aquilegia vulgaris *is a good example of a perennial species that maintains itself by self-sowing.*

Achillea filipendulina
Four-year-old, established plants need dividing otherwise they become too congested and their centres start declining. When dividing, remove the centre parts and replant the healthy, outside portions, thereby maintaining bright displays.

Sedum spectabile
One of the easiest plants to propagate. It divides readily: you do not even have to dig it up, just slice off a section of the plant with roots, replant, and it takes. The younger the plants the better because vigorous new growth guarantees strong colour and scent, which will attract masses of butterflies.

③

Stachys byzantina
Grown for its gorgeous velvety foliage, but it can quickly start looking quite ragged. Either divide annually, or take cuttings.

④

Sisyrinchium striatum
Each leafy shoot dies after producing a flowering shoot, but self-sown seedlings are abundant and can be transplanted into fresh soil when small to maintain the display.

Phlox paniculata
Phlox are alarmingly prone to eelworm. To guarantee a continuous healthy show, take root cuttings annually. Note: if you use this technique for variegated types, they will immediately revert to green; divide instead.

⑥

Alchemilla mollis
A prolific self-seeder, excellent as an edging plant, but the seedlings get everywhere. To stop things getting out of hand, trim down all but one of the flower heads in late summer, collect its seed, and sow in a cold frame. When mature, plant out where required.

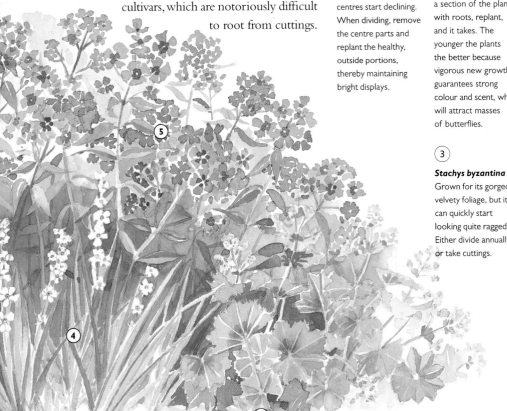

PROPAGATING TECHNIQUES
HERBACEOUS PERENNIALS

Techniques that increase the stock of perennial plants range from the simplest methods of division to the slightly more adventurous techniques of grafting. None of these procedures is particularly difficult, most will give satisfyingly rapid results and very little is required in the way of tools and equipment.

SEED

The best time to sow most perennial seed is in late winter or early spring. However, members of the families Primulaceae and Ranunculaceae, such as hellebores, always germinate freely if sown fresh, but much less so if spring-sown.

In the wild, germination is frequently delayed until conditions are perfect, and some seed has a built-in inhibitor that prevents germination until soil and weather conditions are suitable. Some wait until spring rains provide sufficient moisture for growth

Sowing seed ....

Plunging pots of sown seed in a plunge bed is a convenient way of storing until germination. It prevents pots from tipping and spilling their contents and reduces temperature fluctuations.

▶ 1 Sow the seed thinly and evenly on the surface of the seed compost and cover with a 6mm (¼in) layer of fine grit. This prevents the seed drying out and makes it easier to water evenly and to remove weeds or moss.

▶ 2 Water the pot and plunge in an open frame, shaded from hot sun. Do not cover unless there is excessive rain, but keep evenly moist until germination. If germination occurs before the last frosts, move the seedlings into a greenhouse.
Prick out seedlings into individual pots as soon as the first true leaves appear, and place in a closed cold frame until re-established. Then harden off and place in an open frame or plunge bed until large enough to set out. If germination does not occur in the first year, retain the pot and keep it watered. Many species germinate erratically, more than one season after sowing.

and these often have tough seed coats that only break down when soaked. Lupins and many other members of the pea family (Leguminosae) are like this and, in cultivation, must be soaked or have their hard coats pierced by abrading or nicking. Others need chilling and then warmth to mimic winter followed by spring before they will germinate. Chilling can be achieved by placing the pot in the bottom of a domestic refrigerator (not a freezer) for up to three weeks. Most seed that requires chilling needs exposure to temperatures no lower than 1–5°C (34–41°F); they positively do not need freezing. The natural way is often the easiest way and for most perennials, sowing in late winter and exposing the pots to frost in an open frame is usually sufficient to break dormancy. If in doubt as to the best time for sowing, sow half in autumn and half in spring.

Some robust perennials can be sown directly into the soil as for annuals and vegetables, and these also often provide self-sown seedlings. These can be pricked out into pots in the normal way, or left to develop and then moved to their flowering position. Unlike annuals, few hardy perennials need heat for germination, although many will germinate more quickly in warmth, at 15–20°C (59–68°F), in a propagator. Label the seed and seedlings at all stages of growth, ideally with the date of sowing and source of the seed, as well as the name of the plant.

Prick out seedlings into individual pots as soon as the first true leaves appear, and place in a closed cold frame until re-established. Then harden off and transfer to an open frame or plunge bed, until large enough to set out.

If germination does not occur in the first year, retain the pot and keep it watered; seedlings may appear the following year, or even the year after that.

DIVISION

Division is an essential part of perennial gardening and is used both to increase stock and to keep plants in good health with maximum flowering potential. Division produces offspring that are identical to the parent, which can seldom be guaranteed when new plants are raised from garden-collected seed. Nearly all perennials that spread from a central crown to form a mat or clump are perfect candidates for division. Those with a deep taproot or single central stem are generally unsuitable for division and, for these, stem or root cuttings are usually a better option.

Division is safest if performed in the spring, just before new growth commences. This is especially the case in areas with hard winters, since spring division gives the plants a complete growing season to become well established, generate a new root system and produce plenty of growth buds at the crown. Some spring-flowering plants may be divided in autumn, or immediately after flowering, as long as they are kept well watered if the weather remains dry for a prolonged period.

Damp, warm, overcast weather provides the optimal conditions for re-establishment. Always use healthy stock plants as any pests or diseases will be carried over to the divisions. When dividing older plants, discard the old woody centres, re-planting only young, vigorous growth from around the edges of the clump.

Techniques for division

There are several slightly different techniques of division, depending on the growth habit of the original plant and the number of divisions required.

The simplest way is to dig up the plant and break it into pieces either by hand or by inserting two forks back-to-back and levering them apart. This is ideal for fibrous-rooted plants whose roots are not entwined.

An alternative method of division is to disentangle the roots carefully and separate the clump into individual portions, each with a single shoot or crown. Such small divisions are best potted up and grown on in a cold frame before planting out. Shake the soil from the roots and then gently manipulate individual crowns with the fingers until they fall apart. It is often easier, especially for plants grown in heavier soils, to wash the soil from the roots in a bucket of water; the individual

Division . . . .

There are several techniques for division, depending on the original plant and the number of divisions that are required. The simplest is suitable for clump-forming and fibrous-rooted plants, such as asters.

▶ **1** Lift the plant with a spade or fork, including the entire root zone if possible, when the new shoots reach about 5cm (2in) long. Section large clumps with a spade, then tease out small pieces by hand, each with about half a dozen new shoots and a mass of fibrous roots. Discard old material from the centre of the clump.

▶ **2** Replant the divisions immediately, with the growing points at the same depth as they were originally. Set them in at spacings of about 30cm (12in). Water in thoroughly.

▶ **3** If the root ball is very dense, tangled or congested, lift the entire root ball, and insert two garden forks back-to-back at the centre of the clump. Use a levering action to prise the clump firmly but gently apart.

crowns should then become clearly visible and will separate very easily with minimal damage to the roots.

Tough-rooted plants, such as hostas, can be hosed clean of soil and the selected crowns separated with a sharp knife. A rather crude method is to slice them into two to four pieces with a sharp spade, but this not only wastes material but also increases the risk of a fungal infection entering the broken-off roots.

Dividing rhizomatous perennials ....

Division of bearded iris, as shown here, can be done in early autumn but is best done just after flowering. They need dividing every three years or so to keep them flowering well.

► **1** After flowering, lift the clump of rhizomes, shake off any excess soil, and separate into sections by hand. Select plump young rhizomes with healthy roots and discard the old rhizomes.

◄ **2** Section the plump young rhizomes into 5–10cm (2–4in) lengths with a sharp knife, ensuring that each has a healthy fan of leaves at one end. Trim the slender fibrous roots by one third of their length.

► **3** Trim the leaves to a mitre about 15cm (6in) long; this will reduce wind rock when planted.

◄ **4** Set the rhizome into the soil so that the slender fibrous roots are buried, and the rhizome itself is buried to no more than half its depth. When replanting groups of iris rhizomes, make sure they are set so that all the leaf fans face in the same direction.

Basal cuttings ....

Take basal cuttings from vigorous shoots as the first leaves begin to unfurl. Cut off with a sharp knife, with a small piece of harder, semi-woody material at the base. Trim off the lowest leaves and insert in pots or trays of moist cutting compost. Place in a cold frame or propagator out of direct sun. Keep the compost moist. When rooted, after about 3–5 weeks, pot up separately.

Division of rhizomatous perennials

Plants with substantial rhizomes, such as irises or bergenias, can be cut up into individual portions provided that each section of rhizome has at least one growing point. Rhizomatous plants such as bergenias can be cut up into relatively small sections, about 4cm (1½in) long, provided that each portion has a bud on it.

Larger divisions can be replanted into the soil once it has been refreshed with well-rotted organic material. It is important that rhizomes are set back in to the soil at the same depth as they were previously. For some genera, such as *Iris* (*see left*), the rhizomes grow naturally at or just above the soil surface and will rot if planted too deeply. If the weather is hot and dry, or the divisions are small, pot them up and keep them in a closed cold frame for 2–3 weeks. Then harden off before setting them out.

CUTTINGS

Taking cuttings produces plants that are identical to the parent. It is also a useful technique for propagating a 'sport' or mutation – a shoot that differs from all the others on the same plant, such as one that has produced variegated leaves. It is important only to use pest- and disease-free material when taking cuttings. Any disease present in the parent plant will be transferred to the new ones, and material infested with pests is likely to be weakened and will not establish well, if at all. There are several different methods of taking cuttings.

Basal cuttings

Basal cuttings are an excellent way of increasing many perennials. With some plants, such as the *Aster* × *frikartii* cultivars, it is the only practical method and it is also ideal for most members of the family Compositae, such as *Artemisia,* as well as the Labiatae, including *Nepeta* and *Stachys.* Basal cuttings are also particularly useful for plants with hollow stems, such as delphiniums, since the base of the new growth is solid and makes perfect cutting material, unlike the mature stems.

The cuttings are taken in spring as the new shoots emerge, but before the leaves are unfurled. Shoots used for cuttings are soon replaced and the plant is unharmed.

Basal material is not so readily available once the plants have reached their full growth and any that does appear is usually rather drawn or etiolated because of the tall stems around it. Plants such as violas can be induced to produce new basal growth later in the season by shearing the plant over after the first flush of bloom. The resulting new shoots are ideal material for basal cuttings.

This method of propagation can also be used for a number of tender perennials, among them chrysanthemums and argyranthemums, are traditionally propagated by basal cuttings. The old plants are lifted in autumn before they are caught by the frosts, and overwintered in a frost-free shed or greenhouse, bedded in just-moist compost or peat substitute. They are usually given a little extra warmth in late winter or very early spring to force them into growth. When new basal shoots appear, they are removed and treated as ordinary basal cuttings. Basal cuttings of half hardy and tender plants should be rooted at 15°C (59°F), grown on in warmth and hardened off before setting out.

Pre-rooted cuttings

Although taking basal cuttings is neither a difficult nor a lengthy process, there is a quicker variation – small, prerooted stems known as 'Irishman's cuttings'. It is often possible to find a few shoots that have already sent out one or two roots by searching around the margins of the clump. If necessary, trace the stem down below the surface of the soil. Sever the cutting below the rooted section and then pot up into proprietary cutting compost, being careful not to damage the existing roots. Proceed then as for basal cuttings.

Plants that are amenable to this process include *Aster*, *Anaphalis* and *Mimulus*, as well as many other mat- or carpet-forming, stem-rooting perennials.

Stem tip cuttings

Taking stem tip cuttings is a productive means of increasing a wide range of perennials. Cuttings are taken from the tips of healthy, non-flowering, semi-mature or mature shoots, between early summer and autumn. In genera such as *Penstemon*, which root very easily, shoots can be cut into a number of usable sections at almost any time during the growing period.

For most perennials, stem tip cuttings strike easily without the need to stimulate rooting by using hormone rooting compound. Dipping the bottom 1cm (½in) of the cutting in rooting preparation is

Stem tip cuttings

Stem tip cuttings are best taken early in the day, when plants are most turgid (full of water). Place them in a polythene bag to reduce water loss and prevent wilting before insertion.

▶ 1 Using a sharp knife or secateurs, cut the stem tip from the plant, at about 7.5–12.5cm (3–5in) long.

◀ 2 Trim the cutting to 5–7.5cm (2–3in) long, with a straight cut just below a node. Neatly trim the lower leaves from the bottom third of the cutting.

▶ 3 Insert the cuttings to the depth of the lowest leaves, around the edge of a prepared pot of cutting compost. Make sure that the leaves do not touch each other or the compost surface. Cover the pot with a sealed polythene tent, or place in a propagator, preferably with bottom heat at 15°C (59°F). Heating is not essential but speeds rooting. A mist unit is useful for large-scale propagation.

Aftercare
Provide good light but shade from direct sunlight. Check regularly and remove any fallen leaves or rotted material as soon as seen. If left in place, they will spread infection to the healthy cuttings. Cuttings that root during the summer should be potted up straightaway, but those that do not develop roots until late autumn are left in place until spring. Keep young plants in frost-free conditions over winter.

nevertheless helpful because the compound contains a fungicide which helps to inhibit rots.

The gentle bottom heat provided by a propagator or soil-warming cables is not essential but speeds up the rooting process. A 15°C (59°F) temperature is suitable. For large scale propagation a mist unit is useful.

ROOT CUTTINGS

As all gardeners know when digging out dandelions, or ground elder, if just a little piece of root is left, it is likely to come up as a new plant. In essence, this is the same process as that of taking root cuttings, except that in this case the gardener deliberately exploits the plant's capacity to regenerate itself from its root and produce a new individual that is identical to its parent.

The plants that respond best to this technique are those with thick roots, some of which are not amenable to increase by division or by cuttings. They can be

Root cuttings . . . .

Taking root cuttings during the plant's dormant period is a suitable way of increasing those plants that do not lend themselves to propagation by division or cuttings.

◄ **I** Dig up the plant and remove a few pencil-thick roots. Wash the soil from the root cuttings and rub off small fibrous roots. Cut the roots into 5–7.5cm (2–3in) lengths, making a straight cut at the top (the end nearest to the crown) and a sloping one at the base, so that it is easy to see which way up to insert the cutting.

► **2** Plant the pieces of root vertically into a prepared pot of moist cutting compost, with the straight cut just below the level of the compost. Top-dress with a 5mm (¼in) layer of grit. Label with the name and date.

◄ **3** For plants with very slender roots, the technique varies a little. Section the roots into 7.5–12.5cm (3–5in) lengths. Lay them horizontally on the surface of a prepared tray of compost and just cover to their own depth with sieved compost. Top-dress with a 5mm (¼in) layer of grit.

taprooted plants, such as the sea hollies (*Eryngium*), or plants which have thick, widely spreading roots, like the Californian tree poppies (*Romneya*). Some more slender-rooted plants, such as the Pasque flower (*Pulsatilla*) can also be propagated in this way. Root cuttings are taken during the dormant period, in late autumn or early winter.

There are several common reasons for failure of root cuttings. It is important to make sure that the root cutting is inserted with the correct orientation. Root tissue is programmed to produce shoot growth from its upper end and root growth from its lower end. This is why a root cutting is made with a straight cut at its top end and a sloping cut at the bottom end. It serves to ensure that the cutting is inserted the right way up. For plants with very slender roots the technique is modified by inserting them horizontally. Cuttings of slender roots must be longer than those of the usual thickness, as otherwise they do not contain sufficient food reserves for the development of new growth. If planted vertically, they are likely to rot before the new growth reaches the compost surface.

Overwatering commonly leads to failure. If kept too moist, the root cuttings are likely to rot before they have had a chance to make new growth. After insertion, place the tray or pot of cuttings in a cold frame or greenhouse and keep it just moist; the pots will only need a little watering, if any, until new growth begins.

The last reason for failure is probably impatience. In spring, the roots will send up new topgrowth, but may do so before they are properly rooted. Before attempting to pot up, always check to make sure that the cuttings are well rooted. They are very unlikely to be successful if moved before a good network of fibrous roots has formed.

If only a few new plants are required, it is often possible to scrape away some of the soil from the margins of the plant and remove just a few roots, thus not disturbing the parent plant.

A crude method of increase – effectively a means of taking root cuttings *in situ* – is sometimes used with oriental poppies (*Papaver orientalis*). Here, you need to sheer off the top-growth of the plant just below the surface of the soil with a spade. When new plants arise from the top of the severed roots, separate them and re-plant immediately.

GRAFTING

Grafting is seldom used with herbaceous perennials, with the exception of the cultivars of *Gypsophila paniculata*, such as 'Bristol Fairy' and 'Flamingo', which are difficult to root from cuttings. The nature of the material does not lend itself to complicated grafts and a simple wedge graft, made in late spring, is sufficient. A two-year-old plant of the species is raised from seed to act as the rootstock.

Once the graft union has been made, transfer the pot to a propagator, with gentle bottom heat. Keep the compost just moist, watering from below if necessary. New roots and the graft union should form within 4–6 weeks. Wean gradually from the propagator and grow in a cool, frost-free place with good light but out of direct sun. Remove the grafting tape when new growth resumes and pot on when plants are well established.

LAYERING

Layering is a technique that is mainly used for woody subjects, such as shrubs, but a few perennials can also be increased in this way, in particular *Dianthus*, such as pinks and border carnations. After flowering, prepare for layering by cultivating the soil around the plant to a depth of about 7.5cm (3in). Incorporate peat (or substitute) and sharp sand to improve the drainage and aeration of the soil in the rooting area.

Layering pinks and border carnations ....

Layering is a traditional and simple means of increasing border carnations and pinks. After flowering, the plants produce vegetative shoots that will root within 5–6 weeks.

◄ Select a sturdy, low-growing stem. Strip the stem of leaves, leaving about 4–5 pairs at the stem tip. Make a nick in the stem with a sharp knife to form a tongue that extends from the first bare, leafless node to just below the next node towards the parent plant. Bend the stem over onto the prepared soil surface and pin it down with a U-shaped piece of wire. Hold the stem tip upright by tying it to a vertical piece of split cane. Cover the stem with soil. When the stem has rooted, sever from the parent plant and either pot it up to grow on, or transfer to its permanent position.

Grafting ....

Grafting herbaceous material, like the *Gypsophila* cultivar shown here, is a fairly simple technique although it does require planning to raise the rootstock material.

▶ **1** Lift the rootstock and select a single stout root, about 1cm (⅓in) thick, and cut about 12.5cm (5in) or so of root from the parent plant.

▶ **2** Trim off any small fibrous roots and reduce any large lateral roots to about 1cm (½in) long. With a straight top cut and a slanting bottom cut, trim the rootstock to 7.5–10cm (3–4in) in length. Make a vertical cut, 1cm (½in) deep in the top of the rootstock. Set the rootstock in a prepared pot of cutting compost with the top 2.5cm (1in) above the compost surface.

▶ **3** To prepare the scion, take a sturdy non-flowering shoot, 4mm (⅛in) in diameter, from the desired cultivar and trim to 4–7.5cm (1½–3in) long. Trim the base of the scion to a wedge-shape to match the cleft in the rootstock.

▶ **4** Insert the scion into the rootstock, matching up the cut surfaces. Bind with grafting tape and keep in a propagator with bottom heat until the graft has taken.

33

DIRECTORY OF
HERBACEOUS PERENNIALS

Below are key tips on a selection of herbaceous perennials that are particularly suitable for propagation. Unless otherwise specified, follow the detailed instructions given under the propagation section on pages 28–33.

Key

H   Height
S   Spread
🌱   By seed
🌱   Germination
☀   Time to maturity
✎   By division

Acanthus

(Bear's breeches)   Acanthaceae

Some 30 species of mostly hardy herbaceous perennials, grown for their strongly architectural form and tall spikes of flowers, with papery hood-like bracts, in summer. The flowers are excellent for cutting. They tolerate most types of soil in sun or light shade, but grow best in deep, fertile soils. Those described are hardy.
A. mollis. Large, lobed, glossy, dark green leaves and white flowers with purple bracts. Late summer. H to 1.5m (5ft), S 1m (3ft).
A. spinosus. Narrow, deeply cut, spiny leaves, and white flowers with purple bracts from midsummer onwards. The **Spinosissimus Group** has very deeply divided, spiny, greyish green leaves with white spines and midribs. H to 1.2m (4ft), S 60–90cm (2–3ft).

Acanthus spinosus

PROPAGATION

🌱 spring, in a cold frame. Sow the large seeds in individual pots. Germination is more rapid at 15–20°C (59–68°F) in a propagator. Do not transplant once the taproot has developed. Will self-sow if left on the plant and can be a nuisance. Dig up self-sown seedlings as soon as possible. Any part of the root left in the ground will re-shoot.
🌱 14 days.   ☀ 3 years.
✎ spring or autumn, with care. Divisions re-establish slowly.   ☀ 2 years.
Root cuttings – winter. Use deep pots to minimize root disturbance when planting out.   ☀ 3 years.

Achillea (Yarrow)   Compositae

About 85 species and many cultivars of hardy, evergreen and herbaceous perennials, valued for their aromatic, often finely divided, grey-green or silver-grey foliage and corymbs of tiny, daisy-like flowers. Those described here tolerate a range of soils in sun or dappled shade. Most have flowers that are suitable for drying.
A. millefolium. Has tiny flowers throughout summer, in shades of lilac, lavender, cerise to deep red. H 60cm (24in), S 60cm (24in).

Achillea 'Moonshine'

A. 'Moonshine' has yellow flowers. H and S 60cm (24in).
A. ptarmica (Sneezeweed). Bears white flowers throughout summer. 'Boule de Neige' has double flowers; 'The Pearl' has pompon-like blooms.
H to 60cm (24in), S 30cm (12in).
A. 'Taygetea', syn. A. aegyptica. Evergreen with heads of yellow flowers in summer. H 60cm (24in), S 45cm (18in).

PROPAGATION

✎ spring. Divide mature plants every 3–4 years to maintain vigour.   ☀ 14 months. Basal cuttings – spring, while shoots are still young. Valuable for short-lived, or woody-based species and cultivars, such as A. 'Moonshine' and A. 'Taygetea'.   ☀ 2 years.
🌱 autumn or spring, in a cold frame. Plants may not come true but this is a useful method for mixed-coloured forms.
🌱 1–4 months,   ☀ 1–2 years.

Anaphalis (Pearly everlasting) Compositae

About a hundred species of hardy, clump-forming perennials with silver foliage and white 'everlasting' flowers during summer. They need moist but well-drained soil in full sun.
A. margaritacea. Produces yellow-centred flowers from midsummer to autumn. H to 60cm (24in), S 60cm (24in).
A. triplinervis. Yellow-centred flowers in mid- to late summer above silver-grey leaves. H to 90cm (36in), S to 60cm (24in).

PROPAGATION

✎ spring.   ☀ 15 months.
Basal cuttings – spring,   ☀ 15 months.
🌱 preferably sown fresh. Autumn or spring, in a cold frame. This is the quickest method of propagation. Germination is more rapid at 15–20°C (59–68°F) in a propagator.
🌱 1–3 months,   ☀ 1 year.

Anenome x hybrida 'Max Vogel'

Artemisia absinthium

Aster x novae-angliae

Anemone
Ranunculaceae

Some 120 species of hardy to half-hardy perennials, with tuberous, rhizomatous, fibrous, or fleshy roots. Larger species, grown for their mounds of palmate foliage and cup-shaped flowers, are suited to an herbaceous border. Grow in moist but well-drained, fertile soil, in sun or dappled shade. (See also Bulbs, Corms and Tubers directory, pp. 64–65.)

A. x hybrida, syn. A. x elegans, A. japonica (Japanese anemone). Hardy suckering perennial bearing semi-double, pale pink flowers in late summer and autumn. 'Honorine Jobert' has pure white flowers. H 1.2–1.5m (4–5ft), S 60cm (24in) or more.

PROPAGATION
Root cuttings – early winter. Remove thicker roots and cut into 5cm (2in) lengths. ☀ 2 years.

✂ spring. Divide when the soil is not too dry and therefore not crumbly – success can be assured if divisions are re-planted without the soil falling off. Divide A. hybrida with care. ☀ 6 months.

🌰 as soon as ripe in a cold frame; germination can be erratic. Less common perennial species, such as A. rivularis, are best propagated by seed.

Anthemis
Compositae

Some100 species of annuals and mostly hardy perennials with feathery leaves and white, yellow, or orange, daisy-like flowers borne over long periods in summer. Grow in light, well-drained soil in sun. They are short-lived, so propagate regularly.

A. punctata subsp. cupaniana. Hardy and mat-forming with silver-grey leaves. White daisies in early summer. One of the easiest plants to increase (see propagation). H 30cm (12in), S to 90cm (36in).

A. tinctoria (Golden marguerite, Ox-eye chamomile). A hardy species with golden yellow daisies during summer. 'E.C. Buxton' has pale lemon-yellow flowers. H 90cm (36in), S 90cm (36in).

PROPAGATION
Basal cuttings – spring, 4cm (1½in) long. Some, such as A. punctata subsp. cupaniana, can simply have pieces snapped off and put in the ground where they will usually root. ☀ 16 months.

🌰 spring, in a cold frame. Cultivars may not come true. Some, such as A. tinctoria and A. sancti-johannis, self-sow. Transplant or pot up while still small. 🌱 2–3 weeks. ☀ 1 year.

Artemisia
Compositae

Some 300 species of annuals, perennials, subshrubs, and shrubs. Many of the perennial species and cultivars are valued in the garden for their silver foliage; few have attractive flowers. Those described are hardy. Grow in well-drained soil in sun.

A. absinthium 'Lambrook Silver'. A woody-based perennial with deeply cut silver leaves. H to 90cm (36in), S 60cm (24in).

A. lactiflora (White mugwort). Clump-forming, with jagged, dark green leaves and panicles of creamy-white flowers from midsummer to autumn. H 1.5m (5ft), S 60cm (24in).

A. ludoviciana (Western mugwort). Rhizomatous, with clumps of narrow, silver-white leaves. 'Silver Queen' is lower-growing. 'Valerie Finnis' is shorter still, with silver leaves. H 60–120cm (2–4ft), S 60cm (2ft).

PROPAGATION
Cuttings – greenwood or heeled semi-ripe cuttings in late summer/autumn. All cuttings are best taken from young growth and shoots should be free of flowers and buds. A. absinthium takes best from late-summer cuttings. Soft tip cuttings of A. a. 'Lambrook Silver' are taken in spring. Overwinter young plants at 5°C (41°F). ☀ 15 months.

✂ spring. Only suitable for clump-forming artemisias, such as A. ludoviciana. ☀ 15 months.

🌰 autumn or spring in a cold frame. Cultivars do not come true. 🌱 2–3 weeks. ☀ 1 year.

Aster
Compositae

About 250 species of annuals, biennials, and perennials, bearing daisy-like flower heads with yellow discs. The hardy perennials and their cultivars are valuable for their long flowering season, from late summer to autumn. Grow in deep, fertile, moist but well-drained soil in sun. A. amellus tolerates drier soil than A. novae-angliae and A. novi-belgii. Discard self–sown seedlings; they are rarely as good as their parents.

A. amellus. Bears corymbs of lilac-blue flowers in late summer and autumn. Cultivars with pale pink to violet flower-heads are available. H to 60cm (24in), S 45cm (18in).

A. x frikartii. Pale to dark blue-violet flower heads with a central orange-yellow disc. Late summer to autumn. H 35–75cm (14–30in), S 30cm (12in).

A. x novae-angliae (New England aster). Rhizomatous perennial producing violet flower heads from late summer to autumn.

35

HERBACEOUS PERENNIALS A-Z: ASTER

Astrantia major

Bergenia cordifolia

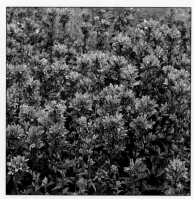

Campanula glomerata

There are many cultivars, in white through shades of pink, deep red, violet, and lilac-blue. H 1.2–1.5m (4–5ft), S 45–60cm (18–24in).
A. × novi-belgii (Michaelmas daisy, New York aster). Produces violet flowerheads, with cultivars in colours from creamy white through pink to deep crimson and violet. H 1–1.2m (3–4ft), S 45–60cm (18–24in).

PROPAGATION
✄ spring. Divide *A. novae-angliae* and *A. novi-belgii* every 3 years to maintain vigour.
☀ 6 or 18 months.
Basal cuttings – spring. A few asters, in particular *A. amellus* and *A. × frikartii* and its cultivars, cannot be divided and must be increased by basal cuttings. ☀ 18 months.
🌰 autumn or spring. Sow fresh.
Pre-chill spring-sown seed. Cultivars do not come true.

Astrantia (Masterwort)   Umbelliferae
Some 10 species of hardy perennials with umbels of tiny flowers surrounded by conspicuous papery bracts. Grow in fertile, moist but well-drained soil in sun.
A. major (Masterwort). Clump-forming with deeply lobed leaves, and green or pink flowers surrounded by white, often pink-tinged bracts. Early to midsummer.
'Sunningdale Variegated' has yellow-variegated leaves.
H to 90cm (36in), S 45cm (18in).

PROPAGATION
✄ spring or autumn. ☀ 14 months.
🌰 autumn or spring. Sow fresh in a cold frame. Cultivars are unlikely to come true. Astrantias frequently self-sow, providing a ready supply of seedlings.
🌱 3 weeks. ☀ 1 year.

Bergenia (Elephant's ears)   Saxifragaceae
Some eight species of mostly hardy, rhizomatous, evergreen perennials, grown for their leathery leaves and bell-shaped flowers in spring. There are many cultivars with flowers in white (**B. 'Bressingham White'**, **B. 'Silberlicht'**) through shades of pink (**B. 'Schneekönigin'**) to crimson and red-purple (**B. 'Abendglut'**, **B. 'Ballawley'**). Useful as ground cover in sun or part-shade, in moist but well-drained soil.
B. cordifolia. Glossy dark green leaves, flushed purple in winter, and pale to deep pink flowers. Late winter or early spring.
H 60cm (24in), S 70cm (28in).
B. purpurascens. Green leaves tinted purple beneath; purple flowers in spring. H 45cm (18in), S 30cm (12in).

PROPAGATION
✄ autumn or spring. ☀ 1 year.
Rhizome cuttings – winter. Cut rhizomes into 2.5cm (1in) sections, each with a dormant bud which is often hidden under a scale. Set horizontally in cutting compost and keep moist. This method will give large quantities of plants but they will take longer to come into flower. ☀ 2 years
🌰 autumn or spring in a cold frame. Pre-chill spring-sown seed. Cultivars do not come true.
🌱 1–3 months. ☀ 2–3 years.

Campanula (Bellflower)   Campanulaceae
About 300 species of annuals, biennials, and perennials, most with bell-shaped flowers borne over long periods. Those described are hardy. They need fertile, moist but well-drained soil, in sun or light shade.
C. glomerata (Clustered bellflower). White, lavender, or blue-violet flowers, in summer.
'Superba' is taller with rich violet-purple flowers. H 45cm (18in), S indefinite.
C. lactiflora (Milky bellflower). Has white to pale blue, or blue-violet flowers, in midsummer. **'Prichard's Variety'** has violet-blue flowers. H 1.2m (4ft), S 75cm (30in).
C. persicifolia (Peach-leaved bellflower). Open spires of white or blue flowers. Early to midsummer.
H 45–75cm (18–30in), S 30cm (12in).

PROPAGATION
✄ spring. Clump-formers, such as *C. persicifolia*, and rhizomatous campanulas, such as *C. glomerata*, are best increased by division. Re-plant only young growth from the edges of the clump. ☀ 1 year.
🌰 autumn or spring. Pre-chill spring-sown seed for 3 weeks. Some self-sow. Cultivars do not come true and should be increased by basal cuttings.
🌱 2–6 weeks. ☀ 1 year.
Basal cuttings – spring, ☀ 1 year.

Centaurea
(Hardhead, Knapweed)   Compositae
About 450 species of annuals and perennials. A few are valued for their foliage and flowers. Grow in well-drained soil in sun.
C. hypoleuca. Has divided, pale green leaves and bears pink flowerheads during summer.
'John Coutts' has deep pink flowerheads. H 60cm (24in), S 45cm (18in).
C. montana. Vigorous and rhizomatous, and bears blue flowers from early to midsummer. H 45cm (18in), S 60cm (24in).

PROPAGATION
✄ spring or autumn. Clump-formers are easily divided. Divide regularly, every 2–3

Chrysanthemum x *superbum*

Delphinium 'Oliver'

Dianthus 'Dora'

years, to maintain vigour.   ☀ I year
🌰 autumn or spring. Pre-chill spring-sown
seed for 3 weeks. Many self-sow.
🌱 2–6 weeks.   ☀ I year.
Stem cuttings – autumn (*C. cineraria*),
overwinter under glass.   ☀ 9 months.

Chrysanthemum   Compositae

Some 20 species of annuals and perennials,
most of which are now placed by botanists
in the genera *Dendranthema*, *Leucanthemum*,
and *Tanacetum*, but are retained here for
convenience. **C. x *morifolium*** (Florists'
chrysanthemum) is now *Dendranthema* x
grandiflorum. Grown in borders and for
cutting and exhibition; most are half-hardy or
frost-tender. The hardy perennials need moist
but well-drained, fertile soil, in sun.
C. *rubellum*, syn. *Dendranthema zawadskii*.
Has given rise to the **Rubellum Group**
hybrids that bear daisy-like, single or double
flowers, in a range of colours, from late
summer to autumn. Half-hardy. H 60–75cm
(24–30in), S 45cm (18in).
C. x *superbum*, syn. *C. maximum*, (Shasta
daisy). Now properly *Leucanthemum* x
superbum. Masses of white daisies over long
periods in summer. Hardy. H 90–120cm
(3–4ft), S 45cm (18in) or more.

PROPAGATION
Basal cuttings – winter or early spring,
5cm (2in) long. Most can be increased by
this method, which is particularly good for
C. x morifolium, cuttings of which should be
taken under glass.   ☀ 6 months.
🔪 spring or autumn. Discard older material
from the centre of the clumps. Hardier
species can be more readily increased by
division in spring.   ☀ 6 months.

🌰 spring, for Rubellum Group hybrids, at
15–20°C (59–68°F).
🌱 I month.   ☀ 6 months.

Cortaderia (Pampas grass)   Gramineae

Genus of 24 species of large, tussock-
forming, evergreen and semi-evergreen
grasses grown for their impressive habit and
large, long-stemmed, silky-plumed
inflorescences in late summer.
C. *selloana*. This hardy species forms tussocks
of arching leaves and produces large, silvery,
often pink-flushed, pyramidal plumes in late
summer. It can be raised from seed, but
inflorescences, which may take several years
to be produced, are very variable.
H to 3m (10ft), S. 1.5m (5ft).

PROPAGATION
🔪 mid-spring, as new growth begins.
Separate sections from the extremity of the
clump with a sharp spade, and either divide
further by hand or re-plant as a clump. The
leaf margins are razor-sharp, so wear gloves
and remove foliage to make handling easier.
☀ 2–3 years.
🌰 spring. Cultivars will not come true.

Delphinium   Ranunculaceae

About 250 species of hardy annuals,
biennials, and perennials, and many garden
hybrids, grown for their mainly blue flowers,
although cream- and pink-flowered variants
are also available. The **Elatum Group**, the
most common in cultivation, produce one
main spike of flowers, with a central eye or
'bee', in early and midsummer. The
Belladonna Group bear branched spikes of
flowers in early and late summer. Grow in
fertile, moist but well-drained soil in sun.

PROPAGATION
Basal cuttings – spring, 5–7.5cm (2–3in) long,
with gentle bottom heat. For the Elatum and
Belladonna Group hybrids, this is the usual
means of increase.   ☀ 14 months
🔪 spring. Cut through the crown with a
sharp knife, leaving each section with roots
and at least one bud. Pot up and grow on.
☀ 14 months
🌰 late summer to autumn, or spring, at
15–20°C (59–68°F). Germination can
be erratic.
🌱 I–4 months.   ☀ 6–12 months.

Dianthus
(Carnation, Pink)   Caryophyllaceae

About 300 species of annuals, biennials, and
often short–lived perennials. The many
cultivars of hardy, evergreen border
carnations and old-fashioned and modern
pinks are the most suitable for herbaceous
borders. Cuttings are the most common
method of increase; seed is only used for
annual and biennial species, or when raising
new cultivars.

PROPAGATION
Stem tip cuttings – summer, of non-flowering
shoots. Pinks can be increased by 'pipings'.
Pull the stem so that it parts at a leaf joint,
and treat as ordinary cuttings.   ☀ I year
Layering – summer, after flowering. For
border carnations and pinks that do not root
easily from cuttings.   ☀ I year.

Dicentra   Fumariaceae

Some 19 species of hardy annuals and
perennials, which may be taprooted,
tuberous, or rhizomatous. Dicentras are
grown for their fern-like foliage and for their

37

Dicentra spectabilis

Echinops bannaticus 'Taplow Blue'

Epimedium x *rubrum*

pendent, heart-shaped flowers. A number of named cultivars is available with flowers of creamy white, and shades of pink to deep carmine or crimson. Grow in moist, fertile, leafy soil in partial or dappled shade.
D. eximia. Rhizomatous, with narrowly heart-shaped, white, pink or pink-purple flowers, in late spring, often repeating through to autumn. H 60cm (24in), S. 45cm (18in).
D. spectabilis. Fleshy-rooted, with pink and white flowers in late spring and early summer. H 1–1.2m (3–4ft), S 45–60cm (18–24in).

PROPAGATION
✄ early spring. Clump-formers, such as *D. eximia*, are easily divided. *D. spectabilis* is best increased by cuttings. ☀ 1 year.
☘ autumn or spring, in a cold frame or at 15–20°C (59–68°F). Pre-chill spring-sown seed for 3 weeks. *D. spectabilis* and its white form, 'Alba', can both be grown from seed; the latter usually comes true.
🌱 1–3 months. ☀ 1 year.
Cuttings – take root or basal cuttings of *D. spectabilis* in spring.

Echinacea (Cone flower) Compositae
Some nine species of hardy, rhizomatous, spreading perennials, grown for their daisy-like flowers. Grow in fertile soil, in sun or part-day shade. An easy genus to increase, all species can be propagated in the same way.
E. purpurea, syn. *Rudbeckia purpurea*. Has red-purple ray florets around a central golden-brown disc, from midsummer to autumn. Cultivars and seed-raised hybrids are available with white, purple, or crimson flower heads, some with orange or orange-brown discs.
H to 1.5m (5ft), S 45cm (18in).

PROPAGATION
Basal cuttings – spring. ☀ 1 year.
☘ autumn or spring, sown fresh.
E. purpurea cultivars are unlikely to come true. All tend to self-seed.
🌱 1–4 months. ☀ 1 year.
✄ spring or autumn. They resent root disturbance and may be slow to re-establish.
☀ 6–18 months.

Echinops (Globe thistle) Compositae
About 120 species of mostly hardy annuals, biennials, and perennials, grown for their foliage and globular flower heads. Grow in well-drained, not too fertile soil, in sun. Division of the strong thick roots is difficult.
E. bannaticus. Woolly stems, spiny grey-green leaves, and blue flowerheads in late summer. 'Taplow Blue' has brighter blue flowerheads. H to 1.2m (4ft), S 60cm (2ft).
E. ritro. Spiny leaves with white hairs and blue flower heads in late summer. 'Veitch's Blue' has darker blue blooms in several flushes. H 60–90cm (2–3ft), S 45cm (18in).

PROPAGATION
Root cuttings – winter, 4–5cm (1½–2in) long. ☀ 18 months.
☘ autumn or spring, in a cold frame or seedbed, or at 15–20°C (59–68°F). Self-sows freely. Pot up seedlings in deep pots to minimize root disturbance. Offspring of cultivars are variable.
🌱 1–4 months. ☀ 18 months.

Epimedium Berberidaceae
Some 25 species of hardy, rhizomatous, evergreen or deciduous perennials, grown for their foliage and flowers. Grow in fertile, moist but well-drained soil in partial shade.

E. x *versicolor* tolerates sun and drier conditions. If grown in leafy, woodland-type soil, epimediums spread to form large stands which are easily divided. In spring it is best to wait until they have flowered. Alternatively, divide them in autumn so that they can settle down before the next flowering time.
E. grandiflorum, syn. *E. macranthum*. Has green leaves, bronze-flushed when young, and white, pink, yellow, or purple flowers in spring. H to 30cm (12in), S 30cm (12in).
E. x *rubrum*. Has dark red and yellow flowers in spring, and red leaves in autumn. H 30cm (12in), S 30cm (12in).
E. x *versicolor*. Produces coppery young leaves, with pink and yellow flowers in spring. H 30cm (12in), S 30cm (12in).

PROPAGATION
✄ autumn or after flowering. ☀ 1 year.
☘ autumn. Spring sowing may delay germination; pre-chilling for 3 weeks helps.
🌱 1–12 months. ☀ 1 year.

Erigeron (Fleabane) Compositae
About 200 species of hardy annuals, biennials, and perennials grown for their daisy-like flower heads in summer. The named cultivars have a colour range from pink (*E.* 'Dimity'), lilac-pink (*E.* 'Charity'), to violet (*E.* 'Dunkelste Alle', syn. 'Darkest of All'). Many will layer if trailing stems are covered with soil. Grow in well-drained soil in sun.
E. karvinskianus, syn. *E. mucronatus*. Produces white flowers that age to red-purple. H to 30cm (12in), S 90cm (36in) or more.

PROPAGATION
Basal cuttings – spring, 2.5–5cm (1–2in) long, with bottom heat, at about 15°C (59°F).
☀ 14 months.

Eryngium giganteum

Gentiana asclepiadea

Geranium 'Ann Folkard'

spring. Divide clump-forming species every 2–3 years to maintain vigour. ☀ 6 months.

in spring, in a cold frame. Seed is most satisfactory for the species, especially *E. karvinskianus*, which self-sows prolifically, producing many usable seedlings. ☠ 2–3 weeks. ☀ 14 months.

Eryngium (Sea holly)   Umbelliferae

About 230 species of mostly hardy, usually prickly, annuals, biennials, and perennials with attractive foliage and umbels of often metallic-hued flowers. The perennials are taprooted, making division difficult. Grow in well-drained, fertile soil in sun.

E. giganteum. Large, metallic-blue flowers with spiny, silvery bracts in summer. H 90cm (36in), S 45cm (18in).

E. x oliverianum. White-veined leaves, and bright blue flowers from midsummer to autumn. H 90cm (36in), S 45cm (18in).

E. x tripartitum. Many small blue-violet flowers with silvery grey-blue bracts, in midsummer and autumn. H to 90cm (36in), S 50cm (20in).

PROPAGATION

Root cuttings – winter, 5cm (2in) long. If the plant is expendable, lift and take off the roots, otherwise dig down and carefully remove a few roots from the side of the clump. *E .giganteum* should be increased from seed. ☀ 18 months.

autumn (preferably) or spring, in a cold frame, or at 15–20°C (59–68°F). Prick out into deep pots and plant out as soon as possible to minimize root disturbance. ☠ 1–4 months. ☀ 18 months.

spring. Take extreme care to avoid

damaging the deep, thick taproot. Root cuttings are preferable. ☀ 12–24 months.

Euphorbia (Spurge)   Euphorbiaceae

Some 2000 species, ranging from annuals to trees. Care should be taken when cutting or handling these plants as they produce a latex–type sap that can cause skin irritation and is dangerous and painful if it gets into the eyes. The hardy species include clump-forming perennials, like *E. amygdaloides* and *E. polychroma*, shrub-like perennials, such as *E. characias*, and prostrate perennial succulents, like *E. myrsinites*. Several, such as *E. griffithii* and *E. sikkimensis*, have glassy, red or pink young stems.

PROPAGATION

spring. Rhizomatous species and those with a spreading or clump-forming habit are easily divided. ☀ 12–18 months.

Cuttings – spring or autumn. Basal (*E. polychroma*), tip (*E. palustris*) and lateral (*E. griffithii*) cuttings can all be tried as some are more successful than others with certain species. Dip cut surfaces in charcoal to reduce bleeding. ☀ 18 months.

autumn or spring, in a cold frame. Offspring of cultivars are often very close, if not identical, to the parent. Pre–chilling and then some warmth, 15–20°C (59–68°F), may speed germination. Move self–sown seedlings when still small. ☠ 1–4 months. ☀ 12–18 months.

Gentiana (Gentian)   Gentianaceae

About 400 species of annuals, biennials, and perennials, the majority of which are considered alpines *(see p.83)*. The most commonly seen of the larger herbaceous

perennials, *G. asclepiadea*, is best grown from seed, although it can be divided carefully in spring, and basal cuttings are sometimes successful. It needs humus-rich, fertile, moist but well-drained soil, in part shade.

G. asclepiadea (Willow gentian). Bears trumpet-shaped, blue, occasionally white flowers, from mid- to late summer–early autumn. H to 90cm (36in), S 45cm (18in).

G. lutea (Yellow gentian) has a thick taproot and can only be increased from seed.

PROPAGATION

autumn, in a cold frame. Pre-chill spring-sown seed, then germinate at 15–20°C (59–68°F). Needs light for germination. *G. lutea* takes several years to reach maturity. ☠ 1–4 months. ☀ 18 months.

Geranium (Hardy cranesbill)   Geraniaceae

Some 300 species of annuals, biennials and perennials. They grow in most soils in sun or shade; smaller species require good drainage.

PROPAGATION

Between them, they are propagated by the complete range of techniques, including layering in summer (e.g. *G. procurrens*). The clump- or mat-forming types can be increased by division in spring. Many can be increased by cutting off part of the overground rhizome and potting it up. *G.* 'Ann Folkard' and similar, scrambling hybrids can be increased by stem cuttings taken in summer. *G. sanguineum* can be grown from root cuttings. Most species can be increased from seed in autumn or spring, and many cultivars, although not all, produce plants that are close to their parents, e.g. *G. wallichianum* 'Buxton's Variety'.

Geum chiloense

Gunnera manicata

Helleborus orientalis

Geum   Rosaceae

About 50 species of hardy perennials, grown for their single or semi-double flowers, produced throughout the summer. The best way to increase existing stock is by division but many cultivars, such as *G. chiloense* 'Lady Stratheden' and 'Mrs J. Bradshaw', come reasonably true from seed. Most are easily grown in fertile, well-drained soil, in sun.

PROPAGATION

✎ spring. Replant directly. In dry weather, pot up and plant out once the plant has re-established. ☼ I year.

🌰 autumn or spring. For best results, sow in a propagator at 15–20°C (59–68°F) or germination is likely to be slow or erratic.
🌱 1–4 months. ☼ 14 months.

Gunnera (Chilean rhubarb)   Gunneraceae

Some 40–50 species of giant, rhizomatous and diminutive, creeping perennials.
G. manicata. Almost hardy, but needs a deep mulch of leaf litter in cold areas. Grow in moist, fertile, humus-rich soil, in sun or dappled shade. Provide good shelter from cold winds. Division is the most effective method of increase. H 1.8m (6ft), S 2.1m (7ft).

PROPAGATION

✎ spring. Many gunneras are huge and impossible to dig up and divide in the conventional sense. The best method of propagation is to cut pieces from the edge of the clump, pot up in a large pot and in a fibrous compost, and keep moist.
☼ 2–3 years
🌰 autumn, as soon as ripe, at 15–20°C (59–68°F). 🌱 I month.
☼ 4–5 years.

Gypsophila   Caryophyllaceae

About 100 species of mostly hardy annuals and perennials, few of which are in cultivation. Most species can be easily grown from seed but cultivars of *G. paniculata* need to be increased vegetatively. Unfortunately, they are difficult to grow from cuttings and need to be wedge-grafted. Grow in deep, well-drained, slightly alkaline soil in sun.
G. paniculata (Baby's breath). Hardy perennial, with grey-green leaves, bearing clouds of tiny white flowers in summer.
'Bristol Fairy' has double white flowers.
'Flamingo' has pale pink blooms.
H 90–120cm (3–4ft), S 90–120cm (3–4ft).

PROPAGATION

🌰 spring at 15–20°C (59–68°F), or in a seed bed, when germination takes a bit longer.
🌱 2–4 weeks. ☼ 18 months.
Cuttings – spring or early summer, of young side shoots, with a heel. ☼ 14 months.
Wedge-grafting – summer, onto seed-raised rootstock of *G. paniculata*. Appropriate for 'Bristol Fairy' and 'Flamingo'. ☼ I year.

Helenium (Sneezeweed)   Compositae

Some 40 species of annuals, biennials, and mostly hardy, fibrous-rooted, clump-forming perenniasl with daisy-like flowerheads over long periods in summer. Cultivars are available in shades of yellow ('Butterpat'), orange ('Wyndley'), bronze-mahogany ('Moerheim Beauty'), and crimson-red ('Bruno'). All perennials and their cultivars are most easily increased by division.

PROPAGATION

✎ autumn or spring. Discard the woody centre. Divide routinely every 2–3 years.
☼ 3 or 15 months.

Helleborus (Hellebore)   Ranunculaceae

Some 15 species of rhizomatous perennials with cup- or saucer-shaped flowers in winter or early spring. Most are hardy or nearly so and thrive in leafy, humus-rich, fertile soil that does not dry out, in partial shade. Many named cultivars are available, and hybrids often occur where several species are grown together. *H. argutifolius* and *H. foetidus* are difficult to divide and should be raised from seed. Most cultivars of *H. orientalis* will not come totally true from seed, although many will come close to the original. For true reproduction, division is the safest method. This is also true for *H. niger*.
H. niger (Christmas rose). From early winter to spring produces white flowers that are sometimes flushed pink. 'Potter's Wheel' has large, pure white flowers with a green eye. H to 30cm (12in), S 45cm (18in).
H. orientalis (Lenten rose): Bears green-white flowers, flushed purple to pink, from midwinter to spring. H and S 45cm (18in).

PROPAGATION

🌰 autumn, as soon as ripe, in a cold frame. Prick out in spring. Pot up self-sown seedlings and grow on before replanting.
🌱 I month. ☼ 2 years.
✎ autumn, or in spring, after flowering. Separate into individual crowns with a sharp knife. Pot up and grown on in light shade. Slow to re-establish. ☼ 2 years.

Hemerocallis (Day lily)   Liliaceae

Some 15 species of mostly hardy perennials, some of which are evergreen or semi-evergreen. Grown for their flowers, lasting only a day, but produced throughout summer. There are numerous named

Hemerocallis 'Pink Prelude'

Hosta fortunei

Kniphofia 'Little Maid'

cultivars, which must be increased by division. They prefer fertile, humus-rich, moist but well-drained soil, in sun.

PROPAGATION

✄ spring. Tease apart by hand. Replant larger pieces and pot up the smaller ones.

☀ 15 months.

🌰 autumn or spring. Species only.
Pre-chill spring-sown seed for up to 3 weeks.

❦ 2 months, ☀ 2–3 years.

Heuchera Saxifragaceae

About 55 species of evergreen or semi-evergreen perennials, grown for their flowers and foliage. Most in cultivation are hardy. Species can be grown from seed or divided. Most forms divide very easily and can be planted straight back into the soil as long as it is not too dry. Named cultivars and hybrids are increased by division; *H. micrantha* var. *diversifolia* 'Palace Purple' can be grown from seed. Other cultivars do not come true.

H. micrantha. Lobed leaves marbled green and grey. It bears tiny white flowers in early summer. **var.** *diversifolia* **'Palace Purple'** has bronze-purple leaves. H 60cm (24in), or more, S 45cm (18in).

H. sanguinea (Coral bells). Lobed, rounded leaves, marbled dark and pale green, and bears red flowers, in summer. H 30cm (12in), S 30cm (12in).

PROPAGATION

✄ autumn or spring. Divide by hand, or cut with a knife; ensure that each piece has buds and roots. Pot up and grow on until established. ☀ 14 months.

🌰 spring, in a cold frame. Germination is quicker at 15–20°C (59–68°F).

❦ 1 month. ☀ 14 months.

Hosta (Plantain lily) Hostaceae

About 40 species of hardy perennials with numerous cultivars and hybrids, grown mainly for their foliage; many also have racemes of fragrant flowers in summer. Leaves range from small to large and come in all shades of green, through to blue-green, blue-grey, and grey-green, some variegated with gold, cream, or silver.

PROPAGATION

✄ spring. Lift plants and wash all the soil from the roots. Cut into individual crowns with a sharp knife and pot up the divisions.

☀ 2 years.

🌰 autumn or spring. Species only.

❦ 1–3 months. ☀ 2 years.

Iris Iridaceae

About 300 species of rhizomatous and bulbous perennials *(see also Bulbs, Corms and Tubers Directory, pp.68–69)*. The hardy, rhizomatous, summer-flowering bearded irises have sturdy rhizomes on or near the soil surface and fans of sword-shaped leaves. There are many cultivars, with large flowers having distinct standards and falls, with a 'beard' of hairs at the centre of the each fall petal. The other major group are the beardless irises, which include *I. spuria, I. sibirica* and their cultivars, with delicate flowers and narrow leaves.

PROPAGATION

✄ for rhizomatous irises, divide in summer, immediately after flowering. Divide clump-forming irises, such as *I. sibirica*, in spring, just as or just before new growth begins.

🌰 autumn, preferably as soon as ripe, or in spring, in a cold frame. Species only.

❦ 1–3 months. ☀ 3–4 years.

Kniphofia (Red-hot poker, Torch lily)
Liliaceae/Aloaceae

Some 68 species of rhizomatous, clump-forming perennials with upright, cylindrical racemes of small tubular flowers. It is mostly cultivars that are grown and they must be increased vegetatively.

PROPAGATION

✄ late spring. Tease crowns apart, cutting if necessary, then pot up and grow on until they are large enough to be planted out.

☀ 16 months

🌰 spring, in a cold frame. Species only.

❦ 2–4 weeks. ☀ 3–4 years.

Lychnis (Catchfly) Caryophyllaceae

Some 20 hardy species, most of which are perennials, grown for their flowers, and, in some species, for their silver foliage. They thrive in well-drained, fertile soil in sun. Grey-leaved species tolerate dry soils. Most species produce copious seed and will self-sow, providing plenty of useful seedlings, many of the colour forms coming true.

L. chalcedonica (Maltese cross). Bears brilliant scarlet flowers in early or midsummer. H to 1.2m (4ft), S 30cm (12in).

L. coronaria (Rose campion). Has grey leaves and a succession of magenta flowers in late summer. It is short-lived and best propagated each year. **'Alba'** has white flowers. **'Oculata'** has pink-eyed, white flowers; both come reasonably true from seed, unless pollinated by the magenta-flowered species. H 80cm (32in), S 30cm (12in).

PROPAGATION

🌰 spring, in a cold frame, seed bed, or *in situ*. Many self-sow freely.

❦ 2–4 weeks. ☀ 3–16 months.

Lychnis coronaria

Miscanthus sinensis

Paeonia 'Lovely Rose'

🔧 spring. Division is only suitable for clump-forming species, such as *L. chalcedonica*.
☀ 1–2 years.

Meconopsis (Blue poppies)   Papaveraceae

Some 43 species of hardy annuals, biennials, and perennials, noted for their blue poppy-like flowers; there is also yellow (*M. chelidonium*) and dusky red (*M. napaulensis*). Many of the perennials are short-lived or die after flowering. Most produce abundant seed and readily self-sow. Move seedlings as soon as possible, before the taproots begin to form. A few, such as *M. grandis*, can be divided after flowering. Likes a cool, moist atmosphere. Grow in leafy, open, moist but well-drained, neutral to slightly acid soil, in dappled shade.
M. betonicifolia (Tibetan blue poppy). Bears pendent, bright blue flowers in early summer. H 1.2m (4ft), S 40cm (16in).
M. grandis (Himalayan blue poppy). Bears nodding, blue to red-purple flowers in early summer. H to 1.2m (4ft), S 60cm (2ft).
M. x sheldonii. Bears pale to deep blue flowers in late spring–early summer. H to 1.5m (5ft), S 60cm (2ft).

PROPAGATION

🌰 as soon as ripe, in late summer. Overwinter seedlings in a well-ventilated cold greenhouse or frame; they are very susceptible to damping off. *Meconopsis* seed needs light for germination; do not cover.
🌱 1–4 months.   ☀ 18 months.

Miscanthus   Gramineae

Some 20 species of mostly hardy, clump-forming perennial grasses, grown for their foliage and silky flower panicles in late summer. Grow in moist but well-drained, not-too-fertile soil in full sun. The cultivars are most often grown; division is the best method of increasing them.
M. sinensis. Bluish green leaves and silvery, hairy flower panicles in late summer or autumn. Smaller cultivars include **'Variegatus'**, with leaves striped white and pale green, and **'Silberfeder'**, with silvery, pink-flushed flower panicles that persist through winter. H to 4m (12ft), S 1m (3ft) or more.

PROPAGATION

🔧 mid-spring, just as new growth begins. Large clumps can be divided by spading off a section and then dividing this by hand.
☀ 2 years.
🌰 spring, in a cold frame. Not suitable for cultivars.
🌱 2–4 weeks.   ☀ 2–3 years.

Nepeta (Catmint)   Labiatae

About 250 species of hardy and half-hardy perennials with aromatic leaves and spikes of flowers. The most common tolerate a range of well-drained soils, in sun or light shade.
N. x faassenii, syn. *N. mussinii.* Aromatic, grey leaves and spikes of lavender-blue flowers throughout summer. **'Six Hills Giant'** is similar, but much larger, reaching 90cm (3ft) tall. H 45cm (18in), S 45cm (18in).

PROPAGATION

Basal cuttings – spring. Or shear over after flowering, and take cuttings from the resultant new growth in late summer.
☀ 15 or 10 months.
🔧 spring. Water until established.
☀ 15 months.
🌰 autumn, in a cold frame or seed bed. Cultivars may not come true.   ☀ **2 years.**

Paeonia (Peony)   Paeoniaceae

About 33 species of mostly hardy, long-lived, tuberous-rooted perennials and shrubs, most of which are cultivated, as well as thousands of named cultivars, derived mainly from *P. lactiflora.* They have single, semi-double, or double flowers in early summer, in white and pink to rich crimson. Need deep, well-cultivated, fertile soil that is humus-rich and reliably moisture-retentive, in sun or light dappled shade.

PROPAGATION

🔧 autumn or early spring. Divisions re-establish slowly. Prepare the planting site thoroughly; incorporate organic matter. Keep well watered until re-established.
☀ 2–3 years.
Root cuttings – winter.   ☀ 3 years.
🌰 as soon as ripe, in autumn or in early winter. Suitable for species only. Retain pots undisturbed if germination does not occur in the first spring.
🌱 up to 2–3 years.   ☀ 3–4 years.

Papaver (Poppy)   Papaveraceae

About 70 species of annuals, biennials, and perennials grown for their silky, bowl- or cup-shaped flowers. Grow in fertile, well-drained soil in a sunny site.
P. orientale (Oriental poppy). Has divided leaves, scarlet flowers, in early summer. Many cultivars are available, with including (**'Perry's White'**) white and (**'Allegro'**) scarlet.
P. bracteatum. Similiar to *P. orientale* but with stiff habit.

PROPAGATION

Root cuttings – autumn or early winter, 5cm (2in) long. Either dig up the whole plant and discard it after taking cuttings, or dig

Papaver bracteatum

Pulmonaria angustifolia

Rudbeckia fulgida

down beside it carefully and remove only a few roots. Leaves appear before new roots; do not pot on until well rooted. ☀ 2 years.
❦ spring, in a cold frame. Transplant seedlings when small to minimize root disturbance. Cultivars of *P. orientale* are unlikely to come true from seed but can be increased from root cuttings.
❦ 2 weeks. ☀ 2 years.

Penstemon   Scrophulariaceae

Some 250 species of perennials and sub-shrubs, grown for their foxglove-like flowers which, in most border perennials, are borne from midsummer to autumn. Cultivars with a wide colour range, and of varying hardiness, are available. The hardiest include
P. 'Andenken an Friedrich Hahn' (wine-red), **'Appleblossom'** (pale pink) and **'Evelyn'** (rose-pink). The larger cultivars are grown mainly as perennials, while many of the species are grown as alpines. They are some of the easiest plants to root. Grow in well-drained, fertile soil in sun *(see also Alpines and Rock Garden Plants directory, p.80)*.
P. campanulatus, syn. *P. pulchellus*. Bears violet flowers in early summer. Hardy to about -5°C (23°F). This species is a parent of many modern hybrids. H to 60cm (24in), S 45cm (18in).

PROPAGATION

Cuttings – early or midsummer. Any part of the stem will root. Take stem tip cuttings at any time the plant is in growth.
☀ 12 months.
❦ autumn or spring. Species only. Cultivars will not come true and should be increased by cuttings. Many species self-seed freely.
❦ 1–4 months. ☀ 3–15 months.

Phlox   Polemoniaceae

Some 67 species of annuals, evergreen or herbaceous perennials, and a few shrubs. The hardy border phlox, cultivars of *P. maculata* and *P. paniculata*, are grown for their large fragrant flowers, borne in mid to late summer. Grow in moist but well-drained, fertile soil, in sun or partial shade. Phlox are very susceptible to stem eelworm; do not take propagating material from infested plants.

PROPAGATION

⚒ autumn or spring. Divide healthy clumps only, and discard old material from the centre of the clumps. ☀ 12 months.
Basal cuttings – spring. From healthy clumps only. Stem eelworm will be passed on if present on parent plants. ☀ 12 months.
Root cuttings – early autumn or winter. Root cuttings are usually free from eelworm infestation. ☀ 12 months.

Pulmonaria (Lungwort)   Boraginaceae

Some 14 species of hardy, rhizomatous perennials, grown for their funnel-shaped flowers, in shades of blue, pink, violet, red, or purple; some also have attractive spotted foliage. Grow in moist, leafy soil, in dappled or partial shade. All pulmonarias are best divided, although they grow readily from seed. In clumps of cultivars which have self-sown, different flower colours are likely to be present. Take cuttings from rogue plants if you like the colour; otherwise remove them.
P. angustifolia (Blue cowslip). Intense, deep blue flowers in spring.
H to 30cm (12in), S 45cm (18in).
P. rubra. Bears red to salmon-pink flowers in late winter and spring, above green leaves.
H to 40cm , S to 90cm (36in).

PROPAGATION

⚒ spring, after flowering. Wash soil from the roots and the plant will fall into natural divisions. Remove old rootstock and shorten the leaves. Pot up and plant out once they are growing strongly. ☀ 12 months.
❦ spring, in a cold frame. Species only. Cultivars self-sow, but are rarely true to type.
❦ 1 month. ☀ 12 months.

Rudbeckia (Coneflower)   Compositae

About 20 species of annuals, biennials, and hardy, rhizomatous perennials grown for their flowerheads with cone-shaped central discs, produced over long periods in summer. Grow in moist but well-drained soil, in sun or dappled shade. Division is the most satisfactory way of increasing these plants. Cuttings work well but may take longer. Seed is becoming increasingly available commercially but often produces slight variations in flower colour and pattern.
R. fulgida (Black-eyed Susan). Bears orange-yellow flowers with a dark brown central disc. Late summer to autumn.
H 90cm (36in), S 45cm (18in).
R. laciniata. Bears pale yellow flower heads with a greenish disc, from midsummer to autumn. **'Goldquelle'** is shorter, with double, lemon-yellow flower heads.
H 1.5m (5ft) or more, S to 1m (3ft).

PROPAGATION

⚒ spring or autumn. ☀ 18 months.
Basal cuttings – spring, 5cm (2in) long. Older shoots often already have a few roots attached to them. ☀ 18 months.
❦ spring, in a cold frame. Species only. Pre-chilling helps germination.
❦ 2–3 weeks. ☀ 8 months.

43

Salvia × *superba*

Sedum spectabile

Sidalcea malviflora

Salvia (Sage)   Labiatae

About 900 species of annuals, biennials, subshrubs, and perennials, some rhizomatous or tuberous-rooted. They are grown for their two-lipped, tubular flowers and their aromatic foliage (*see also Herbs directory, p.169*). The hardy border perennials prefer light, not-too-fertile, moist but well-drained soil, in sun. Commercially available seed can be used for propagating the species and some selected clones. Some salvias, such as *S. sclarea*, happily self-sow, providing enough seedlings for most purposes.
S. nemorosa. Dense spikes of white, pink, or violet-purple flowers in midsummer. Leaves are notched and wrinkled. **'Lubecca'** and **'Ostfriesland'** are more compact with violet and blue-violet flowers respectively. H to 1m (3ft), S 60cm (2ft).
S. × *superba*. Spikes of intense blue-violet flowers from midsummer to autumn. H 90cm (3ft), S 45cm (18in).
S. × *sylvestris*. Has wrinkled, scalloped leaves, and spikes of pink-violet flowers in early to midsummer. **'Mainacht'**, syn. 'May Night', has indigo-violet flowers with purple bracts. H 75cm (30in), S 30cm (12in).

PROPAGATION
✂ spring. Tuberous-rooted *S. patens*, which is not reliably hardy, can be lifted in autumn; divide before replanting in spring. ☀ 12 months.
Cuttings – basal in spring, stem-tip in early summer. Woody-based perennials – semi-ripe cuttings in late summer. Also take semi-ripe cuttings of more tender species to protect against winter loss. Overwinter semi-ripe cuttings in a frost-free frame or greenhouse. ☀ 12 months.

🌱 surface-sow in spring, in a cold frame. Suitable for species only. For more tender species, such as *S. patens*. Sow at 16–18°C (61–64°F). Cultivars rarely come true.
🌱 2–3 weeks. ☀ 1–2 years.

Sedum (Stonecrops)   Crassulaceae

Genus of some 400 species of fully hardy to tender, annuals, biennials, perennials, and shrubs, many of which are small alpine plants (*see also Alpines and Rock Garden Plants directory, p.85*). The larger, hardy species and their cultivars are valued for their handsome leaves, in spring and summer, and for their small, star-shaped flowers, in late summer and autumn. They prefer not-too-fertile, well-drained, neutral to slightly alkaline soil in sun.
S. spectabile, syn. *Hylotelephium spectabile* (Ice plant). This has fleshy, grey-green leaves and wide, slightly domed heads of pink flowers, in late summer and autumn. **'Brilliant'** has deep pink flowers. **'Septemberglut'**, syn. 'September Glow', has rich pink flowers. H 45cm (18in), S 45cm (18in).

PROPAGATION
Cuttings – spring, summer, or autumn. Stem or basal cuttings root easily. Leaf cuttings also grow readily; insert one or more leaves vertically in cutting compost in a propagating case; gentle bottom heat speeds rooting. ☀ 16 months.
✂ spring, ☀ 16 months.

Sidalcea (Prairie mallow)   Malvaceae

Genus of around 20 species of hardy annuals and perennials valued for their silky-petalled, cup-shaped flowers. Those most often grown are cultivars or hybrids and are best increased by vegetative means, such as division, to ensure that plants come true. They need light, moist but well-drained, fertile soil, in a sunny position.
S. malviflora (Checkerbloom). Produces clumps of glossy leaves and spires of pink flowers in midsummer. **'Elsie Heugh'** has pink flowers. **'Loveliness'** is lower-growing, with soft pink flowers. H to 1.2m (4ft), S 45cm (18in).

PROPAGATION
✂ spring or autumn. Lift and wash away the soil, then divide by hand, using a sharp knife if necessary. Split larger clumps with back-to-back forks. ☀ 14 months.
🌱 spring or autumn, in a cold frame. Species only; cultivars may self-sow, but do not come true.
🌱 2–3 weeks. ☀ 12 months.

Thalictrum (Meadow rue)   Ranunculaceae

Some 130 species of hardy and tender, tuberous or rhizomatous perennials. Several are hardy border perennials that are valued for their sometimes glaucous foliage and their tiny flowers with large, fluffy clusters of stamens and pistils. Grow in moist but well-drained soil in dappled shade, or in sun where soil remains moist.
T. aquilegifolium. Divided, pale green leaves and bears fluffy heads of rose-lilac flowers, in early summer. H 1m (3ft), S 45cm (18in).
T. delavayi, syn. *T. dipterocarpum*. Dainty, pale green foliage on purple-flushed stems, and panicles of white or lilac flowers in mid- to late summer. H 1.2m (4ft), S 60cm (2ft).

PROPAGATION
✂ spring. Replant immediately or pot up small divisions and grow on. Spreading plants,

Tradescantia Andersoniana Group

Veronica spicata

Yucca gloriosa 'Variegata'

such as *T. minus*, are easily divided. Small
clump-formers are not so easy.
☀ 12 months.
🌰 as soon as ripe or in spring, in a cold
frame. Many, such as *T. aquilegifolium*, self-sow.
Seedlings should be moved while still young.
🌱 2–3 weeks. ☀ 1–2 years.

Tradescantia   Commelinaceae
Genus of some 65 species of evergreen
perennials valued for their three-petalled
flowers with conspicuous stamens, borne
from early summer to autumn, and often
also for their attractive leaves. Those featured
are hardy. They prefer moist but well-drained,
fertile soil, in sun or dappled shade.
T. Andersoniana Group. This hardy selection
forms clumps of fleshy, jointed stems and
lance-shaped leaves, usually green, often
purple-tinted. Cultivars come in a range of
colours: '**Isis**' and '**Zwanenburg**' have deep
blue flowers, '**Osprey**' has white flowers with
blue filaments, '**Karminglut**', syn. '**Carmine
Glow**' has rich carmine-pink flowers.
H 45–60cm (18–24in), S 45–60cm (18–24in).

PROPAGATION
🔪 autumn or spring. ☀ 12 months.

Veratrum   Scrophulariaceae
Genus of some 45 species of hardy,
rhizomatous perennials mainly grown for
their foliage; they also produce spires of
small, star-shaped flowers. The leaves are
large and ovate and bright emerald-green as
they emerge in spring. Grow in deep, moist
but well-drained, fertile soil in partial shade,
with shelter from winds. Growing from seed
is not difficult – just lengthy. For the first year
of germination all growth is below ground, so

do not throw away the pot. Take care in
handling *Veratrum* as all parts are toxic.
V. album (False or White hellebore). White,
sometimes green-tinted flowers in summer.
H 1.8m (6ft), S 60cm (2ft).
V. nigrum. Produces maroon, flowers, in mid-
to late-summer. H 1.2m (4ft), S 60cm (2ft).

PROPAGATION
🌰 sow as soon as ripe in a cold frame. Grow
on in a nursery bed.
🌱 in spring. ☀ 3–4 years.
🔪 autumn or early spring, ☀ 2–3 years.

Veronica (Speedwell)   Scrophulariaceae
Genus of 250 species of annuals and woody-
based, sometimes rhizomatous perennials.
The hardy species are grown for their spikes
of white, pink, or blue flowers in summer.
Grow in moist but well-drained, fertile soil in
sun or dappled shade. Most are very easy to
increase by division.
V. gentianoides. Spikes of blue flowers in early
summer, and rosettes of glossy leaves.
H to 45cm (18in), S 45cm (18in).
V. longifolia. Produces tall, dense spikes of
blue to lilac-blue flowers, in late summer.
H 1.2m (4ft), S 30cm (12in).
V. spicata. Spikes of blue flowers throughout
summer, above narrow, hairy leaves.
subsp. *incana* has silver-hairy leaves and deep
violet-blue flowers.
H 30cm (12in) or more, S 45cm (18in).

PROPAGATION
🔪 autumn or spring. Discard the woodier
central portions. ☀ 1 year.
🌰 autumn or spring, in a cold frame. Many of
the larger species, such as *V. longifolia*, self-sow
and provide a ready supply of seedlings.
🌱 1–3 months. ☀ 1–2 years.

Yucca   Agavaceae
Some 40 species of evergreen, woody-based
perennials, shrubs, and trees, many of which
are frost-tender. They are grown for their
creamy-white flower panicles, up to 2.5m
(8ft) tall, and their architectural habit. Hardy
species need sharp drainage and full sun.
Outside of North America, yuccas must be
hand-pollinated for seed production.
Y. filamentosa (Adam's needle). Hardy species
with stiff, narrow leaves that have curly
threads at the margins. Flowers in mid- to
late summer. H 80cm (32in), S to 1.5m (5ft).
Y. flaccida Hardy with short, spreading
rosettes of narrow, blue-green leaves.
Flowers in mid- to late summer.
H 50cm (20in), S to 1.5m (5ft).
Y. gloriosa (Spanish dagger). Less hardy than
Y. flaccida, but with sharp drainage tolerates
temperatures to about -5°C (23°F). It has
blue-green to dark green leaves. '**Variegata**'
has leaves with yellow margins. Flowers in
late summer. H 1.8m (6ft), S to 1.8m (6ft).

PROPAGATION
🌰 spring, at 13–18°C (55–64°F). Subtropical
and tropical species need higher temperatures
to germinate.
🌱 1–2 months. ☀ 4–5 years.
Cuttings – autumn. Take stem cuttings from
sideshoots, and root in a propagator. Keep
frost-free in winter. Pot up in spring.
☀ 6 years.
Root cuttings – winter, 5cm (2in) long,
planted vertically. Rather than lifting the
whole plant, dig down beside it and remove
a few thick roots. ☀ 6 years.
🔪 spring. Suitable for yuccas with a
suckering habit, such as *Y. filamentosa*.
☀ 2–3 years.

ERNS

Ferns have long been popular as house and
conservatory plants, but in recent years hardy
ferns have once again become more widely
grown in gardens. Ferns complement almost
any garden style – whether planted in a shady
mixed border for contrast, or grouped in a
dark, damp corner where little else will grow,
their wonderful form and texture is almost
indispensable. In addition, ferns have the
advantage of giving some interest all year round,
many wintergreen species remaining handsome
until flattened by snow. The natural reproduction
of ferns is quite different to that of flowering
plants, and propagating them yourself provides
an opportunity both to increase stocks and to
observe a most fascinating process at first hand.

◄ *Massed plantings of* Matteucia
struthiopteris *provide a wonderful
effect in a shady border; this
particular fern can be increased
by division or spores.*

WHY PROPAGATE
FERNS?

Despite their bold, architectural shapes and subtle range of shades, ferns remain one of the most under-utilized of all the plant groups available to modern gardeners. While a single specimen can look quite magnificent they are best grown in clumps and, having mastered the basic propagation techniques, you will soon be able to rear any number of plants.

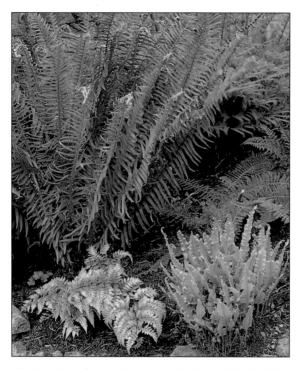

The ferns shown here and opposite can be increased by the full range of propagation techniques.

All ferns likely to be grown in the home or garden are perennials and, given the correct growing conditions, are exceptionally long-lived. So, quite unlike other perennials, which need propagating to maintain health, vigour and flowering, the main reason for propagating ferns is simply to increase numbers.

Ferns are not difficult to propagate. Sexual reproduction involves a recombination of the genes that determine physical appearance, so the offspring are seldom identical to either their parent or each other. In many cases this is of no importance, but selected garden forms often do not come true from spores and must be increased by vegetative methods.

INCREASING BY DIVISION

Where only a few additional specimens are required, this is the best method of increasing stocks. Division of mature plants inevitably causes some disturbance and is best carried out during spring. Species with creeping rhizomes, like *Adiantum venustum*, can be cut into sections and most will grow as long as they have some growing points. Species that form an upright crown, or shuttlecock, of fronds must be separated so that each individual crown remains intact if division is to be successful.

OPTING FOR SPORES

For mass multiplication of ferns it is most efficient to propagate from spores – a mature plant can produce one thousand million spores in one season! Increasing from spores is not difficult and the process itself is fascinating.

The life cycle for sexual reproduction is clearly divided into two generations. The generation we see as the fern plant is known as the sporophyte, which produces spores, usually on the underside of the fronds. Spores germinate and grow into a free-living structure, the prothallus, or gametophyte, which is the second generation. It is on this structure that the male and female sexual organs are found and gametes produced. As the male gametes must swim in a film of water beneath the prothallus to fertilize the female egg cells, an adequate moisture level is essential during this stage of reproduction.

After fertilization, the new fern is produced. The new plant parasitizes the now redundant prothallus, using its nutritious tissues to get a good start in life until it can produce its own root and the first leaf begins to function to provide it with a food supply.

ADDITIONAL RESOURCE

Mass production of ferns is sometimes possible from bulbils, and these offspring will almost invariably be identical to the parent. Bulbils tend to be produced most prolifically on *Polystichum setiferum* cultivars in wet summers or on adequately watered plants.

Interestingly, there is never any outward sign of a bulbil on the leaf bases of the Hart's-tongue fern, *Asplenium scolopendrium*, yet when treated correctly, nearly every leaf base will produce at least one fern.

'Living Antiques'

Some ferns have mutated to produce very attractive crested or finely divided plumose fronds. They seldom come true from spores and must be propagated vegetatively, which is generally a slow process. With some of the best cultivars, division is only possible when one or more side crowns are produced. Some cultivars have been propagated by this method since Victorian times. Identical to the original, they are often referred to as 'living antiques'. Polystichum

setiferum *'Plumosum Bevis'* and Athyrium filix-femina *'Clarissima' are good examples.*

Polystichum setiferum
'Plumosum Bevis'
with unfurling fronds.

1

Polystichum munitum
This species produces spores which ripen and may be sown in late summer. It forms shuttlecock crowns and can also be increased by careful division of side crowns in spring.

2

Athyrium niponicum var. pictum f. metallicum
A form that occasionally produces bulbils, and may be divided. Spores produce green- and coloured-leaved offspring in almost equal numbers, so select the most highly coloured variants.

3

Asplenium scolopendrium Crispum Group
These cultivars are generally unsuitable for division and produce variable offspring from spores. They can, however, often be induced to form bulbils on the base of the fronds.

4

Polystichum setiferum Divisilobum Group
Unlike the parent species, these cultivars often form bulbils along the frond midrib which can be sown to produce offspring identical to the parent plant.

PROPAGATING TECHNIQUES
FERNS

*The techniques of increasing ferns by division or from bulbils differ only
slightly from those used when dividing perennials or increasing bulbs from bulbils.
Spore propagation, however, is unique to the fern family. It may appear complex at first
but, in practice, the steps of the procedure are actually very simple.*

DIVISION

Most ferns can be propagated by division at the beginning of the growing season. Species with creeping rhizomes, such as *Adiantum venustum* and *Polypodium* species, can be cut into a number of sections. Most pieces will grow if you make sure that there are two to three healthy fronds on each division, with a 5cm (2in) ball of soil around each plantlet.

Many ferns have erect rhizomes with an upright crown, or shuttlecock, of fronds. Separate crowns with a knife, or prise apart using two forks. It often takes at least a year for the parent plant to recover.

Replant large divisions immediately. Pot up small ones in well-drained loamless compost, with added slow-release fertilizer. Protect for about three months in a sheltered spot, until established, and do not overwater.

BULBILS

Some ferns produce bulbils along the midribs of the fronds. With hardy ferns, these fronds may be layered onto the soil surface in autumn while still attached to the parent plant and left until spring, when the rows of little plantlets can be pricked out into seed trays.

Bulbils on leaf bases

Some ferns, notably *Asplenium scolopendrium* and its cultivars, can be propagated from leaf bases. This is very useful for sterile cultivars, such as *A. scolopendrium* 'Crispum'. In spring, wash the soil from an established plant to expose the old leaf bases. They may appear to be dead, but snap them off at their point of attachment to the main rhizome and you will see live tissue. Surface sterilize a tray of seed compost as if sowing spores (*see opposite*). Wash the leaf bases, then stick them in the compost bottom up, that is, the end that was

attached to the rhizome pointing upwards. Replant the parent. Place the tray in a clean plastic bag and keep in a light place at 15–20°C (59–68°F). After three months, one or several bulbils should develop on each leaf base. They will be ready to plant out the following spring.

Bulbils . . . .
Tender ferns, such as *Asplenium bulbiferum*, and hardy ferns where the fronds cannot be layered to the soil, may be propagated by pegging down fronds individually into seed trays.

▲ **1** Cut the frond from the plant and peg it into a seed tray of low-nitrogen compost or peat.

▲ **2** Place the tray in an inflated, sealed polythene bag. Keep at 15–20°C (59–68°F) in good light.

▲ **3** When the young plantlets reach 4–5cm (1½–2in) high, with 2–3 tiny fronds, prick out into potting compost. Lift the plants individually with a widger, ensuring that each has a good clump of soil attached to the root ball.

▲ **4** Pot up singly into 7.5cm (3in) pots, setting the root ball into a dibbled hole in the centre of the pot, at the same level as it was in the seed tray. Young plants are usually ready to plant out in 6–9 months, in early summer.

PROPAGATING FERNS FROM SPORES

Most true species of fern can be easily increased from fresh spores.

Collecting spores

Inspect the underside of the fronds for sori (the spore-bearing structures) from midsummer onwards. These are usually covered by a flap of tissue (the indusium). If, with the aid of a hand lens, shiny globules can be seen underneath it, the sporangia (the spore-containing structures) have not shed their spores. If the sporangia are pale, they are probably not ripe, so wait a few days until they darken. If the sporangia are shaggy, they have almost certainly shed their spores, so select another frond. Debris from old sporangia can be confused with fresh spores. If in doubt, scrape the 'spores' onto a piece of white paper and examine them with a hand lens. Spores can be recognized by the thousands of minute grains of uniform size.

When the sporangia are ripe, break off a section of frond and put it in a clean, dry envelope; after 2–3 days, dust-like spores will have dropped to the bottom. Clean any debris from the spores, as it can lead to contamination. In a draught-free room, tip the spores onto a piece of paper, hold at 45° and tap gently. Pieces of debris move down rapidly, spores very slowly: practice will tell you when the spores have separated. Return them to a fresh envelope or sow immediately.

Spore storage

Many spores can be stored in a cool place for several months, but *Osmunda* and *Lygodium* species must be sown within a few days of collection. Storage in a refrigerator can prolong the viability of all spores.

Sowing spores

Fill a seed pan with seed compost and sterilize by pouring boiling water gently over the surface through muslin to scald it thoroughly. Cover immediately with plastic film to prevent contamination by air-borne fungi, moss or fern spores. Sow the spores 24 hours later. Choose a draught-free room and a clean surface that can be swabbed down with industrial spirit. Spores are best sown as soon as possible after collection, when viability is highest. If possible, sow spores of the same species from different sources, mixed together.

Spores

Most ferns ripen spores in late summer. Success in propagation depends on following the steps below carefully, and maintaining high standards of hygiene throughout.

◀ **1** Prepare a label with the fern name and date of sowing, and set it on one side of the pot. Carefully tap the spores from a clean piece of paper to give a very thin covering to the compost surface. Place the pot immediately into a new polythene bag and seal it. Keep at a temperature of 15–20°C (59–68°F), in indirect light.

▶ **2** About 6 weeks later, a green film will appear on the surface of the compost. By the following spring, the prothalli should be easily distinguishable. To grow them on, you will need to lift small patches with the point of a knife.

◀ **3** Set out the patches of prothalli 1–2cm (½–¾in) apart, in depressions in a prepared pot of seed compost. Return to a clean, sealed plastic bag. Continue to keep the culture closed until tiny, erect fronds appear. Harden them off gradually.

▶ **4** Prick out the tiny ferns into a seed tray or modular tray of seedling compost. Water gently and cover with a plastic dome until the little ferns are established. After a few months, recognizable ferns about 5cm (2in) high can be potted on into individual pots.

This helps to ensure cross-fertilization thus increasing the genetic diversity so that the resulting ferns are likely to be more vigorous.

From sowing to planting out usually takes 2–3 years. If the culture is contaminated with moss, tease it out with tweezers and water from below with a solution of potassium permanganate. If algae invade, some ferns may yet survive. Although contamination may spread rapidly, it can be checked with a fungicide.

DIRECTORY OF
FERNS

Below are key tips on selected ferns that are particularly suitable for propagation. Unless otherwise specified, follow the detailed instructions given under the propagation section on pages 50–51.

Key

H   Height
S   Spread
B   By bulbils
✎   By division
Sp   By spores
PO   Time to planting out

Asplenium (Spleenworts)   Aspleniaceae

About 700 species of evergreen and rhizomatous, terrestrial, epiphytic, or rock-dwelling ferns. Relatively few are cultivated, but these include **A. bulbiferum** (Hen-and-chicken fern) and **A. nidus** (Bird's nest fern). Both are commonly grown as houseplants. **A. scolopendrium** (Hart's-tongue fern) and **A. trichomanes** (Maidenhair spleenwort) are both hardy species ideal for a well-drained, shady border.

PROPAGATION

✎ not normally recommended for this group. If attempted, pot up divisions into a gritty, sharply drained propagating medium. PO 3–4 months.
Sp ripen in late summer. Spores from the cultivars of *A. scolopendrium* will give rise to variable progeny. PO 2–3 years.

Asplenium scolopendrium

B – leaf bulbils of *A. bulbiferum* can be grown in the usual way. Bulbils are the best method of multiplying cultivars of *A. scolopendrium*. They are very rarely found on the fronds, but can almost always be stimulated to grow on the leaf bases (see p.50).
PO 6–12 months.

Athyrium   Woodsiaceae

About 100 species of deciduous, terrestrial or rock-dwelling ferns with erect or creeping sometimes branched rhizomes and variable attractive fronds. **A. filix-femina** (Lady fern) and its cultivars, and **A. niponicum var. pictum f. metallicum** syn. 'Pictum' (Japanese painted fern), both of which are hardy, are the most commonly grown. They need damp or wet, shady conditions and are ideal for pool sides.

PROPAGATION

✎ the only way to propagate the cultivars called 'living antiques' that ensures the continuation of a true clone.
PO 6 months.
Sp ripen in late summer. Cultivars will produce variable progeny. *A. niponicum* var. *pictum* f. *metallicum* produces approximately 50 per cent green-leaved and 50 per cent purplish-leaved offspring. PO 1–2 years.

Blechnum gibbum

B very rarely produced, but, with luck, can be spotted with a hand lens on the pinnules or the pinnule stalks. Harvest bulbiferous leaves and keep warm in a closed case or polythene bag. PO 1–2 years.

Blechnum   Blechnaceae

Some 200 species of rhizomatous and evergreen, terrestrial or epiphytic ferns, some of which are grown as houseplants: **B. gibbum** (Miniature tree fern) for example. **B. spicant** (Hard fern), **B. chilense**, syn. *B. tabulare*, and **B. penna-marina** are all hardy plants suitable for growing in the garden. They prefer a site in leafy, acid soil in a damp, shady border.

PROPAGATION

✎ spring, for creeping species like *B. penna-marina* and, to a lesser extent, *B. chilense*. Species with upright rhizomes, like *B. spicant*, can be separated with care. PO 3 months.
Sp ripen in late summer. Use an acidic propagating mixes for spore sowing. PO 2–3 years.

Dryopteris (Male fern, Buckler fern, Wood fern)   Dryopteridaceae

About 200 species of rhizomatous terrestrial ferns. They are mainly deciduous but may stay green in sheltered sites. There are also many cultivars, most of which are hardy and suited to growing in the garden in well-drained or damp positions. They can tolerate modest amounts of direct sunshine.

PROPAGATION

✎ as growth begins in spring. Most have upright rhizomes and, with age, produce side-crowns around the side of the main crown, which can be separated in the usual way. PO 3–6 months.
Sp late summer. Spore-raised progeny from cultivars of *D. affinis* (Golden male fern)

Matteuccia struthiopteris

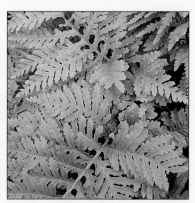

Polypodium vulgare

come true to type. Cultivars of other species come fairly true, except for the crested cultivars, which are less reliable. PO 2–3 years.

Gymnocarpium   Woodsiaceae

Genus of five species of hardy, terrestrial, deciduous ferns with long, creeping rhizomes which may colonize areas rapidly where conditions suit them.

G. dryopteris (Oak fern). With distinctive triangular fronds, to 18cm (7in) long, this species establishes rapidly in sites of dappled shade, in leafy, well-drained soil.
H 20cm (8in), S indefinite.

PROPAGATION

✎ all species have creeping rhizomes and are easily split up. PO 3–6 months.
Sp easy from spores, but division is so successful that spore propagation is rarely necessary. PO 2 years.

Matteuccia   Woodsiaceae

Between two and four species of hardy, deciduous ferns with erect or creeping rhizomes and short, trunk-like bases.
M. struthiopteris (Ostrich fern). The most widely grown of the genus. It is ideal for wet, shady borders or shady pool sides.
H 1.7m (5½ft), S 1m (3ft).

PROPAGATION

✎ Although *M. struthiopteris* has an erect crown, or 'shuttlecock', it also produces a creeping rhizome. New crowns are produced at random, 15–30cm (6–12in) away from the parent plant. Separate and replant in a new site immediately.
PO Immediately.
Sp early spring. Stumpy, black, unhealthy-

looking, spore-bearing fronds are produced at the centre of the shuttlecock in late summer. In autumn, the outer green fronds wither rapidly but the sporing fronds stand erect all winter. The spores ripen in late winter. Sow immediately or store in a refrigerator. PO 2–3 years.

Onoclea   Woodsiaceae

Genus of one or two species of hardy, rhizomatous, deciduous ferns.
O. sensibilis (Sensitive fern) This is the widely grown species with triangular or more lance-shaped, divided, pale green fronds. It is suitable for growing in wet and shady positions in the garden. H 60cm (24in), S indefinite.

PROPAGATION

✎ spring. *O. sensibilis* spreads vigorously, and is easily divided. PO Immediately.
Sp early spring. Sporangia are borne on specialized fronds that resemble pipe cleaners – dark sticks covered with small beads near the tip – and are produced in late summer. Spores are green and ripen in late winter. Sow immediately or store in a refrigerator. PO 2 years.

Osmunda   Osmundaceae

About 12 species of hardy and tender, rhizomatous and sometimes trunk-forming, deciduous ferns.
O. regalis (Royal fern). The most commonly grown, it is hardy, forming impressive large 'shuttlecocks' of pale blue-green fronds. It makes a magnificent large specimen for wet areas and pool sides and will tolerate direct sun if given adequate moisture at the roots.
H 1.8m (6ft), S 4m (12ft).

PROPAGATION

✎ spring. Many species, including *O. regalis*, produce a huge rootstock that can be cut into pieces for growing on. Ensure that individual crowns are clearly separate as failures are not uncommon. PO Immediately.
Sp produced in early summer in specialized clustered structures, either at the tip of otherwise normal fronds, as in *O. regalis*, or on specialized fronds, as with *O. cinnamomea*. Spores are green and should be sown immediately or stored in a refrigerator. PO 2–3 years.

Polypodium   Polypodiaceae

Some 75 species of terrestrial, epiphytic, or rock-dwelling ferns, with creeping, often surface rhizomes. The genus includes a few hardy species and their cultivars. Most are wintergreen but some, e.g. *P. cambricum,* syn. *P. australe,* become leafless during the summer months. They thrive in well-drained borders, with or without direct sun.

PROPAGATION

✎ The commonest method of increase. All species have creeping rhizomes that can be readily cut. Use a free-draining compost. PO Immediately.
Sp late summer or autumn for most species; spores of *P. cambricum* ripen through midwinter. Sporangia of *P. cambricum* are yellow when ripe, making quite a feature in the winter garden. The cultivars do not come reliably true from spores.
B very rare but occasionally produced all over the upper surface of the fronds of *P. vulgare* 'Elegantissimum'. They are difficult to strike but worth trying in low-nutrient compost or peat substitute.

BULBS, CORMS AND TUBERS

In gardens, the term 'bulb' is generally used to include corms, tubers, and rhizomes. Plants with these subterranean storage organs have a relatively brief period of growth and flowering – the majority in spring and early summer – followed by a long dormancy below ground. This means that bulbs can be used to prolong the season of interest by enhancing the dull periods before other plants peak or when they are past their best. They can also be used in formal spring displays, as well as in containers, both indoors and out. However, bulbs create the most memorable effects when naturalized *en masse* in short turf or beneath trees and shrubs – reason enough to propagate your own.

◄ *Important bulbous plants, such as tulips and hyacinths, are propagated by a range of techniques that are specific to bulbs.*

WHY PROPAGATE
BULBS, CORMS AND TUBERS?

Whether naturalized in grass, incorporated in a border scheme or planted in containers, for maximum impact bulbs should be grown in generous clumps. Since they can be expensive, and the choicer varieties are often only available in limited quantity, it is simple good husbandry to master the technique of multiplication for yourself.

Few sights can match the joy that the first bulbs of spring bring, heralding the start of another gardening year with their fresh colours and often rich perfumes. Of course, bulb displays are not confined to this early flourish and throughout the season there are choice specimens to covet. They are all very different, but have one thing in common – the bigger the clump, the better they look. By propagating your own bulbs, such massed plantings can be achieved very cheaply. From seed, bulbs usually take four to seven years to reach maturity, or even longer in large species. Fortunately for those gardeners who lack the necessary patience, there are a number of alternative techniques that are usually much quicker in producing results.

GROWING FROM SEED

Bulbs are expensive. Seed collected from your own plants is free and, having been produced under local conditions, is more likely to succeed in your garden. Given suitable growing conditions, most species will produce seed, and the offspring will usually be the same as the parent plant. Hybrids and named cultivars, even if fertile, rarely reproduce themselves and their offspring will display mixed combinations of characteristics. Nevertheless, such seed can be sown for interest and may produce offspring that are unique to your garden.

There are a variety of bulbs and cormous plants shown here that will need a variety of techniques to propagate.

DIVIDING CLUMPS

Many bulbs produce offsets that can be separated off to increase stocks. Division is essential for some species, since, if clumps become overcrowded, they eventually cease flowering. Lift such clumps when dormant, separate loose bulbs, remove old debris, and replant parent and offspring into fresh soil or a new site.

CUTTINGS AND CUTTAGE

Several more specialized techniques may be used to increase the stock of a wide range of bulbs. Scaling, chipping, scoring, scooping, sectioning and cuttings are all options which involve causing intentional damage to a specific part of the bulb, which in turn responds by producing offsets or bulblets from dormant buds. It includes scaling, chipping, scooping, scoring and sectioning. All of these techniques demand perfect hygiene and although they are more commonly used by commercial growers, they can, with practice, be mastered to great advantage by the amateur gardener.

Tulip-Breaking Virus

This virus is spread by sap-sucking aphids, and causes feathering, streaking or flaming on the ground colour of the petals of tulips. Its effects are most famously seen on the Rembrandt tulips depicted by the Dutch painters of the 17th century. The virus is not transmitted by seed, and these old varieties can be maintained only by propagating from offsets. The Rembrandts will, however, form a source of virus infection and, for this reason, must be grown in

isolation away from other tulips and other susceptible bulbs, such as lilies.

The feathered markings of *Tulipa* 'Striped Bellona' are typical of those induced by the tulip-breaking virus.

They are a very effective way of bulking up the numbers of your stocks, and ideal where massed plantings are needed.

Taking cuttings from true bulbs is not an option, since their leaves and stems do not have the ability to form root initials. However, cuttings are a very economical way of increasing tuberous-rooted plants, such as dahlias. If induced into growth early in the year, basal cuttings taken from the resulting shoots will produce flowers later the same season.

① Tulipa species
Unlike the highly bred cultivars, which either do not produce seed or do not come true, many small *Tulipa* species can produce flowers from seed in their third or fourth year.

② Anemone blanda
The knobbly tubers divide naturally to form large clumps. For more rapid increase, section the tubers into 1 cm (½in) pieces when dormant, but do not allow them to dry out.

③ Muscari
Many of the grape hyacinths in cultivation are true species and are easily increased by seed and often self-sow. They will flower in their second or third year.

④ Tulipa 'Red Riding Hood'
As with most other *Tulipa* cultivars, this produces offset bulblets at the base of the mother bulb. Increase your stock by separating bulblets and grow them on in a nursery bed.

⑤ Narcissus
Only species and new cultivars of *Narcissus* are raised from seed. Cultivars are propagated by separation of offset bulbs in early or late summer, and larger bulbs can be sectioned or twin-scaled.

PROPAGATING TECHNIQUES
BULBS, CORMS AND TUBERS

Division is one of the simplest means of bulb propagation and raising plants from seed is another option, producing large numbers of offspring, although these can take some time to reach flowering size. However some bulbs do not readily produce offsets or set seed and for these there is a range of alternative propagation techniques.

WHAT IS A BULB?

The term 'bulb' is often rather loosely applied to a variety of plants that have a specialized, subterranean food-storage organ and a periodic growth habit which makes it possible for them to survive, while dormant, during an inclement period of either severe cold or high temperatures without moisture. On the return of suitable growing conditions, the stored nutrients allow the plant to make immediate and rapid growth. This rapid growth ensures that the plant can flower and set seed in the short time available before the next season's dormancy is enforced by the return of unsuitable growing conditions, whether they are cold and wet or hot and arid.

Included in this category are true bulbs, corms, tubers and rhizomes. Since all these food-storage organs also contain growth buds, at the base of the scales, or on the surface of corms, rhizomes and tubers the gardener is able to use them as material for a wide range of vegetative propagation techniques.

Bulb types ....

Bulbs, corms, tubers and rhizomes are all subterranean food-storage organs, but their appearance and structure – and hence the methods of propagation appropriate to each – vary considerably. You will need to know which type you are dealing with in order to select the correct propagation technique in each case.

1 A bulb is a compressed stem and its fleshy scales are modified leaves. The scales have growth buds at their bases and enclose the flower bud initials that will produce the coming season's flowers. The papery tunics are the dried remains of previous season's scales. Some bulbs, like lilies, are composed of a large number of scales, while others have only two or three, as with *Fritillaria*. Other examples of scaly bulbs include, *Hippeastrum* and *Narcissus*.

2 A rhizome is a horizontally growing stem, usually narrow and elongated, which sends up leaves or flower stems at intervals from buds produced along the rhizome or at its tip. Many grow below the soil surface, while others, such as *Iris* and some rhizomatous anemones, are partly exposed.

3 A corm is the swollen base of a stem in which reserve food materials are stored. It is usually rather flattened or compressed and solid, with buds on its upper surface at the base of the previous year's growth. New corms are produced annually on top of the old one. Examples of cormous plants include *Crocus*, *Gladiolus* and *Freesia*.

4 A tuber is the swollen part of an underground stem. Usually rounded, it may have various protrusions or depressions containing growing buds in shallow axils, often spirally arranged over the surface, as in *Tropaeolum*. The tubers of *Anemone* are hard, knobbly and somewhat flattened. Some tubers have buds only at the top, where old growth has died back, as in *Dahlia* and *Cyclamen*.

BULBS FROM SEED

Relatively few bulbous plants raised from seed will flower within a year, but *Tigridia pavonia*, *Dahlia* and *Freesia* are among those that do. The seeds of these plants must be sown in warmth, in late winter or very early spring, and good growing conditions must be maintained, with appropriate feeding in the later stages. For most hardy bulbous plants, however, seeds should be sown in late summer or early autumn, as the process of germination is initiated by the falling temperatures at this time of year.

Sowing seed

Sowing seed collected from the bulbs in your garden is an inexpensive way to produce large numbers of plants, although the young bulbs will take several years to reach flowering size.

▶ **I** Fill a clay or plastic pot with compost to within about 2.5cm (1in) of the rim. Sow the seeds evenly and thinly on the surface of the compost and cover with sieved compost to a depth roughly five times the diameter of the seed. Top with a layer of coarse grit to just below the pot rim, to deter algae and liverwort growth and prevent disturbance of the seed by heavy rain. Label with the plant name and date. Plunge the pot to its rim in the open ground, or in an open frame with a sand base, in a position out of direct sun.

Aftercare
Once seedlings have germinated, grow them on in good light, with shade from hot sun, and keep them evenly moist until the leaves show signs of dying back. Stop watering and keep dry during the dormant period. Resume watering only when signs of new growth are visible. Natural rainfall usually provides sufficient moisture, but, in dry periods, additional water may be required. Keep a glass or plastic frame light at hand to be used during severe weather and dormancy.

▶ **2** If growth has been vigorous, pot the small bulbs into trays or individual pots of potting compost in the late summer of their first year, then replace the pots in the frame. Most bulbs will take two growing seasons before they are ready to be potted on. Leave them in their pots and apply a half-strength, balanced liquid feed during their second growing season.

Smaller bulbs will be ready to be planted out at the end of their second year and may bloom in their third. Most of the larger hardy bulbs may be planted out in the garden at the end of their third year.

Division

Detaching the smaller daughter bulbs from large bulbs, such as *Crinum*, is essential to maintain vigour and flowering, as well as being a useful way in which to increase your stocks.

▶ In spring, just before growth begins, lift the clump, retaining as much as possible of the massive root system. Shake off loose soil, and remove any that is compacted, using a jet of water from a hose pipe. Separate large individual bulbs from the clump by hand, or, if necessary, use back-to-back forks to prise congested clumps apart. Gently pull away offsets from the base of the mother bulb, retaining as many roots as possible. Pot up the offsets singly into sandy potting compost, with the growing point just above the surface of the compost, and grow on for one or two seasons before planting out in their permanent flowering site. Replant the parent bulbs directly into the flowering site, setting them out at appropriate spacings.

The majority of bulb seed does not require any pre-sowing treatment. A few plants, such as some *Iris*, have hard, impermeable seed coats that benefit from nicking or chipping so that water can penetrate to initiate germination. To do this, use a sharp knife to remove a small piece of the seed coat and expose the pale interior, then sow in the usual way.

Some species, like the South African *Gladiolus*, which originate in areas where bush fires are commonplace, require smoke treatment to initiate growth. They do not need heating, but should simply be placed in a sieve suspended in smoke from a garden bonfire for 15–20 minutes. The chemicals in the smoke destroy the germination inhibitors.

Cyclamen seed is best sown as soon as ripe, but, if sowing dry seed, soak for 24 hours in tepid water to which a single drop of household detergent has been added, then rinse before sowing.

Sowing and growing on
A loam-based seed compost mixed with one quarter part by volume of sharp sand or seed–grade perlite is a suitable medium in which to germinate most bulb seeds. For seed of woodland bulbs, add an additional quarter part of sieved leaf mould.

Offsets . . . .

Many bulbs produce numerous small offsets around the mother bulb, and removing these to grow on individually is one of the easiest methods of propagation.

◄ **1** When the bulbs or corms of *Narcissus, Crocus* or *Colchicum* become overcrowded, lift the clumps during the dormant period. Separate the bulbs from the soil or compost and then gently pull offset bulbs from the mother bulbs. Rub off the old dry tunics and dried remains of root. Select only plump bulbs and offsets with no sign of damage or disease. Mother bulbs and larger offsets may be replanted directly into fresh soil or a new site.

► **2** Grow on smaller offsets in pots or in a nursery bed, for one or two growing seasons. Plant them at twice their own depth, at least one bulb width apart.

Bulbils and bulblets . . . .

Collect leaf axil bulbils as they ripen during summer, before the parent plant dies back. They will be dark brown and will come away easily when fully ripe. To collect stem bulblets, lift the parent bulb when the flowering stem has died back after flowering or cut the dry stem from the parent bulb. Pick off the bulblets carefully, to avoid damage to any small roots that may already have formed.

◄ **1** Set bulbils on the surface of a prepared pot of compost, pushing them into the surface to no more than one quarter of their height. Cover with a layer of grit, so that it barely covers the nose of the bulbil. Grow on in a cold frame. The following autumn, pot up individual bulbs separately, or if growth has been vigorous, set the whole pot out in the flowering site.

◄ **2** Plant bulblets at twice their own height in a prepared pot of compost and top-dress with a layer of grit. After care is as for bulbils (*see above*); both will take 2–5 years to flower.

Alternative techniques for seed

A few genera and species germinate more reliably using other techniques. Seeds of many genera in the family Amaryllidaceae have flat seeds of a papery texture that root easily in moist soil before sprouting. Float them on the surface of water in a saucer, or sow onto damp flannel or kitchen tissue. Keep out of direct sun, at 16–25°C (61–77°F). Do not allow to dry out, even for a short time. Viable seed should sprout within 4–10 days. When the leaf is 5–8cm (2–3in) long, transfer the seedlings to an open, sterilized compost to grow on.

In some genera, like *Nerine* and *Crinum*, the seeds may germinate while still attached to the flower stem and immediately develop small bulbs that produce first roots and then leaves. These may be removed and treated as small plants to be grown on in the same compost as used for the parent plant.

DIVISION

When grown in favourable conditions, many bulbs produce numerous offsets or daughter bulbs which, through over-crowding and competition for nutrients, eventually deteriorate and become non-flowering. So, as well as increasing your stock, division is also necessary to maintain vigour and flowering potential.

There are several slight variations in technique when dividing different bulbs. Bulbs like *Crinum, Nerine* and *Amaryllis belladonna* form substantial clumps with a mass of fleshy roots and often produce several offset daughter bulbs from the base of large mother bulbs.

Anemones have different types of rootstock. Divide the finger or twig-like rhizomes of *Anemone nemorosa* and its cultivars during the dormant season, by simply breaking them apart at the natural joints. The knobbly tubers of *A. blanda, A. coronaria* and the De Caen and St Brigid cultivars may be cut or broken into small pieces not less than 1cm (½in) in diameter, prior to replanting in autumn.

BULBILS AND BULBLETS

A number of bulbous plants, including *Tritonia* and, especially, *Lilium* species, produce stem bulbils in the leaf axils on the aerial parts of the stem, or bulblets on the underground-rooted portions of the stem. Both provide an easy and convenient means of propagation and offspring are identical to the parent plant.

Scaling ....

Scaling is a useful method of propagation for bulbs that produce numerous and/or clearly defined scales that can be separated easily from the parent bulb. *Lilium* is the prime example, and as the bulbs can be expensive to buy, it is well worth propagating your own during the dormant season from plants already growing in the garden.

◄ **1** Between late summer and autumn, select a sound, healthy bulb with plump scales. Pull the outer scales away from the parent bulb's basal plate. Reject any that are soft and flabby, or dried and wrinkled. Place the scales in a plastic bag of fungicide powder and revolve it gently to coat them thoroughly. Empty out the scales and dust off any surplus fungicide.

◄ **2** Transfer the scales to a clean plastic bag with about four times their own volume of a mix of equal parts peat and sharp sand, vermiculite or perlite. Shake gently to ensure even distribution. Inflate the bag, seal with a wire tie and put in a dark place, at about 16–25°C (61–77°F). Inspect periodically, and remove any scales that show signs of rotting.

◄ **3** When small bulbs appear at the base of the scales, after about 4–12 weeks, separate them from the compost. Remove the bulblets from any scales that have become soft, but leave firm scales in place. Pot each scale in a small pot of well-drained potting compost, and top-dress with a 5mm (¼in) layer of grit, so that the scale tip is just at the surface. Grow on in a shaded cold frame.

◄ **4** At the end of the first growing season, separate out the bulblets, pot them on individually and return them to the cold frame. The following spring, if large enough they can be set out in their permanent positions in the garden. Alternatively, grow the bulblets on in pots for a further year before planting them out.

Chipping ....

This method of propagation is useful for increasing stocks of *Hippeastrum* and other bulbs that are not easy to divide and/or do not set seed. Cutting the bulb into chips stimulates it to produce bulblets in response to the injury. Success depends upon meticulous hygiene at all stages to prevent disease penetrating the cut surfaces.

◄ **1** Choose a healthy, mature bulb and cut off the roots and nose using a sharp knife, which has first been sterilized using methylated spirit. The roots should be sliced off immediately below the basal plate. The length of the section of nose removed must be no more than one quarter of the overall length of the complete bulb.

◄ **2** Place the bulb nose-end down on the work surface and slice in half vertically, cutting down through the basal plate. Repeat until you have 16 chips, ensuring that each has a segment of basal plate attached (smaller bulbs will yield 4–8 chips). Soak the chips in fungicide for about a quarter of an hour, stirring occasionally to ensure good penetration.

◄ **3** Place the chips in a plastic bag containing moistened vermiculite (1 part water to 2 parts vermiculite by volume is sufficient). Seal the bag and place it in a warm, dark place at about 20–25°C (68–77°F), for around 12 weeks. Young bulblets will develop from the basal plate between the chips.

◄ **4** Once they are large enough to handle, or have begun to form roots, you can separate the bulblets and pot them up individually into small pots of potting compost. Otherwise, plant the chip and bulblets in their entirety so that the bulblet nose is just below the surface of the compost.

Twin-scaling ....

As with chipping, good hygiene is essential throughout the twin-scaling process to prevent disease entering the cut surfaces of the bulb segments.

◄ I The procedure for twin-scaling is essentially the same as for chipping, except that each segment is further divided into pairs of scales, each with a tiny section of basal plate.

► 2 The bulblets appear from between the pairs of scales. Chipped or twin-scaled bulbs take about 2–3 years to reach flowering size.

CUTTAGE

There are several techniques that fall under the general heading of 'cuttage', all of which cause intentional damage to the bulb, corm, or tuber to encourage the production of small offsets from dormant buds. All these are slightly more specialist techniques that demand greater care, attention to detail and good hygiene.

Scaling

Lilium species and cultivars are often increased by this method. It can also be used on bulbs of *Fritillaria* species, which generally have only a few scales, but these are usually clearly defined and easily separated by making a vertical cut between them with a scalpel blade.

After separating from the parent bulb and dusting with fungicide, the scales may be planted directly into trays of propagating compost. Bury them to half their height with the tips uppermost, and cover with sphagnum moss or a polythene sheet. Keep them moist and shaded, at about 21°C (70°F) for 4–12 weeks, then transfer to a cold frame to grow on.

Chipping and twin-scaling

Chipping is often used to increase cultivars of *Hippeastrum* and it is equally suitable for increasing other true bulbs, especially those that do not divide readily, or which do not set seed. Twin-scaling, often used to increase *Narcissus* and *Galanthus* (snowdrops), is similar to chipping, but involves reducing the cut sections to pairs of scales. Since both of these methods involve cutting through the flesh of the bulbs, good hygiene is essential at all stages to minimize the risk of contamination of cut surfaces by disease. All work surfaces and cutting blades should be sterilized by swabbing them with methylated spirit.

Scooping ....

Scooping is a good method for propagating hyacinth cultivars, which produce few offsets and do not come true from seed. Only the simplest of tools – an old spoon with a specially sharpened edge – is required.

◄ I Hold the bulb upside down and scoop out the central section of the basal plate with the sharpened edge of a spoon. Take good care not to damage the outer rim of the basal plate. The depth of the scoop is critical: aim to remove only as much basal-plate tissue as is necessary to expose the lowest point of the scale leaves. Dust the cut surface with fungicide.

◄ 3 Small bulblets will form over the cut surface of the mother bulb after about 12–14 weeks. They should be left in place for the next stage of the process.

◄ 2 Set the prepared bulbs in a tray of sand, with the cut surface uppermost. Place the tray in a warm, dark place, at 25°C (77°F), for about a week. Then moisten the sand in the tray to prevent desiccation of the bulbs.

◄ 4 Plant the mother bulb upside down in a pot of gritty, sharply drained potting compost with the nose of the young bulblets just below the compost surface. The bulblets will produce leafy growth in spring. In late summer, when the leaves die down, lift, separate and pot up individually. The plants will flower in 3–4 years.

Scoring . . . .

Similar to scooping, scoring is a relatively simple procedure. Make two V-shaped incisions at right angles to each other across the basal plate of the bulb. Dust with fungicide and treat as for scooped bulbs. The bulblets will take 2–3 years to reach flowering size.

Scooping and scoring

Scooping and scoring are techniques that involve injuring the basal plate to promote the production of small bulblets. They are most commonly used for bulking up hyacinth cultivars, which are slow to form offsets and would not come true from seed, even if any were produced. Scooping is generally the more productive method. Commercially, a special curved tool is used, but an old spoon with a sharpened edge will perform the job equally well. In late summer, select healthy bulbs about 8–10cm (3–4in) in diameter. Scoring produces a smaller number of slightly larger bulblets.

CORMELS

A number of genera, particularly *Gladiolus*, produce numerous cormels, usually around the junction of the old and new corms, which are insurance against the death of the parent. These do not usually grow to flowering size unless separated from the parent. Lift the parent corm, complete with its stem, in late summer or early autumn, as it dies back after flowering. Store in a dry, frost-free place over winter. In late winter or very early spring, separate the small cormels from the parent.

Cormels . . . .

The parent corm will produce numerous cormels of varying size. Plant them in trays half-filled with potting compost, 2.5cm (1in) apart and with their growing points uppermost. Then fill the trays so that the growing points are just below the compost surface. Grow on in a frost-free bulb frame or greenhouse. They will take about 2–3 years to reach flowering size.

Dividing *Dahlia* tubers . . . .

The tubers of *Dahlia* species and cultivars can be divided to produce flowering plants in the same year. Start the tubers into growth before division to ascertain which tuber or tubers have viable growths.

▲ **1** Set the tubers on the surface of a tray of compost in warmth, mist over and keep warm and slightly moist. The new growth emerges just where the top of the tuber meets the old, dried stem. When the 'eyes' are clearly visible, section the parent tuber using a sharp knife, so that each section has one eye or shoot, with one or more plump, healthy tubers attached. Dust the cut surfaces with fungicide.

▶ **2** Set each division in a pot of potting compost, with the base of the shoot just at surface level and the growing tip above the surface. Grow on and plant out in the flowering site when all danger of frost has passed.

CUTTINGS AND SETTING FROM TUBERS

Several genera that have tubers, such as *Dahlia*, *Tropaeolum* and *Begonia*, may be propagated by basal cuttings, using much the same technique as for herbaceous perennials (*see pp.30–31*).

The process begins in late winter or very early spring. Bring the tubers into growth, in warmth, and when the shoots have reached about 5–10cm (2–4in) in length, trim them from the tuber together with a heel of basal tissue. Dip the cut surface in hormone rooting powder and then pot up the shoots into an open, moist compost. Enclose both the pot and the plant in a plastic bag and keep in a warm, light place until growth indicates that the shoots have rooted, when the small plants can be potted up or planted out individually. This technique will produce plants of flowering size the same year.

DIRECTORY OF
BULBS, CORMS AND TUBERS

Below are key tips on a selection of bulbs, corms and tubers that are particularly suitable for propagation. Unless otherwise specified, follow the detailed instructions given under the propagation section on pages 58–63.

Key

H   Height
S   Spread
PD   Planting depth for bulbs
B   By bulbils
🌰   Seed
🔧   By division
🌱   Germination
✹   Time to maturity

Allium (Onion)   Liliaceae

Some 700 species of hardy, bulbous or rhizomatous, spring, summer, or autumn-flowering perennials, ranging from dwarf species, 5cm (2in) tall, to robust species of 2m (6ft) in height. Flowers are bell-, star- or cup-shaped, borne in spherical or hemispherical umbels, above clumps of basal, narrow or strap-shaped leaves. Large species are best purchased as bulbs initially and then increased from garden-collected seed. Require an open, sunny situation.

Large species

A. aflatunense. Dense, spherical umbels, 10cm (4in) across, of pink-purple flowers, in summer. H 1m (3ft), S 12–15cm (5–6in), PD 5–10cm (2–4in).

A. cristophii, syn. *A. albopilosum, A. christophii.* Grey-green leaves and open umbels to 20cm (8in) across, of metallic, pink-purple flowers in early summer. H to 60cm (24in), S 20cm (8in), PD 5–10cm (2–4in).

A. giganteum. Produces star-shaped, lilac-pink flowers in dense umbels to 10cm (4in) across, in summer. H to 2m (6ft), S 20cm (8in), PD 5–10cm (2–4in).

Small species

The following species increase easily and soon form clumps:

A. beesianum. Bears open, 2.5cm (1in) wide umbels of bell-shaped, blue or white flowers in late summer or early autumn. H to 20cm (8in), S 7cm (3in), PD 5–10cm (2–4in).

A. moly (Golden garlic). Produces dense rounded umbels, 5cm (2in) wide, of golden yellow, star-shaped flowers in summer. H to 20cm (8in), S 7cm (3in), PD 5–10cm (2–4in).

PROPAGATION

🌰 as soon as ripe, in an open frame.
🌱 6–12 weeks.   ✹ 1–3 years for small species; 4–6 years for large species.
🔧 early autumn. Divide established clumps of small species. Separate offset bulblets for larger species.

Amaryllis   Amaryllidaceae

One species of bulb.

A. belladonna. Funnel-shaped, pink flowers in autumn, followed by long, strap-shaped wintergreen leaves. Needs well-drained soil at the base of a warm wall. Mulch in winter where temperatures fall below -5°C (23°F). H 60cm (24in), S 10cm (4in), PD nose at soil level.

PROPAGATION

🔧 midsummer. Divide established clumps or separate offsets.   ✹ 1–2 years.
Cuttage – late summer with mature bulbs. Scoop, or section into quarters.
✹ 2–3 years.

Anemone (Windflower)   Ranunculaceae

About 120 species of hardy or half-hardy, tuberous, rhizomatous, or fibrous-rooted perennials, usually with finely cut foliage and cup- or bowl-shaped flowers in spring, summer, or autumn. (*See also herbaceous perennials directory, p.35.*)

A. blanda. Knobbly, woody tubers bearing slightly cupped, many-petalled, blue, pink or white flowers in spring. Hardy. H 15cm (6in), S 15cm (6in), PD 5–8cm (2–3in).

A. coronaria. Knobbly tubers producing erect plants with shallowly cup-shaped, white, blue or red flowers in spring. Includes the **St Brigid anemones**, with double flowers, and the single-flowered **De Caen anemones**, both with flowers in a wide range of colours. Hardy. H 30cm (12in) or more, S 15cm (6in), PD 5–8cm (2–3in).

A. nemorosa (Wood anemone). Short, slender, finger-like, creeping rhizomes that in spring, produce delicate, cup-shaped, white flowers. Dark green, ferny leaves. Variants which bear lavender-blue flowers are also available. Hardy. H to 15cm (6in), S 30cm (12in) or more.

Allium aflatunense

Anemone coronaria

Arum italicum

Begonia Pendula Group

Colchicum speciosum

PROPAGATION

🌱 as soon as ripe, in an open frame. Cultivars do not come true.

🌿 slow, unpredictable and erratic.

☀ 2 years.

🔧 summer, when dormant. Break finger-like rhizomes at the joints. Cut tubers into sections not less than 1cm (½in) in diameter. Do not allow to dry out.

Arum (Cuckoo pint)   Araceae

Some 26 species of tuberous, herbaceous perennials, with large, attractive leaves and flowering spathes followed by spikes of fleshy berries.

A. italicum. Arrow-shaped, deep green leaves are veined white, and pale green spathes appear in late spring or early summer. They are followed by poisonous, orange-red berries. 'Marmoratum' has leaves marbled with a mixture of cream and pale green. Hardy. H 30cm (12in), S 20cm (8in), PD 15–25cm (6–10in).

PROPAGATION

🌱 when ripe, in a cold frame. Extract seed from berries wearing gloves as the flesh of the berries may irritate skin.

🌿 2–10 weeks. ☀ 4–7 years to flower; good foliage within 1–2 years.

🔧 mid- to late summer. ☀ 2–3 years.

Begonia   Begoniaceae

About 900 species of mainly frost-tender, annuals, perennials, and shrubs, with tubers, rhizomes, or fibrous roots. Begonias are grown for foliage and flowers, both in a range of colours, for bedding, as pot plants, and in hanging baskets. A complex genus, divided into seven horticultural groups, of

which only the most important tuberous or rhizomatous types are described here. All need fertile, humus-rich compost and some shade from hot sun.

Rex-cultorum begonias. These are usually rhizomatous and mainly evergreen plants. They are grown as houseplants for their colourful, often beautifully textured foliage. Optimum temperature; 21–24°C (70–75°F).

Tuberhybrida and **Multiflora begonias.** These grow from tubers and are dormant in winter. They are cultivated as houseplants for their usually brilliantly coloured flowers. Some are also suitable for using as summer bedding. Start into growth at 16–18°C (61–64°F).

Pendula begonias. Tuberous with a pendent habit that makes them ideal for hanging baskets. Best at 16–18°C (61–64°F).

PROPAGATION

🌱 late winter–early spring at 16–20°C (61–68°F). Mix with fine sand and surface-sow.

Tubers – late winter. Section tubers of Multifloras, each piece with a growth bud. Basal cuttings – spring, all types. 6–8cm (2½–3in) long. Start stock plants into growth at 16°C (61°F) in early spring.

Chionodoxa (Glory of the snow) Liliaceae

Genus of six species of hardy bulbs, bearing racemes of blue and white, star-shaped flowers in spring. Their leaves are linear and basal. Grow in any well-drained soil in sun or light, dappled shade. They often self-seed.

C. forbesii, syn. *C. luciliae* (hort.), *C. seihei, C. tmolusi.* Produces stems bearing white-centred, blue flowers above erect to spreading leaves in spring. H to 20cm (8in), S 2.5cm (1in), PD 8cm (3in).

PROPAGATION

🌱 early autumn, as soon as ripe, or mid-winter, in a cold frame.

🌿 in spring. ☀ 2–4 years.

🔧 late summer–early autumn. Separate offsets from established clumps.

☀ 1–2 years.

Colchicum (Autumn crocus, Naked ladies)
Liliaceae

Some 45 species of mostly hardy corms bearing goblet-shaped flowers, often with attractive chequered markings, in late summer, autumn, or winter. Leaves appear after flowering is over and are often large and coarse, so site colchicums where they will not swamp smaller plants. Those described below thrive in a range of soils, in sun or in light, dappled shade. They may also be naturalized in grass.

C. autumnale (Meadow saffron). Pinkish lavender flowers in autumn; white or double-flowered variants are available. Hardy. H 15cm (6in), S 8cm (3in), more when in leaf, PD 10cm (4in).

C. speciosum. Produces pale to deep pink-purple flowers in autumn. Hardy. H 18–20cm (7–8in), S 8–10cm (3–4in), more when in leaf, PD 10cm (4in).

PROPAGATION

🌱 early autumn, in a cold frame. Transfer to a nursery bed at the end of their second year and grow on.

🌿 in spring. ☀ 4–6 years.

🔧 mid- to late summer. Divide established clumps every third or fourth year to maintain vigour. Remove offsets at the same time and replant immediately.

☀ 1–2 years.

Crinum x *powellii*

Crocus tommasinianus 'Whitewell Purple'

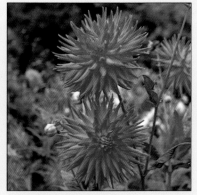

Dahlia 'Biddenham Sunset'

Corydalis
Papaveraceae

Some 300 species of hardy annuals, biennials, and rhizomatous or tuberous perennials, a few of which are evergreen. Those featured are herbaceous. They have brittle, finely divided, fern-like leaves, often blue- or grey-green, and produce spurred, tubular flowers in early spring or summer. A few are difficult to grow – even in the shelter of an alpine house – but those described here tolerate sun or dappled shade, and thrive in moist but well-drained, humus-rich soil.

C. cashmeriana. Tuberous perennial bearing dense racemes of intense blue flowers, with curved spurs, above bright green foliage in early summer. It prefers cool damp conditions and part-shade.
H to 25cm (10in), S to 15cm (6in).

C. fumariifolia. Tuberous perennial with glaucous leaves and racemes of azure or purple flowers, with triangular spurs, in late spring and early summer. It enjoys similar conditions to *C. cashmeriana*.
H to 15cm (6in), S 10cm (4in).

C. lutea. Mound-forming, rhizomatous perennial with fern-like, pale green leaves. It produces a succession of yellow flowers, with blunt spurs, from spring to autumn.
H to 40cm (16in), S to 30cm (12in).

PROPAGATION
🌰 as soon as ripe, in a cold frame. Seed rapidly loses viability if allowed to dry out.
🌱 in spring. ☀ 2–3 years.
✂ after flowering. Tubers divide naturally after flowering and can be lifted and separated when dormant. Tubers of *C. cashmeriana* may be carefully separated when in full growth if immediately replanted and kept moist. ☀ 1–2 years.

Crinum
Amaryllidaceae

About 130 species of mostly tender bulbous perennials, bearing very showy, funnel-shaped flowers on leafless stems in spring, summer, or autumn. They usually have strap-shaped basal leaves. All need fertile, sandy but humus-rich soil and sun. Tender species are ideal for containers in the home or conservatory.

C. x powellii. This bears pale or dark pink flowers in late summer. Hardy, given sharp drainage, a sheltered sunny site and a winter mulch. In very cold areas, grow in large tubs and overwinter in the greenhouse.
H 1.2–1.5m (4–5ft), S 30cm (12in), PD nose at soil level.

PROPAGATION
🌰 as soon as ripe at 21°C (70°F). Practical only for the very patient gardener.
🌱 in spring. ☀ up to 15 years.
✂ in spring. Lift and separate offsets and replant immediately. ☀ 2–3 years.
Cuttage – spring. Scoop or section.

Crocosmia (Montbretia)
Iridaceae

Seven species of cormous perennials forming clumps of narrow, ribbed, sword-shaped leaves and bearing branched spikes of funnel-shaped flowers in late summer. Several named cultivars are available with flowers in shades of yellow to deep scarlet-red. Most cultivars are hardy to at least -5°C (23°F), *C. x crocosmiiflora* and *C. masoniorum* to about -10 to -15°C (14–5°F). All need humus-rich, moist but well-drained soil in sun or part-shade, with a winter mulch until well established.

C. x crocosmiiflora. Bears slender, branched spikes of orange or orange-yellow flowers in late summer–early autumn. H 60cm (24in), S 8–10cm (3–4in), PD 8–10cm (3–4in).

C. masoniorum. This species bears upright, orange-red flowers in arching spikes in mid- to late summer. H to 1.2m (4ft), S 8–10cm (3–4in), PD 8–10cm (3–4in).

PROPAGATION
🌰 as soon as ripe, or between winter and early spring, in sandy compost in a cold frame. Cultivars do not come true.
🌱 in spring. ☀ 3–4 years.
✂ in spring. Separate offsets or divide congested clumps, before growth begins.
☀ 1–2 years.

Crocus
Iridaceae

Some 80 species of cormous perennials that produce goblet-shaped flowers between late autumn and late spring. They have mainly linear leaves, mostly with a distinct central silver stripe. A wide range of variants is available, with flowers of many sizes and in colours, including striped or marked with contrasting colours, and often with conspicuous styles. Some, such as cultivars of *C. nudiflorus* and *C. tommasinianus*, may be naturalized in turf. Those most commonly grown thrive in sun in light, well-drained soil. PD 8–10cm (3–4in).

PROPAGATION
🌰 as soon as ripe, in late summer–autumn, in sandy compost in an open frame. Cultivars do not come true. Some species self-seed.
🌱 in spring. ☀ 3–4 years.
✂ in mid- to late summer, when dormant. Separate offsets or divide congested clumps. *C. nudiflorus* produces stolons which provide a rapid means of increase. ☀ 1–3 years.

Eranthis hyemalis

Erythronium californicum 'White Beauty'

Fritillaria meleagris

Dahlia   Compositae

Some 30 species of tuberous-rooted herbaceous perennials and many thousands of cultivars, grown for their exuberantly coloured flowers in late summer and autumn. There are ten recognized flower types which vary greatly in appearance from single to pompon- or waterlily-like. In frost-prone areas, the tuberous roots are lifted when the leaves have turned black after the first frost, and overwintered in frost-free conditions. Bedding dahlias are raised from seed; the remainder from cuttings or divisions. Grow in fertile, humus-rich, moist but well-drained soil in a sunny site.

PROPAGATION
🌱 between late winter and early spring, at 18–20°C (64–68°F). Prick out into individual pots when two true leaves have formed, and pot on successively. Pinch out stem tips when three leaf nodes have formed, to promote branching.
🌱 5–10 days.   ☀ 5–6 months.
🔧 mid- to late winter or early spring. Bring stored tubers into growth in gentle warmth and with careful watering. As dormant buds swell, section tubers so that each has at least one growing point.   ☀ 4–5 months.
Basal cuttings – late winter or early spring. Bring tubers into growth at 15–18°C (59–64°F). Take cuttings when shoots are 7–8cm (3in) long.   ☀ 4–5 months.

Eranthis   Ranunculaceae

Some seven species of hardy perennials with knobbly tubers and finely divided leaves, bearing cup-shaped, yellow flowers in winter and very early spring. Grow in moist but well-drained soil in sun or light shade.

E. hyemalis (Winter aconite). This bears rich yellow flowers in late winter and early spring, with a ruff of bright green leaves immediately beneath. H 8–10cm (3–4in), S 5cm (2in), PD 5cm (2in).

PROPAGATION
🌱 as soon as ripe, in late spring, in an open frame. Seed has short viability and is rarely available commercially. Self-sows freely. Cultivars do not come true.
🌱 14–21 days.   ☀ 1–3 years.
🔧 when dormant, immediately after flowering. If tubers are allowed to dry out they will be difficult to re-establish.
☀ 1–2 years.

Erythronium   Liliaceae

About 22 species of hardy, spring- to early-summer-flowering bulbs. They have pendent flowers with reflexed petals, and conspicuous stamens. They need moist but well-drained, leafy soil in a cool site in partial shade. Do not allow bulbs to dry out before planting.
E. californicum 'White Beauty'. Has creamy white flowers, each with a red basal ring in spring. H to 35cm (14in), S 10cm (4in), PD 10cm (4in).
E. dens-canis (Dog's-tooth violet). White or pale pink-purple flowers in spring, above bronze-marbled leaves. H to 15cm (6in), S 10cm (4in), PD 10cm (4in).

PROPAGATION
🌱 in autumn, in an open frame. Cultivars do not come true.
🌱 in spring.   ☀ 4–6 years.
🔧 mid- to late summer or immediately after flowering. Separate offsets or divide established clumps and replant immediately.
🌱 1–2 years.

Freesia   Iridaceae

Genus of about six species of tender cormous perennials, with hundreds of cultivars bred for the cut-flower market. They usually bear fragrant, funnel-shaped flowers in a wide range of colours in late winter and spring. The leaves are linear and grow in fans at the base. In areas that experience winter frost, they should be grown in a greenhouse; prepared bulbs for summer flowering can be planted outdoors. Grow in sandy, slightly acid, humus-rich soil. H 20–40cm (8–16in), S 2.5–5cm (1–2in), PD 8cm (3in).

PROPAGATION
🌱 in autumn, at 13–18°C (55–64°F) for species. Sow seed of cultivars in late winter, and grow on at 16–20°C (61–64°F).
🌱 10–14 days.   ☀ 18–24 months for species, 8–10 months for cultivars.
🔧 separate offsets when dormant, in autumn.   ☀ 1 year.

Fritillaria   Liliaceae

About 100 species of mostly hardy bulbous perennials, usually with subtly coloured, often chequered, tubular to bell-shaped flowers. Most flower in spring or early summer. Some small species need protection from rain when dormant and are grown in a bulb frame. The fleshy bulbs produce offsets or rice-grain bulbils. Those described here are suitable for the open garden.
F. imperialis (Crown Imperial). Bears large bell-shaped flowers in shades of yellow, orange or red in early summer .Needs well-drained soil and sun. Hardy, but prone to rot in very moist soils.
H 1.2–1.5m (4–5ft), S and PD 20cm (8in).

Galanthus nivalis

Gladiolus communis subsp. *byzantinus*

Hyacinthus orientalis 'Blue Magic'

F. meleagris (Snake's head fritillary). Pendent, square-shouldered, chequered white, pink or purple flowers in spring. It needs moist, fertile, heavy soil in sun or dappled shade. Hardy. H 30cm (12in), S 5–8cm (2–3in), PD 10–15cm (4–6in).

PROPAGATION

🌱 in autumn, or as soon as ripe, in an open frame. Except for *F. imperialis* and other large species, grow on in pots for 2 years.

🌱 in spring. ☀ 3–7 years, depending on size.

🔧 separate offsets or sow rice-grain bulbils when dormant, in autumn. Pot up or line out in a cold frame. ☀ 1–3 years.

Bulb scales – the bulbs of several species are made up of 2–10 fleshy scales. Separate the scales when dormant, and set in sandy compost. Water sparingly and carefully until established. Plant out the following autumn. ☀ 1–3 years.

Galanthus (Snowdrop)   Amaryllidaceae

Genus of 15–20 species of hardy bulbous perennials with single or double, pendent, pear-shaped, often green-tipped, white flowers, mostly in late winter–early spring, although a few are autumn-flowering. Most are easily grown in light dappled shade, in leafy, humus-rich, even heavy, soil that does not dry out too much in summer. Snowdrops can be difficult to establish from dry bulbs, and are best divided in the green, and replanted at their original depth.

G. nivalis (Common snowdrop). Bears green-tipped, white flowers in late winter-early spring. Several cultivars are available with larger, double, or yellow-marked flowers. H 10–15cm (4–6in), S 10cm (4in).

PROPAGATION

🌱 as soon as ripe, in a shaded frame. Snowdrops hybridize freely, and established clumps will self-seed.

🌱 2–3 weeks. ☀ 3–4 years.

🔧 immediately after flowering. ☀ 1 year.

Cuttage – Scoop or quarter when dormant. ☀ 1–3 years.

Gladiolus   Iridaceae

About 180 species of cormous perennials with spikes of open, funnel-shaped flowers and fans of linear leaves. Hybrids and cultivars are the most often grown, valued for their exuberant spikes of brilliantly coloured flowers in summer. They are ideal for cutting for flower arrangements. Gladioli are classified into three main groups – *Grandiflorus*, *Nanus* and *Primulinus* – and the flower sizes range from giant, at 14cm (5½in) or more across, to the miniatures, with flowers to 6cm (2½in) wide. They need fertile, very well-drained soil, in a warm, sunny site, with shelter from strong winds. Provide support. Plant 10–15cm (4–6in) deep, in spring. Most are half-hardy or tender and need lifting before the first frosts in autumn, but a few, such as *G. communis* subsp. *byzantinus* with magenta flowers and *G. italicus*, syn. *G. segetum* with deep purple-pink flowers, are hardy.

PROPAGATION

🌱 spring, in a cold frame for hardy species; at 15°C (59°F) for half-hardy and tender species.

🌱 in spring. ☀ 1–3 years

🔧 autumn, when lifting. Separate cormlets from the parent corm and store in dry, frost-free conditions overwinter. Plant out in

spring in drills in a nursery bed. Lift again in autumn, as for adult corms. They may reach flowering size in their second year; if not, grow on for a third season, lifting before frosts, as before. ☀ 2–3 years.

Hyacinthus (Hyacinth)   Liliaceae

Genus of three species of hardy bulbous perennials. The legion cultivars of hyacinth, derived from the species *H. orientalis*, are available with single or double flowers, in a range of colours from pure white to indigo-blue, through pink, orange, and yellow. They bloom between late winter and spring; specially prepared and forced bulbs bloom in early to midwinter. They are easily grown in any well-drained soil in sun or light shade. H 20–30cm (8–12in), S 8–10cm (3–4in), PD 10cm (4in) in open ground, nose at soil level in containers.

PROPAGATION

🌱 as soon as ripe, or in autumn in a cold frame. Species only; cultivars rarely set seed.

🌱 in spring. ☀ 4–6 years.

Cuttage – bulbs may be scooped or sectioned when dormant. ☀ 2–3 years.

Iris   Iridaceae

Some 300 species of mostly herbaceous bulbs and rhizomatous or fleshy-rooted perennials grown for their flowers, which consist of 'falls' and 'standards' and are often very impressive. Most are hardy but some require specific conditions in order to do well. Classified botanically into a number of subgenera; the most important bulbous irises are described here. (*For Bearded and Rhizomatous irises, see p.41.*)

Iris xiphium 'Professor Blaauw'

Leucojum aestivum

Lilium regale

Xiphium irises

I. latifolia, syn. *I. xiphioides* (English iris). Bears white, blue, or violet flowers in early summer. Enjoys moist but well-drained soil. Hardy. Bulbs may be left *in situ* through the winter. H 25–60cm (10–24in), S to 15cm (6in), PD twice bulb's height.

I. x hollandica (Dutch iris). This has white, blue, violet, yellow, bronze or apricot flowers from late spring to midsummer. Hardy but protect with cloches where winters are harsh. Lift bulbs as the leaves wither if grown in damp, heavy soils. H 25–60cm (10–24in), S to 15cm (6in), PD twice bulb's height.

I. xiphium (Spanish iris). With pale or dark blue (like **'Professor Blaauw'**), occasionally yellow or white, flowers in late spring and early summer. Hardy, but prefers warmer, drier conditions than Dutch or English irises. Bulbs are best lifted after foliage dies, to be replanted in autumn. H 40–60cm (16–24in), S to 15cm (6in), PD twice bulb's height. Grow Dutch, English and Spanish irises in neutral to alkaline, well-drained soil in a sunny position.

PROPAGATION

as soon as ripe, in autumn in a cold frame. Offspring from hybrids and cultivars will not come true.

in spring. 3–5 years.

autumn. Lift established clumps and separate offsets. Grow on in a nursery bed. 1–3 years.

Reticulate irises

I. reticulata. This bears violet-blue flowers, with a yellow ridge on the falls, in late winter or early spring. Several excellent cultivars are available, including **'J S Dijt'**, **'Harmony'** and **'Katherine Hodgson'**. All are suitable for a rock garden in well-drained, neutral to alkaline soil in sun. Hardy and the most easily grown of the Reticulate Group, many of which need bulb-frame or alpine-house protection. H to 15cm (6in), S to 5cm (2in), PD twice bulb's height.

PROPAGATION

as soon as ripe, or in autumn in a cold frame. Seed is rarely available for cultivars, and garden-collected seed will not come true.

in spring. 3–5 years.

late summer. Numerous bulblets are produced at the base of the bulb. Separate and grow on in pots or in a nursery bed. 1–3 years.

Leucojum (Snowflake) Amaryllidaceae

Some 10 species of mostly hardy bulbs, grown for their snowdrop-like flowers in spring or autumn. They have narrow, strap-shaped to linear leaves. Plant in moist but well-drained soil in sun; *L. aestivum* and *L. vernum* are best grown in moist soil that does not dry out.

L. aestivum (Summer snowflake). Bears pendent white flowers with green tips in spring. Hardy. H to 60cm (24in), S 10cm (4in), PD 8–10cm (3–4in).

L. autumnale. Produces bell-shaped white flowers in summer and autumn. Hardy. H to 15cm (6in), S 8cm (3in), PD 8–10cm (3–4in).

L. vernum (Spring snowflake). Green-tipped, white flowers in early spring. Hardy. H to 30cm (12in), S 8cm (3in), PD 8–10cm (3–4in).

PROPAGATION

in autumn in an open frame.

in spring. 2–4 years.

early summer. Lift established clumps and separate offsets. 1–2 years.

Lilium (Lily) Liliaceae

Genus of about 100 hardy and half-hardy bulbous species and many hybrids. They produce beautiful, trumpet- or funnel-shaped, bowl-shaped, or turkscap flowers, in early, mid- or late summer, and autumn, usually on long, slender stems that are clad with short, linear leaves, sometimes in distinct whorls. Many are highly fragrant. Most lilies prefer moist but well-drained, neutral to acid soil in sun, with the roots in cool shade. Lily bulbs are composed of fleshy, overlapping scales; a few also produce rhizomes and several bear bulbils in the leaf axils or on the stem. Those described below are hardy.

L. bulbiferum. Bears umbels of upright, bowl-shaped, orange flowers, which are spotted maroon or black. Early to midsummer. Produces leaf axil bulbils. Tolerant of alkaline soils. H to 150cm (5ft), S 30cm (12in), PD 2–3 times bulb's height.

L. candidum (Madonna lily). Produces sweetly scented, trumpet-shaped white flowers in midsummer. Needs neutral to alkaline soil. H to 180cm (6ft), S 30cm (12in), PD just beneath soil surface.

L. lancifolium, syn. *L. tigrinum* (Tiger lily). This has nodding, rich orange-red turkscap flowers, with dark spots and papillae at the throat, in late summer and early autumn. It produces bulbils in the leaf axils, and on the rooting stem. H to 150cm (5ft), S 30cm (12in), PD 2–3 times bulb's height.

L. regale (Regal lily). Bears scented, trumpet-shaped white flowers flushed with purple.

Muscari armeniacum

Narcissus, 'February Gold'

Ornithogalum umbellatum

It blooms in midsummer and prefers full sun.
H to 200cm (6ft), S 30cm (12in), PD 2–3
times bulb's height.

PROPAGATION

For all vegetative methods of propagation,
use only virus-free stock.

🌱 as soon as ripe in a cold frame. Hybrids
and cultivars do not come true. Lilies show
two distinct types of germination. Some, like
L. regale, produce growth above the compost surface within 2–4 weeks (epigeal germination); others, like *L. bulbiferum,* first
produce a small bulblet below ground
before topgrowth emerges (hypogeal germination), usually after a cold period. Retain
pots, undisturbed, for at least 18 months if
germination is not immediate.

🌱 variable from 2–4 weeks to 18 months.
☀ 2–4 years.

Leaf axil bulbils – late summer. Detach and
sow immediately. ☀ 1–3 years.

Stem bulblets – separate as the leaves and
stem wither after flowering. Plant bulblets
immediately. ☀ 1–3 years.

Scaling – between late summer and early
spring, when dormant. Suitable for all species
and hybrids. ☀ 3 years.

🔪 of established clumps between autumn
and spring. Some lilies increase readily,
producing several new bulbs each year. Lift
and divide every third or fourth year to
relieve congestion. ☀ 1–2 years.

Muscari (Grape hyacinth)   Liliaceae

About 30 species of mostly hardy, mainly
spring-flowering bulbs with spikes of blue
flowers on leafless stems. The leaves are
linear and fleshy, and can grow surprisingly
long. They need well-drained soil in sun.

M. armeniacum. Bright blue flowers with
white-rimmed mouths in spring. Hardy.
H to 20cm (8in), S 5cm (2in), PD 10cm (4in).
M. comosum **'Plumosum',** syn. 'Monstrosum'.
Violet flower spikes, comprising tassel-like
sterile flowers. Frost hardy. H to 30cm (12in),
S 8–10cm (3–4in), PD 10cm (4in).

PROPAGATION

🌱 as soon as ripe, or in autumn in an open
frame. Many species self-seed freely.

🌱 in spring.   ☀ 3–5 years.

🔪 late summer-autumn. Most readily
produce numerous offsets. Lift and divide
established clumps regularly to relieve
congestion and promote vigour.
☀ 1 year.

Cuttage – bulbs may be scooped or
sectioned when dormant. The most effective
method of increasing sterile forms rapidly.
☀ 2–3 years.

Narcissus (Daffodil)   Liliaceae

Some 50 species and thousands of cultivars
of mostly hardy bulbous perennials bearing
characteristic trumpet-shaped flowers in
shades of yellow, with ruffs often of a
different shade. The myriad cultivars of
Narcissus are among the most rewarding and
easily grown of spring-flowering bulbs and,
with careful selection, blooms may be had
from late winter with **N.** 'February Gold',
almost until early summer, with **N.** *poeticus*
and its cultivars. A few less common species
flower in autumn. *Narcissus* is divided into 12
horticultural divisions, ranging in form from
the trumpet and large-cupped daffodils to
the small-cupped and split-corona types, and
those – often fragrant – *Narcissus* that bear
heads of several flowers. Nearly all are

excellent as cut flowers. Most thrive in sun
or light shade, in any moderately fertile soil
that remains moist during the growing season.
Smaller species generally need more sharply
drained soils. *Narcissus* range in height from
about 10cm (4in) for the smallest species,
like **N.** *bulbocodium,* to about 50cm (20in) for
the most robust species and cultivars. Plant
all at 1–3 times the bulb's height.

PROPAGATION

🌱 as soon as ripe, or in autumn in an open
frame. Many species self-seed and will
hybridize. Seed is the most practical method
for small species, some of which rarely produce offset bulbs.

🌱 in spring.   ☀ 3–5 years.

🔪 late summer. Separate offsets from parent
bulbs. Lift and divide established clumps and
replant immediately.   ☀ 1–2 years.

Cuttage – large bulbs may be scooped or
sectioned when they are dormant. Also by
twin-scaling.   ☀ 2–3 years.

Ornithogalum (Star of Bethlehem)

Liliaceae

About 80 species of mostly hardy, spring- or
summer-flowering bulbous perennials with
star-shaped, usually white flowers, often
marked or striped green outside. Grow in
well-drained soil in full sun; *O. umbellatum*
tolerates light shade.

O. nutans. Nodding, one-sided racemes of
green-striped, silver-white flowers in spring.
Hardy. H to 60cm (24in), S 5cm (2in),
PD 10cm (4in).

O. umbellatum. Bears star-shaped white
flowers in broad racemes in early summer.
Increases rapidly and can be invasive. Hardy.
H 20cm (8in), S 5cm (2in), PD 10cm (4in).

Scilla siberica

Sternbergia lutea

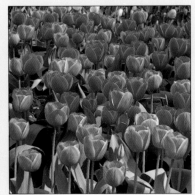

Tulipa 'Ad Rem'

PROPAGATION

🌰 autumn or spring, in a cold frame. Grow seedlings on for 2 years, do not allow to go dormant in the first season.

🌱 in spring. ☀ 3–4 years.

🔪 late summer. ☀ 1–2 years.

Cuttage – scoop or section bulbs of larger species when dormant. ☀ 2–3 years.

Scilla (Spring squill)　　Liliaceae

About 90 species of mainly hardy, spring- or summer-flowering bulbs grown for their star-shaped, usually blue, occasionally white or pink, flowers. They have linear to elliptic leaves that are sometimes channelled. They need well-drained soil and sun or light, dappled shade.

S. siberica (Siberian squill). This produces pendent, bright blue, bell-shaped flowers in spring. **'Spring Beauty'** has deep blue flowers. Hardy.

H to 20cm (8in), S 5cm (2in), PD 8cm (3in).

PROPAGATION

🌰 autumn or as soon as ripe in an open frame.

🌱 in spring. ☀ 3–5 years.

🔪 autumn. Lift established clumps, separate offsets and replant immediately.

☀ 1–2 years.

Cuttage – bulbs may be scooped or sectioned when dormant. ☀ 2–3 years.

Sternbergia　　**Amaryllidaceae**

Genus of eight species of mainly autumn-flowering bulbous perennials, most of which are cold hardy but dislike winter wet. They are grown for their crocus-like flowers that usually emerge before the leaves. The leaves are linear to strap-shaped. Needs light, well-

drained soil in a warm, sunny, sheltered site, preferably at the base of a wall or similar. It flowers best if provided with a warm, dry summer dormancy.

S. lutea. Shining yellow, goblet-shaped flowers in autumn. They appear at the same time as the leaves, which elongate after flowering. Frost hardy. H 15cm (6in), S 8cm (3in), PD 10–15cm (4–6in).

PROPAGATION

🌰 autumn, in a cold frame.

🌱 in spring. ☀ 3–5 years.

🔪 late summer. Lift established clumps, divide and replant immediately.

☀ 1–2 years.

Cuttage – mature bulbs may be scooped or quartered when dormant. ☀ 2–3 years.

Tigridia　　Iridaceae

Genus of 23 species of frost-tender cormous perennials with bell-shaped or, more usually, iris-like flowers, mainly in shades of white, yellow, pink, orange and red, and often with marks or mottling in contrasting colours. The leaves are narrowly lance-shaped to sword-like, mostly in a basal cluster. They need well-drained, preferably sandy soil, in a sunny position. In cold areas, lift before first frosts.

T. pavonia (Peacock flower, Tiger flower). Bears orange, yellow, pink or white flowers, with contrasting, darker central marks, in mid- to late summer. H 50–60cm (20–24in), S 10cm (4in), PD 10cm (4in).

PROPAGATION

🌰 autumn, or spring, at 13–18°C (55–64°F). Careful watering and feeding, without over-heating, will ensure large bulbs that may be flowered in their second year.

🌱 in spring. ☀ 2 years.

🔪 late summer–early autumn. Separate offsets and replant immediately or store in dry, frost-free conditions and replant in spring. ☀ 1–2 years.

Tulipa (Tulip)　　Liliaceae

Some 100 species and thousands of cultivars of mostly hardy bulbous perennials with linear to broad leaves that are green to blue-green and may have darker stripes. The many cultivars of *Tulipa* are grown in bedding, in borders and containers, and for cut flowers. They bloom between early spring and early summer. The genus *Tulipa* is divided into 15 horticultural divisions, with flowers ranging in shape from cup-shaped, bowl-shaped or goblet-shaped, to the classic ovoid flowers of the **Darwin hybrids,** and the frilled and dissected blooms of the **Parrot tulips.** Flowers are available in a huge range of colours from almost black to white. Most thrive in sun in any well-drained, fertile soil. Aside from the true species and most of the **Kaufmanniana hybrids,** tulip bulbs are best lifted as the leaves wither after flowering, and stored dry until replanting in autumn. Plant all at a depth of 10–15cm (4–6in).

PROPAGATION

🌰 as soon as ripe, or in autumn in an open frame. Suitable for species only; the cultivars and hybrids seldom set seed, and do not come true.

🌱 in spring. ☀ 3–7 years.

🔪 summer. Separate offsets from the parent bulbs after lifting. Grow on in a nursery bed. Some species tulips produce bulblets on the ends of long stolons. Lift and separate them from the stolons in autumn. ☀ 1–2 years.

71

ALPINES AND ROCK GARDEN PLANTS

A precise definition is elusive, but in the popular imagination alpines are dwarf plants, usually free-flowering and tolerant of low winter temperatures. Gardeners often convert to growing them after witnessing a riotously colourful Swiss mountain meadow in early summer or tiny plants decorating apparently barren rock slides.

Many alpines are easy to grow; others present a challenge. Regular propagation ensures that you have ample numbers of easy alpines to give to friends while maintaining your stock of those that are more challenging to grow.

◄ *The rock garden provides niches for both true alpines and rock plants and is kept well stocked by a range of propagating techniques.*

WHY PROPAGATE
ALPINES AND ROCK GARDEN PLANTS?

The range of techniques for increasing alpines is as wide as the plants themselves are diverse. Depending on the available facilities, many alpines can be propagated throughout the year. A mist unit and a heated propagating bench do much to extend the propagating season and certainly speed root development, but are by no means essential.

Seeds of alpine species come true but may not be set in cultivation – for these, vegetative methods must be used.

Many alpines have growth habits adapted to their specialized habitats, and these give clues to the propagator. For example, some Himalayan androsaces have runners that produce new plantlets like a strawberry plant (peg down the tips and detach the rooted rosettes); some, like soldanellas, occur in alpine turf, forming mats of surface roots which are easily divided. Some mat- and cushion-formers produce new shoots with vestigial roots that develop further only when moisture and a suitable substrate are present, but otherwise shrivel away. For these, Irishman's, or pre-rooted, cuttings are ideal.

If a plant is happy with its garden siting, self-sown colonies may appear without help from the gardener. Such natural effects can be captivating, but one species often prospers at the expense of its more delicate neighbours – a good reason to rescue less vigorous plants by propagating fresh stocks to replant elsewhere. Not all plants set viable seed in cultivation, however,

and for these, and for named hybrids and cultivars, vegetative methods must be used. A few alpines can only be propagated at specific points in their growth cycle (*see the plant directory, pp. 80–85*).

MULTIPLYING FROM SEED

Raising alpines from seed is by far the most important means of propagating and is usually the only practical method of increasing rare or newly introduced species.

Seedlings vary in vigour or adaptability to certain conditions. Furthermore, seed-raised plants are virus-free, a particularly important consideration with susceptible genera such as *Primula*. Some species hybridize freely (saxifrages, for instance), so there is always the potential to produce exciting new cultivars.

DIVISION OF CLUMPS

Division is appropriate for almost any plant that forms multiple rootstocks or a clump of basal shoots, or that spreads by underground stolons. Success is almost guaranteed if divisions are given due care until they are re-established. Irishman's cuttings – a modification of division – are used for mat- or cushion-formers that root as they spread.

TAKING CUTTINGS

Shrubby alpines can be increased by various types of cuttings. Perennial alpines that are unsuitable for division may be propagated by stem tip cuttings. Most

Alpines in Tufa

Crevice-dwelling alpines (such as Porphyrion *saxifrages and* Silene acaulis) *often grow more compactly and flower more freely in tufa – a porous limestone deposit – than in soil. Recently propagated material is essential – established root systems are too bulky to introduce successfully. Hose down the tufa to remove the outer shell of sludge-like material. Drill a planting hole, 10cm (4in) deep. Shake the roots free of soil and insert them using a funnel of stiff card. Trickle in tufa debris around the roots. Water in well and*

cap with tufa fragments around the plant collar.

This compact, crevice-dwelling saxifrage thrives and flowers freely when planted in tufa.

rosette-forming species can be increased by detaching individual rosettes from the edge of the plant. For those with thicker roots, propagation by root cuttings is possible. A few alpines can be increased by leaf cuttings. Relatively few alpines are increased by leaf cuttings but, using healthy, young mature material, the technique is successful with the somewhat fleshy leaves of some sedums and with members of the family Gesneriaceae, such as *Haberlea* and *Ramonda*.

① *Aurinia saxatile* 'Citrinum'
The species can be raised from seed, but if you find its chrome-yellow too bright, grow this paler-flowered cultivar and keep it healthy and floriferous by propagating regularly from cuttings.

② *Phlox douglasii* cultivar
The evergreen mats of foliage eventually become less floriferous at the centres; keep them compact by trimming after flowering and take cuttings from the resulting new shoots to replenish your stock.

③ *Aubrieta deltoides* cultivar
Aubrietas are very free-flowering and often self-seed, but self-sown seedlings usually produce inferior flowers to selected cultivars. Propagate named forms by softwood or semi-ripe cuttings or by division.

④ *Helianthemum* cultivar
Helianthemums are not always reliably hardy. Insure your stock by propagating regularly from softwood or semi-ripe cuttings and overwinter young plants in frost-free conditions under glass.

⑤ *Iberis sempervirens*
This evergreen subshrub can be increased by softwood or semi-ripe cuttings, but since they develop an extensive root system they may need potting on several times before they can be planted out.

ALPINES AND ROCK GARDEN PLANTS

The techniques for propagating alpines and rock garden plants are essentially the same as those for other plant groups, except that, in most cases, the material used is much smaller in scale. The other most important modification to ensure success is to use sharply drained propagating mediums to suit the special needs of alpine plants.

ALPINES FROM SEED

Generally speaking, sow seed as soon as it is ripe or on receipt from a seed-distribution outlet; Ranunculaceae especially (*Anemone, Pulsatilla, Ranunculus*) come up quickly if sown barely ripe but erratically if dried off. Fresh seed is critical in some cases (notably *Celmisia*) – conversely, with plants from low rainfall areas, it matters much less, though seeds can germinate irregularly over several years. If possible, sow stored seed before late winter or germination may be delayed a further year. With rare species, save seed pots for three years before discarding, if space allows, since germination can be erratic. One of three pre-treatments may be necessary. In all cases, sow immediately after treatment.

Stratification

The seed is exposed under moist conditions to temperatures around freezing point to break its dormancy. Either mix the seed with moistened sand in a container or sow it as normal (*see right*); in both cases, place in the bottom of a refrigerator for 1-3 months. In areas with cold winters, sowing in late autumn and leaving the pots outdoors in an open frame is easier.

Soaking

This technique is used for older seeds that are large enough to be handled individually. As well as hydrating dried seed, chemical inhibitors in the seed coat may be leached out. Quarter-fill a tumbler with tepid water, add the seeds and a drop of household detergent (to help the seed to sink). Change the water after twelve hours, leave a further twelve hours, then sow as normal. *Sorbus* seeds should be soaked in vinegar; *Lupinus* seeds need to be immersed in hot – but not boiling - water, and then allowed to cool.

Alpines from seed ....

For most purposes, sowing seed in a 9cm (3½in) pot will provide sufficient seedlings for planting out in the rock garden and giving away to gardening friends.

◀ **1** Fill pots to within 1cm (⅛in) of the rim, tap firmly to settle the compost and firm gently with a presser board.

► **2** Sow the seed evenly over the surface. Cover the seed with a 3–5mm (⅛–¼in) layer of washed grit. Water overhead or place the pots in a shallow container filled with 5cm (2in) of water for half an hour, allowing the compost to become moist by capillary action. Fine seed is best sown onto the grit surface – watering or rainfall will wash it down to the right level.

▲ **3** Place the pots outdoors in an open frame; genera sensitive to overhead watering (*Dionysia* especially) need the shelter of an alpine house or a covered frame, while tiny seeds of alpines that suffer if allowed to dry out (such as those of the Ericaceae) should be kept humid in a closed propagator.

Scarification

Some seeds have hard seed coats that need breaking down before germination can take place. Large seeds can be rubbed with emery paper; smaller ones can be mixed with sharp sand and shaken in a screw-top jar.

Most seed is best sown in 9cm (3½in) pots. Deep-rooted plants, however, especially those that form underground tubers, benefit from being left in the same pot until they go dormant after a second season of growth; the seed of these should be sown in deep pots, which are available from specialist suppliers. Prepare a seed compost of two parts sterilized loam (or John Innes No. 1), one part 2–4mm (⅟₁₆–⅛in) lime-free grit and one part horticultural grade vermiculite or perlite, all parts by volume. (Substitute ericaceous compost for the loam for lime-hating plants.)

Most alpines germinate from late winter as the temperatures rise. Good light is needed once the seedlings emerge. Keep the compost moist and protect the seedlings from strong sun, particularly under glass. As a general rule, prick out seedlings into 6cm (2½in) pots once the first true leaves are apparent, using the same potting mixture (*for exceptions to this rule, see the plant directory, pp. 80–85*). Once the seedlings are well established, apply a dilute liquid fertilizer.

DIVISION

Division is one of the simplest and most reliable of techniques and is used for clump-forming perennials. Most can be divided either in early spring or early autumn. Semi-deciduous, summer-flowering genera such as *Campanula* are best divided in early spring, while *Primula* and others that experience fresh growth in autumn are best divided in early autumn. Alpines with a summer dormancy habit are best divided before new root growth is underway, generally in late summer.

To lift large fibrous-rooted plants grown in the open garden, insert two handforks back to back and prise the plant apart. On plants with tangled roots, cut the crown into sections, washing off old soil and dipping the roots in silver sand before replanting. Small plants may be pulled apart by hand, but well-rooted sections are best cut with a knife. Most divisions can be planted out immediately at the same depth as before. Pot up smaller divisions and grow on in a cold frame; replant only when substantial new root growth appears.

For plants in containers, always replant in fresh compost, protecting them from hot or windy weather using shaded cloches or a closed cold frame. The divisions may appear etiolated once separated from the surrounding clump. To counteract this, plant them deeper than their previous level. For *Hepatica* and some suckering species of *Cassiope* that resent disturbance, a two-stage process is sometimes used: after flowering, make a deep cut into the crown of the plant with a spade, insert a thin slate into the cut, then leave the plant until the following spring before lifting the division. This stimulates the production of new roots before the new plant is lifted and separated and enables the division to establish more quickly.

Irishman's, or pre-rooted, cuttings

This is a technique for alpines with a creeping habit but which form a woody rootstock that does not lend itself to conventional division. It can also be used for plants spread by runners or produce offsets. The best results from pre-rooted cuttings are achieved when root growth is active between early spring and mid-autumn.

Irishman's, or pre-rooted, cuttings . . . .

Irishman's cuttings are, in effect, an easy short-cut to producing small pre-rooted plants that require the minimum of aftercare to guarantee success.

▲ **1** Lift a section from the edge of the plant, cutting it free either immediately below the developing root mass or along any runner that connects it to the core of the plant. Trim away any dead, damaged or excess foliage to leave a small crown of shoots (*see right*).

◀ **2** Dip in a fungicide solution then pot up in a sandy compost, with the lowest leaves just at the compost surface. Top-dress with grit.

CUTTINGS

Cuttings are usually taken from mid-spring through to mid-autumn, but can be rooted earlier using a soil-warming cable or heated propagator. Softwood cuttings are taken in spring, semi-ripe cuttings in summer, and ripewood or hardwood cuttings from late summer to mid-autumn. With rare species it is worth taking cuttings at any time if the parent plant starts to show signs of distress.

When taking cuttings of alpines, use sharp scissors or a razor blade, to avoid crushing plant tissues. In most cases, coarse, lime-free horticultural sand, sterilized by rinsing with boiling water poured through muslin, is an adequate rooting medium, packed into 9cm (3½in) pots. Allow the sand to cool completely before inserting the cuttings. Add a little slow-release fertilizer to the base of the container, so that the cutting may be kept in the container for a month or so after rooting. Some alpines show superior rooting rates in a less free-draining mixture of equal parts of perlite and fine composted bark.

Softwood cuttings

Softwood and stem tip cuttings are taken from new growth, produced in the first half of spring, after flowering. They are liable to wilt if not dealt with immediately. The optimum time for taking them is early morning or on cool, overcast days when plant tissue is most turgid. To produce cuttings later in the season, cut back a proportion of the plant to promote new shoots for use any time up to late summer.

Semi-ripe and hardwood cuttings

Semi-ripe and hardwood cuttings are taken from midsummer to late autumn. Semi-ripe shoots are firm to the touch at their bases but still in active growth. Ideally, you should use short side shoots, 5–10cm (2–4in) long. Pull them away from the main shoot with a heel, then trim the heel neatly. Hardwood cuttings are used when shoot growth for the year is completed, which is often indicated by the formation of an apical bud. Take a cutting 5–10cm (2–4in) long, with a heel. Alternatively, cut just above a node, trim the cutting below its lowest node and cut off the lower leaves. Wound the base of the cutting by removing a sliver of bark about 5mm (¼in) long.

Insert the cuttings in the rooting medium, then place them in a closed propagator or cover them with plastic bags supported by canes. Species intolerant of high humidity are best if left uncovered, but under cold greenhouse protection.

Dipping the cuttings in a rooting compound can help rooting. Most rooting compounds also contain fungicide, though it is still important to check at least weekly to remove any cuttings that show signs of rotting or fungal attack. Softwood cuttings will root in two to six weeks; semi-ripe cuttings may take two months or more. Hardwood cuttings will probably not form roots until the spring after they were taken.

Softwood cuttings ....

Softwood cuttings root more readily than other types of cutting, but need more aftercare. Do not allow them to wilt at any stage, and root them in gentle heat and good light.

► **1** Take cuttings about 2.5–7cm (1–3in) long from the tip of non-flowering shoots with a straight cut just below a node.

◄ **2** Trim off the lower leaves to about a half or a third of the overall length of the cutting.

► **3** Insert to the depth of the lowest leaves into the rooting medium. Firm in gently. Ensure that the leaves do not touch each other .

◄ **4** Seal in a plastic bag, keeping the plastic clear of the leaves with split canes or wire hoops.

Lift out the small plantlets with care, pot up using the same compost as the parent plant and, in warm weather particularly, grow them on under glass for a week before hardening them off in a semi-shaded area. Rather than disturb recently rooted material just before the onset of winter, it is advisable to leave all but the earliest to root in their pots until the following spring.

Using individual rosettes as cuttings.
Numerous alpines form neat domes or cushions comprising many small rosettes. These can be propagated by snipping off tiny – as little as 3mm (⅛in) diameter – shoots from the periphery of the clump about a month after flowering (in earliest summer for many alpines). Only the new growth is required, and all persistent dead leaves along the length of the stem must be meticulously trimmed away as far as possible, leaving a small shoot core (the rosette) at the end of a stem 5–15mm (¼–½in) long. Insert in sand up to the base of the rosette. Rooting normally follows after three weeks. When potting on, make a small hollow in the compost, drop the young plantlet into it and back-fill with silver sand. When watering, always avoid wetting the foliage.

LEAF CUTTINGS

This method principally applies to *Ramonda myconi* and its relatives (e.g. *Haberlea*, *Jankaea* and *Lewisia*). Remove mature leaves from the parent plant in early spring or (preferably) late summer; it is not necessary to tear away the base of the leaf stalk (petiole) as is sometimes recommended. Insert the cuttings upright in moist sand in a propagator, or in a pot enclosed in a plastic bag, and keep them shaded. Rooting should occur in four to six weeks. Pot the plants up two to six weeks after a small rosette has appeared at the base of the parent leaf.

ROOT CUTTINGS

Alpines with long, thickened roots can be increased by root cuttings. Lift the plant soon after the onset of dormancy – generally in midsummer (*Dodecatheon*, *Pulsatilla*) or autumn (*Phlox*, *Verbascum*). Shake the roots free of soil or compost. Select younger, thicker roots – those nearest the crown are best for forming new plants - and cut into sections 5cm (2in) long. For the continued health of the parent plant, remove no more than one-third of the roots for propagation.

Material for the different types of cuttings .....
The figures below indicate the type of material that is used for various types of cuttings. The dotted lines represent the depth of insertion for each type.

▲ 1 Take stem tip cuttings, 2.5–7cm (1–3in) long, from herbaceous plants in the spring.

▲ 2 Take rosette cuttings, up to 10–15mm (½in) long, in early to midsummer.

▲ 3 Take leaf cuttings from entire, healthy, young leaves in spring or late summer.

▲ 4 Take softwood cuttings, 2.5–7cm (1–3in) long, in spring.

▲ 5 Take semi-ripe cuttings, 5–10cm (2–4in) long, in midsummer.

▲ 6 Take ripewood (hardwood) cuttings, 5–10cm (2–4in) long, in late summer or autumn.

Trim the cuttings with a straight cut at the end nearest the crown and an angled cut at the base, to ensure correct insertion, then trim off side roots, treat the cut surfaces with fungicide and insert vertically in sandy compost, covering them with a 1cm (½in) layer of grit. Place the cuttings in a closed cold frame or in the greenhouse until top-growth is well underway, usually about a month later. Top-growth often appears before a new root system is well established, so check that the cuttings are well rooted before potting them up.

DIRECTORY OF
ALPINES AND ROCK GARDEN PLANTS

Below are key tips on a selection of alpine and rock garden plants that are particularly suitable for propagation. Unless otherwise specified, follow the detailed instructions given under the propagation section on pages 76–79.

Key

H Height
S Spread
🌰 By seed
🌱 Germination
☀ Time to maturity
🔧 By division

Aethionema (Stone cress) — Cruciferae

About 40 species of hardy, evergreen and semi-evergreen subshrubs and woody-based perennials with prolific flowers in spring and early summer. As the roots dislike being disturbed, division of plants is rarely a successful method of increase.

A. grandiflorum, syn. *A. pulchellum*. Evergreen subshrub with fragrant pink flowers. H and S to 30cm (12in).

PROPAGATION

🌰 as soon as ripe in midsummer or when available. Self-seeds freely.

🌱 1–6 months. ☀ the following spring. Softwood cuttings – summer. Clip over after flowering and use the new shoots that arise as a result. When side shoots appear on the young plant, cut back the main stem by one-third; this will promote bushiness.

Androsace (Rock jasmine) — Primulaceae

Over 100 species, most of which are mat- or cushion-forming, hardy, evergreen perennials, valued for their tiny flowers. Some thrive in the open garden; others, like the high-alpine Aretian cushion-formers, either demand scree conditions or rock crevices with protection from excess winter rainfall, or are grown in an alpine house. Seed generally needs stratification and is the principal method of propagation.

A. sempervivoides. Stoloniferous mat-former with leathery, glossy leaves that bears fragrant pink flowers in spring. H to 5cm (2in), S to 20cm (8in).

A. vandellii. Aretian cushion-former with silver-grey, hairy leaves. It bears white flowers in spring. Some plants flower so freely that the foliage is obscured, and the size of the flowers varies; select accordingly. H to 5cm (2in), S to 12cm (5in).

PROPAGATION

🌰 as soon as ripe or before late winter. Prick out seedlings as soon as the first true leaves appear.

🌱 3–6 months. ☀ 2–3 years. Rosette cuttings – early to midsummer. Root single rosettes and avoid wetting the foliage.

by watering from below. ☀ 1 year. Stolons – after flowering. Stoloniferous species usually produce 4–5 stolons which root on contact with the top-dressing. They take about 1–2 months to root well. ☀ 1 year.

Armeria (Thrift) — Plumbaginaceae

Some 80 species of cushion- or mound-forming, evergreen perennials with hardy rosettes of linear leaves, grown for their slender-stemmed, spherical flower heads in spring or summer. They need well-drained, not-too-fertile soil, in sun. They hybridize freely, so vegetative propagation is the preferred method of increase to ensure that the new plants are true to type.

A. juniperifolia, syn. *A. caespitosa*. Neat hummock-former with grey-green leaves and white, pink, or pink-purple flowers in spring. H to 8cm (3in), S 15cm (6in).

A. maritima (Sea thrift). Forms clumps of dark green leaves, and bears white, pink, or dark red-purple flowers, in spring and summer. H to 20cm (8in), S to 30cm (12in).

PROPAGATION

Cuttings – summer. Root single rosettes or branchlets bearing 3–5 rosettes, taken with a heel of older wood at the base.

☀ 9 months.

🔧 early spring. ☀ 6 months.

Aubrieta — Cruciferae

Some 12 species of evergreen, mat- or mound-forming, hardy perennials, grown for their four-petalled, cross-shaped flowers, which are borne in profusion in spring. They are easily grown in any well-drained soil in a sunny position. Usually it is the numerous, free-flowering cultivars that are found in cultivation. Recommended cultivars include: **'Dr Mules'** with violet flowers; **'Joy'** with

Androsace vandellii

Aubrieta deltoides 'Dr Mules'

Aurinia saxatilis

Campanula carpatica 'Blue Clips'

Cyclamen hederifolium

mauve double flowers; and **'Red Carpet'** with deep red flowers. Cut back after the main spring flowering – they will often flower again in summer. H 5cm (2in), S to 60cm (24in).

PROPAGATION

Cuttings – softwood or semi-ripe, in summer or early autumn. Avoid any woody material and keep part-shaded and uncovered. ☀ the following spring.

✎ early autumn after re-growth following cutting back. Split with a spade and replant immediately, watering well until established. ☀ 6–8 months.

Aurinia   Cruciferae

Some seven species of hardy biennials and woody-based, evergreen perennials of which *A. saxatilis* and its cultivars are the most commonly cultivated. They are valued for their heads of small yellow flowers, borne above the foliage in mid-spring. They grow in any well-drained soil in sun.

A. saxatilis, syn. *Alyssum saxatile*. Produces masses of bright yellow flowers in spring and has mounds of hairy, grey-green leaves. **'Plenum'** has double flowers; **'Citrinum'** produces soft lemon-yellow flowers. **'Dudley Nevill'** has attractive buff-yellow blooms. All are best sheared back after flowering to maintain a compact habit. H 20cm (8in), S 30cm (12in) or more.

PROPAGATION

🌰 late summer. Species only.

Ⓨ 10–14 days. ☀ 8–12 months.

Cuttings – summer. Softwood cuttings of new side shoots formed after cutting back. Line out, uncovered, in a cuttings frame. ☀ 10 months.

Campanula (Bellflower)   Campanulaceae

About 300 species of annuals, biennials, and perennials, with bell-shaped flowers, including many dwarf species and cultivars that are suitable for a rock garden or alpine house. (*See also the Herbaceous Perennials directory p. 36.*) Some are short-lived or monocarpic and a few self-seed or sucker too freely for all but the largest rock garden. The most robust rock garden species thrive in sun or dappled shade, in moist but well-drained soil.

C. carpatica. Hardy mat-former with bell-shaped, white, blue, or violet flowers during summer. **'Blue Clips'** and **'White Clips'**, with blue and white flowers respectively, are smaller and more compact than the species. H and S 30cm (12in) or more.

C. **'Joe Elliott'**. Dwarf in habit, this hardy plant bears large mid-blue, bell-shaped blooms in abundance during summer; the very generous display means that cuttings are hard to find during its long flowering period, so it is best to divide specimens frequently or take cuttings in mid-spring. H 8cm (3in), S to 20cm (8in).

PROPAGATION

✎ early spring, before flowers form. ☀ 3–6 months.

Softwood cuttings – early to mid-spring, before flowers form. ☀ 6–8 months.

🌰 as soon as ripe or in autumn.

C. 'White Clips' comes almost true from seed.

Ⓨ in spring. ☀ 6–8 months.

Cyclamen   Primulaceae

About 19 species of tuberous perennials, a few of which are small plants, well-suited to growing a rock garden. Selected forms are sometimes increased by sectioning a tuber

with multiple growing points, although this technique is specialized and rather risky. Those described need well-drained, not-too-fertile, humus-rich soil, in dappled shade. Establish colonies beneath shrubs or trees to provide dry conditions needed during summer dormancy.

C. coum. Hardy. Bears small, white, pink to carmine flowers with rounded, dark green, often silver-marked leaves, in late winter or early spring. It exhibits numerous leaf forms, some breeding largely true, e.g., the **Pewter Group**, which have heavily silvered leaves. H to 8cm (3in), S 10cm (4in).

C. hederifolium, syn. *C. neapolitanum*. Autumn-flowering hardy species, with flowers in white and many shades of pink, and leaves that are dark green, often heavily silver-patterned and flushed purple beneath. May self-seed. H 12cm (5in), S 15cm (6in).

PROPAGATION

🌰 as soon as ripe in late summer, in a loamless compost. Fresh seed is distributed by some specialist suppliers within weeks of harvesting. Stored seed should be soaked and well rinsed. Seedlings emerge when the species concerned comes into leaf and produce only one leaf in first year. Keep part-shaded and moist after sowing. Shelter seedlings from strong wind and insulate the frame in severe winter weather. ☀ 18–24 months.

Daphne   Thymelaeaceae

Over 50 species (and numerous hybrids and cultivars) of slow-growing, deciduous and evergreen shrubs, valued for their often very fragrant flowers. Some alpine species seldom set seed (which is poisonous) in lowland

Daphne petraea 'Grandiflora'

Dianthus deltoides

Dryas octopetala

gardens, but can be propagated – depending on species – by layering in spring or early summer (*see p.108*), by semi-ripe cuttings in mid- or late summer (some slow to root and grow on), or by apical-wedge grafting in winter or summer (*see p.111*). The choice of rootstock is critical if grafted plants are not to become over-vigorous. Grow in moist but freely drained, approximately neutral, humus-rich soil, in sun.

D. blagayana. Prostrate, hardy evergreen with trailing branches bearing fragrant creamy-white flowers in spring. It is easily layered. H to 38cm (15in), S to 90cm (36in).

D. petraea 'Grandiflora'. Compact, slow-growing, hardy evergreen with scented, rosy pink flowers in spring. It is usually grafted (*D. tangutica* and *D. longilobata* are preferred rootstocks) in late winter or high summer. If, however, this plant is to be grown in tufa, the bulkiness of the rootstock makes grafting unsuitable so semi-ripe cuttings are necessary. They are slow to grow away, often not rooting properly for 6 months. H 10cm (4in) or more, S 25cm (10in).

PROPAGATION
Layering – prostrate species and cultivars. Layer new growth, about 4–8 weeks after flowering. Leave for a year before severing from the parent plant. ☀ 1 year.
Semi-ripe cuttings – midsummer.
☀ 12 months.
Grafting – *D. petraea* 'Grandiflora'. Choose a seedling rootstock with a stem diameter of 4–5mm (¼in) and cut off below the cotyledons. Insert a 2cm (¾in) scion, with a wedge-shaped base 1cm (½in) long. Spray with fungicide, bandage firmly with grafting tape, and place in a closed propagator at

18°C (64°F). Midsummer grafts will not need artificial heat. Union takes around a month, after which the plants are hardened off.
☀ 9–15 months.

Dianthus (Carnation, Pink) Caryophyllaceae
Over 300 species, including a number that are suitable in scale for a rock garden, raised bed or trough. (*See also the Herbaceous Perennials directory p.37 and the Annuals and Biennials directory p.18.*) Most rock garden species, some of which are short-lived, are grey-leaved, evergreen perennials with a neat mat-, cushion- or mound-forming habit, bearing diminutive flowers in spring and early summer. Many named cultivars are available and must be increased by cuttings. Most need gritty, sharply drained, neutral to alkaline soil in sun.

D. alpinus. Short-lived cushion-former, bearing pink to crimson flowers in summer. H 8cm (3in), S 10cm (4in).

D. deltoides (Maiden pink). Short-lived, mat-former with often dark-eyed, white, pink, or red flowers with toothed petals, in summer. Fresh or stored seed germinates abundantly. H to 20cm (8in), S 30cm (12in),

D. pavonius, syn. *D. neglectus*. Neat, free-flowering mat-former with pale to deep-pink flowers in early summer. It needs acid soil. H 8cm (3in), S 20cm (8in).

PROPAGATION
🌱 autumn to early spring, in an open frame. Expect the seedlings to vary and select accordingly. Compact, large-flowered seedlings can then be increased by cuttings.
🌱 spring. ☀ 12 months.
Cuttings or pipings – after flowering.
☀ 8–10 months.

Dryas (Mountain avens) Rosaceae
Just three species of hardy, prostrate, evergreen subshrubs with leathery, wrinkled, dark green leaves and cup- to bell-shaped flowers. *D. octopetala* is the most commonly cultivated. All are easily grown in gritty humus-rich soil in sun.

D. octopetala. Mat-forming subshrub with oak-like foliage, and up-turned, cup-shaped creamy-white flowers in early summer, followed by feathery seed heads. H 10cm (4in), S 90cm (36in) or more.

PROPAGATION
🌱 as soon as ripe. Germinates poorly and uncertainly unless sown fresh.
🌱 spring. ☀ 2 years.
Ripewood cuttings – late summer, 5–8cm (2–3in) long. ☀ 10 months.
Irishman's cuttings – at any time, preferably in the growing season. ☀ 6–8 months.
Layering – spring. Strip away the dead winter foliage before layering. Detach rooted layers in autumn.
☀ 6 months, flowering the following year.

Edraianthus (Grassy bells) Campanulaceae
Over 20 species of tuft-forming, herbaceous and evergreen perennials, generally short-lived. They have grass-like leaves and bell-shaped flowers in summer. They need sun in sharply drained, gritty, alkaline soil.

E. pumilio, syn. *Wahlenbergia pumilio*. Cushion-forming perennial, with delicate, bell-shaped flowers in early summer that can be almost any shade of blue when raised from seed. H 2.5cm (1in), S 10cm (4in).

PROPAGATION
🌱 as soon as ripe or in late winter. Dislikes root disturbance except at the seedling

Gentiana verna

Iberis sempervirens 'Weisser Zwerg'

Lewisia cotyledon

stage, so place plants in their permanent positions as early as possible.

Ψ unlikely before mid-spring.
☀ 15 months minimum.
Softwood cuttings – from basal shoots either before the flowers form (early spring) or more readily after flowering. (Disbud spring cuttings if flowers form in same year.)
☀ 12 months.

Gentiana (Gentian)   Gentianaceae

About 400 species of hardy annuals, biennials, and perennials, the last group including many alpines, with trumpet- or five-pointed flowers in intense shades of blue (*see also p. 39*). They need humus-rich, moist but well-drained soils; the autumn-flowering species almost invariably need acid soils. Except in climates with cool, damp summers, most need protection from hot sun.

G. acaulis, syn. *G. excisa*, *G. kochiana* (Trumpet gentian). Bears blue flowers late spring to early summer. Often flowers more reliably in fertile, loamy soil. H 8cm (3in), 25cm (10in).

G. sino-ornata. Bears blue flowers, striped blue and white outside, in autumn. The foliage dies down in winter to clusters of shoots with plump roots (thongs), which are easily divided. H 7cm (3in), S to 30cm (12in).

G. verna (Spring gentian). Short-lived, forming mats of evergreen rosettes that are clothed in spring with tubular, sky-blue flowers. Subsp. *balcanica*, is more vigorous, usually longer-lived and free-flowering, blooming in its second year and for several years thereafter. H 5cm (2in), 10cm (4in).

PROPAGATION

🌰 as soon as ripe or no later than midwinter or germination will be delayed a year. Sow *in situ* or prick out the seedlings early to avoid root damage.

Ψ spring.   ☀ 12–24 months.
✎ after flowering or in early autumn. Divide *G. sino-ornata* just before growth restarts in early spring.   ☀ 12 months.
Cuttings – late spring. Take basal cuttings of non-flowering shoots 2–3cm (¾–1¼in) long, severed close to the crown and detached cleanly just below a node. Rooting occurs fastest at 10–15°C (50–59°F).
☀ 12 months.

Helianthemum (Sun rose)   Cistaceae

Some 110 species of small, evergreen and semi-evergreen subshrubs and shrubs, grown for their often vividly coloured, saucer-shaped flowers and silver or grey-green foliage. A few are not reliably hardy in very cold, wet winters, and all prefer light, well-drained soil in a warm sunny site. Several named cultivars, about 20–30cm (8–12in) tall and across, are available with single or double flowers, in white, yellow, orange ('**Ben Nevis**'), pink ('**Rhodanthe Carneum**'), and carmine ('**Ben Hope**'). Trim the plants back after blooming.

H. oelandicum subsp. *alpestre*. Hardy, neat mat-forming species that has downy, grey-green leaves and produces yellow flowers from spring to summer. H 10cm (4in), S 20cm (8in).

PROPAGATION

Softwood or semi-ripe cuttings – in early, or mid- to late summer respectively. Encourage bushiness and cutting material by pinching out stem tips in spring. Overwinter cuttings in frost-free conditions in their first year.
☀ 10–12 months.

Iberis (Perennial candytuft)   Cruciferae

About 40 species of annuals, perennials, and evergreen subshrubs, several of which are ideal for rock gardens. They are grown for their heads of cross-shaped flowers in late spring or early summer. Cultivate in not-too-fertile, well-drained soil in sun. Cut back once the flowers begin to fall.

I. sempervirens. Evergreen, mat- or mound-forming species with small, dark green leaves. It bears heads of small white flowers in spring. '**Weisser Zwerg**', syn. '**Little Gem**', is much more compact and well-suited to the smaller rock garden. H 30cm (12in), S 30cm (12in).

PROPAGATION

Softwood or semi-ripe cuttings – early and midsummer respectively. The root system is extensive, so pot on frequently or plant out before the second repotting.
☀ the following spring.

Lewisia   Portulacaceae

Some 20 species of evergreen and deciduous, rosette-forming perennials, grown for their cup-shaped, often vividly coloured flowers, in spring or summer. They need sharply drained soil, and protection from rain and snow in winter – plant them on their sides in crevices in a rock garden or wall, or by growing in an alpine house.

L. cotyledon. Evergreen perennial with flowers of white, yellow, orange, and pink-purple. **Cotyledon hybrids** are robust with flowers in very vivid colours. They are variable from seed, but produce many attractive shades. Good colour forms can be increased by offsets. H 15–30cm (6–12in), S 25–40cm (10–16in).

Lithodora diffusa 'Heavenly Blue'

Phlox subulata

Pulsatilla vulgaris

PROPAGATION

as soon as ripe, or in autumn/early winter. Use a peat-based compost mixed with 50% grit and some perlite. Keep seedlings frost-free. As they are brittle prick out carefully either singly or into seed trays – the seed-tray seedlings will need moving up in to 7cm (3in) pots by late spring.

☀ 9 months.

Offsets – midsummer. Detach with 1cm (½in) of stem, treat with rooting hormone, and keep under shaded glass in a peat-based potting compost.

☀ 9 months.

L. rediviva (Bitter root). Deciduous perennial that is summer dormant. It bears funnel-shaped, white or pink flowers in early spring and summer and has linear to spoon-shaped dark green leaves. H 5cm (2in), S 10cm (4in).

PROPAGATION

early autumn. Space-sow seeds under glass; they will germinate over winter. Keep just moist until the seedlings die down naturally. No further water is necessary until re-growth is apparent after about 4 months. Leave in original pot for a further year, giving occasional liquid feeds during the second spring. Pot the carrot-like crowns individually into 7cm (3in) pots in mid-autumn.

🌱 3–6 months.   ☀ 2–3 years.

Lithodora   Boraginaceae

Some seven species of evergreen shrubs and subshrubs that produce funnel-shaped, usually intense blue flowers, in late spring and early summer. The acid-loving *L. diffusa*, especially its cultivar 'Heavenly Blue', is the most commonly grown. It needs well-drained, humus-rich soil.

L. diffusa, syn. *Lithospermum diffusum*. Prostrate evergreen, producing deep blue flowers in late spring and summer. The flowers of **'Heavenly Blue'** are profuse, and deep azure. H 15cm (6in), S 60–75cm (24–30in).

PROPAGATION

Semi-ripe cuttings – mid- to late summer. Use an ericaceous cutting compost. A mist unit will increase rooting percentage.

☀ 7–8 months.

Phlox   Polemoniaceae

Some 67 species of annuals and mainly perennials, including a number of small, mat- or cushion-forming species for the rock garden (*see also the Herbaceous Perennials directory, p.43*). There are numerous named cultivars that will brighten the rock garden in late spring. They need well-drained, not-too-fertile soil, in sun. Those described are hardy.

P. bifida (Sand phlox). Neat, evergreen mound-former, that is clothed in lacy-petalled, usually white or lavender flowers. H 15–20cm (6–8in), S 15cm (6in).

P. douglasii. Low, mound-forming evergreen with white, blue, or pink flowers in spring. **'Crackerjack'** has crimson flowers, while those of **'Iceberg'** are palest lilac. H 15–20cm (6–8in), S 30cm (12in).

P. subulata. Forms evergreen mats or cushions studded with star-shaped flowers, in a range of colours, usually red or purple, but also violet, pink, or white. **'Tamaongalei'** is a striking white and bright pink cultivar. H to 15cm (6in), S to 60cm (24in).

PROPAGATION

Softwood cuttings – after flowering the mats benefit from a light cutting back and the resultant clippings should contain new shoots, 2–3cm (¾–1¼in) long, which root easily. *P. bifida* has firmer, larger shoots that root best in equal parts peat and silver sand.

☀ 8–12 months.

Pulsatilla   Ranunculaceae

Around 30 species of hardy perennials forming clumps of finely divided leaves, and bearing bell- or cup-shaped, usually very silky-hairy flowers, in spring or early summer, followed by silky seed heads. Often long-lived but resentful of transplanting except in dormancy. Grow in well-drained soil in sun.

P. halleri. Bears lavender or purple, silky haired, bell-shaped flowers in late spring. It is best with very good drainage and protection from winter rains and snow. H 15–35cm (6–14in), S 15–20cm (6–8in).

P. vulgaris (Pasque flower). More robust than *P. halleri* and bears nodding, bell-shaped, silky flowers in white, or shades of red, pink, or purple. H and S 25cm (10in).

PROPAGATION

as soon as ripe in early summer, or store in the bottom of the refrigerator; old seed germinates erratically. Cover the feathery 'tails' with 1cm (½in) of grit, to deter theft by birds. Prick out in early spring, and pot into deep pots to reduce chances of disturbance when planting out.

🌱 4–8 weeks if sown fresh.

☀ 2–3 years.

Root cuttings – autumn. Root cuttings present some risk to the parent. Cut thick roots into 3cm (1¼in) sections. Keep at about 10°C (50°F). Adventitious buds develop after 2 months, but leave plantlets *in situ* until spring.   ☀ usually 2 years.

Saxifraga burseriana 'Gloria'

Sedum spathulifolium '**Cape Blanco**'

Sempervivum arachnoideum

Ramonda   Gesneriaceae

Just three species of hardy, evergreen perennials with rosettes of leaves and, in late spring or early summer, flowers like those of the related African violets. Grow in an alpine house or in vertical rock crevices in partial shade. They dislike exposure to winter wet which will make the rosettes rot if it is allowed to accumulate in them.

R. myconi, syn. *R. pyrenaica*. This produces lavender, pink, or white flowers in late spring. The leaves are dark green. It is the easiest species to grow. H 10cm (4in), S 20cm (8in).

PROPAGATION
Leaf cuttings – early autumn. Often used to increase selected colour forms.
☀ 12–24 months.
✂ early autumn. Wash the dense root system free of compost, then root individual rosettes. ☀ 12 months.
🌰 as soon as ripe. Surface sow the dust-like seed onto the surface of milled sphagnum, then place the pot in a polythene bag to maintain high humidity. Keep out of direct light. Water from below. Prick out only when the seedlings have developed several leaves and are about 1–2 cm (½–¾in) across.
🌱 2 weeks. ☀ 3–5 years.

Saxifraga (Rockfoil)   Saxifragaceae

Complex genus of about 350 species of mostly rosette-forming, evergreen or semi-evergreen perennials, and many hybrids, often with complicated parentage, but sometimes easier to grow than the species. Plants in cultivation range from the easily grown **Mossy saxifrages**, with mats of soft mossy, bright green leaves, to high-alpine rock-, scree- and cliff-dwellers that form

tight, firm rosettes of often lime-encrusted leaves (the '**Silvers**'). Division is best reserved for the vigorous **Mossy hybrids**; many of the smaller rosette-formers have a single 'neck' or are difficult to re-establish.

S. burseriana '**Gloria**'. Rosettes of grey-green leaves and large white flowers at the end of winter. H to 5cm (2in), S 15cm (6in).

S. cochlearis '**Minor**' Lime-encrusted with red-spotted white flowers. Neat in a trough or raised bed. H 10cm (4in), S 15cm (6in).

S. '**Tumbling Waters**' Cascades of small white flowers in spring. As with several others, the rosette dies after blooming, but is replaced with daughter rosettes. H 45cm (18in), S 30cm (12in).

PROPAGATION
Rosette cuttings – 4–10 weeks after flowering. Root in silver sand at 10-15°C (50–59°F). If taken too early, the fragile rosettes may fall apart during preparation.
☀ 12 months.
🌰 autumn, in an open frame. Hybrids do not come true, although many are fertile and unexpected colour forms occur in the resulting seedlings.
🌱 spring. ☀ 2–3 years.

Sedum (Stonecrop)   Crassulacea

Around 400 mostly succulent species, not all hardy or long-lived, but with many suited to the rock garden in scale and hardiness. Most bear tiny star-shaped flowers in summer or autumn. They need well-drained soil and sun.

S. spathulifolium '**Cape Blanco**', syn. *S. s.* 'Cappa Blanca'. Forms a wide, low mound of bloomed, grey leaves, spangled with heads of star-shaped yellow flowers in summer. H 10cm (4in), S 45–60cm (18–24in).

PROPAGATION
Cuttings of non-flowering shoots – early to midsummer. Exceptionally easy to root, even rosettes knocked accidentally onto the surrounding soil may form new plants.
☀ 12 months.
✂ spring or late summer.
☀ 6 months.

Sempervivum (Houseleek)   Crassulaceae

Some 40 species, and hundreds of cultivars, of hardy, fleshy, rosette-forming perennials valued mainly for their foliage, although many are also very handsome when bearing their flat-topped heads of star-shaped flowers in summer. The flowered rosette dies after flowering finishes, but surrounding rosettes erupt with short stolons that soon fill the gap with satellite rosettes. Grow in sun in sharply drained, gritty soil of low fertility.

S. arachnoideum (Cobweb houseleek). Rosettes of leaves cobwebbed with white hair and flowering columns topped by starry pink flowers. H 5–8cm (2–3in), S to 30cm (12in) or more.

S. tectorum (Common houseleek). Produces large rosettes of very fleshy, purple-tipped, blue-green leaves and has red-purple starry flowers on hairy stems. H 10–15cm (4–6in), S 45–50cm (18–20in).

PROPAGATION
Offsets – spring or early summer. Once the stolons have developed new rosettes, sometimes with vestigial roots, these can be severed and grown on separately. Those with congested rosettes can have groupings of rosettes from the edge of the cushion pulled off and rooted in a sandy compost.
☀ 12 months.

CONIFERS AND HEATHERS

Conifers and heathers are interesting and versatile plants that deserve a place in every garden. They provide form, structure and continuity while giving a year-round display of colourful flowers, foliage and cones. There are species and cultivars in every form and for every situation: majestic sequoias to dominate the skyline, exquisite dwarfs for the rock garden and carpeting heathers to brighten the darkest winter days.

Propagating heathers is easy, rewarding and economical, using only the simplest of equipment and the most basic techniques. Conifers can be as easy as heathers or they can be challenging, a test for the best propagator. Here are all the techniques you will ever need.

◄ *Despite their infinite variety in form and colour, conifers and heathers can be increased by a range of mostly very simple propagating techniques.*

WHY PROPAGATE
CONIFERS AND HEATHERS?

Highly prized for their year-round impact, conifers and heathers deserve a place in every garden. Choice specimens can be expensive yet are easy to propagate at home, so why not bulk up one or two store-bought plants and grow your own hedge, exchange unusual varieties with friends, or simply expand your border display.

Most ornamental cultivars of conifers and heathers do not come true from seed; increase relies on vegetative methods.

It is well worth while producing a reserve stock of both conifers and heathers. Although most conifers are hardy plants adapted to harsh conditions, casualties can occur in all gardens. Tall heathers, such as *Erica arborea* and *E. australis*, are similarly vulnerable, and mat-forming types, which tend to become bare at the base after a few years, are best replaced regularly with fresh stock. With conifers there is also the attraction of raising your own hedges and saving a lot of money in the process.

EXCITING POSSIBILITIES

Seed is the key to variety. Some conifer species have unstable genes that are capable of producing plants of widely differing size and habit. Hence, there is always the chance that a new form will emerge.

Most garden heathers, however, are cultivars and can only be reproduced vegetatively. Fortunately, the techniques involved are so easy that propagation from seed is rarely practised except to produce new hybrids.

SHORTCUTS

Cuttings are the simplest way of reproducing conifer cultivars though they must be taken from young plants. Heathers are equally easy, but a heated propagator is necessary for those taken early and for tender varieties.

Pines, cedars, firs, and spruces are almost impossible to strike from cuttings and so are usually grafted. Exceptions are the prostrate and dwarf firs and spruces which do root, albeit slowly, from softwood cuttings.

LOW-MAINTENANCE OPTION

Layering and dropping are two useful techniques for increasing heathers, provided the plants have an area of bare soil around their bases. Dropping is also an ideal way to rejuvenate heathers that have become leggy and bare at the base. Both methods are more reliable and easier than cuttings, since the young plants are rooted while still attached to the parent

Overcoming Seed Dormancy

The cones of most conifers ripen in their first year, opening to release the seed before winter. If the seed germinated immediately, the seedlings would face the rigours of winter. A natural dormancy period that is broken by a period of cold, prevents the seed from germinating until the spring, when the young plant has a full season to establish itself and form overwintering buds that will produce the next year's growth. Storing seeds of conifers such as the pines, Abies *and* Picea, *at 2–4°C (36–39°F) in the refrigerator for four weeks mimics this process and assists even germination.*

Abies koreana, the Korean fir, is a species of conifer that can be grown from seed, as discussed above.

plant and so need much less aftercare; although young plants should always be kept watered and weed-free as a matter of course.

Many dwarf conifers, especially prostrate or arching variants, can also be layered successfully, provided that young or juvenile shoots are selected. They invariably root quicker than older wood.

(1)

Taxus baccata 'Hibernica'
Yews are slow to propagate from seed, which can take 2 years to germinate. Heeled semi-ripe cuttings root in 2–3 months, making this a productive method for both species and cultivars.

(2)

Abies balsamea, dwarf cultivar
Prostrate and dwarf cultivars of *Abies* root reasonably easily from softwood cuttings; larger cultivars are propagated by side-veneer grafting onto A. grandis or A. procera. Only species are increased by seed.

(3)

Thuja occidentalis cultivar
Cultivars of T. occidentalis include golden-leaved, dwarf, upright, and weeping forms; all are increased by semi-ripe or ripewood cuttings. The species makes good hedging, and ample numbers can be grown cheaply from seed.

(4)

Chamaecyparis lawsoniana cultivar
Chamaecyparis lawsoniana often mutates and has given rise to over 500 mostly seed-raised variants. Once a sport or mutant has arisen, however, it must be increased vegetatively.

(5)

Chamaecyparis lawsoniana 'Elwoodii'
This upright cultivar makes a good screen in the garden. It is one of the easiest of variants to root either from semi-ripe or from ripewood cuttings, so raising sufficient numbers yourself is an economical proposition.

PROPAGATING TECHNIQUES
CONIFERS AND HEATHERS

Although most conifers are relatively straightforward to raise from the seed which they hold in their woody cones, there are also a number of other techniques available to the home propagator. Cuttings of both conifers and heathers will strike quite readily, provided they are taken from young stock at the correct time of year.

There are three main methods used to propagate conifers: seed, cuttings and grafting. Each method has its benefits, and each requires a different set of techniques and skills. Heathers are usually grown from cuttings or from various types of layers; seed is usually used only to produce hybrids.

SEED

The majority of conifers hold their seeds in woody cones. Most ripen in their first autumn, opening to release the seed before the cone falls. Conifers from dry, fire-prone areas, such as California (many pines and cypress species), retain the cones unopened for up to twenty-five years as part of a natural survival strategy.

Junipers and yews have fleshy cones (commonly referred to as 'berries') that are respectively either blue-black or red when ripe. Seed from these can be slow to

germinate, taking up to three years, and both genera are more quickly propagated from cuttings. Some conifers (such as *Taxus, Juniperus, Araucaria* and all members of Podocarpaceae) have both male and female cones on separate plants so that both need to be present before seed can be produced.

Cones are green when immature and change to a brown or purple colour when ripe. Collect them just before they start to open, from late summer onwards. The seed can be extracted by placing the cones in a paper bag and keeping them in a warm, dry place such as an airing cupboard until they open. Tap out the seed onto a clean piece of paper. If the cones refuse to open, soak them in water overnight and then repeat the procedure. The seed that is found in the lower part of the cone is the most likely to germinate.

Soak the seed overnight in clean water; any still floating on the surface by morning should be discarded as it is probably not viable.

To extract the seed from yews and junipers, squash the ripe berries between thumb and forefinger. Wash the seed in tepid water and dry it on kitchen paper.

Conifer seed can be stored dry at 4°C (39°F) in airtight containers in the bottom of a refrigerator until the early following spring and then sown.

Stratification

The majority of conifer seed germinates best after three to four weeks' cold storage at 0–5°C (32–41°F) in a domestic refrigerator before being sown. This mimics conditions found in the wild and overcomes dormancy. Mix the seed with a little damp peat, vermiculite or perlite in a polythene bag. Alternatively, first sow the seed, then place the pots in the bottom of the refrigerator.

Choice of cutting material . . . .
Always take cuttings from shoots with a distinct growing point. Bun-shaped forms may be produced if lateral or feather shoots, especially from yellow-leaved cultivars, are selected.

◀ If the shape of the parent plant is to be maintained, select the cuttings from the leading shoot or from epicormic growth (where present) on the main stem or branches. If horizontal side shoots are used, prostrate plants will result; in this case a leading shoot may form only after several years, if at all.

Fill 12cm (5in) pots with standard seed compost. Place the seed on the surface, then cover it with its own depth of compost. Mix the fine seed of species such as *Sequoia* and some cypresses with a little fine sand and surface-sow. For the large seed of conifers such as *Araucaria*, sow one seed per 8cm (3in) pot.

Place the pots in an open frame outdoors and pot up the seedlings when they are large enough to handle.

CUTTINGS

Most conifers can be propagated from cuttings. *Juniperus, Taxus, Thuja, Cryptomeria* and other genera mentioned in the directory all root relatively quickly in a cold frame or in a pot tented with a polythene bag.

It is important to use young healthy specimens as a source for cuttings; once they are over six years of age, *Picea* and *Pinus* become increasingly difficult to root. All conifers root faster if the stock plants are young, disease free and vigorous. Junipers and cypresses root more easily from cuttings with juvenile foliage than from those with adult leaves.

Heather cuttings are taken in the same way as conifer cuttings, but you do not need to wound the base; it is sufficient to remove the lowest leaves.

Timing and types of cuttings

Conifer cuttings are usually taken from the time when the current season's growth begins to turn from green to brown. Most are best from semi-ripe cuttings taken between late summer and early autumn (most genera and cultivars.) Early-summer (softwood) cuttings may be more successful for *Abies* and *Picea*; late-winter (fully ripe) cuttings suit junipers and *Metasequoia*.

Early (softwood) cuttings of *Abies* and *Picea* need a closed, heated propagator to root successfully; cuttings taken in the late winter or early summer also need the protection of a greenhouse or unheated propagator. Watch them throughout the summer when they are more at risk of drying out or being scorched by the sun.

Heather cuttings can be taken at any time during the growing season. All cuttings taken from midsummer onwards are best taken with a 'heel', a piece of bark from the main stem of the parent plant.

The later in the season you take the cutting (and the harder the wood), the slower the rooting process will be. With bottom heat, both conifer and heather cuttings taken early in the season (softwood) should root within six weeks. Cuttings taken around midsummer (semi-ripe) should root by the following spring; late summer and autumn cuttings (fully ripe) by the following autumn.

Prepare a well-drained, sterile cuttings compost of equal parts peat (or alternative) and grit, sharp sand or perlite or vermiculite. A layer of sand or perlite on the top helps prevent fungal infection and the growth of liverworts and mosses.

Semi-ripe and fully ripe conifer cuttings ....

Whether propagating directly into a cold frame itself or placing a cutting-filled container in a cold frame, make sure that the surroundings are scrupulously clean, in order to minimize the risk of disease while the cuttings produce roots. Protect the cuttings in winter by insulating the cold frame, and in summer by airing and shading the frame.

▲ **1** If possible, take a cutting with a 'heel', a small section of wood from the main branch. Grasp the stem near its point of origin, and pull it sharply away, tearing off a small piece of bark.

▲ **2** Trim this with a sharp knife. Strip off the lower leaves, and remove the tip of the cutting if this is very soft.

▲ **3** Make 2.5cm (1in) holes, 5cm (2in) apart, in the cuttings medium either directly in a cold frame or in a pot; then insert the cuttings. Place the pot in the cold frame, then shut the lid.

▲ **4** Once the cutting has rooted well, replant it in a 7.5–10cm (3–4in) pot, while it becomes further established, or transplant it to its final position in the garden.

Semi-ripe conifer cuttings with a heel . . . .

A cutting taken with a heel has a firm base to protect it against rots. It also has a high capacity to produce roots from the exposed, swollen base of the current season's growth.

◄ **1** Pull a vigorous shoot away from the parent stem, with a heel.

▼ **2** Trim off any leaves on the bottom third of the cutting.

For most conifers, cuttings should be 8–12cm (3–5in) long; for heathers and some dwarf conifers, cuttings can be only 5cm (2in) long, or even shorter if suitable material is not available.

Softwood cuttings

These are taken early in the season, but only when the terminal bud is clearly visible – cuttings taken earlier do not have sufficient food reserves to survive until rooting occurs. On conifers, trim the cuttings at the base just below a node and strip off the lower leaves.

Dip both conifer and heather cuttings in fungicide and dab the bases in hormone rooting powder (or dip the base of the cutting in a hormone solution), then insert them up to a third of their length in the cuttings medium. Spray the cuttings with fungicide and place them in a closed propagator at 21°C (70°F). Inspect them regularly for any signs of fungal diseases and remove any affected cuttings. Spray the remainder with fungicide to prevent the spread of disease.

GRAFTING

Grafting is a more challenging technique used for propagating conifer cultivars and species that are very difficult to strike from cuttings or raise from seed. *Ginkgo* and large-growing cultivars of *Abies*, *Cedrus*, *Picea* and *Pinus* are often propagated by grafting. The best time for grafting conifers is in late winter before the onset of active growth. Side-veneer grafting is most commonly used for conifers (*see also p. 113*).

Side-veneer grafting

Rootstocks for grafting should be two- or three-year-old, pot-grown seedlings of the same or a closely related species. All pines are mutually compatible, provided the needles are borne in bundles of the same number.

Coax the rootstock out of dormancy by bringing it into a cool greenhouse about three weeks before grafting. Keep it dry, however: you do not want to encourage active growth that would result in too great an upsurge of resin.

Scions should be collected either from the terminal shoots or from strong upright shoots of the specimen to be propagated. They should be 8–12 cm (3–5in) long and from the previous season's growth. Keep the stems in a plastic bag in the refrigerator until ready to graft.

Cut back the rootstock to within 7cm (3in) of the base. Remove a sliver of wood about 2.5cm (1in) long from near the base of the rootstock. Cut the scion just below a pair of buds, then remove a 2.5cm (1in) sliver of wood from its base to match that of the rootstock. Bring the exposed sections of pith together and bind them with grafting tape. Ideally, the scion and rootstock will be of the same thickness. Where the rootstock is thicker, align rootstock and scion at one side, thus bringing into contact the cambium layers (the layer of cells just beneath the bark). Seal the union with grafting wax.

Keep the grafted conifer humid at 15°C (59°F) until the scion produces fresh growth, normally within four weeks. Pinch out any shoots that arise on the rootstock below the grafting joint. Cut back the rootstock to just above the graft union when the scion is growing well.

LAYERING HEATHERS

Layering is a successful method of propagating heathers and dwarf conifers, provided the surrounding soil is fairly friable. The layers take about a year to develop good roots, after which they can be severed from the parent plant and planted out or potted up. Layering is best done in autumn. Heathers can also be increased by mound layering in spring, but both methods will only be successful on plants that have strong, sturdy stems.

In all cases, the principle is the same: to bring the stems into contact with soil and so encourage rooting at that point. The stems of most other shrubs need wounding in some way to encourage root production, but this is not necessary with heathers.

Heathers from cuttings . . . .

The best time to propagate heathers from cuttings is when there are plenty of vigorous, non-flowering shoots available. This most probably will be in summer.

◀ **1** Take semi-ripe cuttings 2.5–4cm (1–1½in) long from the top of a non-flowering shoot.
Make a straight cut at the bottom.

▶ **2** Strip off the leaves from the lower half of the stem.

◀ **3** Fill the tray with cuttings compost. Insert the cuttings to the depth of the lowest leaves. Place tray in a closed cold frame.

In autumn, dig a shallow trench around the perimeter of the plant. Mix the excavated soil with sharp sand and peat or garden compost to make a friable mixture.

Spread out the outer stems of the heather and sprinkle in the soil mixture. Hold the stems in place with wire bent into a U-shape.

Mound layering

Mound layering is a modification of simple layering (*see p.92*). Prepare a sandy, friable mixture of garden soil, sand and peat or garden compost. Cut out any dead or woody stems, then spread the remainder apart with your fingers and mound the soil around them. Cover the stems to within about 2.5–5cm (1–2in) of their tips. Keep the mound well watered during dry spells in summer. Replenish the mound if heavy rainfall washes some of the soil away. The shoots should root by late summer, when they can be separated from the parent plant and potted up or planted out.

Dropping

Heathers that have been allowed to become woody at the base are best increased by dropping. Dropping is done in the dormant season, since it involves lifting the plant, a procedure that normally checks growth. The whole plant is buried in a planting hole large enough to accommodate the root ball, with the stem tips 2.5–5cm (1–2in) above soil level.

Dropping heathers . . . .

Unless heathers are trimmed regularly after flowering, they tend to become sparse and leggy with age, producing unattractive tufts of foliage at the ends of bare stems that are particularly ineffective as ground-cover. In this case, dropping is a simple and productive way of renewing your stock.

◀ **1** In late winter to early spring lift the entire plant, keeping the rootball intact. Cut back any straggly or congested stems.

◀ **3** The shoots can be arranged in the planting hole in one of two ways: so that they form a straight line, which is easy to keep weed-free; or in a bowl shape.

◀ **2** Sink the plant in a hole with 2.5–5cm (1–2in) of the stem tips above soil level. Mix the excavated soil with sand and peat and work it in around each stem. Roots will develop by the following autumn. Pot them up or plant them out.

◀ **4** Heathers arranged in a bowl shape should have their stems evenly spread around the circumference of the planting hole, if possible.

DIRECTORY OF
CONIFERS AND HEATHERS

*Below are instructions and special propagating tips on selected conifers
and heathers. Unless otherwise specified, follow the detailed instructions given under
the propagation section on pages 90–93.*

Key

H   Height
S   Spread
🌰   By seed

Conifers

Abies (Silver fir) Pinaceae

About 50 species of hardy, evergreen
conifers with a pyramidal habit and single,
linear, flattened leaves, spirally arranged or
in two ranks and often with distinctive pale
silvery-blue bands beneath. Mature cones
are upright, resinous, usually purple, and
break up at the end of the first year. Useful
as specimen trees or for windbreaks. Grow
in sun in neutral to acid, well-drained soil.
A. balsamea f. *hudsonia.* Makes a dense,
conical mound. H 60cm (24in), S 1m (3ft).
A. nordmanniana (Caucasian fir). Cultivars
include dwarf and prostrate forms. **'Golden
Spreader'** is prostrate and golden-leaved.
H 1m (3ft), S 1.5m (5ft).
A. koreana (Korean fir). Bears purple cones
prolifically at a young age, and is suitable
for small gardens. .
H to 10m (30ft), S to 6m (20ft).

A. pinsapo **'Glauca'.** Makes a fine specimen
tree with dark glaucous foliage. H 25m
(80ft), S to 8cm (25ft).
A. procera **'Compacta'.** One of the best blue-
foliaged dwarfs. H 1m (3ft), S 1.5m (5ft).

PROPAGATION
🌰 species only. Collect in autumn before
cones start to break up. Sow immediately
outdoors or in an open frame. Seed does
not store well.
Grafting – larger cultivars only. Using a side-
veneer graft in late winter, graft on to 2-year
old rootstocks of *A. grandis* or *A. balsamea.*
Softwood cuttings – for dwarf and prostrate
cultivars. Collect cutting material in early
summer, treat with rooting hormone and
root in a propagating case.

Araucaria Araucariaceae

Genus of 20 species of evergreen conifers,
only one of which is reliably hardy. Grow in
well-drained soil with shelter from cold wind.
A. araucana (Monkey puzzle, Chile pine).
One of the most characteristic of conifers
with an unusual branching habit, symmetrical
dome, and sharp-pointed, leathery, dark
green leaves. Good as a specimen or in a
group. H to 25m (80ft), S to 10m (30ft).

PROPAGATION
🌰 collect the large seeds from beneath
female trees in autumn. Sow immediately in
individual pots and keep in a cold frame or
greenhouse. Lay the seed horizontally on the
surface – do not cover, and keep moist.

Calocedrus Cupressaceae

About three species of evergreen conifers.
C. decurrens (Incense cedar). Fairly common
in cultivation and hardy. It is an upright, fast-
growing tree with tough, scale-like, aromatic,
dark green leaves. It is resistant to root rots
and is not very fussy about soil or site.
'Berrima Gold' has sprays of yellow foliage.
H to 40m (130ft), S to 9m (28ft).

PROPAGATION
🌰 collect cones when they turn red-brown
in autumn, dry, and separate seed. Store
seed dry at 3°C (37°F) for 21 days, then
sow outdoors in a seedbed or in pots in
an open frame. Species only.
Cuttings – early autumn. Semi-ripe cuttings
root slowly in a cold frame or propagator.

Cedrus (Cedar) Pinaceae

Genus of 4 species of hardy, evergreen
conifers with slender, needle-like foliage that
varies from green to blue; there are also
golden and deep blue cultivars. Young trees
are pyramidal or conical, and fastigiate and
weeping forms are available. All species make
excellent specimens for large gardens. Grow
in an open site in well-drained soil. *C. libani*
'Sargentii' is a good weeping form while
'Comte de Dijon' is a slow-growing dwarf.
C. atlantica **'Glauca'** has deep blue-grey
foliage, and *C. deodara* **'Aurea'** has foliage
that is golden in spring and summer. Mature
cones are barrel shaped, and upright; they
ripen in their second year and break up on
the tree. H to 40m (130ft), S to 10m (30ft).

Abies koreana

Cedrus libani

Chamaecyparis lawsoniana 'Ellwoodii'

Cryptomeria japonica

Ginkgo biloba

PROPAGATION

🌿 species only. Collect cones as they start to open and extract the seed by drying. Store dry seed at 3°C (37°F) until early spring and then sow in seedbeds or in pots in an open frame. Seedlings are variable as the species hybridize but good forms can be selected for foliage colour.

Grafting – cultivars are grafted onto rootstocks of the same species or seedlings of C. deodara, using a side-graft in late winter.

Chamaecyparis (False cypress)
Cupressaceae

Genus of five species and usually three recognized varieties of hardy, evergreen conifers with aromatic, paired, scale-like leaves in flattened sprays, small rounded cones and characteristic nodding tips. The species and their cultivars are widely used as specimens, hedges, or screens. Best in neutral to slightly acid, well-drained soil in sun.

C. lawsoniana (Lawson's cypress). Has over 500 cultivars – most originating as chance seedlings. There is an almost limitless choice of dwarfs, ground-covers and weeping and upright forms, offering blue, golden, or variegated foliage. **'Ellwoodii'** is dense and conical. H 3m (10ft). **'Ellwood's Gold'** has gold-green juvenile foliage and forms a small, compact tree. H to 3m (10ft). **'Kilmacurragh'** has bright green foliage and a narrow habit. H to 15m (50ft), S 2–5m (6–15ft).

C. obtusa 'Crippsii'. Dense sprays of golden foliage and makes a fine specimen. H 15m (50ft), S 8m (25ft).

C. pisifera 'Boulevard'. Makes a small conical shrub when young and has soft blue juvenile foliage. H 10m (30ft), S 5m (15ft).

PROPAGATION

🌿 collect in autumn before cones open. Sow outdoors in seedbeds or in pots in an open frame. Germination is erratic. Species only. Cuttings – autumn to spring. The best way to propagate all the species and cultivars. Shoots with juvenile foliage root most readily, as semi-ripe or ripewood cuttings, in a cold frame. Most species can be rooted in the same way. C. nootkatensis, C. obtusa, and their cultivars should be taken in late winter to early spring.

Cryptomeria
Taxodiaceae

One or two hardy evergreen species that tolerate most soils and sites.

C. japonica (Japanese cedar). Fast-growing tree with awl-shaped leaves and rounded cones. H to 23m (80ft), S to 6m (20ft). **'Cristata'** has flattened, crested growths. **'Elegans'** is a large bushy shrub with bronze-purple foliage in winter. H 8m (25ft), S 4m (12ft).

PROPAGATION

Cuttings – early autumn to spring. Take heeled semi-ripe cuttings, wound at the base, and root in a cold frame or propagator.

x Cupressocyparis
Cupressaceae

Single hardy hybrid between Chamaecyparis and Cupressus. Grow in deep fertile soil in sun or partial shade.

x C. leylandii (Leyland cypress). Has long, flat sprays of foliage, nodding leading shoots, vigorous growth, and a columnar habit. Cultivars are among the most widely planted and fastest growing conifers and are often used for hedging and screens. **'Haggerston Grey'** and **'Green Spire'** are commonly grown, while **'Robinson's Gold'** is one of the

best gold-leaved cultivars. All are propagated by cuttings. H to 35m (120ft), S to 5m (15ft).

PROPAGATION

Cuttings – collect at almost any time between late summer and early spring. Both heeled and nodal cuttings give good results.

Cupressus (Cypress)
Cupressaceae

About 20 species of evergreen conifers. Most are conical, with scale-like foliage in three-dimensional sprays. Persistent cones often retain the seed. Grow in any well-drained soil in full sun.

C. arizonica var. glabra 'Pyramidalis'. Has bluish green new growth. H to 15m (50ft), S to 5m (15ft).

C. macrocarpa 'Donard Gold' and **'Goldcrest'**. Both good golden forms. H to 5m (16ft), S to 2.5m (8ft).

C. sempervirens 'Stricta'. Fastigiate form of the Italian cypress. H 20m (70ft), S 3m (10ft).

PROPAGATION

🌿 species only. C. sempervirens is variable from seed. Fastigiate forms are best grown from cuttings. Cones are ripe when they turn dark brown, and open if dried in gentle heat. Sow in pots in a cold frame or greenhouse after storing for 4 weeks at 3°C (37°F). Cuttings – early to late autumn. Take heeled, semi-ripe cuttings, treat them with rooting hormone, and root in a cold frame or greenhouse.

Ginkgo
Ginkgoaceae

Single species of hardy, deciduous conifer. Grow in fertile, well-drained soil in sun.

G. biloba (Maidenhair tree). Broad, fan-shaped, bright green leaves. Autumn colour is a clear buttery yellow. Male and female

Juniperus communis

Metasequoia glyptostroboides

Picea glauca var. albertiana 'Conica'

cones are borne on separate trees – the plum-like female fruits have an unpleasant odour. H to 30m (100ft), S to 8m (25ft).

PROPAGATION
Cuttings – midsummer. Collect semi-ripe cuttings, treat with rooting hormone and root in a propagator. Those taken from the shorter lateral shoots will form leaders in their second year.

Juniperus (Juniper)   Cupressaceae
Some 45–60 species of hardy to frost-hardy, evergreen conifers. Grow in well-drained soil in sun or light shade. Junipers are variable and versatile. Foliage can be adult (scale-like) or juvenile (sharp, needle-like); sometimes both types appear on the same plant. Habits of both cultivars and species vary.
J. procumbens. Completely prostrate (H to 75cm/30in); *J.* x *media* 'Pfitzeriana' is an open vase-shaped shrub (H 1.2m/4ft); while some cultivars of *J. communis* and *J. chinensis* are narrow and conical (H to 20m/70ft, S to 6m/20ft), but very varied. The foliage colour in the cultivars also varies with almost every hue of blue, green or grey available.
J. squamata 'Blue Carpet.' Forms a dense blue mat. H 30cm (12in), S 3m (10ft).
J. virginiana 'Grey Owl'. Has silvery grey foliage and a spreading, vase-shaped habit. H 2–3m (6–10ft), S 3–4m (10–12ft). The seed is in a fleshy fruit and can take up to 3 years to ripen. Seed germinates erratically over a long period, so most junipers – species and cultivars – are propagated by cuttings. Prostrate species and cultivars sometimes layer themselves, and these can be lifted before new growth begins in spring.

PROPAGATION
Cuttings – juvenile forms are the easiest but those with adult foliage can also be rooted successfully. Cuttings can be taken as ripewood cuttings in midwinter to early spring, or as semi-ripe cuttings from late summer to early autumn. Cuttings of *J. communis*, its cultivars, and other prostrate species are best taken late in the year, while those of the more upright species and cultivars are best taken in early spring.

Larix (Larch)   Pinaceae
Genus of 14 species of hardy, fast-growing, deciduous conifers, with needle-like leaves, clustered or spirally arranged. Grow in deep, well-drained soil in sun. Larches are often used in shelter belts or woodland gardens to provide protection for more tender plants; in gardens, they are also valued for their foliage colour. They turn shades of old gold in autumn and the spring foliage is the brightest sea-green. Cones persist on the tree for many years although the seed is shed in the first year. Cuttings are very difficult to root and seed is the best method of increase. H 1–30m (3–100ft), S 1–6m (3–20ft).

PROPAGATION
❦ collect cones before they open in autumn, dry, and extract the seed. Store dry seed at 3°C (37°F) until early spring, then sow outside in a seedbed or open frame.

Metasequoia   Taxodiaceae
Genus of a single hardy species. Provide humus-rich, well-drained soil in a sunny site.
M. glyptostroboides (Dawn redwood). A fine deciduous conifer, with red-brown bark and opposite pairs of linear, soft green leaves that

turn pink or gold in autumn. The tight pyramidal habit and the buttresses that form on the older trees make this a fine specimen for medium- and large-sized gardens. Cones ripen in 1 year and open on the tree. H to 40m (130ft), S to 5m (15ft).

PROPAGATION
Cuttings – hardwood, in mid- to late winter. Root in a frame, preferably with bottom heat. They root within 4 months. Softwood cuttings collected in early summer and rooted in a propagator are also successful. Collect all cuttings from either terminal or upright shoots.
❦ collect seed as soon as cones start to open and sow immediately in a cold frame or greenhouse. Seed usually germinates within 2 weeks.

Picea (Spruce)   Pinaceae
About 35 species of hardy to frost-hardy, evergreen conifers, distinguished from firs by their narrow, single, usually forward-pointing, spirally arranged needles and their pendent cones. Grow in sun in any deep, moist but well-drained soil, preferably neutral to acid. The foliage is usually dark green, but there are blue cultivars, such as *P. pungens* 'Koster', and golden-leaved cultivars, like *P. orientalis* 'Aurea'. Some, such as *P. glauca* var. *albertiana* 'Conica', form conical shapes, others make low mounds or 'buns'; there are also weeping, fastigiate, or prostrate forms. Sizes vary from H 15cm (6in) to 40m (130ft), S 50cm (20in) to 12m (40ft). Cones ripen and shed their seed in the first year.

PROPAGATION
❦ for species. Collect cones when they turn brown, dry, and extract the seed. Sow in

Pinus mugo 'Winter Gold'

Podocarpus salignus

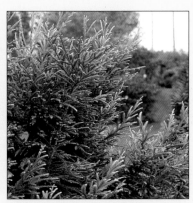

Sequoia sempervirens 'Adpressa'

seedbeds outdoors or in a cold frame. Grafting – late winter. Larger cultivars are grafted using a side-graft with *P. abies* as a rootstock.

Cuttings – dwarf cultivars, such as *P. mariana* 'Nana', *P. abies* 'Little Gem'. Take softwood cuttings in midsummer, avoiding strong growth, and root in a propagator.

Pinus (Pine)   Pinaceae

About 110 species of hardy to frost-hardy, evergreen conifers, usually easily recognized by their bundles of needles. Most have whorled branches and are fast-growing, conical when young and dome-shaped at maturity. They make good individual specimens, and smaller species and some cultivars are suitable for rock and heather gardens. Grow in sun in any well-drained soil. Cones sometimes remain closed on the tree for many years. Cuttings are almost impossible to strike unless very young plants are used.
P. mugo (Mountain pine, Swiss mountain pine, Dwarf pine). Hardy, round to spreading tree. **'Winter Gold'** has golden winter foliage. H to 3.5 (11ft), S to 5m (15ft).
P. sylvestris **'Aurea'** (Scots pine). Hardy, golden conifer; colour stronger in autumn and winter. H to 15m (50ft), S to 9m (28ft).

PROPAGATION
collect cones in autumn when they are brown; dry, and extract the seed. Most species benefit from 12 weeks stratification at 4°C (39°F). Sow into seedbeds outdoors or in pots in a cold frame in early spring. Grafting – cultivars are grafted onto rootstocks of the same species or other species with the same number of needles. Use a side-veneer graft in late winter.

Podocarpus (Podocarps)   Podocarpaceae

About 100 species of evergreen, coniferous shrubs or trees, but with only a few hardy species in cultivation. Tolerant of many soils, but prefer sun and shelter from cold wind.
P. salignus. Drooping branches and long, glossy, narrowly lanceolate leaves.
H to 20m (70ft), S to 9m (28ft).

PROPAGATION
Cuttings – late summer to early autumn. Heeled and semi-ripe, the lower half lightly wounded. Treat with rooting hormone and root in a cold frame or propagator. They root slowly.

Prumnopitys   Podocarpaceae

Genus of 10 species of evergreen, yew-like coniferous shrubs or small trees with long, arching branches and linear, glossy green leaves that are bluish underneath.
P. andina syn. *Podocarpus andinus* (Plum yew). Fast-growing and hardy; can resemble *Taxus baccata*. H to 20m (70ft), S to 8m (25ft).

PROPAGATION
Cuttings – late summer to early autumn. Take heeled semi-ripe cuttings, with the lower half lightly wounded, treat with rooting hormone and root in a cold frame or propagator. They are slow to root.

Sequoia   Taxodiaceae

One hardy, evergreen conifer species. Grow in well-drained soil in sun or light shade.
S. sempervirens (Redwood, Coast redwood). Has red-brown bark and broad, scale-like leaves. Suitable only for larger gardens. H to 112m (365ft), S 9m (20ft). **'Adpressa'** can be grown as a dwarf shrub. H to 9m (28ft), S to 6m (20ft). Cones ripen in the first year.

PROPAGATION
collect cones when they begin to turn yellow, dry them and extract the seed. Store at 3°C (37°F) for 3 weeks, then sow in a cold frame. Keep seedlings moist.
Cuttings – midwinter. Take ripewood cuttings and root in a cold frame. Leaders will form after 2 years.

Sequoiadendron (Wellingtonia, Big tree)
Taxodiaceae

One hardy, evergreen conifer species. Plant in sun or light shade in well-drained soil.
S. giganteum. Has thick, furrowed, red-brown bark and scale-like to awl-shaped leaves. Suitable only for larger gardens. The cones ripen in their second year.
H to 80m (260ft), S to 10m (30ft).

PROPAGATION
collect in autumn and sow immediately in a cold frame, seedbed or pot. Seed germinates readily without pre-treatment. Cuttings – early autumn. Small cuttings of epicormic shoots (those that arise directly from the trunk) root easily in a cold frame.

Taxodium   Taxodiaceae

Genus of three species of hardy, deciduous conifers, similar to *Metasequoia*, but with alternate leaves. Grow in moist or wet soil, preferably slightly acid, in sun or part shade.
T. distichum (Bald cypress, Swamp cypress). Foliage turns brick-red in autumn. Cuttings are difficult to strike so seed is the best method. H to 40m (130ft), S 9m (28ft).

PROPAGATION
collect cones as they turn purple in autumn, extract seed and sow immediately in a seedbed outdoors, or in a cold frame.

Thuja orientalis 'Elegantissima'

Thujopsis dolabrata 'Aurea'

Tsuga canadensis 'Jeddeloh'

Taxus — Taxaceae

Between three and ten hardy species of long-lived, evergreen conifers, recognized by their flat, linear, glossy, dark green leaves and the fleshy, bright red fruits. Tolerant of a wide range of soils and situations, they also respond well to clipping and are extensively planted as hedges and in formal situations. *T. baccata* (Yew). Has many cultivars ranging from the dark green, columnar **'Fastigiata'** (Irish yew) to the wide-spreading, golden-leaved **'Washingtonii'**. Yews are difficult to propagate from seed (although bird-sown seedlings can sometimes be found) but cuttings strike readily. H 10–20m (30–70ft), S 8–10m (25–30ft).

PROPAGATION

Cuttings – autumn. Take heeled, semi-ripe cuttings with a small portion of 2-year-old wood at the base. Treat with rooting hormone, wounded lightly at the base and root in a cold frame. They root within 2–3 months. Cuttings taken from side shoots do not form leaders but can be used as ground-cover.

Thuja — Cupressaceae

Genus of five species of hardy, fast-growing, conical, evergreen coniferous trees. Grow in well-drained soil in full sun; protect from cold winds. The small, scale-like, usually dark, glossy green leaves are in flattened sprays, and very strongly scented. Small, woody cones ripen in their first year and release the seed on the tree. Cultivars include dwarfs, weeping and fastigiate forms with colours from yellow and gold to green and variegated. *T. occidentalis* **'Rheingold'** (H 1m/3ft) and **'Golden Globe'** (H 1m/3ft) are both good golden forms.

Thujas are easy to propagate from seed and from cuttings.
T. orientalis **'Elegantissima'**. Conical bush with foliage that turns from yellow to green then bronze over winter. H 5m (15ft), S 6m (20ft).

PROPAGATION

❦ species. Collect cones in early autumn as they turn brown, then dry and extract the seed. Sow immediately in a seedbed outdoors, or in a cold frame.
Cuttings – autumn to early winter. Take heeled, semi-ripe cuttings and root in a cold frame. They will root over winter.

Thujopsis — Cupressaceae

One species of hardy, evergreen conifer, similar to *Thuja,* but distinguished by rounded cones and fleshier, flattened sprays of waxy leaves that are bright green above and marked with white beneath. Seedling offspring are variable and slow-growing, so cuttings are the preferred means of increase. *T. dolabrata.* Conical, dark green tree. H to 20m (70ft), S to 9m (30ft). **'Aurea'** has golden foliage. H to 15m (45ft). **'Nana'** is a dwarf form. H 1m (3ft), S 80cm (32in).

PROPAGATION

Cuttings – midwinter. Root ripewood cuttings, collected from erect shoots, in a cold frame.

Tsuga (Hemlock) — Pinaceae

Up to 11 species of hardy, evergreen conifers, with flattened, narrow, usually linear leaves, arranged radially or in two ranks, and with silver-white bands beneath. They are related to *Picea,* but have softer foliage, and the leading shoot remains pendent while the tree is still growing. *Tsuga* has tiny, almost spherical male cones, and small ovoid to almost spherical female cones that become pendent at maturity. They resemble the cones of the spruces (*Picea*), but with fewer scales, and turn from shades of purple to brown when ripe, usually in late autumn. Grow in humus-rich, moist but well-drained soil in sun or light shade.
T. canadensis (Eastern hemlock, Canadian hemlock). Linear leaves, fresh green at first, later dark green, with two broad white bands beneath. H to 25m (80ft), S 10m (30ft). It has given rise to several cultivars that are useful for smaller gardens.
'Aurea' is a slow-growing, compact cultivar with golden yellow young leaves that become darker through the season. H to 8m (25ft) eventually. **'Jeddeloh'** forms a hemispherical specimen. H to 1.5m (5ft), S slightly broader. *F. pendula,* syn. 'Pendula', is slow-growing and mound-forming with pendent branches. H to 4m (12ft). The dwarf cultivars are sometimes used for bonsai. They are propagated by cuttings, since they become too vigorous if grafted on to seedling rootstock.
T. heterophylla (Western hemlock). Aromatic, very glossy, dark green leaves, of varying sizes arranged on each side of the shoot. It is a fine specimen tree for larger gardens and makes excellent hedging.
H to 40m (130ft), S to 10m (30ft).

PROPAGATION

❦ for species. Collect brown cones, dry, and extract the seed. Sow in spring, in seedbeds outdoors or in a cold frame.
Cuttings – take semi-ripe cuttings in late summer or autumn, treat with rooting hormone, and root in a propagator.

Calluna vulgaris 'Foxhollow Wanderer'

Daboecia cantabrica 'Bicolor'

Erica vagans 'Valerie Proudley'

Heathers

Calluna (Heather) Ericaceae

A single species of hardy, evergreen shrub, *C. vulgaris*, with thousands of cultivars. All need humus-rich, acid soil and are best in open sites in full sun. Heathers have tiny flowers, concealed by coloured sepals, and dense, scale-like leaves. H to 50cm (20in), S to 75cm (30in). Only a few of the cultivars can be described here. **'Gold Haze'** has yellow foliage and white flowers. **'Robert Chapman'** has bronze-yellow foliage turning orange in winter, and bears pink flowers in late autumn. **'Silver Queen'** has grey foliage and deep mauve-pink flowers. **'Foxii Nana'** is dwarf; H to 7cm (3in). **'H. E. Beale'** has long spikes of double pink flowers in late summer to early autumn. **'Kinlochreul'** has double white flowers.

PROPAGATION

Cuttings – late summer. Take 2.5–5cm (1–2in) heeled, semi-ripe cuttings from the lateral shoots below the main shoots. Root in a cold frame or plastic-covered pot. Cuttings can also be taken in early winter, after flowering, from new growth. Root in a greenhouse or propagator, with bottom heat.

Daboecia (Irish heath) Ericaceae

Genus of two species of hardy to half-hardy, evergreen shrubs. All grow best in acid soils in full sun but will tolerate neutral soils and partial shade. *D. cantabrica*, syn. *D. polifolia* (Irish heath or St Dabeoc's heath) is a hardy species, and along with its cultivars and hybrids, is the most common in cultivation. All have short racemes of relatively large, urn-shaped flowers at the tips of stems bearing lance-shaped, lustrous, dark green leaves. **'Bicolor'** has white, magenta, and pink flowers, some striped, often with all these colours on the same raceme. **'Jack Drake'** bears bright purple flowers, and **'Waley's Red'** has deep magenta blooms.
H 25–40cm (10–16in), S to 65cm (26in).

PROPAGATION

Cuttings – mid- to late summer. Take heeled semi-ripe cuttings, 2.5–5cm (1–2in) long, from lateral shoots that arise below the main shoots. Root in a cold frame or plastic-covered pot.

Erica (Heaths) Ericaceae

Some 700 or more evergreen shrubs with a few hardy species. They have bell-shaped flowers, with colour in the petals rather than in the sepals, and whorls of mostly linear, needle-like leaves. Species and cultivars can be selected to give a brilliant display of colour almost throughout the year. All grow best in well-drained, acid soil in full sun, although *E. carnea*, *E. vagans* and their cultivars tolerate some lime.
E. arborea (Tree heath). Has needle-like, dark green leaves, and bears pyramidal racemes of honey-scented white flowers in spring. **'Aurea'** has golden foliage. H to 2m (6ft), S 1.5m (5ft), often more.
E. carnea, syn. *E. herbacea* (Winter heath). Has linear, dark green leaves and bears slender, urn-shaped, pink-purple flowers in late winter and early spring. Most cultivars bloom between winter and mid-spring. **'Foxhollow'** has soft pink flowers and foliage that is a bronze-tipped, pale yellow to deep orange, in winter. **'Myretoun Ruby'** has deep crimson flowers in mid- to late spring. **'Springwood White'** has white flowers and brilliant green foliage.
H to 40cm (16in), S to 55cm (22in).
E. cinerea (Bell heather). Has linear, dark green leaves and produces spikes of urn-shaped, white, pink, or purple flowers throughout summer. **'C. D. Eason'** has magenta flowers. **'Fiddler's Gold'** has golden then red foliage and pink flowers; **'Hookstone White'** bears white flowers.
H to 60cm (24in), S 80cm (32in).
E. x darleyensis (Darley Dale heath). Has comparatively broad, lance-shaped green leaves and produces spikes of urn-shaped or cylindrical, white or pink flowers, from late winter to early spring. **'Darley Dale'** has cream-tipped foliage in spring, and bears soft pink flowers; **'J. W. Porter'** has green leaves, tipped red and cream, and bears deep pink-purple flowers. **'White Perfection'** has white flowers and green leaves.
H 30cm (12in), S 60cm (24in).
E. vagans (Cornish heath). A spreading shrub with dark green, linear leaves. It bears pink or white bell-shaped flowers from midsummer to autumn. **'Birch Glow'** has deep pink flowers. **'Valerie Proudley'** has white flowers and yellow foliage.
H 40cm (16in) or more, S 75cm (30in).

PROPAGATION

Cuttings – early to midsummer. Take heeled, lateral cuttings 2.5–5cm (1–2in) long. Cuttings from tree heaths should be 5–8cm (2–3in) long. Cuttings of *E. carnea* and its cultivars root better if taken from the tips of the flowered shoots in early summer. Layering – early spring, for dropping or mound layering.

SHRUBS, TREES AND CLIMBERS

Trees and shrubs are the backbone of the garden. They are often long-lived plants that make a strong statement, or that provide valued backdrops to others of more transient beauty.

Climbers are woody-stemmed plants that attach themselves either to another plant (as in the wild) or to some kind of support by various means, whether this be twining stems, leaf stalks or specialized aerial roots.

Such is the diversity of this group of plants that a wide range of propagation techniques can be used for multiplying. While most can be raised by seed or cuttings, some must be grafted, and for others layering is a possibility.

◄ *Shrubs are a group of long-lived woody plants that do not usually need frequent propagation; when this is required, a wide range of techniques can be exploited.*

WHY PROPAGATE
SHRUBS, TREES AND CLIMBERS?

The backbone of the garden, this important group of plants introduces an element of three-dimensional structure into planting schemes. Specimens draw the eye and thus should always be of the best quality. Propagation will allow you to build up a reserve to replace leggy plants or those that have outgrown their allotted space.

Many ornamental shrubs and trees are cultivars that must be raised by vegetative means; they seldom come true from seed.

This group tends to be expensive, since several years are often needed to produce a saleable plant, and many garden centres now stock only the most popular and easily propagated cultivars. Gardeners can therefore provide a valuable service by keeping up stocks of those unusual varieties that may not be viable to propagate on a commercial scale, as well as providing themselves with insurance against winter losses.

In addition, many trees and shrubs are slow-growing but ultimately large plants. Once they outgrow their allotted space it is often better to discard them or to pass them on to friends with larger gardens rather than resorting to drastic pruning that may not be successful. Replace them with smaller, newly propagated specimens. Similarly, climbers can often become unmanageable with time and are best replaced.

PRIMARY METHODS

All species can be propagated by seed and this is often the best method to use, particularly for trees, as this assures healthy, disease-resistant stock. However, seed production and germination can both be adversely affected by the climate.

Cuttings are a more reliable method of reproducing the characteristics of any given parent plant and are also useful for exploiting growth that 'sports' (*see box on opposite page*). However, some difficult genera, such as *Berberis*, require the rather more specialized technique of mallet cuttings.

ADDITIONAL TECHNIQUES

Subjects that do not strike readily from cuttings can be grafted, a technique that also boosts vigour if a strong-growing rootstock is used. Subjects include selections of *Camellia reticulata* and rhododendrons, as well as maples, birches and beeches. The allied technique of budding is generally used for hybrid roses.

Betula species
All birches can be propagated by seed, although cultivated plants are likely to produce variable offspring because birches hybridize so readily. Side-veneer grafts or softwood cuttings are used to increase cultivars.

Tree peony
Tree peony species *Paeonia lutea* and *P. delavayi* can be increased by fresh or scarified seed. Named cultivars are increased by apical-wedge grafting in the late summer onto *P. officinalis* or *P. lactea* rootstocks.

Sambucus nigra 'Guincho Purple'
Coloured- or cut-leaved variants of elder are propagated mainly by hardwood cuttings. Cuttings of the hollow stems are taken with a heel, mallet, or just below a node to avoid exposing the pith.

Cotinus coggygria 'Royal Purple'
Coloured-leaved variants of *Cotinus* can be propagated by softwood cuttings in early summer, but French layering in spring is the most productive method. Layers will be well-rooted by autumn.

Climbers and shrubs that produce long branches near ground level can be layered or, if a branch will not reach the ground, air layered. As a variation, plants that are already mature or that have become straggly can be 'dropped', a technique in which the whole plant is almost completely buried so that only the tips of the branches show – this encourages the stems to root.

Some shrubs produce shoots at ground level which can be divided, almost like a herbaceous perennial. Others have running roots just below the soil surface, with growth buds that can make new plants.

Sports and Reversion

Variegated plants usually arise as a sport or mutation on a green-leaved parent species. Other sports may vary in form or habit, or in leaf, flower or fruit colour. They very rarely come true from seed and must be increased vegetatively, usually by cuttings of one sort or another or by grafting. Sometimes a branch of the sport reverts back to the normal green type. Since this is almost invariably more vigorous than the mutated form, it is advisable to check regularly

and remove reverted shoots when you see them. If left, the sports will eventually dominate the plant.

The shrub *Elaeagnus pungens* 'Maculata' must be propagated vegetatively.

(5)

Euonymus fortunei 'Silver Queen'
Taking semi-ripe cuttings in the summer is one of the easiest and most convenient methods for evergreen *Euonymus*, whether species or cultivars. They root easily, without wounding or hormone rooting treatments.

(6)

Physocarpus opulifolius 'Dart's Gold'
Although they do not come true from seed, cultivars can be increased by a range of other methods, including division of suckers, and by semi-ripe or hard-wood cuttings.

PROPAGATING TECHNIQUES
SHRUBS, TREES AND CLIMBERS

The most rewarding method of propagating shrubs, trees and climbers is almost certainly from seed, one of the simplest techniques available to produce something that will have a long-lasting place in the garden or landscape from the very beginning of its life. However, for speedier results, there are plenty of other effective ways of multiplying.

SEED

The seed of most woody plants can be collected in autumn, by which time it has ripened sufficiently for sowing. Rhododendron seed is carried in pods that release the seed only after frost, so these are best gathered while still green in early autumn and stored in a paper bag until they open. *Acer* seeds should also be harvested while still green; if left until fully ripe they develop a hard coat that inhibits germination. *Hamamelis* 'shoots' its seed once mature, so this too is best gathered while the seed capsules are still green.

Squash fleshy berries to release the seed, then wash it in tepid water and dry on kitchen paper. Plants like crab apples, which enclose their seeds in firm fruits should be cut open so that the seeds can then be picked out. Sticky seeds that are difficult to handle, such as *Pittosporum,* can be separated by mixing with fine sand.

Nearly all seed is best sown the first spring after it has been gathered. Store the seed in clearly labelled paper bags in a cool, dry place through the winter, or dry it and keep it in airtight containers in the door of a refrigerator. In order to produce viable plants of slow-growing shrubs such as rhododendrons, it is necessary to sow seed in autumn so that the seedlings' first growing season lasts as long as possible. This permits the formation of winter buds that will produce the following year's growth.

Pre-sowing treatments

Some seed benefits from further preparation prior to sowing. In nature, many seeds undergo a period of winter dormancy; this is a natural survival mechanism that prevents seeds from germinating until suitable weather conditions for growth return in the spring.

Scarification . . . .

For successful germination, it is often necessary to treat hard-coated seeds so that water intake is speeded up and germination occurs without hindrance.

◄ Nick or shave off part of the hard outer coats of large seed such as oak (*Quercus*) to allow water to penetrate more easily. It is vital that only the hard outer coat is cut into; any damage to the seed embryo within is likely to prove fatal. Abrade the coat of smaller seed in a jar lined with emery paper; alternatively, rub them between two pieces of emery paper.

Sowing in containers . . . .

As young seedlings are highly vulnerable to disease, it is vitally important that the container into which they are sown is absolutely clean and that the compost is fresh and sterile.

► Fill the container or seed tray to overflowing with seed compost or similar, then level it with the brim using a piece of flat wood. Firm the compost gently, especially in the corners, to remove any air pockets. Sow the seed thinly on top of the compost and cover with the seed's own depth of sieved compost. Top-dress the compost with a layer of grit. Cover the container with glass or similar to keep the compost moist while the seed germinates, and put the container in an open frame or in a well-ventilated, cold greenhouse. Germination can be erratic, and seedlings may not emerge for 2 years or more. Remove any cover on the container as soon as any seedlings appear.

Stratification

In the case of most plants that grow in cool temperate climates, seed needs a period of cold to overcome dormancy before it will germinate. This process of chilling is known as 'stratification'. In areas with cold winters, it can be achieved by sowing the seed as normal in late autumn or winter, and placing the containers in an open frame outdoors. As soon as the seedlings begin to germinate, bring the containers into a cold greenhouse.

A more reliable method is to mix the seed with moistened peat or perlite in a clear polythene bag and place it in the bottom of a refrigerator. For the majority of species, chilling to 0.5–5°C (33–41°F) is sufficient to break dormancy; if allowed to freeze solid, the seed embryo will almost certainly die.

The length of the chilling period required varies depending on the species. Most hardy deciduous species will need chilling for six to eight weeks, others may need as little as three to four weeks or as many as twelve. Seed should be sown as usual the moment signs of germination are seen, so check it regularly for signs of emergence without opening the polythene bag.

Scarification

Some species delay germination by forming a hard protective coat around the seed. This must be breached or broken down so that the embryo can imbibe the water necessary for germination to occur. Seed of the pea family (Leguminosae) has a hard and shiny coating, particularly after a hot summer, and this is best broken down by covering the seed with hot – but not boiling – water, then allowing it to soak over twenty-four hours before sowing as normal.

The hard coat of large seed can be abraded with a file or nicked with a sharp blade. In the latter case, it is vital that just a small section of the seed coat is shaved away with a shallow cut. A deep cut that penetrates the embryo may well be fatal. Smaller seeds can be rubbed gently between two sheets of emery paper, or shaken in a lidded jar lined with emery paper.

Sowing

Sow the seed in containers or seed trays containing a proprietary loamless or loam-based seed compost or a mixture of equal parts sterilized loam, peat (or

Sowing outdoors in a seedbed ....

An outdoor seedbed is constructed using a frame of side boards, 20–22cm (8–9in) deep; the bed is 1m (3ft) wide so that it is narrow enough to reach from both sides.

▲ Dig the seedbed thoroughly, then rake to a level surface with a fine tilth. Sow the seeds in drills or broadcast-sow them in blocks. Cover the seeds with grit. By the following spring they should have germinated.

alternative) and sharp grit or sand, to which a slow-release fertilizer has been added at the manufacturer's recommended rate. Firm the compost gently, sow the seed thinly and evenly on top, and cover with its own depth of compost. To offset the growth of mosses and lichens and to prevent the compost surface from forming a cap of compacted soil during this time, top-dress it with a layer of coarse grit. Put the pots in an open frame or in a well-ventilated cold greenhouse.

Germination can be erratic, and seedlings may not emerge until the second spring, so keep the compost just moist and do not discard the pots if seedlings do not appear in the first season.

Once the seedlings are large enough to handle, prick out into individual pots, taking care to handle seedlings only by their seed leaves to avoid damage to the fragile roots and stems.

Sowing in a seedbed outdoors

Where large numbers of plants are needed, for example, for hedging, seed may be sown in a specially prepared seedbed outdoors. Seed sown outdoors generally needs less aftercare than that sown in containers, and can be grown on for a further year *in situ* without disturbance.

In the season before sowing, dig over a bed to a spade's depth and incorporate well-rotted organic matter and grit. Just before sowing, rake the bed to a fine tilth and sow seed evenly. Cover the seed to its

Semi-ripe cuttings . . . .

This technique is used to propagate a wide range of deciduous and evergreen shrubs. Each cutting should have a woody base but be soft towards the tip.

▶ 1 Cut a leading shoot just below a node at the base and just above a node at the tip, so that it is 10–15cm (4–6in) long. Remove the lowest pair of leaves with a straight cut flush to the stem, then cut the lowest remaining leaves in half with a straight cut across the centre of the leaf.

▲ 2 To increase the chances of rooting, wound the base of the stem by cutting away a shallow sliver of bark, 1–2.5cm (½–1in) long, from one side. Then dip the base of the cutting in a hormone rooting powder.

▲ 3 Around the edge of a 12.5cm (5in) pot of cuttings compost, insert the cuttings almost to the depth of the lowest leaves. Ensure that the leaves do not touch. Place in a propagator, if bottom heat is needed, or in a cold frame, while the cuttings root.

own depth with soil, then top with a 1cm (½in) layer of coarse grit. Water thoroughly and label each drill with the name of the plant and date of sowing.

Keep the seedlings weed free and water as necessary. Check for and treat any pests and diseases as soon as seen. After a year's growth, if plants are large enough, transplant directly to their permanent site. Otherwise, transfer to a nursery bed and grow on for a further year.

CUTTINGS

Most woody plants can be propagated by cuttings. For some, cuttings can be taken at any time during the growing season, while for others, timing is critical. The equipment needed depends on the degree of ripeness of the cutting: softwood cuttings need the warmth and humidity of a propagator; hardwood cuttings may be rooted in open ground. Softwood cuttings need more

attention during rooting and establishment but root quickly, and a high percentage generally succeeds.

Use an inert rooting medium of equal parts peat or sterilized crushed bark with sharp sand or perlite. Use pots not less than 12.5cm (5in) across (small pots dry out more quickly and are susceptible to wide temperature fluctuations; both will inhibit rooting).

To ensure a good supply of cutting material, prune a section of a tree, shrub or climber hard a year ahead to stimulate the growth of vigorous new shoots.

The cuttings of some shrubs such as viburnums and azaleas have a tendency to die off during the first winter after rooting. For these, take cuttings as early in the season as possible to provide the longest possible growing season before the first period of dormancy.

Softwood cuttings

In spring or early summer, in the early morning when plant tissues are at their most turgid, take cuttings about 5–10cm (2–4in) long, cutting just above a node. (Water the plant the previous evening, if the weather is dry.)

Hardwood cuttings . . . .

Hardwood cuttings should be propagated in a site out of full sun and sheltered from drying winds. Cultivate the soil well. Make a trench a spit deep with one vertical side and one sloping one. Line the trench to a depth of 2.5cm (1in) with sharp sand.

◀ 1 Take cuttings of pencil thickness (thinner stems will tend to dry out before callusing occurs). Remove any soft tips, cutting just above a leaf joint. Trim the base of the cuttings just below a joint to make cuttings about 15cm (6in) long. (Long, vigorous stems may yield two cuttings.)

▶ 2 Dip the bases of the cuttings in rooting powder, then insert them in the trench up to about two-thirds of their length. If soil heave occurs during frosty spells, gently firm in the cuttings with your foot. Hardwood cuttings of some evergreens, such as box, lavender and *Lonicera nitida* can also be rooted in the open ground. Remove the lower leaves as for other types of cuttings. It is important not to allow these to dry out, so cover them with cloches or root them under a polytonal.

Put the cuttings in a polythene bag to prevent moisture loss. They must not be allowed to wilt.

Trim the cuttings just below the lowest node and remove the lower leaves to leave three or four at the tip. Clematis stems can be simply be cut halfway between the nodes to make nodal cuttings (*see right*); each stem will yield several cuttings. Immerse the cutting in a fungicide solution then dip the base in hormone rooting powder.

Insert the cuttings in the cuttings medium up to half their length so the leaves do not touch each other. Put them into a mist propagation unit or into a closed, heated propagator. If the propagator is large, tent the pots with polythene bags supported by canes.

Check periodically for signs of fungal disease. Remove any affected cuttings and spray the remainder with fungicide. The cuttings should root in two to three weeks, after which they can be potted up and gradually hardened off. Alternatively, if cuttings are taken later in the season, add a little slow-release fertilizer to the rooting medium to avoid having to pot them up immediately. Potting up can then be delayed until the following spring.

Semi-ripe cuttings

Semi-ripe cuttings need to be taken in mid- to late summer, just as the base of the current year's growth is beginning to turn woody. They are prepared as for softwood cuttings, but are rooted in an unheated propagator or closed cold frame. Alternatively, take the cutting with a 'heel' (*see below*). Grasp the stem at its point of origin and then pull it sharply away from

Nodal and inter-nodal cuttings ....

Most woody plants are cut just below a node, that is the point on a stem where a leaf, shoot or flower arises. A stem cut at a node is less vulnerable to fungal rots than one cut farther up.

▲ **Nodal cutting**
Make a straight basal cut about 3mm (⅛in) below a node on the stem to be propagated. Remove the lowest pair of leaves.

▲ **Inter-nodal cutting**
This type of cutting, with its basal cut made halfway between nodes, is most commonly used when propagating fuchsias and clematis.

the main stem with a small tail of bark attached. Carefully trim the bark, using a sharp knife.

Mallet cuttings (*below*) are used for shrubs such as *Berberis* with hollow or pithy stems that are reluctant to root if taken in the usual manner. By including a small piece of the previous year's growth, the cutting is assured of sufficient food reserves to root successfully.

Hardwood (fully ripe) cuttings

Hardwood or fully ripe cuttings are taken at the end of the growing season for evergreens, and just after leaf drop for deciduous plants. Most deciduous cuttings can be rooted in open ground or in a frame; evergreens are best in a shaded cold frame. Add a slow-release

Heel cuttings ....

A heel cutting is a side shoot that is pulled away from the main stem together with a small piece, or 'heel', of woody material from the main stem.

◄ Holding the main stem firmly in one hand and the side shoot in the other, pull the side shoot down sharply so that the shoot comes away with a 'heel' from the main stem. Remove the lowest pair of leaves and neaten the heel, using a sharp knife. Dip the basal cut in a hormone rooting powder. Then insert it in a cuttings compost while it initiates root production.

Mallet cuttings ....

This type of cutting, with its large woody plug from the main stem at the base of the side shoot, is invaluable for cuttings that would otherwise be vulnerable to rotting organisms.

◄ Using a pair of sharp secateurs, cut the main stem straight across just above the side shoot to be propagated. Then make a second, straight cut about 2cm (¾in) below the first cut. Remove any leaves at the bottom of the side shoot, and dip the basal cuts in hormone rooting powder. Then insert the mallet cutting into cuttings compost.

Leaf-bud cuttings ....

To ensure success for this technique, always use healthy, vigorous stems of the current season's growth, which will have a high capacity to root.

▶ Cut a semi-ripe stem from the parent plant and cut it into sections, just above each leaf. Shorten the base to leave a length of stem about 2.5cm (1in) below the leaf. Thereafter, treat leaf-bud cuttings as for semi-ripe cuttings, although the application of hormone rooting powder is not generally necessary.

fertilizer to the rooting medium, since the cuttings will stay in place for a year or more before transplanting.

Prepare a mix of equal parts grit and leaf mould or garden compost. Remove the soil in the frame and replace it with a 15cm (6in) depth of the rooting medium. Alternatively, fill pots with the same mixture.

Take cuttings about 20cm (8in) long of the current season's growth and remove the tips, cutting just above a node. Trim the cuttings at the base just below a node to make a cutting about 15cm (6in) long. For species with pithy stems, take heel cuttings, as described under semi-ripe cuttings (*see p.107*). On evergreens, remove all but the top three or four leaves. Treat the bases of the cuttings with rooting hormone. Insert the cuttings up to two-thirds of their length in the cuttings medium. They will callus over during the winter and begin to root from the following spring. During winter, insulate the frame during cold weather with sacking. Ventilate during mild periods. During spring and summer, ventilate on warm days and water during dry spells. Lift and pot up rooted cuttings in autumn.

Leaf-bud cuttings

Leaf-bud cuttings are commonly used to propagate camellias and *Mahonia*, which have growth buds in the leaf axils. By this method, a number of cuttings can be produced from a stem. Leaf-bud cuttings are best taken in late summer to early autumn.

Eye cuttings

Eye cuttings are similar to leaf-bud cuttings and are used most commonly for vines (*Vitis*) that 'bleed' copiously if the stems are cut while the sap is rising and the plants are in active growth. Take them in winter when the plants are fully dormant. On plants where the eyes (dormant buds) are widely spaced, each cutting can be of a single eye, as for camellias. Where they are closer together, allow two or three buds per cutting. This method can be used for other deciduous climbers such as *Actinidia deliciosa*.

LAYERING

Layering has the great advantage that the layered stem is encouraged to root before being separated from the parent plant, which will continue to provide sustenance until the rooted layer is separated. Layering is best done in early spring, when the sap is flowing and stems are pliable, but may also be performed between late autumn and early spring. It is vital that the soil around all forms of layers is kept moist and weed free during the rooting period.

The year before making a layer, prune a low branch back hard in autumn or spring to encourage flexible young shoots, which root more easily than older material. Just before making a layer, improve the soil around the base of the plant by working well-rotted organic matter and grit into the soil. (When layering

Layering ....

Layers take up to a year to root, and most will be ready for transplanting in the autumn or spring after layering. The layered stem is cut back just behind the wound, then replanted.

▲ Select a vigorous shoot from low down on the plant and bring into contact with the soil. At the point where the stem meets the soil, wound it by cutting a small tongue of bark in the underside of the stem. Dab hormone rooting powder beneath the tongue with a soft brush. Remove all leaves and side shoots from behind the wound, then peg down the stem with U-shaped piece of wire. Insert a cane next to the layer and tie the rest of the stem to this (the bending of the stem encourages rooting). Bury the pegged-down piece of stem with a little friable soil. Layers take up to a year to root.

Serpentine layering ·

This technique is similar to simple layering except that the stem is wounded and pegged down at multiple points near a node, with at least one leaf bud between each wounding site.

▲ Wound the lower part of the stem by making several angled incisions, 2.5–4cm (1–1½in) long. Peg these to the ground at intervals. The resulting plants, usually rooted by autumn, will be smaller than those produced by simple layering and must be potted up and grown on in a cold frame rather than being planted out immediately.

ericaceous plants, ensure that the grit and compost is lime-free and acid.) There are several types of layering:

Simple layering

This, as its name suggests, is the simplest form of layering. Layers that are made in early spring should

Tip layering ·

The hole for tip layering should be 7.5–10cm (3–4in) deep and have one almost vertical side farthest from the parent plant and a sloping one at the point nearest to the parent plant.

▶ In spring, bring down the tip of a long, arching shoot to ground level. At the point where it touches the ground, improve the soil at that point, working in garden compost or leaf mould and sharp sand. Pin down the stem tip and bury well. By autumn, new roots should have formed and the new plant can be cut from the main stem and potted up and grown on.

root by the autumn but should be left in place until the following spring when they can be separated from the parent plant.

Serpentine layering

This is a modification of simple layering that can be used to create several new plants from the same stem and is suitable for climbers such as clematis that produce a quantity of long stems. The timing is the same as for simple layering, except for vines (*Vitis* spp.) and

French layering ·

This technique is carried out over a period of several years. In the dormant season, cut the parent plant back, as for stooling. The stems that emerge are allowed to grow unimpeded during the next growing season. The following spring these stems are reduced to eight or ten in number, and trimmed to equal length.

◀ 1 In spring, once the stems have been trimmed to equal length, spread them out like the spokes of a cartwheel, pegging them to the ground at intervals. This stimulates the production of vertical-growing laterals along each stem.

◀ 2 When these laterals appear, unpeg each 'spoke' stem and cultivate beneath it. Each stem is then pegged down into a long, narrow trench 5cm (2in) deep. When the laterals are 10cm (4in) long, earth up the whole of each 'spoke' stem to a depth of 2.5cm (1in).

◀ 3 Continue earthing up as the laterals grow until they are buried up to 10cm (4in) of their length.

◀ 4 In winter, fork away the soil and sever rooted stems from the parent.

Stooling . . . .

This technique is ideal to raise lilacs, dogwoods, *Amelanchier* and *Cotinus coggygria*. The same healthy parent plant can be mound layered each spring for a succession of new plants.

▲ In the dormant season, cut back all stems hard to within 5cm (2in) of the ground *(above left)*. As soon as any new shoots are 15cm (6in) long, earth them up with friable soil *(above right)*. Continue earthing them up as they grow until 20cm (8in) of stem is buried. In early winter, gently fork away the mounded-up soil and sever the rooted stems below their root system. Pot on or transplant each rooted layer. Cut the parent plant right back again, ready to earth up in spring.

other genera that 'bleed' when sap is actively flowing upwards; these are best done in late winter just before the end of the dormant season.

Tip layering

Tip layering is used primarily on members of the genus *Rubus*. It is best done in early to mid-summer, when the tip growth has just begun to harden.

French layering

An even more productive method is French, or continuous, layering, though it is suitable only for shrubs whose stems remain fairly flexible, such as *Cotinus coggygria* or *Cornus alba*. French layering is a modification of stooling *(see above)*, and also needs forward planning since the young plant that is to be used as propagating material will need one complete growing season to establish itself before preparation for layering takes place.

Air layering

Air layering can be used on shrubs (especially rhododendrons) that do not produce flexible stems near enough to ground level for conventional layering to be an option. In spring, select a sturdy, horizontal stem produced the previous year and remove any leaves and

side shoots along a section about 30cm (12in) in length. Cut a tongue about 2.5cm (1in) long into the wood, pulling the knife towards the stem tip. Pack the cut with moistened sphagnum moss to hold it open, then wrap more damp moss around the stem. Cover this with a polythene sleeve taped to the stem. The layer should root by the autumn. Cut the stem below the rooted section, pot up and grow on in a cool greenhouse until it is well established. (*See also Houseplants, p.137.*)

MOUND LAYERING OR STOOLING

Stooling is a useful method of producing rootstocks in quantity where propagation by seed would be too slow. It is used commercially to produce rootstocks for grafting fruit trees and, for this purpose, permanent 'stool beds' are maintained that are cropped every other year. It is also suitable for ornamental shrubs that respond well to hard pruning, such as *Amelanchier*, *Salix*, *Ribes* and ungrafted specimens of lilac (*Syringa*). It is similar to layering in that the stems are brought into direct contact with the soil, the advantage being that stems within the crown of the plant will also root. It does, however, need planning, since before stooling takes place, a young plant must be planted and allowed to establish for a growing season before cutting back in its first dormant season in late winter or early spring. The resulting growth provides material for rooting.

DROPPING

Dropping is most often used to increase dwarf shrubs, such as rhododendrons, heathers and dwarf cultivars of conifers (*see also Conifers and Heathers, p.95*). In the dormant season, thin out the stems if they are congested to give the remainder sufficient room to produce new roots. In winter or early spring, lift the plant, keeping the root ball intact. Deepen the planting hole and return the plant to it, leaving 2.5cm (1in) of the stems above ground level. Settle the plant in the hole and fill in with friable soil, mixed with leaf mould or garden compost, working it in around each stem. Keep well watered during the growing season.

New roots should have formed by autumn. Remove the soil from around the stems to check for rooting. Sever rooted stems and pot up into a growing medium or line them out in a nursery bed. Grow on until they can be set out in their permanent positions.

GRAFTING

Grafting is a more advanced technique of propagation used for plants that do not root easily by other means of vegetative propagation, and that do not come true from seed. It involves the union of a stem from the plant to be propagated (the scion), taken from the most recent season's growth, with a well-established, strong-growing and compatible rootstock of the same or closely related species, raised either by seed or stooling (*see opposite page*). For grafting to be successful, it is essential that the cambium layer (the layer of actively dividing cells just below the bark) of each is brought into close contact. The cut surfaces should be clean and must not be allowed to dry out, so use clean tools and make the union immediately after preparation.

Seedling rootstocks should be one to three years old; rootstocks from stooled plants should have been grown on for at least a year after being severed from the parent-stock plant. The rootstocks should be either container grown or containerized during the season before grafting is to be carried out.

With a few exceptions, grafting is best done in late winter, towards the end of the dormant season. Deciduous azaleas and selections of *Acer palmatum*, however, which bleed profusely if cut when the sap is rising rapidly, are more successfully grafted in mid- to late summer, *Hamamelis* in late summer. It is essential that the root system of the newly grafted plant does not dry out while the two elements are bonding.

Three weeks prior to grafting, bring the rootstocks into a heated greenhouse to stimulate them gently into growth. Keep the roots fairly dry to encourage root activity and to minimize the speed of upward sap flow. There is a number of variations on the technique of grafting, of which only the simplest and most commonly used are described here.

Apical-wedge or cleft grafting

Apical-wedge or cleft grafting is a straightforward and relatively simple form of grafting.

Prepare for grafting in midwinter by cutting, from the scion, healthy 30cm (12in) lengths of the previous season's growth of pencil thickness. Place in a labelled polythene bag and store in the bottom of a refrigerator. At the same time, earmark suitable rootstocks of a compatible species, also with a pencil-thick stem.

Just before grafting, in late winter, lift the rootstock and wash the soil from the roots. Cut the stem back to about 2.5cm (1in) above the roots, with a straight cut. Make a clean vertical incision in the top centre of the rootstock, about 2.5cm (1in) deep. Trim back the scions to a length of about 15cm (6in), with a straight cut just above a healthy bud at the top and a straight cut at the base. Trim the base to a wedge shape by cutting each side with a sloping cut about 2.5–4cm (1–1½in) long. Push the wedge into the cleft in the top of the scion. Ideally, the scion and the stock should be of equal thickness, but, if they differ slightly, align the cut surfaces so that one edge of the scion is flush with one edge of the stock.

Bind the union with grafting tape, pot up into potting medium and place in a heated propagator at 10–15°C (50–59°F). The graft union will callus over and form within about 5–6 weeks. Once it has taken,

Apical-wedge grafting . . . .

The rootstock and scion must be the same size, preferably pencil thin. For rootstock use a 1–3-year-old seedling tree, cut down to 2.5cm (1in) above the root collar.

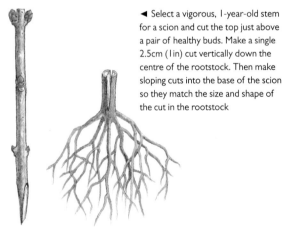

◄ Select a vigorous, 1-year-old stem for a scion and cut the top just above a pair of healthy buds. Make a single 2.5cm (1in) cut vertically down the centre of the rootstock. Then make sloping cuts into the base of the scion so they match the size and shape of the cut in the rootstock

▶ Insert the prepared scion into the cut in the rootstock, neatly aligning the edges on at least one side so there is maximum connection of cambial tissue. Then bind the union with grafting tape and cover it with wax to protect it against disease. Once the graft union has callused over, remove the grafting tape.

Saddle grafting ....

This technique is a good way to propagate rhododendrons, especially large-flowered hybrids. For rootstock, use a 1–3-year-old seedling, usually of *Rhododendron ponticum*.

◀ **1** In winter, bring the rootstock into the greenhouse one month before grafting, and induce into growth. Select a vigorous, non-flowering, pencil-thin shoot of the previous year's growth for the scion and in its base cut an inverted V-shape. Then shorten the rootstock to 5cm (2in).

▶ **2** Starting 2.5cm (1in) from the rootstock base, make an upward, angled cut on either side to match the inverted V-shape on the scion. Push the scion over the rootstock. Secure with grafting tape and keep the plant in a closed, humid, heated propagator until the two elements unite.

remove the grafting tape and harden off gradually. You will then need to grow the new plant on for a further year in a cold frame before planting it out in its permanent flowering position.

Saddle grafting

This method results in strong plants, since a large area of cambium is exposed to form the graft union. It is essential, however, that the scion and stock are of similar thickness. The technique is often used for evergreen rhododendron hybrids, which are usually grafted onto seedling rootstocks of *Rhododendron ponticum*.

About four weeks before grafting, in late winter or very early spring, bring the potted rootstock into a greenhouse and bring gently into growth at about

10°C (50°F). For the scions, take 5–12cm (2–5in) lengths of healthy, one-year-old, non-flowering shoots and store in polythene bags in the bottom of the refrigerator until ready to graft.

Trim the rootstock down with a straight cut, to 5cm (2in) above the surface of the potting medium. Then make two sloping cuts from the top of the rootstock, to form a V-shape. Prepare the scion by making a cut in its base that matches that in the rootstock. Fit the rootstock and scion together and bind with grafting tape. Cut any large leaves in half to minimize water loss. Place in a closed propagator at 10–15°C (50–59°F) and spray weekly with fungicide. The graft union will form within 4–5 weeks. Once the union has taken, remove the tape and harden off gradually. Grow on for a further year in a cold frame before setting out in the planting site; apply a balanced liquid fertilizer monthly.

Side-veneer grafting

Side-veneer grafting is the propagation technique most often used for trees and suits a variety of evergreen and deciduous shrubs.

Bring a potted one- to three-year-old seedling rootstock with a pencil-thick stem into the greenhouse three weeks before you intend to carry out the grafting. Prepare for grafting by cutting back the rootstock stem to 30cm (12in). Starting at about 2.5cm (1in) from the stem base, make a short, inward, downward-sloping cut. Make a second downward cut about 2.5cm (1in) above the first, so that it meets the first cut to form a slight lip.

Select a vigorous, year-old, pencil-thick stem from the scion and trim to approximately 15–25cm (6–10in) in length, cutting just above a bud. At its base, make a shallow cut, 2.5cm (1in) long, on one side of the stem, and make a second angled cut across the base. Match up the scion and rootstock so that the scion fits neatly into the lip cut in the rootstock, with the cambiums in close contact. Bind with grafting tape and then brush with grafting wax to seal the union.

Place deciduous species in a greenhouse at 10°C (50°F) and evergreens in a closed propagator at 15°C (59°F). Union should occur within four to five weeks. Harden off the new plant and, as the scion starts into growth, gradually cut back the rootstock stem to just above the graft union.

112

Side-veneer grafting . . . .

For most hardwood tree species and deciduous shrubs, side-veneer grafting is done just before bud break in mid- to late winter, but *Acer* and *Hamamelis* are propagated in summer.

◄ **1** Prepare the receiving notch on the rootstock as follows. About 2.5cm (1in) from the base, make a short, downward cut at an angle of 45°. About 2.5cm (1in) above this, make a straight, downward cut to meet it and so remove a section of rootstock.

► **2** Cut the same length of bark from the base of the scion and trim the base to fit snugly into the V-shaped channel at the bottom of the rootstock cut. Fit rootstock and scion together. Ideally the cambium layers of both will meet on both sides, but if (as is likely) the scion is slimmer than the rootstock, line up the cambium layers on one side.

◄ **3** Bind the union with grafting tape, which will expand as the union 'takes' and thickens. Wax the graft union. Once the graft has taken, gradually cut back the rootstock until it is flush with the top of the graft union.

BUD GRAFTING

Chip-budding and T-budding are forms of bud grafting used to propagate fruit trees, but are also used for ornamental members of the family Rosaceae. Roses are usually propagated by T-budding in the nursery trade. Bud grafting is done in midsummer, while the plants are still in active growth, onto well-established rootstocks preferably with a stem diameter of at least 1cm (½in). (*See also Fruit, pp. 182–183*).

T-budding

Cut a strong, ripe, healthy stem from the scion and trim off the leaves. Snap off any thorns cleanly. Holding the stem with its growing point towards you, locate a dormant bud. Place the blade of the knife behind it, then draw it towards you, cutting beneath the bud. Pull the knife sharply to tear off a 'tail' of bark by which you then handle the bud. Pull off the pith behind the bud, using the knife if necessary. Make a T-shaped cut in the rootstock, cutting no deeper than the bark. Ease back the bark with the tip of the knife and insert the bud, tail uppermost. Trim back the tail level with the top of the 'T'. Bind the stem with grafting tape. Cut back the rootstock when new scion growth emerges the following spring.

Chip-budding

The principle of chip-budding is essentially the same as that for T-budding, differing mainly in the form of the cuts made in the stock and the shape of the bud-chip taken from the scion. To remove a bud-chip, make a 5mm (¼in) cut, at an angle of 45°, about 2cm (¾in) below the bud. Make a second cut, 4cm (1½in) above the first, sloping downwards and inwards behind the bud so that it meets the first cut. The cut in the rootstock is made to correspond in shape to that of the bud-chip, with a slight lip at the bottom.

DIVISION

Suckering shrubs, such as *Kerria*, which produce quantities of thin, pliable stems can be lifted in spring or autumn and divided like herbaceous perennials. Chop the crown into pieces with a spade or knife and replant the divisions immediately. Alternatively, single suckers can be removed from the margins of the clump and potted up or replanted immediately.

DIRECTORY OF
SHRUBS, TREES AND CLIMBERS

Below are key tips on a selection of shrubs, trees and climbers that are particularly suitable for propagation. Unless otherwise specified, follow the detailed instructions given under the propagation section on pages 104–113.

Key

H	Height
S	Spread
T	Time for rooting
P	Time for planting out
U	Time for graft union to appear
🌰	By seed
🔧	By division

Abelia   Caprifoliaceae

About 30 species of deciduous and evergreen shrubs with tubular flowers.

A. × grandiflora. This hybrid shrub is superior to either of its parents (*A. chinensis* and *A. uniflora*). It has slender, drooping branches with small, glossy, dark green leaves and pink-tinted, white flowers from midsummer to early autumn. Evergreen but becomes semi-evergreen in cold winters. Hardy to -10°C (15°F) or more with shelter from cold winds; it is best against a wall in cold climates. H 2–3m (6–10ft), S 4m (12ft).

PROPAGATION

Softwood or greenwood cuttings – early summer, 6–9cm (2½–3½in) long.
T 8 weeks, P 10 months.

Semi-ripe cuttings – mid- to late summer.

Abelia grandiflora 'Frances Mason'

Nodal cuttings, 10–15cm (4–6in).
T up to 6 months, P 12–15 months.
Simple layering – spring. T 6–8 months, P 12–18 months.

Acer (Maple)   Aceraceae

About 150 species of evergreen and deciduous trees, ranging in size from forest trees to medium- and small-sized specimens. Valued for their leaf shapes, usually brilliant autumn colour and, in some species, such as **A. griseum**, **A. capillipes**, and **A. davidii**, attractively coloured or striated bark. The many different coloured and sized variants of the hardy Japanese maples, **A. japonicum** and **A. palmatum**, are ideal for smaller gardens. H to 8m (25ft), S to 10m (30ft), but many are considerably smaller. Provide moist but well-drained soil and some shelter from cold winds and very hot sun.

PROPAGATION

🌰 if sown as soon as ripe, germinates the following spring. Collect as the 'keys' begin to colour. Sow in a seedbed or open frame. Spring-sown seed may not germinate for a further year. T transfer to nursery bed in first spring, P 12–24 months.

Side-veneer grafting – late winter or

Acer palmatum

midsummer, for selected cultivars, especially of *A. japonicum* and *A. palmatum*.
U 6 or 5 weeks respectively, P 2–3 years.
Chip-budding – early to midsummer, for selected cultivars.
U 6 weeks, P 18–24 months.
Softwood cuttings – spring. Requires some skill but can be successful with *A. palmatum* and the *A. palmatum* Dissectum Group.
T 8–10 weeks, P 24 months.

Actinidia   Actinidiaceae

Some 40 species of mainly deciduous, twining climbers grown for their foliage, flowers, and edible fruit.

A. deliciosa, syn. *A. chinensis* (Chinese gooseberry, Kiwi fruit). (*See the Fruit directory, p.184*). Hardy with deciduous, heart-shaped leaves and clusters of creamy white flowers. **'Blake'** is self-fertile. H 10m (30ft).

A. kolomikta. Slender and hardy, producing dark green leaves splashed with cream and pink variegation. H 5m (15ft) or more.

PROPAGATION

Vine eyes – midwinter.
T 16 weeks, P 18–24 months.
Hardwood cuttings – winter. Take cuttings 20–25cm (8–10in) long.
T 3–4 weeks, P 12–18 months.
Softwood cuttings – early summer. Take basal or nodal cuttings of side shoots, 15cm (6in) long. T 3–4 weeks, P 18 months.
Semi-ripe cuttings – late summer 8–10cm (3–4in) long, with bottom heat, in a closed propagator.
T 4–6 weeks, P 12–18 months.

Aesculus   Hippocastanaceae

About 15 species of deciduous trees and shrubs. Most, including **A. × carnea** (Red horse chestnut) and **A. hippocastanum** (Horse chestnut), are large trees, suited to

Actinidia deliciosa

Betula pendula

Buddleja davidii 'Dubonnet'

parks and big gardens. Grow in well-drained soil in sun or part-shade. Species can be propagated by ripe seed sown in a seedbed outdoors; cultivars are T-budded in summer. *A. parviflora* (Bottlebrush buckeye). Spreading, suckering shrub with candles of red-centred white flowers that are produced freely in midsummer. The palmate leaves turn yellow in autumn. H 3m (10ft), S to 5m (15ft).

PROPAGATION
Root cuttings – midwinter.
T 8–12 weeks, P 24 months.
✎ winter; separate suckers when dormant. Replant immediately.

Andromeda
Ericaceae

Just two species of hardy evergreen shrubs with urn-shaped flowers and narrow grey-green leaves. They need permanently moist, acid soil in sun or light shade.
A. polifolia, syn. *A. rosmarinifolia* (Bog rosemary). Dwarf shrub bearing terminal clusters of urn-shaped, pink or white flowers from late spring to early summer. H 40cm (16in), S 60cm (24in).

PROPAGATION
Softwood cuttings – early summer, 4–6cm (1½–2½in) long.
T 4–5 weeks, P 6–12 months.
Semi-ripe cuttings – late summer, 6–10cm (2½–4in) long.
T 8–10 weeks, P 6–12 months.
Mound-layering – spring.
T 1 year, P 18–24 months.
🌱 as soon as ripe, or in spring. Surface-sow on finely milled moss peat. This method is rather slow but seedlings come true to type. P 24 months.

Aucuba
Cornaceae

Three or four species of evergreen, hardy shrubs with large leaves and attractive fruits. Grows in any soil (except waterlogged) in sun, or light to full shade.
A. japonica. Tough shrub with bold, glossy, ovate leaves and insignificant flowers which give rise to large red berries on female plants. Variegated forms, such as 'Picturata' and 'Sulphurea Marginata'(both female), are more attractive but need more light to grow well. The species can be raised from seed sown in a cold frame in autumn, but it may take several years to ascertain whether offspring are female, berrying forms. H and S 3m (10ft).

PROPAGATION
Ripewood cuttings – early to late autumn. 10–15cm (4–6in) long, with a heel.
T 16–20 weeks, P 30 months.
Semi-ripe cuttings – late summer. 10–15cm (4–6in) long, with a heel.
T 6–8 weeks, P 30 months.

Berberis
(Barberry)
Berberidaceae

Some 200 species of often spiny, deciduous and evergreen shrubs. The hardy barberries are grown for their attractive foliage, which, in deciduous species, often colours well in autumn, and for their cup-shaped flowers and the fruits that follow. There are compact species suitable for small gardens and larger spreading species for bigger areas. Pruning keeps them in check. Most thrive in any well-drained soil, in sun or light, dappled shade.

PROPAGATION
Semi-ripe cuttings – midsummer, under mist or in a plastic tent. Heeled, nodal or mallet cuttings may all be tried. Treat with rooting

hormone. T 4–6 weeks, P 12 months. Ripewood cuttings – 7–10cm (3–4in) long, early autumn in a cold frame. Pre-rooting treatment as above.
T 8–12 weeks, P 18–24 months.
🌱 species only. Separate from the ripe fruit, stratify in boxes of sand over the winter, and sow as soon as signs of germination are seen in spring. P 24–30 months.

Betula
(Birch)
Betulaceae

About 60 species of graceful, deciduous trees of light, airy habit, that grow in almost any soil, but only reach their maximum size in fertile soils. They have attractive stem colours, from white(*B. ermanii*, *B. pendula* and *B. papyrifera*), to pink and shiny orange-brown (*B. albo-sinensis* var. *septentrionalis*); *B. nigra* (River birch) has shaggy, dark brown bark. Many eventually make very large trees up to 18–25m (50–80ft) tall, so choose with care. When grown as multi-stemmed trees, height is reduced and the impact of the stems is increased.

PROPAGATION
🌱 as soon as ripe, in a seedbed or open frame. Germinates in spring.
P 12–24 months.
Grafting – selected cultivars. Side-veneer grafting in late winter.
U 3–6 weeks, P 8–20 months.

Buddleja
Loganiaceae

About 100 species of evergreen and deciduous shrubs and trees. Hardy *B. davidii* and its many cultivars are the most commonly grown. They are very easy to propagate by hardwood cuttings. Other desirable, early-summer-flowering species

Buxus sempervirens 'Chelsea'

Camellia japonica 'Flame'

Clematis 'Jackmannii Superba'

include **B. alternifolia** (hardy), with rounded clusters of lilac flowers, and **B. globosa** (frost hardy), with rounded panicles of orange blooms. These are best propagated by semi-ripe cuttings. H and S to 5m (15ft). Grow in fertile, well-drained soil in full sun.

B. davidii (Butterfly bush). Slender, pyramidal panicles of fragrant white, purple or lilac flowers, from midsummer almost into autumn. Cultivars have more intensely coloured flowers. **'Black Knight'** has deep blue-purple blooms, those of **'Dartmoor'** and **'Royal Red'** are red-purple, and **'Pink Delight'** produces orange-eyed, pink flowers. H 3m (10ft), S to 5m (15ft).

PROPAGATION

Softwood cuttings – early summer; nodal cuttings, 10cm (4in) long.
T 3–4 weeks, P 12 months.
Semi-ripe cuttings – midsummer. Heeled cuttings, 10–12 cm (4–5in) long.
T 4–8 weeks, P 12 months.
Hardwood cuttings – autumn, 20–25cm (8–10in) long.
T 16–20 weeks, P 18–24 months.

Buxus (Box)   Buxaceae

About 70 species of evergreen shrubs and trees, grown for their foliage. Grow in fertile, well-drained soil in partial shade. All can be propagated in the same way.

B. microphylla (Small-leaved box). Dense, hardy shrub. H 75cm (30in), S 1.5m (5ft).

B. sempervirens (Common box). Hardy shrub, ideal for hedging and topiary. Variants include some with golden- or silver-variegated leaves. H and S 5m (15ft).

'Suffruticosa' is a dwarf form which is ideal for hedging and edging. H and S to 1m (3ft).

PROPAGATION

Semi-ripe cuttings – mid- to late summer, 7–10cm (3–4in) long, in a cold frame.
T 12–16 weeks, P 24 months.
Ripewood cuttings – early autumn, 7–10cm (3–4in) long, in a cold frame.
T 20–24 weeks, P 30 months.

Camellia   Theaceae

Genus of some 250 species of evergreen shrubs and trees. The most frequently grown are the named cultivars of *C. japonica* and *C. x williamsii* (*C. japonica* x *C. saluensis*) with flowers in a range of colours from white to deepest crimson, including all shades of pink, and some with splashed and striped petals. Flower forms include single, semi-double, rose-, anemone- and peony-forms. They need leafy acid soil, with some shade from the hottest summer sun, and shelter from cold, dry winds. Most are hardy, but the flowers are not – the earliest bloom in late winter or before, with some cultivars still flowering in mid- to late spring, and the flowers are susceptible to frost. Camellias make excellent wall plants, preferably on a shaded, sheltered wall out of early morning sun. Most *C. japonica* cultivars also thrive in tubs in a cold greenhouse or conservatory.

C. japonica cultivars H to 9m (28ft), S to 8m (25ft), but some are smaller.

C. x williamsii cultivars: H to 5m (15ft), S to 3m (10ft).

PROPAGATION

Semi-ripe cuttings – mid- to late summer; nodal cuttings, 7–10cm (3–4in) long. Root in 50:50 (v/v) peat and sand, or ericaceous cutting compost, with gentle bottom heat, in a propagator. T 7–8 weeks, P 18–24 months.

Leaf-bud cuttings – late summer to early autumn, or late winter.
T 10 weeks, P 18–24 months.
Simple layering – autumn. P 18 months.

Chimonanthus   Calycanthaceae

Six species of deciduous and evergreen hardy shrubs with very fragrant flowers. Will grow in any good garden soil, but best planted in full sun in a warm, sheltered site, so that the new growth will ripen fully to provide a good flowering display.

C. praecox, syn. *C. fragrans* (Winter sweet). Produces beautifully fragrant, waxy, purple-centred, pale yellow flowers, on leafless branches from mid- to late winter. H 4m (12ft), S 3m (10ft).

PROPAGATION

Softwood cuttings – summer. Clones, which are mostly raised from seed, show varying success. T 8–10 weeks, P 24 months.
Simple layering – spring or early autumn.
T up to 2 years.
🌰 sown as soon as ripe germinates in spring. Seed-raised plants may take 5–7 years or more to reach flowering size.
T in spring, P 3–4 years.

Clematis   Ranunculaceae

Some 200 species and over 400 hybrids of mostly deciduous and some evergreen climbers, varying in size and vigour from dwarf to very vigorous species which reach 6m (20ft) or more. Most in cultivation are hardy. There are early-flowering species and their hybrids, flowering in late winter and early spring, and late-summer- and autumn-flowering species, so with careful selection, you can have clematis in bloom over much

Cotinus coggygria 'Royal Purple'

Cotoneaster x watereri

Daphne x burkwoodii

of the year. Grow in fertile, humus-rich soil with the roots in the shade and growth in the sun. Use 'long tom' pots when potting up.

PROPAGATION

Softwood, inter-nodal cuttings – early summer, 7–10cm (3–4in) long.
T 4–5 weeks, P 18–20 months.
Semi-ripe, internodal cuttings – midsummer, 10–12cm (4–5in) long, in a propagator, with bottom heat. T 4–6 weeks, P 18 months.
Serpentine layering – late winter–early spring. T 1 year.
🌱 sown as soon as ripe in a cold frame, germinates in late winter or early spring. Bring under glass on germination. Species only. P 9–15 months.

Cornus   Cornaceae

Some 45 species of mostly deciduous, hardy or frost-hardy, shrubs and trees, including those that are valued for their brilliantly coloured winter stems, such as *C. alba* and its cultivars (H and S 3m/10ft), and those that are grown for their elegant habit and flowers, like *C. capitata* (H and S 12m/40ft), *C. kousa* (H 7m/22ft, S 5m/15ft) and *C. nuttallii* (H 12m/40ft, S 8m/25ft).

PROPAGATION

Hardwood cuttings – late autumn to early winter, 20cm (8in) long, in open ground (*C. alba* and cultivars).
T up to 6 months, P 12 months.
Semi-ripe cuttings – mid- to late summer, 7–10cm (3–4in) long, with a heel, with gentle bottom heat in a propagator.
T 6–12 months, P 2–3 years.
🌱 sown as soon as ripe in an open frame or cold frame, may take 18 months to germinate. P 2–3 years.

Cotinus   Anacardiaceae

Just two species of deciduous trees or shrubs, of which *C. coggygria* and its cultivars are the more widely grown. It does not require a rich soil, flowering more freely and having richer autumn colours on poor soils.
C. coggygria, syn. *Rhus cotinus* (Smoke bush, Venetian sumach). Has rounded green leaves that produce wonderful autumn colours. The feathery flower plumes in midsummer give rise to its common name. **'Royal Purple'** is a less vigorous, smaller, red-leaved cultivar.
H and S 5m (15ft).

PROPAGATION

Softwood cuttings – early summer, 5cm (2in) long. T 6 weeks, P 18 months.
French layering – winter to early spring.
T 9 months, P 12–18 months.

Cotoneaster   Rosaceae

Over 200 species of evergreen, semi-evergreen, or deciduous, shrubs and trees. There is enormous variation in habit, from prostrate, ground-covering species like *C. dammeri* (H 20cm/8in), to those that make excellent wall shrubs, like *C. horizontalis* and *C. microphyllus* (H 1m/3ft). A number, like *C. frigidus* and *C. x watereri* (H to 10m/30ft), make elegant, upright or arching, large shrubs or small trees. Nearly all have tiny white flowers in spring or summer that give rise to berries in a wide colour range. Grow in moderately fertile, well-drained soil in sun or partial shade.

PROPAGATION

Softwood cuttings – early summer, 7–10cm (3–4in) long (deciduous species).
T 5 weeks, P 18–24 months.
Semi-ripe cuttings – late summer to early

autumn, with a heel, 7–10cm (3–4in) long, in a cold frame (evergreens and semi-evergreens). T 3–6 months, P 18–24 months.
🌱 sown when ripe in an open frame or seedbed, may take up to 18 months to germinate. Remove from the fleshy berries before sowing. P 2–3 years.

Cytisus   Leguminosae

About 50 species of deciduous and evergreen shrubs and trees, grown for their often fragrant, pea-like flowers. All *Cytisus* are sun-loving, tolerant of poor, dry soils, and rather short-lived. *C. scoparius* and its cultivars are among the most commonly grown. Use 'long tom' pots when potting up.
C. scoparius (Common broom). Hardy, deciduous, upright shrub with green stems. The species has yellow flowers, but it has produced cultivars of many colours, including bi-colours, through salmon-red to deep crimson. H 1.5m (5ft) or more, S 1.5m (5ft).

PROPAGATION

Semi-ripe cuttings – mid- to late summer, 7–10cm (3–4in) long, in a cold frame.
T 6–8 weeks, P 12–18 months.
🌱 autumn or spring. *C. scoparius* seed produces a mixture of plants with multicoloured flowers. Most are suitable for hedging and similar plantings.
T 7–8 weeks, P 18–24 months.

Daphne   Thymelaeaceae

Some 50 species of deciduous, semi-evergreen, and deciduous shrubs noted for the intense fragrance of their flowers. A number are suitable for a rock garden (*see p. 82*), and some have a reputation for being difficult to grow. Grow in humus-rich, well-

117

Deutzia x elegantissima 'Rosealind'

Eleagnus pungens 'Maculata'

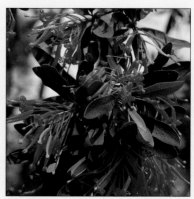

Embothrium coccineum

drained but not dry soil. Most prefer slightly acid soil. Position in sun or light shade.

D. x burkwoodii. Fast-growing, hardy, semi-evergreen with glossy, dark green leaves, and clusters of fragrant, pink-flushed, white flowers in early summer. 'Somerset' has slightly darker flowers and makes an elegant vase-shaped bush. H and S 1–1.5m (3–5ft).

D. mezereum (Mezereon). One of the earliest daphnes to flower, producing its fragrant pink to purplish pink flowers in late winter on leafless stems. *F. alba* has white flowers that show up well on dull winter days. H 1.2m (4ft), S 1m (3ft).

PROPAGATION

Softwood cuttings – early summer, nodal cuttings, 5–10cm (2–4in) long.
T 6–8 weeks, P 12–18 months.
Semi-ripe cuttings – midsummer, 5–10cm (2–4in) long, preferably with a heel, under mist or in a cold frame.
T 5 –14 weeks, P 12–18 months.
Simple layering – preferably spring to early summer. Sever rooted layers in autumn, but do not lift until the following spring.
T 6 months, P 12–24 months.
🌰 sown as soon as ripe in a cold frame, germinates in the first or second spring. Suitable for species, and the most practical method for *D. mezereum*. P 20–24 months.

Deutzia   Hydrangeaceae

Some 60 species of mostly deciduous shrubs that bear cup- or star-shaped flowers in spring and summer. They include a number of beautiful hybrids and cultivars like the pink-flowered *D.* 'Mont Rose', and *D. x elegantissima* 'Rosealind'. Both these are hardy and are suitable for smaller gardens,

reaching only 1.2m (4ft) high. Deutzias are easily cultivated, growing well in all fertile soils, preferably in a sunny site.

D. scabra. Has erect branches covered with peeling, papery bark. The scented, star-shaped white flowers are produced in summer. 'Candidissima' has double flowers. H 3m (10ft), S 2m (6ft).

PROPAGATION

Softwood cuttings – early summer, 7–10cm (3–4in) long. T 3 weeks, P 18–24 months.
Hardwood cuttings – autumn, 25–30cm (10–12in) long.
T 4–6 months, P 12–24 months.

Elaeagnus   Elaeagnaceae

Some 45 species of hardy, evergreen and deciduous shrubs and small trees, grown for their attractive leaves and (some) for their tiny, sweetly scented flowers. *E. x ebbingei* and *E. pungens* and their cultivars are suitable for growing in smaller gardens. Grow in fertile well-drained soil. The evergreens will tolerate some shade.

E. x ebbingei. An autumn-flowering evergreen with glistening, glossy sea-green leaves, covered in silvery scales beneath. 'Limelight' is more compact, with pale green leaves that are yellow and intensely silvered when young. H and S to 4m (12ft).

E. pungens. A spiny-stemmed evergreen with dark green foliage and small, tubular, fragrant white flowers in autumn. 'Maculata' has leaves splashed with deep yellow. H to 4m (12ft), S to 5m (15ft).

PROPAGATION

Semi-ripe cuttings – late summer, 7–10cm (3–4in) long, in a cold frame.
T 4–6 months, P 12–18 months.

Leaf-bud cuttings – mid- to late summer. Sections with a leaf and one or more buds. T 7–8 weeks, P 18–24 months.

Embothrium   Proteaceae

Eight species of evergreen shrubs and trees, only one of which is grown. Frost hardy, it thrives in shelter and dappled sunlight in moist, acid soil.

E. coccineum (Chilean fire bush). Gives a brilliant display of scarlet flowers in late spring and early summer. H to 10m (30ft), S to 5m (15ft).

PROPAGATION

Root cuttings – mid- to late winter, in a cold frame. T 4–5 months, P 18–24 months.
🌰 spring, at 13–16°C (55–61°F), in ericaceous seed compost. P 2 years.
🔧 of suckers, in late winter. Replant immediately.

Escallonia   Crassulariaceae

Genus of over 50 species of evergreen shrubs. Those most frequently grown in gardens are the named cultivars, often of rather mixed parentage, many of the best raised in Ireland by the Slieve Donard Nursery. They bear clusters of white, pink, or red flowers, above dark shiny leaves, throughout summer and early autumn They dislike cold, dry winter winds, and, although not reliably hardy in inland areas, they thrive in coastal regions, where they make good hedges or windbreaks. Escallonias can be grown in any well-drained soil. H and S 1.5–2.5m (5–8ft) or more.

PROPAGATION

Softwood cuttings – early summer, 7–10cm (3–4in) long. T 8–10 weeks, P 18 months.

Forsythia x *intermedia*

Hamamelis x *intermedia* 'Pallida'

Hebe 'Great Orme'

Semi-ripe cuttings – mid- to late summer, 10–12cm (4–5in) long, nodal or with a heel, in a cold frame, or propagator with bottom heat. T 4–5 months, P 18 months.

Forsythia Oleaceae

Some seven species of hardy, deciduous or semi-evergreen shrubs valued for their brilliant yellow flowers, produced before the leaves appear in early spring. The most commonly grown are named cultivars, including those of *F.* x *intermedia*, such as **'Lynwood'** and **'Karl Sax'**. H and S 1.5–2.5m (5–8ft). All are easily grown in moist but well-drained soil.

PROPAGATION
Softwood cuttings – early summer, nodal cuttings, 10cm (4in) long.
T 4–5 weeks, P 18 months.
Hardwood cuttings – autumn, 25–30cm (10–12in) long, in a nursery bed or cold frame. T 4–5 months, P 12–18 months.

Fuchsia Onagraceae

Genus of around 100 species of evergreen and deciduous shrubs, with some 8000 named cultivars. Of the species, *F. magellanica* is the hardiest, and has been used in the breeding of many modern, more or less hardy cultivars, like **'Mrs Popple'** and **'Riccartonii'**. They thrive in both semi-shade and full sun, and in any well-drained soil. In cold winters, nearly all the 'hardy' fuchsias die back to the base and re-emerge in spring, rather like herbaceous perennials.
F. magellanica. Has slender, delicate flowers with a long, scarlet tube and sepals, and violet corollas, borne throughout summer.
Var. *molinae*, syn. 'Alba', has shorter-tubed

white flowers tinted mauve; **'Versicolor'** has scarlet and violet flowers, and its leaves are variegated silver-grey and white, flushed pink and purple. H and S to 3m (10ft); less in areas with cold winters.

PROPAGATION
Most types of cuttings strike freely, but young plants from cuttings late in the season are best overwintered under glass for their first winter, in cold areas.
Softwood cuttings – spring or early summer, nodal or inter-nodal, 7–10cm (3–4in) long. T 2–3 weeks, P 4 months.
Semi-ripe cuttings – mid- to late summer, nodal or inter-nodal, 7–10cm (3–4in) long. T 4–5 weeks, P 16 months.

Garrya Garryaceae

Of the 13 species of evergreen shrubs and trees in the genus, *G. elliptica* is the most commonly found in cultivation. It is tolerant of a range of soils and is well suited to growing against a shady wall.
G. elliptica. Valued for its glossy, dark grey-green leaves, and for its silver-grey catkins in late winter or early spring. Male and female catkins are borne on separate plants, the males being longer and more decorative. For this reason, it is usually best to propagate it vegetatively from a known male plant. **'James Roof'** has catkins 20cm (8in) or more in length. H and S to 4m (12ft).

PROPAGATION
Semi-ripe cuttings – late summer, 7–10cm (3–4in) long, preferably with a heel, in a cold frame. Roots well but cuttings are often lost when transplanted, so insert the cuttings in small pots or modules.
T 7–8 weeks, P 18–24 months.

Hamamelis Hamamelidaceae

Some six species of hardy deciduous shrubs, of which *H. mollis* and *H.* x *intermedia* and their cultivars form some of the most valuable of winter- and early-spring-flowering shrubs. The large leaves turn golden yellow in autumn. They need humus-rich, moist, neutral to acid soil and shelter from cold, dry winds. Use lime-free compost when propagating.
H. x *intermedia.* Cultivars have yellow, orange, or red flowers with crimped petals. **'Arnold Promise'** has bright yellow flowers, **'Diane'** has dark red flowers, **'Jelena'** has copper-tinted flowers, and **'Pallida'** bears soft yellow blooms. H and S to 4m (12ft).
H. mollis (Chinese witch hazel). Produces fragrant, spidery, golden yellow flowers on leafless branches in mid- to late winter. H and S to 4m (12ft).

PROPAGATION
Simple layering – autumn or early spring.
T 2 years.
Softwood cuttings – spring or early summer, 10cm (4in) long, under mist.
T 6–8 weeks, P 12–24 months.
🌢 sown as soon as ripe in a cold frame, will germinate in its first or second winter. Species only. T 2 years.
Side-grafting – late winter, or budding in late summer, onto seedling understocks of *H. virginiana*. For cultivars.
U 16 weeks, P 2–3 years.

Hebe Scrophulariaceae

About 100 species of evergreen shrubs with attractive leaves and spikes of flowers. They range from fully hardy, compact shrubs with small leaves, like *H. pinguifolia* **'Pagei'** (H 30cm/12in), and *H. odora*, syn. *H. buxifolia*

119

Hydrangea macrophylla

Hypericum 'Rowallane'

Kalmia latifolia

(H 1m/3ft), and 'whipcord' types, like the olive-green *H. armstrongii* (H1m/3ft), to larger species with large, often variegated leaves that are not completely hardy inland but which thrive in coastal gardens. These include the half-hardy *H. x andersonii* **'Variegata'** (H 2m/6ft) and garden hybrids of *H. speciosa*, like **'Tricolor'** (H 1.2m/4ft). Of the many named cultivars, *H.* **'Autumn Glory'**, with deep purple flowers from midsummer onwards, and *H.* **'Great Orme'**, with long spikes of pink flowers in summer, have proved to be reasonable hardy and make small shrubs. H and S 1.2m (4ft).

PROPAGATION

Semi-ripe cuttings – late summer–early autumn, 5–10cm (2–4in) long; in a propagator, with gentle bottom heat for less hardy species, or in a cold frame for hardy species. T 4–8 weeks, P 6–12 months.

Hydrangea   Hydrangeaceae

Over 80 species of evergreen and deciduous shrubs and climbers, of which the best known are the many cultivars of *H. macrophylla*. Some of these are offered as pot plants. The majority are frost hardy or fully hardy. They have 'lace-cap' or 'mop-head' flowers (the **'Hortensias'**), in white, pink, or blue; the blue-flowered cultivars produce true blues only on acid soil, becoming muddy pink in alkaline conditions (and vice versa). H and S most reach about 1–1.5m (3–5ft).
H. petiolaris. Deciduous climber that produces creamy white lace-caps in summer. H to 15m (50ft) eventually.

PROPAGATION

Softwood cuttings – early summer, nodal or inter-nodal, 8–10cm (3–4in) long.

T 3 weeks, P 10–15 months.
Softwood cuttings – late spring to early summer, for *H. petiolaris*. Take cuttings of non-flowering side shoots, 8cm (3in) long. T 6 weeks, P 6–12months.

Hypericum   Hypericaceae

Over 400 species of hardy to frost-tender, shrubs, trees, annuals, and perennials, with showy yellow flowers. Those featured are best in well-drained, loamy soil, with some shelter from cold, dry winter winds.
H. calycinum (Rose of Sharon). Hardy evergreen or semi-evergreen shrub making valuable groundcover in shade or sun. Rather too invasive for more manicured areas. H 60cm (24in), S indefinite.
H. **'Hidcote'.** Hardy evergreen or semi-evergreen shrub blooming from midsummer to autumn. H to 1.2m (4ft), S 1.5m (5ft).
H. **'Rowallane.** Frost-hardy, semi-evergreen shrub bearing cupped, deep golden yellow flowers from late summer to autumn. H to 1.8m (6ft), S to 1m (3ft).

PROPAGATION

Semi-ripe cuttings – mid- to late summer, 10–12cm (4–5in) long, preferably heeled, in a cold frame. T 6 weeks, P 9–12 months.
autumn. Lift small rooted pieces (Irishman's cuttings), trim topgrowth and pot individually; overwinter in a cold frame. P 6–8 months.

Ilex (Holly)   Aquifoliaceae

Some 400 species of deciduous and evergreen shrubs and trees, of which the most widely planted are the legion frost-hardy cultivars of *I. aquifolium* (English holly), with prickly leaves, and *I.* **x** *altaclerensis,*

which have spine-toothed or entire leaves. These include many with variegated leaves in shades of gold, creamy white, yellow, or silver and with leaf shapes ranging from smooth and camellia-like (**'Camelliifolia'**) to the spiny **'Ferox'** (Hedgehog holly). They range in habit from fastigiate to pyramidal or rounded. Hollies bear male and female flowers on different plants; both are needed to produce berries. Only vegetative propagation will produce offspring that are identical to the parent. It is possible to raise species from seed sown in autumn in an open frame or seedbed, but they can take 2–3 years to germinate. Grow in moist but well-drained, humus-rich soil in sun or partial shade. H to 25m (80ft), S to 15m (50ft), but many hollies are smaller.

PROPAGATION

Semi-ripe cuttings – mid- to late summer 5–10cm (2–4in) long, nodal or with a heel, in a propagator with gentle bottom heat. Take cuttings before the first frost or they will defoliate. They can also be rooted in early autumn in a cold frame. T 7–8 weeks, P 18–24 months.

Kalmia   Ericaceae

Some seven species of hardy, evergreen shrubs that need similar growing conditions to rhododendrons, and moist but well-drained acid soil. Use ericaceous seed or cuttings composts. All parts are poisonous.
K. latifolia (Calico bush). Dense, glossy-leaved, evergreen with distinctive flowers, borne from late spring to midsummer. They open from crimped, deep red buds, becoming pale to deep pink and cup-shaped on opening. H and S to 3m (10ft) eventually.

Kolkwitzia amabilis 'Pink Cloud'

Lonicera periclymenum

Magnolia stellata

PROPAGATION

❦ spring, at 6–12°C (45–54°F). Seed germinates within a few weeks, and should be pricked out and grown on in a cool greenhouse until 5cm (2in) high. Harden off and grow on in a cold frame, for the first two winters. P 2–4 years.

Simple layering – late summer to early autumn. P 1–2 years.

Kolkwitzia   Caprifoliaceae

A single hardy species of deciduous shrub. *K. amabilis* (Beauty bush). A graceful shrub with long, slender branches, covered for weeks, in late spring and early summer, with foxglove-like, soft pink flowers with a yellow throat. It grows in any well-drained soil and thrives on chalk. **'Pink Cloud'** has darker flowers. H 3m (10ft), S 4m (12ft).

PROPAGATION

Softwood cuttings – spring, 10cm (4in) long, preferably under mist.

T 4 weeks, P 12–18 months.

Greenwood to semi-ripe cuttings – midsummer, 10–15cm (4–6in) long, preferably with a heel, in a cold frame.

T 3 months, P 12–18 months.

Simple layering – late winter to early spring. T 1–2 years.

Lavandula   Labiatae

Some 28 species of hardy to frost-hardy, evergreen, aromatic shrubs and subshrubs. In gardens, *L. angustifolia*, and *L. x intermedia* (English lavender), and their cultivars, are favoured for low-growing hedges, and for dry, sunny, mixed and herbaceous borders. The flower spikes, from mid- to late summer, vary from darkest violet through pink to

white. All thrive in full sun on well-drained soil. They range in size from dwarf forms, like **'Nana Alba'** and **'Munstead'** at H 30–45cm (12–18in), S 30–60cm (12–24in), to **'Grappenhall'**, at H and S 1m (3ft).

PROPAGATION

Semi-ripe cuttings – from mid- to late summer, 8–10cm (3–4in) long, preferably with a heel, in a cold frame.

T 4–16 weeks, P 9 months.

❦ species and some cultivars, like 'Munstead', come true from seed. Sow in spring in a cold frame or cold greenhouse. Stratification in a domestic refrigerator will improve germination. T 6 months.

Lonicera   Caprifoliaceae

About 180 or more species of hardy to half-hardy, deciduous and evergreen shrubs and climbers, many of which are valued for their fragrant flowers; *L. nitida* for its leaves.

L. fragrantissima. Hardy, deciduous or semi-evergreen shrub with strongly scented, white flowers in winter and early spring. H 2m (6ft), S 3m (10ft).

L. nitida. Hardy, evergreen shrub making a dense, low-growing hedge. H and S to 3m (10ft) eventually. **'Baggesen's Gold'** is smaller and has yellow leaves. H to 1.4m (5ft).

L. periclymenum (Common honeysuckle or Woodbine). Vigorous, hardy, deciduous climber that has long been valued for its intensely fragrant flowers, borne from mid- to late summer. **'Belgica'** (Early Dutch) blooms from late spring to early summer, and **'Serotina'** (Late Dutch) blooms from midsummer to early autumn. H to 7m (22ft).

L. x purpusii is similar to *L. fragrantissima*. H to 2m (6ft), S 3m (15ft).

PROPAGATION
Shrubs

Softwood or greenwood cuttings – early to midsummer, for deciduous species take nodal cuttings, 10–12cm (4–5in) long. T 6 weeks, P 18–24 months.

Semi-ripe cuttings – mid- to late summer, for evergreens 10cm (4in) long, in a cold frame. T 12 weeks, P 12–18 months.

Hardwood cuttings – autumn, for deciduous species 25cm (10in) long, in a cold frame. T 6–12 months, P 24 months.

Climbers

Softwood to greenwood cuttings – summer. Nodal cuttings, 10–12cm (4–5in) long.

T 6 weeks, P 18–24 months.

Hardwood cuttings – autumn. 20–25cm (8–10in) long, in a cold frame.

T 6–12 months, P 12–24 months.

Layering – autumn. P 12 months.

Magnolia   Magnoliaceae

Some 125 species of deciduous and evergreen trees and shrubs with unrivalled flowering displays. Many are best in larger gardens. The following hardy species are among the more suitable for smaller and medium-sized gardens. All early-flowering magnolias need shelter from wind and frost to prevent flower damage. They require moist, well-drained, humus-rich, preferably acid to neutral soil, and sun or part shade.

M. denudata, syn. *M. heptapeta* (Yulan). Deciduous shrub or small tree of elegant habit, producing pure white, chalice-shaped flowers, on bare branches in spring. H and S to 10m (30ft) eventually.

M. sieboldii subsp. *sinensis*, syn. *M. sinensis.* One of the smaller deciduous tree

Mahonia x media 'Charity'

Malus 'Profusion'

Philadelphus 'Belle Etoile'

magnolias, bearing lemon-scented, nodding, saucer-shaped white flowers with a centre of red stamens in early summer, which, in favourable seasons, are followed by pendent fruits that display scarlet seeds in winter. H 6m (20ft), S 8m (25ft).

M. x soulangeana. Deciduous shrub or tree with large, goblet-shaped, pure white, pale to deep pink, or purple-flushed flowers, borne with or before the leaves in spring. H and S to 6m (20ft) eventually.

M. stellata (Star magnolia). Compact, free-flowering, deciduous shrub clothed in slender-petalled, star-shaped white flowers, with or before the leaves in spring. H 3m (10ft), S 4m (12ft) eventually.

PROPAGATION
Greenwood to semi-ripe cuttings – mid- to late summer. 8–10cm (3–4in) long, with a heel, in a closed propagator, or under mist, with gentle bottom heat.
T 8–12 weeks, P 2–3 years.
Simple layering – early spring. P 2–3 years.
🌱 sown as soon as ripe, in autumn, in a seedbed, will usually germinate in spring. For all species. P 3–4 years.
Softwood cuttings – early summer (M. x soulangeana forms). Place stem with one or two leaves and buds under mist or in a propagator with bottom heat.
T 8–10 weeks, P 24 months.

Mahonia — Berberidaceae

About 70 species of hardy, evergreen shrubs, valued for their handsome foliage and, in most species and cultivars, their fragrant yellow flowers. Grow in fertile, moist but well-drained soil. They prefer shade but will tolerate sun if the soil is not too dry.

M. x media 'Charity'. An erect, evergreen shrub, with attractive foliage and racemes of fragrant yellow flowers from late autumn to late winter. H to 3m (10ft), S 2m (6ft).

PROPAGATION
Leaf-bud cuttings – late summer to early autumn, in a propagator with bottom heat. T 12 weeks, P 18–24 months.
Semi-ripe or mallet cuttings – late summer to early autumn, 8–10cm (3–4in) long, in a propagator with gentle bottom heat.
T 12 weeks, P 18–24 months.
🌱 sown in autumn in frame, germinates in spring. Species only. P 1–2 years.

Malus — Rosaceae

Some 35 species, and many cultivars, of deciduous trees and shrubs, that include the flowering crab apples. These are mainly small to medium-sized trees; many are ideal for smaller gardens, with flowers in spring and fruits and foliage colours in autumn. The cup-shaped flowers range from white (**M. 'John Downie'**), through pink (**M. floribunda**), to deepest pink-purple, as in **M. 'Profusion'** and **M. x purpurea**, both of which also have red-purple foliage. Those notable for their autumn fruits, which often persist after leaf fall, include **'Golden Hornet'** and **'John Downie'**. Grow in moderately fertile, well-drained soil in full sun or light shade. H 7–10m (22–30ft), S 4–8m (12–25ft).

PROPAGATION
T-budding or chip-budding – summer, onto clonal rootstocks as used for fruit trees (see pp. 82–83). Named cultivars.
U 4–6 weeks, P 12–24 months.
Whip-grafting – winter, as above. U 4–6 weeks, P 12–24 months.

Hardwood cuttings – late autumn to early winter. T 6 months, P 12–24 months.
🌱 sown in autumn, in a seedbed outdoors, usually germinates in spring. Species only. May take 10 years to reach flowering size. P 12–24 months.

Paeonia — Paeoniaceae

Some 30 species of mostly hardy, mainly herbaceous perennials but with several tree peonies, including **P. lutea**, with yellow flowers, and **P. delavayi** with deep red blooms, in early summer. Many hybrids and cultivars are available, derived from **P. suffruticosa** and **P. lutea**. All have erect, woody stems, divided leaves, and bear flowers of many shades and shapes. Grow in deep, fertile soil in sun or light shade; protect from cold winds and spring frosts. H and S to 1.5m (5–6ft).

PROPAGATION
🌱 sown as soon as ripe, in a cold frame, usually germinates in spring, although root growth precedes shoot growth, and this may lead to delayed emergence, especially if seed has been allowed to dry out. P 3–4 years.
Simple layering – spring. P 2–4 years.
Grafting – named cultivars. Usually wedge-grafted in midsummer onto herbaceous peony understock. U 3 months, S 2–3 years.

Philadelphus (Mock orange) — Hydrangeaceae

About 40 species of mainly deciduous shrubs, the most commonly grown of which are named hybrids and cultivars. They have predominantly white flowers, from early to midsummer, valued for their often intense fragrance. **'Beauclerk'**, **'Belle Etoile'**, **'Sybille'**

Potentilla fruticosa

Pyracantha 'London'

Rhododendron 'Bashful'

and **'Virginal'** are hardy and among the most reliable and floriferous. Grow in fertile, well-drained soil in full sun or light shade. H 1.2–3m (4–10ft), S 2–2.5m (6–8ft).

PROPAGATION
Softwood cuttings – early summer, 8–12cm (3–5in) long.
T 3–6 weeks, P 6–12 months.
Hardwood cuttings – late autumn to early winter, 20–30cm (8–12in) long.
T 6 months, P 12 months.

Pittosporum　　　　Pittosporaceae
About 200 species of mostly half-hardy or tender, evergreen shrubs and trees. Grow in fertile, well-drained soil in full sun or light shade; variegation is best in full sun.
P. tenuifolium. Hardy to about -5°C (23°F) in a warm, sheltered site. Evergreen shrub or small tree with chocolate-coloured, scented flowers in spring. Cultivars, with variegated or coloured leaves, are mostly less vigorous.
H 4–10m (12–10ft), S 2–5m (6–15ft).

PROPAGATION
🌰 as soon as ripe in autumn, in a cold frame. Rub away the sticky, viscous coating with dry sand. Germination usually occurs in spring. Species only. P 18–24 months.
Semi-ripe cuttings – late summer, for cultivars. 8–10cm (3–4in) long, with a heel, in a propagator with gentle bottom heat. Small bushy or branched cuttings of less vigorous cultivars can be rooted successfully.
T 10 weeks, P 12–24 months.

Potentilla　　　　Rosaceae
About 500 species of hardy annuals, biennials, perennials, and shrubs. Those most useful in gardens are the many shrubby

cultivars, mostly derived from *P. fruticosa*. These bear saucer-shaped flowers over long periods from early summer until early autumn, in a range of colours. Plant in poor to moderately fertile soil in full sun. H to 1.2m (4ft), S 1.5m (5ft).

PROPAGATION
Softwood cuttings – early summer, nodal cuttings, 10cm (4in) long, in a propagating case. T 6 weeks, P 6–12 months.
Semi-ripe cuttings – mid- to late summer, 8cm (3in) long, in a cold frame.
T 6 months, P 12 months.
Hardwood cuttings – autumn, 8–15cm (3–6in) long, in a cold frame.
T 6 months, P 12–18 months.

Prunus　　　　Rosaceae
Genus of about 400 species of evergreen and deciduous trees and shrubs. The best known are perhaps the legion cultivars of Japanese cherries, *P. dulcis* (almond), and other spring-flowerers like *P. subhirtella*, *P. cerasifera* and cultivars, as well as those grown primarily for their bark, *P. serrula* and *P. maackii*. Named cultivars are nearly all chip- or T-budded, as for fruit trees (see pp. 82–83). Grow in moist but well-drained moderately fertile soil in sun; evergreens tolerate partial shade. There is a wide range of sizes: H from 1–12m (3–40ft), S from 1–6m (3–20ft).

PROPAGATION
🌰 sown as soon as ripe in autumn, in a seedbed or open frame, usually germinates in spring. Species only. P 24 months.
Semi-ripe cuttings – midsummer, for smaller trees and shrubs, including evergreens like *P. laurocerasus*. 8–10cm (3–4in) long, with a

heel, in a cold frame. Some success with Japanese cherries can be expected with this method. T 12 weeks, P 2 years.
Softwood cuttings – late spring to early summer, 5–8cm (2–3in) long, preferably under mist. T 4–6 weeks, P 2 years.

Pyracantha　　　　Rosaceae
Some seven species of thorny, evergreen shrubs, grown mainly as named cultivars and valued for their flowers, foliage, and large, very colourful, yellow, orange, or red fruits in autumn. They are grown as free-standing shrubs, or are wall-trained – especially useful for cool, shady walls. Grow in fertile, well-drained soil and protect from cold winds in frost-prone areas. Depending on how they are trained, H and S to 3m (10ft) or more.

PROPAGATION
Semi-ripe cuttings – mid- to late summer, 10–15cm (4–6in) long, with a heel, in a propagator, with gentle bottom heat.
T 4–6 weeks, P 12–15 months.

Rhododendron　　　　Ericaceae
Genus of between 700 and 800 species and innumerable hybrids and cultivars, *Rhododendron* includes evergreen and deciduous shrubs that range from prostrate dwarfs with tiny leaves 4mm (⅙in) long, to potentially large trees with leaves that reach 75cm (30in) or more in length. There is a wide range of sizes: H from 30cm (12in) to 7m (22ft), S very similar. The azaleas, both evergreen and deciduous, are a subgroup of the genus. The flowering season begins in late autumn or winter and continues into mid- or late summer for the latest-flowering species and hybrids. The earlier flowers are

123

Rhus typhina

Robinia pseudoacacia 'Frisia'

Romneya coulteri

susceptible to frost damage, so the early-flowering species and hybrids are best planted in sites that escape the early morning sun. All need moist but well-drained, humus-rich, acid soil and the majority need dappled shade, and shelter from cold, dry winds; some of the dwarf alpines and the so-called 'iron-clad' hardy hybrids, tolerate more open conditions in sun. Use lime-free potting, cuttings and seed composts for all propagation. As a general guide, propagate large-leaved species by seed or layers; hardy hybrids by cuttings or grafting; deciduous azaleas by layers or grafting; evergreen azaleas and alpine (dwarf) species by cuttings; alpines also by seed.

PROPAGATION

Semi-ripe cuttings – late summer, nodal, 10cm (4in) long, under mist or in a propagator, with gentle bottom heat. They vary considerably in their speed of rooting, from 10 weeks to 3–4 months. P 3–4 years.
Simple layering – spring or autumn. T 2 years.
Side-veneer or saddle grafting – late winter or late summer. Once the graft union has formed, harden off very slowly.
U about 7 weeks, P 24–30 months.
🌱 as soon as ripe, or in spring, at 13–16°C (55–61°F). Sow seed of hardy alpine species in a cold frame as soon as ripe. Surface-sow on finely milled moss peat. (Young seedlings are very sensitive to over-fertilizing.) They hybridize freely and garden-collected seed may not come true. P 2–3 years.
Softwood cuttings – early summer (deciduous Knaphill-type azaleas), in a mist propagator or with bottom heat. Well worth trying but success rate varies according to clone. T 8–12 weeks, P 24 months.

Rhus
Anacardiaceae

Genus of some 200 species of hardy to frost-tender, deciduous or evergreen shrubs, trees, and climbers. They are cultivated mainly for their pinnate leaves, which in deciduous species often colour well in autumn, and their erect, showy fruit clusters. They grow in any moderately fertile, well-drained soil, in partial shade or sun, but autumn colour is best in full sun.
R. typhina (Stag's horn sumach). Deciduous, spreading, suckering shrub with finely divided, pinnate leaves that colour brilliant red, yellow, and orange in autumn. It bears panicles of yellow-green flowers in summer that, on female plants, give rise to conical, red-furry fruit clusters that persist through winter. H 5m (15ft), S. 6m (20ft). **'Dissecta'**, syn. 'Laciniata', is more compact with very elegant, finely cut leaves. H to 2m (6ft).

PROPAGATION

🌱 species only. As soon as ripe in autumn, in a seedbed outdoors. P 2–3 years.
Semi-ripe cuttings – midsummer 10–12cm (4–5in) long, preferably under mist, or root in a propagator, with bottom heat.
T 4–5 months, P 16–18months.
🔧 separate suckers during the dormant period, between autumn and spring. Plant out immediately, or pot up and grow on until the roots are well established, then plant out in autumn or spring.

Ribes
Grossulariaceae

Some 150 species of mainly deciduous shrubs, of which *R. sanguineum* and its cultivars are the most commonly grown. Reliably hardy and floriferous, they thrive in almost any soil in sun or dappled shade.

They can be raised from seed, and will self-seed, but seedlings often produce flowers of washed-out or undistinguished colour.
R. sanguineum (Flowering currant). Vigorous deciduous, spreading shrub with clusters of rosy-pink flowers in spring and aromatic lobed leaves, like those of blackcurrants. **'Tydeman's White'** and **'White Icicle'** have white flower clusters; those of **'Pulborough Scarlet'** and **'King Edward VII'** are dark red. H and S to 2m (6ft).

PROPAGATION

Softwood cuttings – early summer, 8–10cm (3–4in) long. T 8 weeks P 18 months.
Hardwood cuttings – autumn, 25–30cm (10–12in) long. T 4–5 months, P 18 months.

Robinia
Leguminosae

Genus of between 4 and 20 species of bristly or thorny, deciduous trees and shrubs with finely divided foliage and pea-like flowers in spring or early summer. Most are useful for their tolerance of industrial pollution and poor, dry soils. Prefers sun.
R. pseudoacacia. A rapidly growing, suckering tree that is too large for many gardens. H to 15m (50ft), S 5m (15ft) or more. **'Frisia'** has golden leaves. It is more suited to smaller gardens. H to 15m (50ft) eventually.
'Umbraculifera', syn. 'Inermis' (Mop-head acacia) has a round-headed habit, and is thornless. H and S to 6m (20ft).

PROPAGATION

🌱 species only. As soon as ripe in autumn, in a cold frame. Spring-sown seed should be soaked or scarified. P 2–3 years.
Grafting – for cultivars, side-veneer grafting in winter onto seedling understock of the species. U 2–3 months, P 12–18 months.

Rosa moyesii

Rosa 'Gloire de Dijon'

Rosa 'Seagull'

Romneya   Papaveraceae

Just two species of frost-hardy, suckering
subshrubby perennials or shrubs.

R. coulteri (Tree poppy). Upright, deciduous
shrub, with divided, intensely glaucous,
blue-grey leaves, and large, poppy-like
white flowers with golden centres, from
midsummer to autumn. It needs a warm,
sheltered site in sun and may be cut to
the ground in hard winters, but usually re-
sprouts, especially if given a deep, dry winter
mulch. H 1–2.5m (3–8ft), S indefinite.

PROPAGATION

✂ separate suckers in spring. P immediately.

🌱 early spring, at 13–16°C (55–61°F). It will
germinate in 10–14 days. Overwinter young
plants under glass for their first winter.
P 15 months.

Root cuttings – winter, 2.5cm (1in) long, laid
horizontally on the compost. They will shoot
within 2–3 months, but leave undisturbed
until growing vigorously, usually by early
summer.

Rosa   Rosaceae

Although the genus *Rosa* comprises only
some 150 species of evergreen and
deciduous shrubs and climbers, the
extensive breeding and hybridization that
has been carried out – especially over the
last 300 or more years – has given rise to
many thousands of cultivars. The history of
their breeding and parentage is extremely
complex, and hybridizing has given rise to
such diversity of habit, leaf and flower form
and colour, that a system of horticultural
classification has been developed to bring
some order to their multiplicity. The three
main divisions are: species roses, the Old

roses and the Modern roses. The Old roses
are held by most authorities to be those
bred before the First World War and the
major groups include the **Albas**, **Gallicas**,
Damasks, **Centifolias** and their mossy
sports, the Moss roses, as well as more
recent developments like the **Teas**, **Chinas**,
Bourbons, **Portlands** and **Hybrid Perpetuals**.
Many of the Old roses produce only one
glorious flush of bloom in midsummer. The
best known of the Modern roses, many of
which are remontant, or repeat-flowering,
include the large-flowered bushes (the
Hybrid Teas), and cluster-flowered bushes
(the **Floribundas**), as well as the more
recent groups, like ground-cover, miniature,
and patio roses. Both Old and Modern
groups include examples of climbers and
ramblers. Roses are available in a huge range
of sizes and forms: H and S from 30cm
(12in) to 6m (20ft) or more.

Traditionally, nearly all named rose
cultivars are increased by budding in mid-
to late summer onto various rootstocks
that are selected for vigour and suitability
to climate and soil type. For example,
R. multiflora rootstocks prove especially
useful where winters are cold, and perform
reasonably well on relatively poor soils.
R. 'Laxa' is the most widely used rootstock;
it is hardy, almost thornless (and therefore
easy to handle) and performs reliably in a
range of soils and climates. It also has the
advantage that it does not sucker freely. On
other rootstocks, especially *R. canina*, bud-
grafted roses frequently produce suckers
from below the graft union, which must be
removed as soon as seen if they are not to
dominate and eventually out-compete the

grafted cultivar. Commercial rose nurseries
are geared to the large-scale production
of roses by budding. The primary reason
commercial growers use this method of
propagation is that it produces offspring
which are genetically identical to the parent
from which the scion material is taken,
producing saleable stocks – uniform in
habit, vigour and flowering performance –
relatively quickly. For the amateur grower,
when such uniformity is less important, it is
possible to propagate many named cultivars
using the range of techniques outlined
below. It is important, though, to bear in
mind that increasing by these means can
prove difficult. Parents may be reluctant to
root or can give rise to offspring that lack
the vigour of their budded parent. It is
certainly worthwhile experimenting,
however, with any notably vigorous cultivars
that you grow in your garden, and with
roses that are relatively simple hybrids or
cultivars of the species. These would include
cultivars of the shrub roses *R. pimpinellifolia*
and *R. rugosa*, and rampant ramblers or
climbers like 'Seagull', 'Gloire de Dijon'
or *R. filipes* 'Kiftsgate'. The propagation of
roses from seed – at least by the amateur
gardener – is restricted to the true species,
like *R. glauca*, *R. moyesii* or *R. hugonis*. The
species will come true from seed, although
you can expect a range of natural variation,
as with the offspring of any seed-raised
species. Commercial growers raise all new
cultivars from seed, by the process of
hybridization. Given their complex
parentage, offspring will be enormously
variable and the chances of producing a new
cultivar with all the required virtues of good

125

Sambucus nigra

Sorbus aucuparia

Styrax japonica

flower form and colour are remote for amateurs. Breeders take note of the chromosome numbers of parents and then undertake controlled cross-pollination by hand. The resulting seedlings are then grown on for 2 or more years before it becomes clear whether any will produce first-quality blooms. Even then, the hybridization process is only half complete; any promising offspring will subsequently be bulked up by budding, and these are put on trial for several years to assess their overall strengths and weaknesses.

PROPAGATION

 species only. Collect ripe hips in autumn and extract the seed from the flesh. Stratify for 3–6 weeks in a domestic refrigerator and sow in modular containers in a cold frame. They may germinate in the first spring, but can take 12–24 months, so do not discard the containers. P 2–3 years.

 suckering species and cultivars grown on their own roots (e.g. of *R. pimpinellifolia*, *R. rugosa*, and *R. gallica*). Separate suckers when dormant and grow on in a nursery bed. P 1–2 years.

Simple layering – after flowering, in summer. Suitable for many climbers and ramblers, and vigorous cultivars with flexible stems, such as Alba and Damask roses.
T 12 months, P 12–24 months.

Hardwood cuttings – early autumn, about 23cm (9in) long. Species and their cultivars, simple hybrids, ramblers, vigorous climbers, and miniature roses. Hybrid Teas and Floribundas may be slow to root by this method. T 12 months, P 2–24 months.

Semi-ripe cuttings – summer after flowering, 15cm (6in) long, in a propagator. Species and

their cultivars, simple hybrids, ramblers, vigorous climbers and miniature roses. Hybrid Teas and Floribundas may be slow to root by this method.
T 6–8 months, P 12–24 months.

Rubus   Rosaceae

Some 250 species of evergreen and deciduous shrubs that include blackberries, hybrid berries, and raspberries, which are grown for their fruit (*see p. 189*). The more ornamental kinds are grown for their flowers and foliage, or for their very attractive winter shoots. Those in cultivation are hardy. They grow in any well-drained, moderately fertile soil, in sun or dappled shade; those grown for winter shoots produce the best results in full sun.
R. 'Benenden'. Smooth-stemmed, deciduous shrub with lobed, dark leaves and large, pure white, cupped flowers in spring and early summer. H and S to 3m (10ft).
R. cockburnianus. Suckering, deciduous shrub whose primary ornamental value is its white-bloomed shoots in winter. It has dark leaves that are white-hairy beneath, and produces small, purple flowers at the stem tips in summer. H and S 2.5m (8ft).
R. thibetanus. Similar to *R. cockburnianus*, with grey-hairy leaves. H and S 2.5m (8ft).

PROPAGATION

Hardwood cuttings – autumn to early winter, 20–25cm (8–10in) long.
T 6–9 months, P 12–24 months.
Simple layering – autumn, for *R.* 'Benenden'.
T 9 months, P 12 months.

 separate rooted suckers of suckering species in early autumn or spring, and replant immediately.

Sambucus   Caprifoliaceae

Some 25 species of hardy, herbaceous perennials and deciduous shrubs and trees. Grow in humus-rich, moist but well-drained soil in sun or light shade. *S. nigra* and *S. racemosa* (Red-berried elder) have a number of cultivars with very attractive foliage, that colours well in autumn. Among the finest are *S. nigra* **'Guincho Purple'**, with deep purple leaves turning red in autumn, H and S 6m (20ft); **'Laciniata'**, with finely cut leaflets turning red and gold in autumn, is a similar size. *S. racemosa* **'Plumosa Aurea'** has very finely cut, golden yellow leaves, that need shade from hot sun; it is ideal for brightening dark corners. H and S 3m (10ft).

PROPAGATION

Hardwood cuttings – late autumn to winter, 25cm (10in) long, with a heel to avoid exposing the pith. T 1 year, P 15 months.

Sorbus   Rosaceae

Some 100 species of hardy, deciduous trees and shrubs, valued for their habit, fruit and leaves. Grow in well-drained soil in sun; most prefer acid to neutral soil. The species come true from seed. Cultivars are propagated by T-budding, chip-budding, in summer, or whip-and-tongue grafting in winter.
S. aucuparia (Mountain ash). Has dark green, pinnate leaves often colouring brilliantly in autumn. Orange-red berries. H 15m (50ft), S 7m (22ft).
S. cashmiriana. White fruit; dark green, pinnate leaves. H 8m (25ft), S 7m (22ft).
S. hupehensis. Pink fruit; blue-green leaflets. H and S 8m (25ft).
S. vilmorinii. Crimson fruit, becoming white; glossy pinnate leaves, H and S 5m (15ft).

Vitis 'Brandt'

Weigela florida 'Variegata'

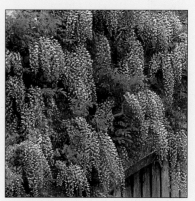

Wisteria floribunda

PROPAGATION

🌱 sown as soon as ripe in a cold frame, usually germinates in spring. Clean from the flesh. P 12–24 months, or more.

Styrax Styracaceae

About 100 species of deciduous or evergreen shrubs and small trees. Plant in moist, humus-rich, neutral to acid soil.
S. japonica. Graceful, deciduous tree with pendent, bell-shaped flowers in early summer. Hardy, but may suffer damage from late frosts, so site with some shade from morning sun. H 10m (30ft), S 8m (25ft).

PROPAGATION

🌱 as soon as ripe. Keep at 15°C (59°F) for 3 months, then transfer to the bottom of a domestic refrigerator for 3 months. Bring under glass when signs of germination are seen. P 18–24 months.
Softwood cuttings – late June to early July, 6cm (2½in) long, in a propagator with gentle bottom heat.
T 6–8 weeks, P 24 months.

Symphoricarpos Caprifoliaceae

About 17 species of hardy, deciduous shrubs that will grow in any well-drained soil in sun. They are grown for their fleshy, round fruit.
S. albus (Snowberry). Small shrub with slender, erect shoots forming dense thickets. Insignificant flowers in summer are followed by large, globose white berries which persist through winter. H and S 2m (6ft).

PROPAGATION

Hardwood cuttings – autumn, 20–25cm (8–10in) long. T 1 year, P 2 years.
🔧 separate suckers when dormant and replant immediately.

Viburnum Caprifoliaceae

About 150 species of hardy to frost-hardy, evergreen and deciduous shrubs. Grow in moderately fertile, well-drained soil in sun or partial shade. This is a versatile genus with many lovely species offering sweetly scented flowers, ornamental fruits, and attractive foliage which, in deciduous species, often colours beautifully in autumn. The white-flowered *V. farreri* (H 3m/10ft) and *V. grandiflorum* (H 2m/6ft) and the pink-flowered *V. x bodnantense* (H 3m/10ft), flower on upright leafless branches from late autumn and in mild spells from winter to spring. *V. tinus* (Laurustinus) is an evergreen shrub (H 3m/10ft), useful as a hedge or specimen, and flowers from late autumn to early spring. Most of the remaining species, including *V. carlesii*, *V. x carlecephalum*, *V. x burkwoodii*, *V. dilatatum* and *V. x juddii*, are spring- and summer-flowering. H to 3m (10ft), S to 2m (8ft).

PROPAGATION

Softwood cuttings – early summer, 8–10cm (3–4in) long. T 4 weeks, P 2–3 years.
Semi-ripe cuttings – mid- to late summer, 8–10cm (3–4in) long, with a heel, in a propagator with gentle bottom heat.
T 4 weeks, P 2–3 years.

Vitis Vitaceae

About 65 species of hardy, deciduous, mostly climbing shrubs, some with edible fruits. Grow in fertile, well-drained soil in sun.
V. 'Brandt'. A vigorous, deciduous climber, with a dual purpose: it produces sweet black grapes in favourable years, and its green leaves colour red and purple, highlighted with yellow veins in autumn. H 7m (22ft).

PROPAGATION

Vine-eyes – winter.
Hardwood cuttings – late winter, 25–30cm (10–12in) long, outdoors or in an open frame. T 12 months, P 18–24 months.

Weigela Caprifoliaceae

Some 12 species of deciduous shrubs, most commonly grown as named cultivars. They bear tubular white, pink or deep ruby-red flowers in early summer. Grow in well-drained soil in sun or light shade.
W. florida. Has dark pink flowers in mid-spring, 'Variegata' has white-margined leaves. H and S to 2.5m (9ft).

PROPAGATION

Softwood cuttings – early summer, 10–12cm (4–5in) long. T 6 weeks, P 18–24 months.
Hardwood cuttings – autumn, 20–25cm (8–10in) long. T 12 months, P 18–24 months.

Wisteria Leguminosae

Genus of 10 species of hardy, vigorous, twining, deciduous climbers. *W. floribunda* (Japanese wisteria) flowers in early summer, and the larger and more vigorous *W. sinensis* (Chinese wisteria) blooms in late spring and early summer. Both bear long, pendent racemes of violet-blue, pink or white flowers, to 30cm (12in) or more in length. Several named cultivars with longer racemes or more strongly coloured flowers are available. Provide support in fertile, well-drained soil in sun or part shade. H 9m (28ft) or more.

PROPAGATION

Serpentine layering – spring. T 1 year.
Softwood cuttings – early summer. Take basal cuttings of side shoots, 8–10cm (3–4in) long. T 6–7 weeks, P 12–18 months.

$\mathcal{H}$OUSEPLANTS

Most gardeners want to bring the garden into the home. Fortunately, there are many plants suitable for growing indoors that can be enjoyed when it is too cold or wet to venture outside. Many tolerate low light levels, while others, such as the cacti and succulents, thrive in the dry atmosphere of centrally heated rooms, provided they have sufficient light.

Most houseplants originate from the subtropical or tropical zone and make rapid growth given the conditions that suit them. Most of the methods described in this chapter will produce new plants much more quickly than for hardy, cool-climate plants. You can easily increase your stocks of houseplants in the comfort of your home when forays outdoors seem unappealing.

◄ *Even naturally long-lived*
houseplants occasionally succumb to
the less than ideal conditions in the
modern home. Propagating them
regularly helps ensure your stock.

WHY PROPAGATE
HOUSEPLANTS?

Although some houseplants can be cherished into a venerable old age, many lose their charms over the years and hence are best replaced from time to time. The satisfaction that comes from propagating those replacements for yourself is tremendous, giving a treasured pot plant the chance of immortality through reincarnation.

Houseplants include a number of plant groups; some are increased by methods seldom used for outdoor plants.

GROWING FROM SEED

A few houseplants are regularly raised from seed, notably *Coleus* and *Cacti*. For some, the treatment is the same as for half-hardy annuals, but others have more specialized requirements. In general, seed will germinate at 5°C (9°F) higher than the average minimum temperature required for growth.

VEGETATIVE TECHNIQUES

Many shrubby houseplants, including some of the succulents, can be increased by cuttings as easily as their hardy counterparts, but most need bottom heat, as supplied by a soil-warming cable or heated propagator, to root successfully. For suitable subjects, large quantities of new plants can also be propagated quickly by leaf cuttings. Indeed, in some cases, a single leaf can be used to produce many offspring.

There are many reasons why you should wish to propagate your own houseplants. First and foremost, since even the best cared for plants need replacing in time, it is far more economical to create your own stocks of reserve plants than to purchase expensive replacements from commercial growers.

Some houseplants, such as *Ficus elastica*, will eventually outgrow their allotted space in the home and so need to be replaced periodically with smaller specimens. Others can lose their natural habit in time when confined in a pot, becoming gaunt, lop-sided or top-heavy as they stretch towards the light. Shrubby houseplants can also develop bare patches down low as they age, caused by the periods of dormancy that gardeners in cold climates must often impose in order to overwinter them successfully.

In their wild habitats, many of the plants that we grow as houseplants are vigorous and more or less permanently in growth. For this reason, most can be increased extremely rapidly, though some form of supplementary heating is generally required.

SIMPLE DIVISION

Houseplants that develop a crown can be increased by division, rather like herbaceous perennials. This procedure is best carried out when the plant has outgrown its container and is just coming into growth in spring. Many orchids can be divided, but the divisions must be of a certain size, so only a few new plants may be produced. Whereas on other plants the old growth is generally discarded, on orchids the

Dracaena marginata 'Tricolor'
This houseplant often becomes bare of leaves at the base, but may be cut back and renewed by rooting leafless stem sections in gentle bottom heat in early summer.

Saintpaulia
The legion cultivars of the African violet do not come true from seed, but are easily increased by single leaf cuttings, which will root within 2–3 weeks in summer.

dormant back-bulbs can also be used for propagation. Some bromeliads and succulents produce a central rosette of leaves around which new plantlets form. The central rosette produces a flowering shoot and then, in many cases, dies off, leaving daughter rosettes behind. These daughter plantlets (offsets) can be removed and grown on.

AIR LAYERING

This is a method of propagation for large plants that, in the wild, would layer themselves in the surrounding soil. This habit can seldom be accommodated in a container, but suitable stems can be encouraged to produce roots by air layering without the need to bring them down to ground level.

Propagation from Plantlets

There are several houseplants that produce completely formed young plantlets which grow whilst still attached to the parent plant. These young plantlets are, in effect, ready-made propagules, and increasing stock from them is usually very simple. Chlorophytum comosum, *the spider plant, is well known for producing cascades*

of young plants on its flowered stems. They root easily if introduced to a pot of compost and pinned down onto the compost surface.

A *Chlorophytum comosum* 'Variegatum' with numerous young plantlets hanging from its stems.

(3)

Chlorophytum comosum
Raising variegated cultivars of the spider plant is so simple that it does not matter that seed is not an option. Increase by division or plantlets at any time of year except winter.

(4)

Echeveria
An example of one of the rosette-forming succulents that produce ready-made propagules in the form of daughter rosettes. They can also be propagated by stem or single-leaf cuttings.

(5)

Aglaonema
This is one of many foliage plants that seldom set seed in cultivation, and rely on vegetative forms of increase. When parent plants become leggy, divide or separate basal suckers in spring.

PROPAGATING TECHNIQUES
HOUSEPLANTS

Since the plants that we choose to containerize and grow indoors come from an extremely diverse range of native habitats, there are a similarly large number of techniques by which they can be propagated. Many of these methods, such as raising begonias from a cut leaf, are extremely simple while others require a little more attention.

Representatives of a huge diversity of plant groups are grown as houseplants, many of which have tropical or subtropical origins. Some are propagated by methods common to other groups, some use modifications of these techniques and a few, like orchids and succulents, use techniques that are unique to their group.

SEED

In most cases, when houseplants can be raised from seed, they are sown in the normal way. The main difference is that higher temperatures are need to germinate and grow on tropical and subtropical species. As a rule of thumb, seed will germinate at 5°C (9°F) higher than the minimum needed for normal growth.

In nature, most cacti and succulents grow in hot, dry conditions in sharply drained soils, restricting their growing cycle to periods when sufficient moisture is available for growth. Similar conditions must be provided for successful seed germination.

Use a proprietary cactus seed compost or make your own by mixing two parts of soil-less seed mix with one part of washed 6mm (¼in) grit.

Water in the seeds by misting with a hand-held sprayer to reduce the risk of overwatering. Sow in late winter so that seedlings make maximum growth to enable them to survive the following winter. Germination will occur at 19°C (66°F) but will be more rapid at 21–27°C (70–81°F).

Sowing seed of cacti and succulents . . . .

The best time to sow seed of cacti and other succulents is from late winter to late spring. Some fine seed is slow to germinate. Some large seeds may need stratifying for 2 days.

► 1 Prepare a 12.5cm (5in) plastic halfpot by placing a layer of broken clay crocks at the bottom, topped off with a 1cm (½in) layer of mixed gravel and charcoal. Fill the pot to within 1cm (½in) of the pot rim with seed compost. Sow the seed thinly and evenly on the surface of the compost. Water in by misting over with a hand-held sprayer.

◄ 2 Barely cover the compost surface with a layer of fine grit. Enclose the pot in a clear plastic bag, inflate and seal, and germinate at a temperature of 19–27°C (66–81°F).

Growing *Tillandsia* by seed . . . .

Most bromeliads are sown in seed compost in a pot as for cacti (*see left*), but *Tillandsia* seed germinates better if sown on a bundle of moistened moss and twigs.

▲ Mix moistened, live sphagnum moss throughout a bundle of conifer twigs, and tie with wire or raffia. Sprinkle seed thinly onto the surface of the bundle. Each tiny seed has a coma, or tuft, of hair and will cling onto the fine strands of damp moss. Water the bundle evenly by misting with a hand-held sprayer. Suspend the bundle in a light, airy place at 27°C (81°F).

Dividing orchids ....

Some orchids can be propagated by dividing into one or more pieces. Division should also be used to re-invigorate a mature plant, especially one that has become potbound.

▲ **1** Lift the entire plant (such as the *Cymbidium* shown here) from its pot and separate it into sections by hand, each with at least three healthy pseudobulbs. Remove the leafless back-bulbs, discarding any shrivelled ones and retaining plump, green ones for repotting. Trim up each section by removing any dead, shrivelled, dark brown roots with a pair of sharp secateurs.

◄ **2** Re-plant each section, setting the oldest pseudobulbs against the back edge of the pot, so that the plump, young ones, which have short, fresh green leaves, lie towards the front centre of the pot. The new growth will then have space to spread forwards in the pot. Ensure that the pseudo-bulbs are planted at the same level as they were before dividing. Fill with orchid compost, tapping the pot gently so that the compost is shaken down around and between the roots.

Propagating *Tillandsia* by seed

Tillandsias are bromeliads that mostly grow epiphytically in nature; they do not grow in soil as other plants do, but attach themselves to tree trunks by a reduced root system that serves as anchorage. The leaves absorb food and moisture from mist and rainfall. To germinate successfully, *Tillandsia* seed needs treatment that mimics conditions found in the wild. One way of doing this is to provide a substrate that is similar to the mossy bark upon which they would germinate naturally. Bundle evergreen conifer twigs and living sphagnum moss together and bind them with raffia or twine. Sprinkle the seed onto the surface and water it thoroughly by misting with a hand-held sprayer. Suspend the bundle in a light, airy but draught-free place at a temperature of 27°C (81°F) and mist over regularly. Seedlings germinate in about 3–4 weeks. When they are large enough to handle, they can be transferred to a 'bromeliad tree' or slab of bark.

DIVISION

Many houseplants, especially clump-forming or herbaceous sorts, like *Chlorophytum* or *Aspidistra*, can be divided in early spring as described for herbaceous perennials (*see p.29*). Water them well, slip the root ball from the pot and separate it into sections by hand. Re-plant the divisions into clean pots containing the same growing mix as that for the parent plant.

Dividing orchids

Some orchids, like *Cymbidium* and *Cattleya,* produce new growth from the ends of rhizomes to form stems that swell to form pseudobulbs, which act as water-storage organs. This type of orchid can often be increased by division. The process differs slightly from normal division in that, as well as a growing point, each piece needs at least three pseudobulbs if the new plant is to be large enough to establish and survive.

A few orchids will fall apart into sections when removed from the pot. If they do not, cut through the rhizome with a sharp knife to separate the sections.

STEM CUTTINGS

Some houseplants can be propagated by stem cuttings, although there are variations on the technique. With orchids like *Dendrobium* the process is simply a matter of cutting leafless stems into sections as shown below, at

Increasing orchids by stem cuttings ....

A number of orchids, such as *Dendrobium* or *Epidendrum*, produce long, cane-like stems, which make excellent material for propagation by stem cuttings.

◄ **1** Divide some of the parent plant into sections, 25cm (10in) long, by cutting its cane-like stems with a straight cut either at the base or just above a leaf node. Further subdivide each section into 7.5cm (3in) pieces, cutting midway between nodes, so that each piece has at least one node.

► **2** Set the pieces neatly on the surface of a seed tray of moistened sphagnum moss and place in a humid environment in good light but out of direct sunlight. The new plantlets should appear after a few weeks.

the beginning of the growing season. Each piece must have at least one node from which a dormant bud will break. They may take several months to root and can then be potted up individually.

Cacti and succulents from stem cuttings

With succulent plants like *Kalanchoe* and *Crassula* (*see right*) the technique for stem cuttings is very simple, although it differs slightly from other stem cuttings. To reduce the risk of rotting, the wound made in the stem base must be allowed to dry out and callus over before insertion and the cuttings must not be too long. Cuttings are best made in spring at the end of the dormancy to allow a full season's growth before the next winter's dormancy.

Select a sturdy stem and remove it from the parent plant with a straight cut just above a bud. Trim it down to 5–7.5cm (2–3in) in length, again with a straight cut at the base, and remove the lowest leaves to leave about 2.5cm (1in) of bare stem. If the wounded stem bleeds, dip it in lukewarm water and staunch the flow from the parent plant's stem by pressing gently with a pad of damp cloth. Avoid all skin contact with the sap; it is highly irritant in many succulent species. Place the cutting in a warm, dry place for about 48 hours.

Propagating by offsets . . . .

Many bromeliads and succulents can be increased by offsets, young rosettes which form at the base of the parent plant that may be detached and rooted.

▶ I For succulents, remove the offset and place the cut end just below the surface of the compost. Top-dress with grit to keep it in place and to help avoid rotting at the neck.

◀ 2 Bromeliads such as *Neoregelia carolinae* produce daughter offsets after the main rosette has flowered and begun to die back. Leave daughter rosettes in place until they reach one-third of the size of the parent rosette before removing at their base with a sharp knife.

Succulents from stem cuttings . . . .

Some cacti and other succulents such as *Crassula* can be increased by stem cuttings taken at the end of the dormant season, in spring (or autumn for winter-growing plants).

▲ I With a straight cut across the base, sever a stem tip bearing 2–3 pairs of leaves, 5–7.5cm (2–3in) long. Remove the lowest leaves, by pulling them off, to retain 2.5cm (1in) of bare stem. Set the cutting in a warm, dry place for about 48 hours to allow the cut to callus over.

▲ 2 Fill a pot with a mixture of equal parts peat and grit or sharp sand. Insert the prepared cutting vertically and centrally in the pot, almost to the depth of the bottom leaves. Top-dress with a 1cm (½in) layer of grit. Then leave in an airy place in light shade, at 18–24°C (64–75°F).

Insert the cutting just deep enough so that it remains upright in the potting medium and top-dress with a layer of grit. Rooting takes place within 2–6 weeks and the young plant should then be potted on when the roots fill the pot.

OFFSETS

Many plant groups that are grown as houseplants, including succulents and bromeliads, are rosette-formers that produce daughter rosettes around the base of the main parent plant. To increase succulents from daughter rosettes, remove the top dressing of grit from base of parent plant. Cut off the daughter offset with a straight cut, using a sharp knife, just where it arises from base of parent. Allow to callus over for about 48 hours in a warm, dry place. Insert the rosette into a prepared pot containing a mix of equal parts peat and grit, with the base just below the surface. Top-dress with grit so that the lowest leaves just rest on the gritty surface. As new growth appears, pot on the young plantlet into standard cactus compost, and top-dress with grit.

Many bromeliads produce rosettes that die after they flower. As the parent rosette begins to die, a new daughter rosette emerges from its base. When the daughter rosette reaches about a third of the size of the

Succulents propagation by leaf cuttings ....

Many rosette-forming succulents can easily be increased from cuttings of entire leaves which can produce new plants from dormant buds at their base.

▲ Remove a healthy, young but fully formed leaf from the parent rosette by either pulling off or cutting off at the base with a sharp knife. Allow the leaf base to callus over. Insert the leaf in a prepared pot of cuttings compost at a slight angle, just deep enough so that the cutting remains in position. Top-dress with a layer of grit. Place in a propagator at 18–21°C (64–70°F). The new plantlet appears at the base of the leaf just above the soil surface.

parent rosette, sever the daughter rosette at the base with a sharp knife. If it has already begun to develop roots, take care to retain them. Set the new rosette into a pot of bromeliad compost, just deeply enough so that it stays in place.

LEAF CUTTINGS

A number of species and cultivars – usually belonging to the families Begoniaceae, Crassulaceae, and Gesneriaceae – grown as houseplants are capable of forming new plantlets from whole leaves or from sections of the leaves. The phenomenon is seldom seen in hardy woody plants because the cell tissues of their leaves cannot differentiate to form roots and buds.

Leaf cuttings of succulents

Many succulents, including rosette-formers like *Echeveria*, *Crassula*, *Gasteria*, *Haworthia*, *Sedum*, and *Pachyphytum*, will produce new plantlets from the base of whole leaves. For most the best time for taking leaf cuttings is in spring, just as the plant resumes active growth. As with stem cuttings of succulents, once the leaf has been removed from the parent plant, it should be set aside to callus over for about 48 hours.

Select plump, healthy, young but mature leaves and pull them from the parent plant at their base, or remove them with a clean cut made with a sharp blade. Almost fill a 5–7.5cm (2–3in) pot with a mix of equal parts fine

moss peat and sharp sand or grit. Set the callused leaf base on the surface of the cuttings mix, and top-dress with a layer of grit.

Place the pot in a partially shaded propagator at 18–21°C (64–70°F). Mist with tepid water to keep the cuttings barely moist (too much water and high humidity will cause rotting).

Rooting takes between three and twelve weeks to occur, although some roots will form on fast-rooting species within a few days. When plantlets appear at the base of the leaf, allow them to grow on for a further two weeks before potting them up in cactus compost.

Leaf sections

A number of cacti and succulents can be increased by leaf sections. These include succulents, like *Sansevieria*, and cacti, like *Epiphyllum*, with flat, leaf-like stems, and *Opuntia*, with flattened pad-like segments. In the last, each pad is used as an individual cutting.

Select a plump, healthy, fully expanded leaf or stem, and cut it into sections, making a clean cut straight with a sharp knife. For easy handling, make sections between 5–10cm (2–4in) long. Allow the wound to callus over. Use the smallest pot that will contain the cutting comfortably and fill it almost to the rim with proprietary cactus compost or a mix of equal parts peat and grit or sharp sand. Gently push the cutting into the surface of the medium, just deep enough so that the cutting does not fall over. Be sure to insert the cutting with the correct orientation. Top-dress with grit to hold the cutting in place and, if necessary, stake it with a split cane to keep it upright.

Leaf sections ....

Cacti such as *Epiphyllum*, and *Schlumbergera* and succulents like *Sansevieria*, which have fleshy, flattened, stem-like leaves, can be propagated by leaf sections.

► Cut a stem-like leaf into sections, 5–10cm (2–4in) long, using a straight cut across the leaf. Prepare a 3.5–5cm (1½–2in) pot by filling it with crocks, gravel and charcoal, to one-third of the pot's depth, and then topping up with gritty compost to within 1cm (½in) of the brim. In each pot, insert one cutting just deep enough for the stem to remain vertical; only the base should touch the compost. Top-dress with grit.

Saintpaulia from whole leaves ················

Saintpaulias, or African violets, can successfully be increased from a complete leaf and its stalk. This can be done at any time of year provided a suitable leaf is available.

◄ **1** From the parent plant, take an entire, healthy, young but fully developed leaf with its leaf stalk. Trim the stalk 2.5–3cm (1–1¼in) below the leaf blade, using a straight cut. Dibble a hole into a pot filled with a mix of equal parts peat and sharp sand. Insert the leaf stalk so that the leaf blade just touches the compost surface.

▶ **2** Cover the pot with an inverted cloche (a cut-off plastic mineral water bottle is ideal). Set in a warm place in good light but away from direct sunlight. New plantlets will appear at the base of the leaf. Remove the cloche cover when they appear. When they are large enough to handle, separate and pot up individually.

Place the pot in a partially shaded propagator at a temperature of 18–21°C (64–70°F). Mist over with tepid water to keep the cuttings just moist.

Each leaf section takes between three and ten weeks to root and begin to grow away. You may find that slow-growing plants do not root properly before winter. If this happens, keep cuttings completely dry during the dormant period; they should begin to grow on the following season.

Taking cuttings from half leaves ···············

Disease can be a major problem when propagating from half leaves so ensure that all tools and other equipment are totally clean and that the parent plant (here *Streptocarpus*) is healthy.

Take an unblemished, mature leaf and cut it longitudinally into two halves by stripping out the midrib. This exposes the leaf veins. Place each leaf half, cut edge downward, in a shallow trench in a prepared seed tray containing a moistened mix of equal parts peat and sharp sand. Seal in an inflated plastic bag or place in a propagator at 18–24°C (64–75°F). The new plants will appear at intervals along the cut edge. When they are large enough to handle, lift, separate and pot up.

Propagating by cuttings of entire leaves

A number of rosette-formers with fleshy leaves, like saintpaulias (African violets) and other members of its group (gesneriads), such as *Sinningia* (gloxinias), are easily increased from cuttings of entire leaves. Select young, healthy, fully formed and undamaged leaves; they can be rooted at 20–25°C (68–77°F) at any time of year, but are best taken during periods of active growth. They take three to four weeks to produce roots and a further eight to ten weeks to form plantlets that are sufficiently large to be potted on.

Saintpaulia leaves will also root if the petiole is placed in water, in a dark glass bottle. This is slightly slower than rooting in compost and the leaf must be potted on as soon as the roots reach 15mm (⅝in) in length; long roots are too easily damaged when potting up.

Cuttings of half leaves

Large-leaved gesneriads such as *Streptocarpus* (Cape primrose) are also capable of producing plantlets from their leaves, although, in this case, slightly different techniques are more successful. The most usual method is from half leaves as shown below left, although they can also be induced to produce new plantlets by scoring through the leaf veins, or sectioning the leaves, as described for begonias.

Propagating from leaf squares

Any plant with the capacity to produce plantlets from their leaves can be increased rapidly by leaf squares but in general the technique is restricted to large-leaved

Propagation from leaf squares ···············

This technique is particularly useful for plants with big leaves, especially begonias, although any leaf that can be propagated vegetatively can be increased in this way.

Take a healthy, young but mature leaf (here *Begonia rex*) and cut out several 1–2cm (½–¾in) squares, each with a strong leaf vein at its centre. Place the cut squares on the surface of moistened compost with the veined side in contact with the compost surface. Carefully pin down each leaf square with wire. Enclose the seed tray in an inflated, plastic bag and seal tightly. Set in a warm place, at 18–24°C (64–75°F), in good light but away from direct sunlight. Remove the cover once the plantlets appear.

Increasing plants from cut leaves . . . .

Plantlet development can be induced in certain plants such as begonias with netted veining on their leaves by making regular slashes across these veins but not cutting up the entire leaf.

◄ **1** Place a healthy, young but mature leaf of a *Begonia rex* flat on a work surface with its underside facing upwards. Make 1cm (½in) cuts at intervals across the main veins.

► **2** Place the leaf, cut side down, on a prepared tray of compost. Pin across the veins to hold the cut edges against the compost surface. Enclose the seed tray in an inflated, plastic bag and seal. Leave in good light but out of direct sunlight, in a warm place at a temperature of 18–24°C (64–75°F). New plants will appear at the cut edges. When they are large enough to handle, lift, separate and pot up individually.

plants with a network of prominent leaf veins, as seen in most large-leaved begonias. The leaves are cut into 2cm (¾in) squares with a sharp blade such as a razor blade; each square must contain a portion of a principal vein. Any torn tissue should be discarded as it will rot and may infect the healthy squares.

The leaf squares are then pinned down on the surface of a moist propagating mix of equal parts peat and sharp sand or perlite with the veins facing downwards. The cut surfaces must make good contact with the propagating mix. Given a temperature of 18–24°C (64–75°F) in a sealed, inflated plastic bag they will root and form plantlets in about six weeks. Make sure that the plastic bag is kept inflated so that it does not touch the leaf squares.

Begonias from scored leaves

Propagating from scored leaves is another technique for large-leaved plants with prominent veins. In this case, the undersides of the leaves are scored across the main veins to a length of 1cm (½in) at intervals about 2.5cm (1in) apart. The whole leaf is pinned down, veins downwards, onto a moist propagating medium.

Buds will form at the site of the wounds, which then produce roots and, after about six weeks, small clumps

of plantlets. The plantlets can be separated carefully and potted up as soon as they are large enough to handle.

AIR LAYERING

Air layering is ideal for propagating stout-stemmed species such as *Ficus elastica*, the rubber plant, or *Monstera deliciosa*, both of which will eventually outgrow their planting situation. The parent plant may be either discarded or cut back hard after propagating its replacement.

Air layers are best made towards the top of the plant, since stems less than two years old root most easily. The illustration below shows a sleeve of clear plastic for clarity, but better results may be obtained by using black-and-white plastic with the white side facing outwards since this reduces undesirable temperature fluctuations within the sleeve. New roots may take several months to form and it is essential that the moss wadding remains moist during the rooting period. If necessary, unwrap the sleeve and re-moisten by misting.

Air-layering a *Ficus elastica* . . . .

Air-layering is an ideal way of replacing leggy plants that have outgrown their allotted space and has the advantage that the new plant forms roots while still attached to its parent.

► **1** Trim the leaves from a straight piece of stem. Attach a plastic sleeve to the stem, fixing its lower end with adhesive tape. Wound the stem by cutting a tongue into it, with an upward, slanting cut, 5mm (¼in) deep and 2.5cm (1in) long. Apply rooting hormone and wedge the tongue open by padding it with moistened sphagnum moss. Wrap the adjacent stem area with a wad of moistened sphagnum moss and roll the plastic sleeve up over it.

◄ **2** Seal the top of the sleeve with adhesive tape. New roots will grow into the wad of moss. When they fill the plastic sleeve, sever the rooted stem section from the parent plant. Gently loosen the moss ball to separate the roots. Pot up into a prepared pot of compost, firming the compost gently around the roots. Place in a semi-shaded place and water sparingly until the new plant is well established.

HOUSEPLANTS

Below are instructions and special propagating tips on individual conservatory and houseplants. Unless otherwise specified, follow the detailed instructions given under the propagation section, on pages 132–137.

Key
H Height
S Spread
🌱 By seed
🔧 By division
🌿 Germination

Achimenes (Hot water plant)
Gesneriaceae

Some 25 species of perennials, and a number of named hybrids and cultivars, with tuber-like rhizomes, that are valued as houseplants for their long-tubed, salver-shaped flowers. The flowers, in a range of colours, are borne above glossy green leaves for long periods in late summer and autumn. Plants become dormant in winter, after flowering. They need bright light with shade from direct sun, and a minimum temperature of 10–15°C (50–59°F).

A. grandiflora. Upright in habit, this has dark green leaves and bears red-purple flowers with white eyes and purple-dotted throats. H and S to 60cm (24in).

A. longiflora. Trailing habit and soft red, lavender, or deep purple flowers. H 25cm (10in), S to 40cm (16in).

PROPAGATION
🔧 early spring.
Time to flowering – 6 months.
Stem cuttings – spring.
Time to rooting – 2–3 weeks.
Time to flowering – 6 months.

Agave (Century plant)
Agavaceae

Over 200 species of succulent perennials with rosettes of fleshy, spine-tipped leaves. A number are valued as houseplants for their architectural form. At maturity, they bear long-stemmed, terminal clusters of funnel-shaped flowers, from the centre of the rosette. Some species die after flowering, but these can take 40 years to bloom and then usually leave daughter rosettes to grow on. All need good light and a very gritty, sharply-drained potting compost. They should be kept almost completely dry in winter.

A. americana 'Marginata'. Slow-growing, with evergreen rosettes of lance-shaped, grey-green leaves with creamy yellow margins. Min. temp. 5°C (41°F). H to 2m (6ft), S to 3m (10ft), much less as a houseplant.

A. victoriae-reginae. Produces exceptionally neat and symmetrical rosettes of plump, fleshy, oblong-triangular, dark green leaves, outlined with white. Min. temp. 10°C (50°F). H and S 50cm (20in).

PROPAGATION
🌱 early spring, at 21°C (70°F). Species only.
🌿 up to 3 months.
Offsets – spring or autumn.
Time to rooting – 2–4 weeks.

Aloe
Liliaceae

About 300 species of evergreen, succulent, rosette-forming perennials grown as houseplants for their sculptural form and racemes of tubular flowers. All species need full light and a sharply drained, loam-based potting compost with added grit. They should be kept almost dry in winter. Those featured need a minimum temperature of 10°C (50°F).

A. aristata. Clumps of stemless rosettes of lance-shaped, dark green leaves, dotted with tiny soft, white spines, and producing orange-red flowers in autumn. H 12cm (5in), S 30cm (12in) often much more.

A. variegata (Partridge-breasted aloe). Has rosettes of firm, green leaves with bands of greenish white. Pink or red flowers are borne on fleshy stems in summer. H 20cm (8in), S 30cm (12in) often much more.

PROPAGATION
🌱 early spring, at 21°C (70°F). Species only.
🌿 up to 3 months.
Offsets – spring to early summer. Offsets can often be separated from the parent with roots already formed.
Time to rooting – 2–4 weeks.

Aspidistra
Liliaceae

Three species of evergreen, rhizomatous perennials of which A. elatior is the most commonly grown. Noted for its tolerance of dry atmospheres, a wide temperature range,

Achimenes 'Primadonna'

Agave victoriae-reginae

Aloe aristata

Aspidistra elatior 'Variegata'

Begonia masoniana

poor soils, and low light, it has long been used as a houseplant, and can make an elegant specimen when well-grown.

A. elatior. Produces long-stalked, lance-shaped, glossy, dark green leaves that arise from clustered rhizomes. The insignificant flowers appear at the leaf stalk bases in late winter or early summer. **'Variegata'** has dark green leaves striped or margined with creamy white. H and S to 60cm (24in).

PROPAGATION

✄ early spring.

Begonia   Begoniaceae

An enormous genus of some 900 species, many of which are grown as houseplants for their foliage or flowers. Most grow best at temperatures of 19–24°C (66–75°F) but, if kept on the dry side in winter, will tolerate 10°C (50°F). All thrive in partial shade and need protection from direct sun. They are divided into several groups.

Rex-cultorum begonias. Evergreen, usually rhizomatous perennials, with asymmetrically ovate to lance-shaped leaves in a wide range of colours, many marked, striped, or margined with dark velvety red, bright pink, silvery green, and other metallic shades. Examples: *B.* 'Duartei', *B.* 'Helen Lewis', *B.* 'Merry Christmas'.
H and S 12–75cm (6–30in).

Tuberous begonias. Deciduous perennials, becoming dormant in winter, producing top-growth annually from a tuber. Some cultivars are used in summer bedding, but many, including the Tuberhybrida, Multiflora, and Pendula types are also grown as summer-flowering houseplants for their large, brilliantly coloured, usually double, satin-

textured flowers. Examples include *B.* 'Billie Langdon', *B.* 'Can-Can', *B.* 'Flamboyant'. H 60cm (24in), S 45cm (18in).

Rhizomatous begonias. Evergreen perennials with creeping rhizomes, grown mainly for their leaves, which often have interesting textures and colours and may be puckered, crested, and/or marked with metallic silver. Examples: *B.* 'Bethlehem Star', *B. imperialis*, *B. masoniana* (the Iron Cross begonia), *B.* 'Norah Bedson'. H 13–50cm (5–20in), S 23–45cm (9–18in).

Semperflorens begonias. Fibrous-rooted perennials with mounds of evergreen, glossy, green or bronze, usually rounded leaves, bearing a succession of small, single or double flowers throughout summer. Often used as summer bedding, they also make long-flowering pot plants for home or conservatory. Examples: *B.* 'Ambassador', *B.* 'Organdy'. H and S 20–40cm (8–16in).

Cane-stemmed begonias. Shrubby, fibrous-rooted, evergreen perennials with long, firm, slender stems bearing asymmetrical, often beautifully coloured and patterned leaves at the stem nodes. The showy flowers are produced from early spring to summer. Examples: *B. aconitifolia*, *B. albopicta* (Guinea-wing begonia), *B.* 'Orpha C. Fox'.
H to 1.2m (4ft) or more, S to 35cm (14in).

Shrub-like begonias. Shrubby, often succulent-stemmed, evergreen perennials valued for their foliage, which is often beautifully coloured and has interesting surface textures. They produce flowers in spring and summer. Examples include: *B. x argenteoguttata* (Trout-leaved begonia) and *B. metallica* (Metallic-leaf begonia). H to 2m (6ft), many smaller, S 22–60cm (9–24in).

Winter-flowering begonias. Compact, bushy, evergreen perennials bearing single, semi-double, or double flowers from autumn to spring. They include the **Christmas begonias** (also known as **Cheimantha** or **Lorraine begonias**) and the **Reiger hybrids.** Examples *B.* 'Kleo', *B.* 'Azotus'.
H 20–45cm (8–18in), S 15–60cm (6–24in).

PROPAGATION

Leaf cuttings – spring or summer. For small-leaved plants: whole leaf cuttings with a leaf stalk. For larger-leaved plants, leaf squares, or scored-leaf cuttings.
Time to rooting – 2–6 weeks.
✄ spring. Semperflorens begonias.
Rhizome sections – summer. Suitable for Rex-cultorum and rhizomatous begonias.
Time to rooting – 4–6 weeks.
Tuber sections – late winter–early spring, as new growth begins. Start tubers into growth at 16°C (61°F) on the surface of a tray of sandy compost. As buds swell, section the tubers with a clean sharp knife so that each section has at least one growing bud and some roots. Dust with fungicide, allow to callus over for a few hours, then pot up into moist compost. Do not water again until growth begins; then water sparingly until plants are growing well. Suitable for tuberous begonias.
Basal cuttings – spring, or for winter-flowering begonias, early summer. Start tubers into growth as for sectioning tubers. When the shoots reach 5cm (2in) long, take basal cuttings, each with a small wedge of tuber at the base. Place in a propagator until well-rooted, then harden off. Suitable for tuberous and Semperflorens begonias.
Time to rooting – 3–4 weeks.

Cattleya labiata

Chlorophytum comosum 'Vittatum'

Cymbidium Strathdon 'Cooksbridge Noel'

Stem tip or stem cuttings – spring or summer. For cane-stemmed and shrub-like begonias. Time to rooting – 2–6 weeks.

❦ late winter-early spring, at 21°C (70°F). Suitable for all species, some tuberous begonias, including Tuberhybrida, Pendula, and Multiflora cultivars, and for Semperflorens begonias. ❦ 15–60 days. Bulbils – set on the surface of a tray of moss peat in spring. Suitable for some species and cultivars of tuberous begonias. *(See also Bulbs, Corms, and Tubers, pp. 64–71.)*

Cattleya
Orchidaceae

Some 40 species and hundreds of cultivars of epiphytic, evergreen orchids with pseudobulbs and short rhizomes. Valued for their showy flowers, they are suitable for a conservatory. They need filtered light, high humidity, and copious watering in summer. After flowering, give a semi-dry rest and water sparingly. Most need a minimum temperature of 5°C (41°F).

C. labiata. Produces racemes of flowers in shades of pink, with ruffled petals and purple lower lips, in autumn.
H and S 30cm (12in).

PROPAGATION

❦ autumn and winter-flowering species in early spring, spring-flowering species in early summer. Divide summer-flowering species immediately after flowering, or in early spring. If divided too late, they will not develop a good root system before growth slows in autumn.
Rhizome sections – each section with at least two or three pseudobulbs, when new shoots and roots appear.
Time to rooting – 6–10 weeks.

Ceropegia
Asclepiadaceae

Over 200 species of perennials including evergreen and semi-evergreen climbers, trailing plants, and many succulents. A number make attractive houseplants, being tolerant of dry atmospheres, and trailing species, like *C. linearis* var. *woodii* are ideal for hanging baskets. They need a well-drained, leafy potting mix, in bright light with shade from hot sun. Provide a minimum temperature of 10°C (50°F).

C. linearis var. *woodii*, syn. *C. woodii* (Hearts on a string, Rosary vine). Produces long, trailing, slender stems bearing small heart-shaped leaves that are green with pale silvery grey-green or purple markings above and purple beneath. It often produces bulbils in the leaf axils.
H 10cm (4in), S indefinite.

PROPAGATION

Stem bulbils – spring or early summer. Detach and set on the surface of potting compost. Time to rooting – 2–4 weeks. Stem tip cuttings – early summer, 10–15cm (4–6in) long. Root in mix of equal parts peat and sand in a propagating case at 20–25°C (68–77°F). Time to rooting 2–4 weeks.

Chlorophytum
Liliaceae

Among some 200 species of evergreen perennials, the variegated cultivars of *C. comosum* are the most widely grown. An almost indestructible plant, it tolerates neglect, poor soils, hot, cool, damp and dry conditions, and low light levels.

C. comosum (Spider plant, Ribbon plant). Forms clumps of narrowly lance-shaped, bright green leaves and bears tiny 6-petalled white flowers on cascading stalks that later

produce plantlets. 'Vittatum' has green leaves with a cream central stripe, 'Variegatum' has white-margined green leaves. H to 20cm (8in), S 30cm (12in).

PROPAGATION

✄ at any time between spring and autumn. Plantlets – separate at any time between spring and autumn. Encourage them to root while still attached to the parent plant by pinning them on to the surface of a small pot of potting mix.
Time to rooting – 2–4 weeks.

Cymbidium
Orchidaceae

About 50 species of terrestrial or epiphytic orchids. The most commonly grown are the winter- or spring-flowering hybrids which number in the hundreds. They produce long arching racemes of flowers in a wide range of colours, and have narrow oval to linear leaves. H in a range between about 30–90cm (12–36in), S to 90cm (36in). The dwarf cultivars that grow to 30cm (12in) high are more suitable for growing as houseplants; avoid the larger sturdy plants that can produce long rush-like leaves to about 1.8m (6ft) tall. Cymbidiums are the easiest of the orchids to grow as houseplants and are able to survive temperatures of 8°C (46°F). They benefit from being stood in the garden in a shady spot during summer; this treatment encourages the formation of flower buds.

PROPAGATION

✄ of large plants in spring. Backbulbs – remove when dividing, pot individually, and keep in a propagator with gentle bottom heat.

Dendrobium nobile

Epidendrum radicaris 'Crucifix orchid'

Epiphyllum 'Gloria'

Dendrobium   Orchidaceae

Over 900 species of deciduous, semi-evergreen, or evergreen, epiphytic and terrestrial orchids, some tiny and moss-like, others with climbing stems to 3m (10ft) in height. The hybrids based on *D. bigibbum* var. *phalaenopsis* and *D. nobile,* are most attractive. Hybrids of the former need a great deal of warmth to flower, whereas those of *D. nobile* are more suitable as houseplants. Those listed need a minimum temperature of 10°C (50°F). Water freely and apply a half-strength balanced fertilizer at every third watering. Shield from direct sun and, in early autumn, gradually reduce the amount of water until early winter; then cease watering completely until late winter.

D. wardiianum. White flowers with purple petal tips and lips marked maroon and yellow. Spring to autumn.
H 30cm (12in), S 15cm (6in).

D. nobile. Rose-pink flowers with a central deep maroon spot, in spring.
H 45cm (18in), S 15cm (6in).

D. infundibulum. Flowers pure white, with yellow spot on the lip, in spring and summer.
H 60cm (24in), S 15cm (6in).

PROPAGATION

Stem cuttings – in spring as growth resumes. Time to rooting 6–10 weeks. Adventitious growths, or keikeis, with their own roots, appear from the nodes. Remove and pot up during the growing season.

Dracaena   Dracaenaceae

About 40 species of evergreen shrubs to tree-like plants with spirally arranged, leathery, glossy, long, linear, and pointed leaves. Some are suited for cultivation as

houseplants if they are kept pruned and are propagated when they become too large. Give full light and provide a minimum temperature of 13°C (55°F). Restrict water during cold periods and in winter.

D. marginata. Has red-margined, dark green leaves. 'Tricolor' has green leaves which are margined and veined red and have a cream stripe. H 5m (15ft), S to 3m (10ft).

PROPAGATION

Air layering – when plant has become leggy, then cut back to soil level.
Time to rooting – 10–16 weeks.
Stem cuttings – cut up main stem into pieces 2.5–5cm (1–2in) long and make into cuttings, using a warm propagator at anytime. Alternatively, take stem tip cuttings.
Time to rooting – 3–6 weeks.

Epidendrum   Orchidaceae

Large genus of over 750 species of terrestrial and epiphytic, evergreen orchids, many of which produce cascades of small flowers. They need some summer shade, high humidity and a minimum of 13°C (55°F). Water copiously in the growing season and very sparingly in winter, when they need as much light as possible.

E. pseudepidendrum. Has green flowers with orange lips, in summer and autumn.
H to 1m (3ft), S 60cm (2ft).

E. secundum. Has long racemes of pink flowers with white and yellow marked lips.
H 60cm (24in), S 30cm (12in).

PROPAGATION

✄ mature plants when pot-bound, as growth resumes in spring.
Stem cuttings – in spring as growth resumes. Time to rooting – 6–10 weeks.

Epiphyllum (Orchid Cactus)   Cactaceae

About 20 species of mostly epiphytic, rainforest cacti. Most of the plants in cultivation are thought to be hybrids; all very similar, with flattened stems notched at the edges, at first growing upright then becoming pendent. Frost tender, they need a minimum temperature of 8°C (46°F). The large flowers are produced in spring and early summer. They are easily grown if they are given richer soil and more water than the desert type cactus. *E.* 'Gloria' has pinkish-red flowers 10cm (4in) across.
E. 'Jennifer Ann' has yellow flowers 15cm (6in) across. *E.* 'M. A. Jeans' has smaller blooms 8cm (3in) across.
H about 60cm (24in), S 50cm (20in).

PROPAGATION

Stem cuttings – sections of the stems or single pads root easily in pots of cutting compost stood on a greenhouse bench.
Time to rooting – 3–6 weeks.

Epipremnum   Araceae

A genus of about eight species of evergreen climbing plants with large heart-shaped or long-pointed leaves. They need temperatures of 18°C (64°F), moisture-retentive, leafy compost, and the support of a moss pole.

E. aureum 'Marble Queen', syn. *Scindapsus aureus* 'Marble Queen'. Evergreen, woody-stemmed climber with leaves streaked with white. H 3–10m (10–30ft) eventually.

PROPAGATION

Stem cuttings – with 2–3 nodes, with a leaf or without, laid on the compost horizontally or inserted upright. Keep warm and humid in a propagator until roots are formed.
Time to rooting – 3–8 weeks.

Euphorbia pulcherrima

Ficus benjamina

Kalanchoe daigremontiana

Euphorbia — Euphorbiaceae

Very large genus of over 1,000 species, including annuals, herbaceous perennials, shrubs, trees, and succulents.

E. pulcherrima (Poinsettia). Upright, evergreen shrub. The poinsettias with the coloured bracts in red, pink, and white, sold by florists, are manipulated with chemical retardants, control of day length, or both. To prevent leaf drop give as much light as possible and a temperature no lower than 8°C (46°F). H and S to 3m (10ft). As a houseplant usually H 20–30cm (8–12in), S 35–40cm (14–16in).

PROPAGATION

Cuttings – possible, although the resulting plants will not be compact like the parent. Stock plants, which have been dried off after flowering in mid-winter, will make small shoots when watered in spring. These can be cut off, the flow of milky sap stopped with rooting hormone powder, and the cuttings then rooted in a warm propagator. Time to rooting – 3–8 weeks.

Ficus (Fig) — Moraceae

About 600 species of mainly evergreen trees, shrubs, and climbers. One of the most well known is the edible fig, *Ficus carica (see p. 185)*. Some species make good foliage houseplants, growing in quite cool conditions in low light. A minimum temperature of 10°C (50°F) is required, possibly more.

F. benjamina (Weeping fig). Slender drooping branches bear small, ovate leaves. H to 2m (6ft), S 1.2m (4ft) as a houseplant.

F. elastica (India rubber tree, rubber plant). Strong growing tree with large, shiny, oval leaves, to 25cm (10in) long. The various forms grown include 'Variegata' which has cream edged leaves mottled grey-green. H to 2m (6ft), S to 50cm (20in) or more.

PROPAGATION

Cuttings – can be rooted fairly easily given a humid environment at 21°C (70°F). With *F. benjamina* take stem tip cuttings 10cm (4in) long, with the lower leaves removed, place around the edge of a pot of compost; they will root in about 6–12 weeks. With *F. elastica*, take stem cuttings with one leaf and a bud (it helps if the leaf is rolled and tied) and put into small pots of compost. Time to rooting – 6–12 weeks.

Air layering – the top section of a leggy *F. elastica* can be rooted using this technique. When adequate roots have formed, cut off and pot up. Time to rooting – 10–16 weeks.

Kalanchoe — Crassulaceae

About 130 species of succulent annuals, perennials, shrubs, climbers and trees. A number make attractive and unusual houseplants, particularly the bushy perennial succulents with fleshy, rounded leaves and bell-shaped to tubular flowers. Provide a minimum temperature of 10°C (50°F).

K. blossfeldiana. Bushy perennial with glossy toothed leaves and clusters of tubular scarlet flowers. The hybrids include red, salmon, and pink. Prefer partial shade. H and S to 40cm (16in).

K. fedtschenkoi. Perennial succulent with upright growth bearing fleshy, oval, notched, blue-grey leaves with little plantlets in each notch. Bell-shaped, brownish pink flowers appear in late winter. Prefers full sun. H to 1m (3ft), S 25cm (10in).

K. 'Wendy'. Perennial succulent with glossy leaves and bell-shaped, deep pink flowers, with yellow rims, in midwinter. A good hanging basket plant in a cool greenhouse. H and S to 30cm (12in).

PROPAGATION

Stem-tip cuttings – for the majority, put in a gritty compost on an open glasshouse bench at a temp. of 17°C (63°F). Keep relatively dry. Time to rooting – 2–6 weeks. With *K. blossfeldiana*, plantlets drop off the leaves naturally and root on compost surface or can be removed and planted. Time to rooting – 2–3 weeks.

Mammillaria — Cactaceae

Some 150 species of mainly spherical cacti, some are cylindrical. Flowering freely, they produce rings of funnel-shaped blooms on their tops. They need a minimum of 5°C (41°F), full sun, and sharply drained compost. Keep dry in the winter to prevent rot.

M. bocasana (Snowball cactus). Clump-forming cactus covered with long white hairs. The flowers, borne in summer, can be cream, or pink, often followed by red seedpods. H 5cm (2in), S indefinite.

M. plumosa. Spherical cactus that forms clumps of individuals, covered with white hair-like spines; in winter it has creamy white flowers. H 12cm (5in), S 40cm (16in).

M. sempervivi. Dark green spherical cactus, with white spines that have white wool between them. Bears cerise-pink flowers in spring. H and S 8cm (3in).

PROPAGATION

🌱 sow in late winter on gritty, loam-based compost. 🌱 2–3 weeks.

Offsets – mature offsets with their own roots; pot individually into cactus compost.

Neoregelia carolinae

Peperomia obtusifolia 'Variegata'

Philodendron bipinnatifidum

Monstera
Araceae

Some 30 species of evergreen climbers. *M. deliciosa* is a good houseplant for large spaces, and thrives in low light. Support with a moss pole and cut back occasionally. Minimum temperature 15°C (59°F).

M. deliciosa (Swiss-cheese plant). Large, shiny lobed and holed leaves are borne on long leaf stalks from a stem 4cm (1½in) thick, from which long brown aerial roots also grow. **'Variegata'** has splashes of white on the leaves. H to 6m (20ft).

PROPAGATION

Leaf-bud or stem-tip cuttings – pot singly and place in a polythene bag in a warm place. Time to rooting – 4–8 weeks.
Air layering – during the growing season.
Time to rooting – 10–16 weeks.

Neoregelia
Bromeliaceae

About 70 species of evergreen, epiphytic rosette-forming perennials which hold closely-packed flowers at the rosette's centre. Needs warm, humid conditions with a minimum of 13° C (55°F) and shade from full sun. Grow in a mix of granulated bark and sphagnum moss. Water with care during the growing season. Keep the centre of the rosette filled with clean water.

N. carolinae. Has rosettes of strap-shaped leaves in the centre of which are tubular, blue-purple flowers, with red bracts. **'Tricolor'** has green leaves striped with white that flush pink with age.
H 20–30cm (8–12in), S 40–60cm (16–24in).

PROPAGATION

Offsets – pot into small containers of the growing mix. Root in a propagator with bottom heat. Time to rooting – 3–6 weeks.

Peperomia
Piperaceae

Around 400 species of annuals or evergreen perennials. Those grown as houseplants are small plants with ornamental foliage. Many are suitable for growing in small pots and there are some with a trailing habit that are good for hanging baskets. The fleshy or succulent species tend to rot when over-watered; keep them just moist. Grow in bright light but protect from full sun. Those described need a minimum of 10°C (50°F).

P. marmorata (Silver heart). Evergreen, bushy perennial with oval, pointed, fleshy, dull green leaves, marked with greyish white and quilted above, reddish below.
H and S to 25cm (10in).

P. obtusifolia **'Variegata'**. Evergreen perennial with thick, fleshy green leaves, irregularly marked yellow to creamy white at the margins. Plants occasionally flower.
H and S 25cm (10in).

PROPAGATION

✂ of large plants, in spring.
Stem cuttings – of large plants, in spring or early summer. Time to rooting – 2–6 weeks.
Leaf cuttings – entire leaves with or without a leaf stalk attached.
Time to rooting – 2–6 weeks.

Philodendron
Araceae

About 120 species of evergreen, often epiphytic, climbing shrubs or trees, grown for their attractive leaves which are heart- or arrow-shaped. They make ideal houseplants and grow in fairly low light. Some support, such as a moss pole, into which the aerial roots can grow should be provided. Grow in humus-rich soil and water moderately, less in cooler situations; provide a minimum

temperature of 15°C (59°F).

P. bipinnatifidum. Erect, robust, tree-like shrub with large, deeply lobed, glossy green leaves, 60cm (24in) long, on stalks 60cm (24in) in length. H to 5m (15ft).

P. scandens (Sweetheart plant). Fast-growing climber with slender stems covered with attractive small light green, heart-shaped leaves. Regular pruning can be necessary.
H 4m (12ft).

PROPAGATION

Stem cuttings – in heated propagator.
Time to rooting – 2–6 weeks.
Air layering – for climbers, during the growing season.
Time to rooting – 10–16 weeks.

Pilea
Urticaceae

Over 200 species of annuals or evergreen perennials, some of which are good foliage houseplants. Grow in well-drained compost, kept just moist in cool periods; provide a minimum temperature of 10°C (50°F).

P. cadieri (Aluminium plant). Evergreen bushy perennial with pointed-oval leaves that have raised silvery patches. H and S 30cm (12in).

P. involucrata. Similar to *P. cadieri*, with oval to round leaves, that have a bronze, corrugated upper surface and red on the underside.
H 15cm (6in), S 30cm (12in).

PROPAGATION

Stem cuttings – spring, in a heated propagator. Time to rooting – 2–6 weeks.

Pittosporum
Pittosporaceae

About 70 to 80 species of evergreen, mostly tender, trees and shrubs.

P. tobira. This makes a small rounded tree, with oval, grey-green leaves, and produces

Rebutia heliosa

Saintpaulia hybrid

Schlumbergera truncata

clusters of fragrant white flowers in late spring. It can be confined to a pot if pruned each year after flowering. Min. temp. 0°C (32°F). H to 4–5m (12–15ft), S to 3m (10ft).

PROPAGATION

in spring. 3 weeks.
Stem tip cuttings – midsummer, in a propagator. Time to rooting – 6–8 weeks.

Rebutia   Cactaceae

About 40 species of spherical or columnar cacti that have green stems with short spines. Seed-grown plants as young as three years old will produce flowers in profusion from their base. They require full sun and well-drained compost. Provide a minimum temperature 5°C (40°F).

R. aureiflora. This has dark green stems, often tinged violet-red, with short sharp spines and a longer soft central spine. Late spring flowers, 4cm (1½in) across, can be yellow, violet, or red. H 10cm (4in), S 20cm (8in).

R. fiebrigii, syn. *R. muscula.* Dark green stems are densely covered with soft white hairs. Flowers of bright orange appear in late spring and are 2.5cm (1in) across. H 10cm (4in), S 15cm (6in).

PROPAGATION

in spring. 2–4 weeks.
Offsets – spring or summer.
Time to rooting – 2–4 weeks.

Saintpaulia (African violet)   Gesneriaceae

Only six species of evergreen, tender perennials. *S. ionantha* has been used to create many hybrids, which are most commonly grown as houseplants. All form rosettes of rounded, long-stalked, hairy leaves. Flowers range through white, pink,

red, purple, and blue, plain or bicoloured some with frilled petals, others double. They need warm growing conditions, a minimum temperature of 15°C (59°F). Keep out of full sun and water carefully – over-wet compost can cause crown rot and careless watering will mark the foliage.
H to 15–20cm (6–8in), S 8–40cm (3–16in).

PROPAGATION

sow on the surface of peaty compost at a temperature of 21°C (70°F).
3–8 weeks.
Leaf cuttings – at any time; select a healthy undamaged mature leaf, shorten the leaf stalk, insert into cutting compost with the leaf blade clear of the compost. Then place in a propagator with bottom heat. Small plantlets, which can be separated and grown individually or left to form a multi-crown specimen, will grow from the base.
Time to rooting – 2–6 weeks.

Sansevieria   Dracaenaceae

Over 50 species of evergreen perennials, usually stemless with stiff, fleshy often variegated or mottled leaves growing from short thick rhizomes. They need a minimum temperature of 10°C (50°F) and grow well in sandy loam compost in sun or shade.

S. trifasciata (Mother-in-law's tongue). Lance-shaped, pointed, erect leaves are banded horizontally with paler green. **'Laurentii'** has yellow margins to the leaves.
H 38–60cm (15–24in), S 50cm (20in).

PROPAGATION

or offsets – for variegated plants (leaf cuttings will revert to green).
Time to rooting – 2–4 weeks.
Leaf cuttings – 8cm (3in) lengths inserted

into sandy compost and put in a propagator will root freely. Time to rooting – 3–8 weeks.

Saxifraga   Saxifragaceae

Over 300 species, most of which are alpines. *S. stolonifera* makes a good houseplant, surviving in poor compost and low light.

S. stolonifera (Mother-of-thousands). Leaves are round, hairy, silver-veined and dark green, reddish purple beneath. It produces long runners with small plantlets on them, making it a good hanging basket plant. Has sprays of small white flowers in midsummer. Frost hardy. H and S to 30cm (12in).

PROPAGATION

Easily grown from potted-up plantlets.

Schlumbergera   Cactaceae

About six species of epiphytic, bushy cacti with erect, then pendent stems made up of flattened, oblong segments with notched margins. Flowers with petals of varying lengths and prominent stamens are produced on the ends of the stems. The compost needs to be humus-rich and well drained. Grows well in shade. Needs less water in cooler periods.

S. truncata (Christmas cactus). Purple-pink flowers in autumn and winter. Min. temp. 10°C (50°F). H and S to 30cm (12in).

PROPAGATION

Stem cuttings – summer, in a shaded greenhouse. Time to rooting – 2–6 weeks.

Sinningia   Gesneriaceae

About 20 species of tuberous perennials. They need warm growing conditions and good light but not direct sun. Use a humus-rich compost, and provide a humid

Stephanotis floribunda

Streptocarpus 'Johannes'

Tillandsia lindenii

atmosphere. Minimum temperature 15°C (59°F). When the plants die down after flowering allow the tubers to dry out, then store them frost-free, until the next spring.
S. speciosa (Gloxinia). This species has many cultivars. They all have bell-shaped flowers of white, purple, or red, including bicolours and spotted. The leaves are large and oval, red-flushed beneath. H and S to 30cm (12in).

PROPAGATION
🌱 sow on the surface of peaty compost in a propagator at 21°C (70°F) in spring.
🌱 3–8 weeks.
Tubers – cut into pieces each with a shoot, or remove shoots from tubers in spring and treat as cuttings.
Time to rooting – 2–6 weeks.

Stephanotis   Asclepiadaceae
Some 15 species of often tall, twining, evergreen shrubs. S. floribunda is commonly grown as a houseplant at a minimum temperature of 12°C (54°F). Use loam-based compost and keep it fairly dry in winter. Clean the leaves regularly to keep scale insects at bay.
S. floribunda. Oval leaves and fragrant white flowers in early summer. Support is required for the vigorous shoots; weak shoots should be cut out in spring. H 6m (20ft) or more.

PROPAGATION
🌱 – early spring. Is sometimes produced in cultivation, borne in large egg-shaped pods. Sow in a heated propagator at 20–24°C (68–75°F). 🌱 30–90 days.
Stem cuttings – of the previous year's growth, root at 18°C (64°F) in a closed propagator with high humidity.
Time to rooting 2–6 weeks.

Streptocarpus   Gesneriaceae
Some 80 species of annuals and perennials most of which have hairy, veined, wrinkled leaves and tubular flowers with five spreading lobes. S. rexii is the parent of many hybrids which are grouped under the name S. × hybridus. Those grown as houseplants require humus-rich compost and a humid atmosphere with some shade. Provide a minimum temperature 15°C (59°F). The leaves can be damaged if splashed when watering, especially at low temperatures.
S. × hybridus. These have clusters of funnel-shaped flowers of various colours, including magenta, pink, salmon, and white, borne above rosettes of long strap-like leaves, velvety on top and smooth on the underside. H 20–35cm (8–14in), S 45–60cm (18–24in) or more.

PROPAGATION
🌱 sow on the surface of peaty compost at 21°C (70°F). 🌱 21–60 days.
Leaf cuttings – selected cultivars. Take from mature leaves either cut across or in half down the main vein, inserting the cut surface into cutting compost.
Time to rooting – 3–10 weeks.

Tillandsia   Bromeliaceae
Nearly 400 species of strange plants that almost plastic. Most are epiphytic under natural conditions and should be fastened to bark or cork with nylon fishing line, and a little moss. Most need bright light, high humidity, and high temperatures in the summer; those with few or no roots need spraying with water twice a day during hot weather and keeping completely dry in winter. Minimum temperature 10°C (50°F).

PROPAGATION
🔧 or offsets in spring.
🌱 in spring, on conifer twig bundles at 27°C (81°F).   🌱 21–28 days.

Tolmeia (Pig-a-back plant)   Saxifragaceae
A single species of hardy perennial that spreads rapidly. As a houseplant, it tolerates low light levels.
T. menziesii 'Taff's Gold'. Has trailing, yellow-splashed foliage. Plantlets grow from buds on the top of the leaf stalks.
H to 60cm (24in), S to 2m (6ft).

PROPAGATION
Leaf cuttings – insert by the stalk or pin down on the propagating medium.
Time to rooting – 2–3 weeks.

Tradescantia   Commelinaceae
About 100 species of evergreen perennials. Some make good, easy to grow houseplants, particularly the trailing species. Provide a minimum temperature of 5°C (41°F) and bright light, but not direct sun.
T. fluminensis (Wandering Jew). Trailing, perennial with leaves that clasp the stem. The oval, fleshy leaves are glossy green on top, and purple beneath. 'Aurea' has longitudinal yellow stripes. H 15cm (6in), S 20cm (8in).
T. zebrina. Trailing perennial with bluish-green leaves banded silver and purple beneath. 'Quadricolor' has leaves striped with green, pink, red, and white.
H 15cm (6in), S 20cm (8in).

PROPAGATION
Cuttings – stem-tip, at any time. Root in water or compost.
Time to rooting – 2–3 weeks.

WATER PLANTS

Water plants are both intriguing and beautiful, and can be appreciated in even the smallest garden if grown in tubs or half barrels. Their diverse leaf shapes and sizes, and sometimes exotic flowers, are exploited to the full when reflected in a mirror of clear, still water. Visual appeal, however, is not their only virtue: aquatics of all types – from deep-water plants to floaters – are absolutely essential in ensuring clear, clean water and providing a habitat for amphibians, fish and other submerged life in the garden pool. Propagation is vital to maintain health and performance, but the techniques are simple and require little in the way of tools and materials.

◄ *Regular propagation of all types of water plants is an essential part of the routine maintenance of a healthy aquatic environment.*

WHY PROPAGATE
WATER PLANTS?

With their feet in the water and their faces in the sun, the majority of water plants grow at a tremendous rate and are, consequently, generally easy to propagate. As in so many other plant groups, younger specimens tend to put on the best show and therefore it makes sense to regularly restock your pond with fresh plants.

Many aquatics need frequent propagation for control and to maintain oxygenating efficiency, or to keep them floriferous.

Most aquatics grow so rapidly that their propagation is more a matter of good husbandry than of increasing quantity. Since space in a water garden is often limited, there is seldom a need for more of the same thing. However, constant renewal of young plants is necessary, for example, to maintain the efficiency of submerged oxygenators, to maximize the flowering of waterlilies and sustain the lush foliage of marginals. The techniques are simple, but the expertise comes in recognizing when to propagate and which method to use.

AQUATICS FROM SEED

Since the majority of aquatics are far more easily increased vegetatively, seed is used mainly for the propagation of annuals such as *Cotula barbata* (bachelor's buttons) and a few marginal and deep-water plants with roots that are difficult to divide, such as *Lysichiton* (skunk cabbage) and *Orontium* (golden club). Although most waterlilies are propagated vegetatively, the dwarf *Nymphaea tetragona* 'Alba' does not produce buds on its root and must therefore be grown from seed.

DIVIDING YOUR STOCK

Although creeping species with long, sappy stems, such as *Veronica beccabunga*, and those with too few buds on the rootstock, like *Lysichiton*, are difficult to divide successfully, for most marginal and deep-water plants division consists simply of splitting the root system into smaller clumps. For some deep-water plants, such as the hardy waterlilies, it involves sectioning the root so that each piece has a growth bud. *Butomus* (flowering rush) produces tiny bulbils in leaf axils on the woody rootstock which can be detached, or left in place on a small section of root.

TAKING CUTTINGS

With the exception of rhizomatous, deep-water plants like waterlilies, the majority of submerged plants can be propagated easily from stem cuttings. No great skill or

Lysichiton americana
The flowering spathes produce a gelatinous mass of seed that germinates freely if surface-sown on wet compost. Removing offsets is possible, but not so easy.

Myosotis scorpioides
Water forget-me-nots form mats of foliage at the pond margin but to maintain good healthy cover, divide regularly in spring. Seed is also easy, sown *in situ* or in wet compost.

Menyanthes trifoliata
Bogbean looks most effective when grown in extensive colonies. Increase your stock by division in spring, or by seed sown as soon as ripe.

Nymphaea species and cultivars
Waterlilies flower best if propagated and replanted in fresh soil every third year or so, or when their containers become overcrowded. Increase cultivars by division or bud eyes, the species also by seed.

Iris sibirica
To maintain flowering potential, propagate every 3–4 years. This and other water irises (*I. laevigata* and *I. ensata*) divide easily after flowering. Alternatively, sow seed in spring.

special equipment is required – simply nipping off the stems between finger and thumb and refloating them is often all that is needed to ensure a supply of new plants.

RUNNERS, OFFSETS AND PLANTLETS

Floating plants often produce runners and offset plantlets freely and these provide a very easy way of renewing your stock.

GROWTH FROM BUDS

Many submerged plants develop special overwintering buds, or turions, at the shoot tips which, if detached and rooted in protected conditions, will provide a simple means of propagation.

Containers for Water Plants

Many aquatics spread so rapidly that they need containment in a small pool. For those needing regular division, growing in a container has the advantage that it is easily lifted, to be replanted when plants become overcrowded. Containers for aquatics are squatter than ordinary ones and have wide, flat bottoms to give extra stability. The sides are constructed in rigid plastic mesh to permit the exchange of gases between compost and water that is essential for healthy root function.

Growing the waterlily 'Mrs George C. Hitchcock' in a container makes it easy to lift and propagate regularly.

PROPAGATING TECHNIQUES
WATER PLANTS

The techniques used for propagating aquatic plants need little in the way of specialist equipment. A watertight container large enough to hold a seed tray is the main requirement – a disused aquarium makes an excellent propagating case – and for seedlings and young plants, a greenhouse or cold frame to protect them from frost.

SEED

Seed of most water plants is sown as soon as ripe in summer or early autumn; it loses viability quickly if it is allowed to dry out. If immediate sowing is inconvenient, store seed in moist peat (or a substitute) in a polythene bag and keep frost-free. *Myosotis*, *Mentha* and *Alisma* are the main exceptions; their seed may be stored cool and dry, but should be sown within six months of harvest.

DIVISION

Several techniques are used for the division of water plants. Most are basically the same as for herbaceous perennials, but the appropriate season extends from early summer to autumn. It is often difficult to disentangle roots from the mesh sides of their container, so be prepared to sacrifice it. All new divisions should be kept in partial shade in a frost-free frame or greenhouse for their first winter.

Marginal plants

Most marginals are divided simply by splitting clumps by hand into two or more portions, as for herbaceous perennials (*see p.29*). Section tough, thick-rooted clumps with a spade. Discard older, less productive, inner pieces and select young, vigorous, outer portions. Pot these up at their original depth into a basket of aquatic compost and immerse in a watertight container with water just covering the crown. Cut back aerial growth to within 5cm (2in) of water level.

Deep-water plants

Division of rhizomes: Fill a small basket with aquatic compost and firm thoroughly. Lift the rootstock and

Sowing seed ....

Seed of deep-water and marginal plants must be sown in conditions similar to those experienced by mature plants in the garden pool. Water levels in the seed container must therefore be controlled and care taken to ensure that the seed and subsequent seedlings are *never* allowed to dry out.

Deep-water plants ▶
Seed of deep-water plants must be submerged completely under water. Cover the base of a watertight bowl with 7.5cm (3in) of aquatic compost, level off and firm lightly. Sow seed thinly and evenly on the surface and cover with 3mm (⅛in) of finely sieved aquatic compost. Water in using a fine rose until the final water level is 2.5cm (1in) above the compost surface.

Marginal plants ▶
For marginal plants, greater control of the water depth around the seed and seedlings is necessary. Fill a seed pan with aquatic compost to within 5mm (¼in) of the rim. Level off and firm the compost gently, then surface-sow the seed thinly and evenly. Cover with 3mm (⅛in) of fine grit, and water in using a fine rose. Place the seed pan in a watertight container and top up with water until it is level with the compost surface.

Aftercare
Place the container in a frost-free greenhouse or frame with part-day sun, to warm the soil, but protect the seedlings from the hottest midday sun. Replenish the water regularly to maintain the same level as at sowing. When the seedlings are large enough to handle, prick out into 7.5cm (3in) pots of aquatic compost and return to the watertight container. Keep deep-water plants under 2.5cm (1in) of water and marginals in water that is level with the compost surface. Grow on until the plants are large enough to transfer to a small aquatic planting basket.

hose it clean of soil. Remove old leaves and cut plump rhizomes into sections, 5–7cm (2–3in) long, each with new growth at its tip. Trim back thin roots. Press the rhizome onto the compost surface, with the growing tip above the surface at the same angle as it was in the water; do not bury it. Top-dress with 2.5cm (1in) of pea shingle and water in thoroughly.

Immerse the basket in a watertight container and fill it with clean water so that the growing point is covered by no more than 5–8cm (2–3in) of water.

Division of tubers: For tuberous waterlilies, cut off individual side shoots flush to the tuber. *Nymphaea tuberosa* forms small protuberances on the tuber which can be snapped off. Dust the cut surfaces with charcoal and press onto the firmed surface of aquatic compost in a 10cm (4in) pot. Then treat as for rhizomes.

STEM CUTTINGS

Stem cuttings are taken from plants in full growth, between early summer and early autumn, and usually root within 2–3 weeks. After insertion, immerse in a watertight container with sufficient water to keep the stems below the water surface, and place in a warm, partially shaded site until rooted. Once rooted, transfer to larger containers and introduce to the pond.

RUNNERS, OFFSETS AND PLANTLETS

Some tropical waterlilies produce small plantlets on the central leaf vein. Remove the leaf from the parent and pin it onto the surface of aquatic compost in a pot so that the leaf is just submerged. Alternatively, support a bowl of aquatic compost beneath the leaf and pin it down while still attached. When roots develop after 3–5 weeks, pot the new plant up into and overwinter at its recommended minimum temperature.

Cyperus papyrus 'Nanus' forms young plantlets in the flower head. Bend over the flower head and immerse it in a shallow container of aquatic compost and water. Within 3–5 weeks, the plantlet will have rooted. Cut away from the parent plant and pot up separately.

TURIONS AND WINTER BUDS

Cut off the specialized shoot tips as they develop in mid-autumn. Using 7.5cm (3in) pots or seed trays, dibble true turions shallowly into the surface of aquatic

Stem cuttings ·····························

▶ **1** For submerged oxygenators, remove young shoots, 15–23cm (6–9in) long, either by hand or with a knife. Bind 8–9 shoots together with florists' wire near the base. Insert each bunch into a 10cm (4in) pot of aquatic compost, with the tie positioned below the surface of the soil.

▶ **2** Set the pots in a bowl of water. When rooted, transfer to the pond. For marginals with long, soft stems, remove healthy stem tips 7–10cm (3–4in) long. Trim just below a node, and remove the leaves from the lowest third. Insert to the depth of the lowest leaves into aquatic compost.

Runners and offsets ·····························

Detaching runners or offsets from the parent plant is a very easy method of propagating floating plants, as the new plants already have their own roots.

▶ **1** For the majority of floating plants the technique of propagation could not be simpler: simply snap off a new runner or offset from the parent plant.

◀ **2** Return the detached runner or offset immediately to the garden pool, where it will grow away rapidly.

compost, or cover hard winter buds with 3–6in (7–15cm) of compost. Just cover the compost surface with water and overwinter in a frost-free place. As growth begins, pot up individually and submerge to their required growing depth. Once they are growing strongly, either set out into planting baskets or into the pool bottom. The turions of floaters, like *Hydrocharis* (frogbit), are simply refloated onto warm shallow water.

151

DIRECTORY OF
WATER PLANTS

Below are key tips on a selection of water plants that are particularly suitable for propagation. Unless otherwise specified, follow the detailed instructions given under the propagation section on pages 150–151.

Key

H Height
S Spread
PD Planting depth
🌱 By seed
🌱 Germination
☀ Time to maturity
✎ By division

Acorus   Acoraceae

Genus of two species of hardy, rhizomatous, marginal and submerged perennials, grown for their sometimes aromatic foliage. For moist soil or shallow water in full sun or light shade.
A. calamus (Sweet flag). Deciduous, with fragrant, sword-shaped, wrinkly margined, olive-green leaves. **'Variegatus'** has olive-green leaves striped cream and yellow.
H to 90cm (3ft), S 60cm (2ft),
PD to 23cm (9in).
A. gramineus. Compact tufts of semi-evergreen, glossy green leaves. The leaves of **'Variegatus'** are striped cream and yellow, **'Oborozuki'**, striped yellow, **'Yodo-no-yuki'**, variegated pale-green.
H 8–35cm (3–4in), S 10–15cm (4–6in),
PD to 23cm (9in).

PROPAGATION

✎ spring. Divide congested clumps every 3–4 years. ☀ 4 months.
Section rhizomes of *A. gramineus* cultivars in 2–5cm (1–2in) lengths. ☀ 15 months.

Alisma   Alismataceae

Genus of nine species of hardy, rhizomatous, marginal perennials, grown for their loose panicles of flowers and basal rosettes of leaves. Needs full sun or light shade.
A. plantago-aquatica (Water plantain). Ribbed, broadly ovate grey to grey-green leaves and tiny, pink-white flowers in summer. H to 75cm (2½ft), S 45cm (1½ft), PD 15cm (6in).

PROPAGATION

Seed – as soon as ripe or in spring, at 15°C (59°F). As the seed will float, cover with a light dressing of compost. Seed may be stored for up to a year.
🌱 2–5 weeks. ☀ 15 months.

Aponogeton   Aponogetonaceae

Some 44 species of rhizomatous, deep-water perennials, one of which is hardy and is grown for its flowers and foliage. Needs full sun or light shade.
A. distachyos (Cape pondweed, Water

hawthorn). Floating, strap-like, green leaves above which are borne forked spikes of fragrant, white flowers with almost black anthers, in spring and autumn. Almost evergreen in mild winters. H 30–90cm (1–3ft), S to 1.2m (4ft), PD 30–90cm (1–3ft).

PROPAGATION

✎ spring. Section rhizomes into 5cm (2in) lengths, each with 2–3 buds.
☀ 24 months.
🌱 as soon as ripe at 13–16°C (55–61°F). Prick out when new tubers are pea-sized.
🌱 3 weeks. ☀ 12 months.

Butomus   Butomaceae

Genus of a single species of hardy, rhizomatous, marginal perennial, grown for its flowers and foliage. Prefers full sun.
B. umbellatus (Flowering rush). This has rush-like leaves, which are bronze-purple becoming dark green as they mature, and scented, cupped, rose-pink flowers in late summer. H to 1.5m (5ft), S 45cm (1½ft), PD to 25cm (10in).

PROPAGATION

✎ spring. ☀ 4 months.
Bulbils – spring. Remove root bulbils and pot individually in small pots of aquatic compost; keep under 2cm (¾in) of water.
☀ 15 months.
🌱 as soon as ripe at 15°C (59°F).
🌱 3–8 weeks. ☀ 18 months.

Calla   Araceae

One species of hardy, rhizomatous, marginal perennial, grown for its foliage and flowers. Prefers full sun.
C. palustris (Bog arum). Dark green leaves and small, white flowers in spring, followed by rounded clusters of red berries in autumn. H 25cm (10in), S 30cm (12in), PD to 25cm (10in).

Acorus calamus 'Variegatus'

Butomus umbellatus

Caltha palustris

Eichhornia crassipes

Elodea canadensis

PROPAGATION

✎ spring. Section rhizomes into 5–10cm (2–4in) lengths, each with a bud, and plant in trays of muddy soil. ☀ 12 months.
🌰 as soon as ripe in late summer at 10°C (50°F). Surface-sow berries in a seed tray and submerge to three-quarters of their depth. Keep wet and frost-free for the winter. ⚘ 6 months. ☀ 12 months.

Caltha   Ranunculaceae

Some 10 species of perennials, including hardy, marginal aquatics valued for their dense clumps of glossy foliage and buttercup-like flowers, borne before the leaves appear in early spring and often producing a second flush in late summer. Prefers full sun.
C. leptosepala. This has dark green leaves and silvery white flowers on leafless stems. It is best at or just above water level in moist soil. H and S 30cm (1ft).
C. palustris (Kingcup, Marsh marigold). Produces dark green leaves and masses of cupped, rich golden yellow flowers on branching stems. H 60cm (2ft), S 45cm (1½ft), PD to 15cm (6in).

PROPAGATION

✎ immediately after flowering. ☀ 9 months.
🌰 as soon as ripe at 15°C (59°F). Seed germinates well if the seed pan is placed under a mist propagator.
⚘ 2 weeks. ☀ 12 months.

Ceratophyllum   Ceratophyllaceae

About 30 species of half-hardy and hardy, submerged, often rootless, aquatic perennials, used extensively as oxygenators for ponds and water gardens. Prefers sun but tolerates partial shade.

C. demersum (Hornwort). Hardy perennial, often semi-floating, with dense whorls of forked, bristly, dark green leaves produced on slender, brittle stems. H and S indefinite, PD 20cm–1.5m (8in–5ft).

PROPAGATION

Stem cuttings – during the growing season. 15–23cm (6–9in) long. ☀ 2 weeks.
Turions – autumn. Break off and weight to the pond bottom to overwinter.
☀ 3 months

Egeria   Hydrocharitaceae

Only two species of semi-evergreen or evergreen, hardy, submerged or floating, aquatic perennials used as oxygenators. They need cutting back regularly to restrict their spread. Require full sun.
E. densa, syn. *Elodea densa* (Argentinian water weed). This species has long, branching stems with whorls of narrow, dark green leaves with pointed tips that usually curl backwards. May produce insignificant white flowers on the water surface in summer. H and S indefinite.

PROPAGATION

Stem cuttings – summer. 15–23cm (6–9in) long. ☀ 3 weeks.

Eichhornia   Pontederiaceae

Seven species of frost-tender, mainly floating, stoloniferous perennials which spread rapidly in warm climates. Suitable for outdoor pools in temperate climates only during the frost-free summer months. Needs full sun and warm water, preferably at 18°C (64°F).
E. crassipes (Water hyacinth, Water orchid). Floating, aquatic perennial with spikes of pale lilac flowers in summer above rosettes of

shiny, rounded to ovate, pale green leaves with swollen, air-filled bases. H 15–23cm (6–9in), S 15–30cm (6–12in).

PROPAGATION

Plantlets – during the growing season. Snap away from the parent plant and re-float immediately. Overwinter young plantlets on wet soil under glass at a minimum air temperature of 7°C (45°F).
☀ 2 months.

Elodea   Hydrocharitaceae

Some 12 species of hardy, submerged, aquatic perennials. *E. canadensis* is widely used as an oxygenator but is invasive if not regularly thinned. Tolerates sun or shade.
E. canadensis (Canadian pondweed). Has many-branched stems bearing oblong, pointed, mid-green leaves. H and S indefinite.

PROPAGATION

Stem cuttings – throughout growing season. ☀ 3 weeks.

Glyceria   Gramineae

About 16 species of rhizomatous, aquatic or marginal, perennial grasses grown for their foliage and flowers in summer. Because the most widely grown variety quickly colonizes moist soils or water margins, it is best confined in a tub or basket. Prefers full sun.
G. maxima var. *variegata* (Variegated water grass). Has arching, flat, linear leaves, strikingly striped with green, cream and white, usually pink-flushed in spring. The grass-like flowers are green to purple-green. H 80cm (32in), S indefinite, PD to 75cm (30in).

PROPAGATION

✎ any time during the growing season. Any division will root easily. ☀ 4–6 weeks.

Hottonia palustris

Houttuynia cordata 'Chameleon'

Lysichiton americanus

Hottonia
Primulaceae

Just two species of hardy, submerged, aquatic perennials, valued both for their attractive primrose-like flowers, held above the water, and for their feathery, light green leaves, which act as oxygenators.

H. palustris (Water violet). Bears spikes of violet flowers well above the surface of the water in summer; the submerged leaves are finely divided, and bright green. Needs sun and clear, clean water. H to 90cm (3ft), S indefinite, PD 20–60cm (8–24in).

PROPAGATION

✂ spring. ☀ 6 weeks.
Stem cuttings – summer. ☀ 8 weeks
Turions – fruits form turions after pollination. Collect in autumn and overwinter in frost-free conditions, on trays of soil covered with 2.5cm (1in) of water. Pot individually in spring. ☀ 6 months.

Houttuynia
Saururaceae

A single species of rhizomatous, marginal perennial flourishing in the wet margins of pools and streams. The species can be invasive, although its variegated cultivars are less rampant. Prefers partial shade.

H. cordata. This has red-stemmed, bluish-green, ovate leaves, with an unusual fragrance when crushed, and bears spikes of small, white flowers with white bracts, in spring. The green-centred leaves of **'Chameleon'** have heavy markings in vivid crimson and cream. H 15–60cm (6–24in), S indefinite, PD to 10cm (4in).

PROPAGATION

✂ spring. Tease the extensive mats of rhizomes apart and replant immediately.
☀ 8–10 weeks.

Lagarosiphon
Hydrocharitaceae

Genus of nine species of hardy to half-hardy, submerged aquatics grown as oxygenators in indoor and outdoor pools and in aquariums. Prefers full sun.

L. major syn. *Elodea crispa* of gardens (Curly water thyme). Hardy, semi-evergreen perennial with narrow, strongly recurved, fresh green leaves borne in spirals along the stem. Thin regularly to restrict growth. H and S indefinite.

PROPAGATION

Stem cuttings – throughout the growing season. 15–23cm (6–9in) long. ☀ 3 weeks.

Lysichiton
Araceae

Genus of two species of hardy, moisture-loving or marginal, rhizomatous perennials grown for their striking, arum-like spathes in early spring, which are followed by architectural leaves. They grow best in deep, saturated soil, but tolerate shallow water. They prefer full sun.

L. americanus (Skunk cabbage). Has yellow spathes in early spring, followed by huge, almost stemless, paddle-shaped, glossy green leaves, up to 1.2m (4ft) high. H 1m (3ft), S 75cm (2½ft), PD 10cm (4in).

L. camtschatcensis. More compact than *L. americanus* with white spathes; also blooms slightly later in spring. H 75cm (2½ft), S 60cm (2ft), PD 10cm (4in).

PROPAGATION

🌰 as soon as ripe at 15°C (59°F). As the spadix rots it forms a gelatinous mess containing ripe seeds. Do not extract the seed, but break up the spadix and surface-sow in a large seed tray of aquatic compost. Submerge the tray to half its depth, and replenish the water regularly.
❦ 4–6 weeks. ☀ 18 months.
Offsets – spring. Separation of young plants that form at the base of older rhizomes is possible, but not easy. Pot up into pots of permanently moist compost and keep shaded until established. ☀ 18 months.

Mentha
Labiatae

Some 25 species of hardy, aromatic, rhizomatous, often invasive perennials, one of which is grown as a water marginal. Prefers a site in full sun.

M. aquatica (Water mint). Has strongly fragrant, oval, serrated, dark green leaves, and dense, terminal whorls of tiny, lilac flowers in summer. H to 90cm (3ft), S 90cm (3ft) or more, PD 15cm (6in) or more.

PROPAGATION

✂ during the growing season.
☀ 8 weeks.
Root cuttings – during the growing season. Place 8cm (3in) long root sections horizontally, just below the surface of aquatic compost, and cover with 2.5cm (1in) of water. ☀ 4 months.

Menyanthes
Menyanthaceae

A single species of hardy, rhizomatous, marginal perennial, grown for its spikes of flowers and spreading foliage.

M. trifoliata (Bogbean, Buckbean). Has creeping rhizomes that often float at the water margins, and bears shiny, clover-like, green leaves with long stalks that clasp the rhizome. Small, white flowers open from pink buds in early summer, sometimes again in autumn. Needs full sun. H 25cm (10in), S indefinite, PD 0–30cm (0–12in).

Menyanthes trifoliata

Myosotis scorpioides

Nymphaea 'Laydeckeri fulgens'

PROPAGATION
⚒ spring, ☀ 6–8 weeks.
🌰 as soon as ripe, at 16°C (61°F). Cover with 2.5cm (1in) of water.
🌱 2–3 weeks. ☀ 6 months.

Myosotis   Boraginaceae
Some 50 species of hardy annuals, biennials, and herbaceous perennials, including a number of attractive marginals. They have hairy leaves and salverform flowers. Needs sun or light shade.
M. scorpioides (Water forget-me-not). Creeping, rhizomatous, marginal perennial with narrowly oval, mid-green leaves, and cymes of bright blue, yellow-eyed flowers in early summer. **'Mermaid'** is more compact and free-flowering. H 23–30cm (9–12in), S 30cm (12in), PD 10cm (4in).

PROPAGATION
⚒ spring. Established clumps are easily divided. ☀ 3 months.
Cuttings – nip off young tips about 5–7cm (2–3in) long. Treat as softwood cuttings.
🌰 early autumn at 15°C (59°F).
🌱 2 weeks. ☀ 6 months.

Myriophyllum   Haloragidaceae
About 40 species of tender and hardy, submerged aquatics with attractive feathery foliage. They are grown as oxygenators and to provide shelter for fish fry. Needs a position in full sun.
M. aquaticum, syn. *M. brasiliense*, *M. proserpinacoides* (Parrot feather). Has slender stems clothed in whorls of blue-green leaves that emerge above the water surface. An excellent scrambler for disguising pool edges, it will root in moist soil at the

pond margin or may be grown in deeper water in baskets. Half hardy grown as a marginal plant, frost hardy as a deep water aquatic. H to 1.5m (5ft), S indefinite, PD to 1.5m (5ft).

PROPAGATION
Stem cuttings – spring. Take cuttings of young growth, 12cm (5in) long. ☀ 3 weeks.

Nelumbo   Nelumbonaceae
Genus of two species of half-hardy and frost-tender, rhizomatous, marginal perennials with circular leaves and flamboyant, waterlily-like flowers borne well clear of the water surface. Lift the rhizomes in autumn and store in damp sand in frost-free conditions. Needs a position in full sun.
N. lutea (American lotus). Has rounded, blue-green, waxy leaves, 40–80cm (16–32cm) across and, in summer, large, fragrant, yellow flowers. H to 2m (6ft), S indefinite, PD to 60cm (24in).
N. nucifera (Sacred or Oriental lotus). Has bluish-green, waxy leaves, to 80cm (32cm) across, and fragrant, pale pink flowers, in summer. There are several superb cultivars, some of which are suitable for half barrels or tubs. H to 1.5m (5ft), S 1.2m (4ft), PD to 60cm (24in).

PROPAGATION
⚒ spring. Ensure that there are at least two buds on each section of rhizome and set horizontally just below the compost surface. Keep at a minimum temperature of 5°C (41°F) or they will not produce shoots.
☀ 6 months.
🌰 spring, at 25–30°C (77–86°F). Cover with 5cm (2in) of water.
🌱 4 weeks. ☀ 15 months.

Nymphaea (Waterlily)   Nymphaeaceae
About 50 species of deep water, usually rhizomatous, sometimes stoloniferous or tuberous perennials, ranging from tropical species, some of which are night-blooming, to hardy species that will survive long periods beneath ice. They have rounded leaves that float on the water surface and may be red-tinged beneath, and have leafless stalks bearing showy flowers usually floating on the water. Many different cultivars are available to suit various depths of water and in a wide range of colours. They need full sun and still water.

PROPAGATION
⚒ throughout summer. ☀ 12 months.
Bud eyes – during the growing season. Section small pieces of root with a single bud and plant in a pot or a seed tray. Cover with 5cm (2in) of water. ☀ 24 months.
Plantlets can be removed from certain tender species and cultivars which are viviparous. ☀ 12 months.

Orontium   Araceae
One species of hardy, marginal or submerged, deep-rooting, rhizomatous perennial. Leaf colour is best in full sun.
O. aquaticum (Golden club). Has waxy, blue-green leaves, silvery beneath, which in deep water float on the surface. In spring, bears slender white spadices with yellow tips. H to 45cm (18in), S to 75cm (30in), PD 37–45cm (15–18in).

PROPAGATION
🌰 as soon as ripe. Sow in midsummer at 18°C (64°F) and cover with 1–2.5cm (½–1in) of water.
🌱 3–4 weeks. ☀ 12 months.

Peltandra undulata

Pontederia cordata

Ranunculus lingua 'Grandiflorus'

Peltandra — Araceae

Genus of two species of hardy, marginal perennials, with prominent surface rhizomes, suitable for muddy margins or very shallow water, in full sun. They scramble over the soil surface, rooting at the nodes.

P. sagittifolia, syn. *P. alba* (White arrow arum). Has long-stalked, bright green leaves and arum-like, white spathes in early summer, followed by fleshy, red berries. H 45cm (18in), S 60cm (24in), PD 20cm (8in).

P. undulata syn. *P. virginica* (Green arrow arum). This is similar to *P. sagittifolia*, but its leaves are strongly veined and it produces greener and narrower flowers that are followed by green berries. H 90cm (36in), S 60cm (24in), PD 20cm (8in).

PROPAGATION

✎ spring. Section rhizomes into 10–20cm (4–8in) lengths as the buds may be well dispersed. ☀ 12 months.

Persicaria syn. Polygonum — Polygonaceae

Some 50–80 hardy and tender species of annuals and usually rhizomatous or stoloniferous perennials, many of which are moisture-lovers. Needs full sun.

P. amphibia, syn. *Polygonum amphibium* (Amphibious bistort, Willow grass). Hardy, semi-aquatic, stem-rooting perennial, useful for pools with fluctuating water levels. Lance-shaped leaves and pink flowers. H 30–60cm (1–2ft), S indefinite, PD 30–100cm (1–3ft).

PROPAGATION

Stem cuttings – spring and summer.
☀ 3 months.
✎ in the growing season. Separate stems that root at the nodes on contact with soil.
☀ 2 months.

Pontederia — Pontederiaceae

Genus of five species of hardy and tender, rhizomatous, marginal and aquatic perennials with spikes of colourful flowers and attractive leaves. Needs full sun.

P. cordata (Pickerel weed). Hardy, with a thick, creeping rhizome and neat habit. It has upright, lance-shaped, glossy olive-green leaves, and bears spikes of soft blue flowers at the top of the stem in late summer. H 45–60cm (18–24in) or more, S to 75cm (30in), PD 12cm (5in).

PROPAGATION

✎ late spring. Divide when the plant begins active growth. Use a very sharp knife because the rather spongy fibrous rootstock is inclined to rot if pulled apart carelessly.
☀ 3 months.
◖ as soon as ripe, at 12–15°C (54–59°F). Seed is best harvested green; it loses viability very quickly.
🌱 1–2 weeks. ☀ 9 months.

Potamogeton — Potamogetonaceae

About 80–100 species of hardy and tender, marginal and deep-water, often vigorous, rhizomatous perennials, with submerged and floating leaves. Some are suitable for growing as oxygenators or aquarium plants. Needs full sun.

P. crispus (Curled pondweed). Hardy and efficient oxygenator with wavy-edged, almost translucent leaves, varying from green to reddish brown. It may be used in cold-water aquariums and outdoor pools. S indefinite, PD 60cm (2ft) or more.

PROPAGATION

Stem cuttings – spring and early summer.
☀ 4 weeks.

Ranunculus — Ranunculaceae

Genus of about 400 hardy and tender, annuals, biennials, and perennials, including moisture-loving and aquatic species that prefer full sun.

R. aquatilis (Water crowfoot). Hardy, submerged, clump-forming perennial with flat, kidney-shaped, floating leaves. White flowers in midsummer. S 60–90cm (2–3ft) or more, PD 15–60cm (6–24in).

R. lingua 'Grandiflorus'. Marginal aquatic with double, buttercup-like golden yellow flowers. H and S 1.5m (5ft), PD 15–23cm (6–9in).

PROPAGATION

Stem cuttings – midsummer after flowering.
☀ 12 weeks.

R. lingua (Greater spearwort). Hardy, marginal perennial with upright red stems and long-stalked, arrow-shaped leaves. The flowering shoots bear linear or lance-shaped leaves, and cupped, yellow flowers in early summer. H 1.5m (5ft), S 2m (6ft), PD 15–23cm (6–9in).

PROPAGATION

✎ spring. Use a sharp knife to divide the thick, rather sappy rootstock.
☀ 3 months.

Sagittaria — Alismataceae

Some 20 hardy and tender, tuberous-rooted, mainly marginal perennials. The leaves may be floating or submerged and are often attractive. Decorative species are useful in wildlife pools; waterfowl eat the tuberous roots. They prefer full sun.

S. latifolia (Duck potato). Hardy, vigorous, marginal perennial with short, branching tubers. It has arrow-shaped to ovate leaves and bears whorls of three-petalled, white

Sagittaria sagittifolia

Saururus cernuus

Sparganium erectum

flowers in summer. H 40–60 cm (16–24in), S 90cm (36in), PD 8–12cm (3–5in).
S. sagittifolia (Japanese arrowhead). Hardy, tuberous perennial with arrow-shaped leaves and handsome, three-petalled, white flowers with a purple blotch at the base. H 90cm (36in), S indefinite, PD 8–12cm (3–5in).

PROPAGATION
✂ spring and summer. ☀ 3 months.
Seed – as soon as ripe, at 15°C (59°F), in a partially immersed seed tray or pot.
❦ 2 weeks. ☀ 9 months.

Saururus   Saururaceae
Genus of two hardy species of shallow-water, marginal, clump-forming perennials grown for their distinctive small, fragrant flowers. Prefers a sunny position but tolerates light shade.
S. cernuus (Lizard's tail, American swamp lily). Heart-shaped, bright green leaves and tiny, fragrant, white flowers in long spikes in late summer. H 30–60cm (12–24in), S 30cm (12in), PD 10cm (4in).

PROPAGATION
✂ spring. Divide every 3–4 years to maintain vigour. ☀ 3 months.
Offsets – summer. Separate offsets from the margins of the clump. ☀ 6 months.

Sparganium   Sparganiaceae
Some 21 species of deciduous or semi-evergreen, mostly hardy, rhizomatous perennials producing slender, rush-like, brown-green leaves and inconspicuous flowers. They are capable of forming large spreading clumps at the water's edge, which make ideal nesting sites and provide winter food for waterfowl.

S. erectum, syn. *S. ramosum* (Bur reed). Hardy, semi-evergreen species with extensive rhizomatous roots bearing rosettes of long, sword-shaped leaves. The branched inflorescence has rounded female flowers beneath several smaller male flowers in the same flower spike. H 90–120cm (3–4ft), S indefinite, PD to 45cm (18in).

PROPAGATION
✂ spring. Divide the tough rootstock with a spade. ☀ 3 months.
❦ as soon as ripe. Extract seed from the prickly round fruit in summer, and germinate at 15°C (59°F) in partially submerged seed pans.
❦ 3 weeks. ☀ 12 months.

Stratiotes   Hydrocharitaceae
One species of hardy, semi-evergreen, submerged and floating, stoloniferous perennial suitable for a sunny pond.
S. aloides (Water soldier, Water aloe). Rosettes of prickly, sword-shaped, olive-green leaves, which rise to the water surface to flower. The cup-shaped, white, male and female flowers grow on separate plants. The rosettes sink after flowering, then produce axillary shoots which resurface in late summer, to grow into new plants with winter buds or turions. H to 50cm (20in), S indefinite, PD 30cm (12in) or more.

PROPAGATION
Runners – spring. Separate runners and re-float immediately. ☀ 3 months.
Turions – autumn. Collect in autumn and overwinter on mud, covered with 15cm (6in) of water under glass at 4°C (40°F). Scatter on the pond surface in spring.
☀ 3 months.

Utricularia   Lentibulariaceae
About 180 species of hardy and tender, epiphytic, terrestrial, and floating, rootless perennials. They are insectivorous. The aquatic species thrive in stagnant water in the wild and need soft (acid) water in cultivation and full sun.
U. vulgaris (Greater bladderwort). Hardy, stoloniferous perennial with narrowly bell-shaped, rich golden yellow flowers carried well above the water surface on strong stems. Small insectivorous bladders are held in a network of feathery, bronzed leaves. H 30cm (12in), S indefinite, PD 30–60cm (12–24in).

PROPAGATION
✂ early summer. Tease apart the mats of floating foliage and refloat immediately.
☀ 6 weeks

Veronica   Scrophulariaceae
Some 250 species of annuals, herbaceous perennials, and mainly deciduous subshrubs including several hardy marginals.
V. beccabunga (Brooklime). Hardy with creeping, fleshy stems bearing spikes of white-centred, dark blue flowers and shining, rounded, fleshy leaves. It is excellent for scrambling over muddy banks, rooting as it goes. H 10–30cm (12in), S indefinite, PD to 12cm (5in).

PROPAGATION
Stem cuttings – midsummer. ☀ 3 months.
✂ summer. ☀ 2 months.
❦ as soon as ripe. Collect the rounded seed capsules and sow immediately at 15°C (59°F) in partially submerged seed trays.
❦ 2 weeks. ☀ 6 months.

$\mathscr{H}$ERBS

Ornamental and useful, herbs combine the delights of the flower garden with the satisfying activity of producing fresh ingredients for the kitchen that are far superior in flavour to their dried or frozen equivalents.

As a bonus, the delightful fragrances of herbs can be enjoyed in passing, making the garden a more relaxing place. Step into the garden and pick a few sprigs of herbs and you enter a different world, alive with invigorating scents and age-old associations.

Above all, herbs are among the easiest of all plants to grow and propagate. This chapter describes how to increase and replenish your collection of herbs of all kinds, for culinary, medicinal and cosmetic applications.

◀ *A mixed herb garden includes annuals, perennials and shrubs that have been propagated by the full range of propagation techniques.*

WHY PROPAGATE
HERBS?

Fresh herbs are far superior to dried or frozen equivalents, with a strength of aroma that gives intense flavour for kitchen use and the highest levels of active ingredients for teas and tonics. Propagating your own herbs gives a wide choice of varieties, and ensures that they are harvested at exactly the right time for optimum freshness.

Most culinary herbs yield better flavours when young and succulent, so propagate regularly to maintain your supply.

Many herbs are short-lived plants that need to be replaced annually or after only a few years. Some are annuals, or are treated as such, or biennials. Others, like rosemary, produce their best growth when young and become woody with age, so are best renewed regularly.

Whatever their ornamental value, herbs can also be treated as a crop. They may be grown like vegetables and sown at intervals, discarded after cropping, or forced for out-of-season use, regardless of their type.

Propagating herbs enables you to grow them in quantity for storing, either dried or frozen, for use in cooking, pot-pourri or herbal remedies throughout the period when they are not available fresh. Herbs include a range of plant types, and the key to propagation is to know what kind of plant – annual, biennial, perennial, shrub – you are dealing with.

ENSURING SUPPLY

Propagation by seed is used for annual and biennial herbs, but can also be used to raise perennials and shrubby types. The advantage is that, for herbs such as

parsley, which are treated as a crop, you can sow them at intervals throughout the growing season to ensure a continuous supply of good-quality material. It also guarantees disease-free plants.

REJUVENATING YOUR PLANTS

Division is the best method for clump-forming perennial herbs and rhizomatous types that can become woody or congested and less productive with age. All plants propagated by this and other vegetative methods will be identical to the parent. Besides increasing your stock, division benefits the plant by stopping it becoming congested and unproductive. Most should be routinely divided every three to five years.

Melissa officinalis **'Aurea'**
Variegated lemon balm will rapidly outgrow a container. It does not come true from seed, so divide in autumn or spring, or try rooting cuttings of non-flowering shoots in water.

Oreganum vulgare **'Aureum'**
Golden marjoram needs renewing every third growing season. Divide in spring or autumn, take basal cuttings in spring, or stem tip cuttings in early summer.

TAKING CUTTINGS

Cuttings can be taken of some perennials and the majority of shrubby herbs. The treatment of those cuttings depends largely on the time of year they are taken, since cuttings struck early in the season are generally in need of more aftercare than those taken a few months later. Softwood cuttings are usually taken in spring, semi-ripe cuttings in summer and stem tip cuttings whenever suitable material is available. In addition, some herbs root more readily from cuttings taken at specific times of the year. A number of the perennial herbs can also be increased by root cuttings.

MOUND LAYERING

This is a useful method for creating replacement stock of shrubby herbs, such as lavender and rosemary. Its primary use is to propagate from plants that have become bare and woody at the base with age.

Herbs in Containers

All of the common culinary herbs – such as rosemary, bay, tarragon, parsley, chives and mint – can be grown as short-term container plants. Strawberry pots are only suitable for growing small herbs that tolerate dry conditions, as competition for space and moisture is fierce when eight or nine plants are grown in the same container. Herbs in pots are in their prime in their first year. Small, shrubby and perennial herbs may look good for a second season, if pruned and well fed. But if you want good quality herbs in subsequent seasons, be prepared to propagate and replant in fresh compost.

A pot of mixed herbs can provide all your culinary needs for most of the year. Potted herbs can be harvested for much of the year.

(3) (5) (6) (8)

Thymus species
To keep thyme cultivars healthy and productive, increase every third summer by softwood or semi-ripe cuttings and replace in spring. Creeping sorts may also be divided in spring or late summer.

(4)

Laurus nobilis
In areas where bay is not fully hardy, insure your stock by taking semi-ripe cuttings or by detaching suckers in summer. Overwinter young plants in frost-free conditions under glass.

(7)

Salvia officinalis Purpurascens Group
As with other sages, purple sage becomes woody and sparse at maturity and needs replacing every 3–4 years. Take softwood cuttings in summer.

(9)

Mentha x gracilis 'Variegata'
Ginger mint needs replacing every third year or so, by division in spring or autumn, or by rooting cuttings of non-flowering shoots in spring, in compost or water.

PROPAGATING TECHNIQUES
HERBS

The term 'herb' covers a very wide range of plant types, and the key to successful propagation is to know what kind of plant – annual, biennial, perennial, shrub – you are dealing with. In some cases, a choice of techniques may be available to you, and it is often worth trying more than one as an insurance against failure.

Herbs are among the easiest of garden plants to grow and propagate and, by propagating regularly, you can be sure of a continuous supply.

SEED

Unlike vegetables, many of the herbs grown in gardens are true species that have not been subjected to breeding programmes. As a result, you can harvest your own seed from year to year. For plants whose leaves are normally harvested regularly (and thus do not flower or set seed), allow a couple of plants to grow unharvested, so that seed is produced from summer onwards.

Gather the seed when ripe and keep it dry in a paper bag until you are ready to sow it in spring or autumn. Many hardy herbs can be sown *in situ*. Rake over the soil to make a fine tilth and make seed drills 2.5cm (1in) deep. Sow the seed either individually or (for especially fine seed) in pinches. Cover the seed and water in well.

Some seed needs warmth to germinate. (*For requirements of individual herbs, see the plant directory, pp. 166–171.*) You can also sow the seed of some hardy herbs in warmth early in the season for early crops. Fill seed trays or 7.5in (3in) containers with a proprietary seed compost and firm it gently. Water the compost and allow it to drain. Sow the seed on the surface and cover to its own depth of compost. Very fine seed need not be covered. Water with a fine-rose watering can and allow to drain. Put the trays or pots into a heated propagator. Once the seedlings are large enough to handle, pot them on and gradually harden them by opening the propagator for progressively longer spells.

The seed of herbs that resent root disturbance and do not transplant easily can be sown individually in modules. Keep the seedlings in these until they are developed enough for planting out in their final positions.

Drying seed heads . . . .
The technique for harvesting and drying seed is essentially the same whether it is to be saved and sown the following year, or put to culinary use in the kitchen.

▶ **1** Harvest seeds promptly just as they begin to change colour from green to brown. If you wait until they are brown and fully ripe the seeds are likely to fall and be lost. On a fine dry day when the dew has dried, cut the seed head with a good length of stalk to provide enough energy for ripening to continue.

◀ **2** Bundle the stalks and seed heads into small bunches and tie with string or soft twine. Hang them upside down in a dry airy place with the seed heads in paper bags secured with string. The seeds will be caught in the paper bag as they ripen and fall.

DIVISION

In spring or autumn, lift clumps and shake them free of soil. Tease them apart, either with your hands or a hand fork. On tough plants, you may need to use a knife. To divide large clumps, the best method is to insert two forks back to back into the centre of the clump and prise it apart into smaller sections. Discard any woody, congested sections (usually from the middle of the clump) and replant the healthiest, most vigorous pieces. Water them in well.

CUTTINGS

Some perennial and most shrubby herbs can be propagated by various types of cutting, and many can be increased by more than one type of cutting as the season progresses by various types of cutting.

Stem tip cuttings: These can be taken from perennials throughout the growing season. Select a non-flowering side shoot and cut it just above a node to a length of 7.5–12.5cm (3–5in). Trim the cutting just below a node and strip away the leaves from the lower third. Immerse the cutting in a fungicidal solution. Dip the base in hormone rooting powder and insert it to a third of its length in a 7.5cm (3in) pot containing a mixture of equal parts grit, perlite or vermiculite and peat. Tent the cuttings with a polythene bag supported by canes.

Softwood cuttings: Softwood cuttings of shrubby herbs are taken from the current season's growth in late spring and early summer and are treated in the same way as stem tip cuttings. Inspect the cuttings regularly for any signs of fungal disease. Discard any affected cuttings and spray the remainder with a fungicide.

Semi-ripe cuttings: Semi-ripe cuttings, also from the current season's growth, are taken from mid- to late summer, just as the base of the current year's growth is beginning to firm and change from green to brown. If the base of the cutting is woody, remove a sliver of bark, about 1–2.5cm (½–1in) long, before treating with a fungicide. Continue as for stem tip cuttings.

Alternatively, where the side shoots are of a suitable length, take heeled cuttings. Grasp the stem at its point of origin and pull it sharply away to tear off a small piece of bark. Trim this with a sharp knife, then remove the lower leaves and continue as for stem tip cuttings.

In warm weather, keep the cuttings shaded. In cool weather, you can speed up rooting by placing them in a heated propagator. Semi-ripe cuttings can be rooted in a cold frame outdoors, though they will be slower to root. Check regularly for fungal diseases and water them to keep them evenly moist.

Forcing herbs for winter use ....

It is possible to extend the season for some herbs with protection. Chives, mint and tarragon naturally die down in winter but can be lifted, divided and forced for winter use.

▶ **I** In early autumn, lift the clump and remove any dead or dying stems. Divide the clump into manageable portions, separating by hand or, for tough-rooted plants, by cutting with a sharp knife.

▶ **2** Pot up the divisions into pots containing a loam-based potting compost. Water in well. Keep in a light, frost-free place and harvest new shoots regularly when they reach about 10cm (4in) high.

Cuttings given bottom heat should root within about four to six weeks. Once they show signs of new growth, pot them up individually and gradually harden them off. Semi-ripe cuttings without bottom heat should root by autumn but are best left undisturbed until spring. Overwinter them in a cold frame and pot them up the following spring.

Root cuttings: Some perennials can be increased by root cuttings. When the plant is fully dormant, in mid- to late winter, lift it and remove a healthy section of root of pencil thickness (you will find that the best material is usually at the centre of the crown). Cut the root into sections about 5–10cm (2–4in) long. To ensure that the cuttings are inserted correctly, cut the top of the root (the end nearest the crown) straight across and the base with a sloping cut. Each root should yield several cuttings. Dust the cut edges with fungicide. Insert them into moist cutting compost with their tops level with the compost surface and cover them with grit or sharp sand. Then, place them in a cold frame until new growth emerges, usually in early spring. Top-growth is often produced before the roots, so check for rooting before potting up. When they are well rooted, pot them up individually and grow them on.

MOUND LAYERING

This is a useful method for shrubby herbs that have become woody at the base and which do not respond well to hard pruning to rejuvenate them.

In spring, prepare a friable mixture of soil, garden compost or leafmould and grit or sharp sand. Mound the mixture around the plant, working it between the stems so that only the topmost 2.5–5cm (2–4in) of the

Planting up a herb wheel ···

Dig over the whole ground thoroughly, removing all weeds and large stones. Then cover the soil with a weed-suppressing, inorganic mulch, such as black plastic sheeting, and on this add a thick layer of ornamental mulch such as coarse bark, pebbles or grit. Define the edge of the wheel and each spoke with bricks or similar edging material, then fill each sector with a different herb.

Planting plan for a culinary herb wheel

Origanum vulgare 'Compactum'
(Compact marjoram)

Coriandrum sativum
(Coriander)

Anethum graveolens (Dill)

Thymus species
(Thyme)

Mentha spicata
(Spearmint)

Anthriscus
cerefolium
(Chervil)

Rosmarinus
officinalis
(Rosemary)

Allium schoenoprasum
(Chives)

Salvia officinalis
(Sage)

Artemisia dracunculus
(Tarragon)

Petroselinum crispum
(Parsley)

shoot tips are visible. Keep the mound thoroughly watered during dry spells in summer. Replenish the mound if heavy rains wash the topmost surface away. The stems will normally have rooted by the autumn. Scrape the surrounding soil away gently with your fingers and sever the new plants from the parent, cutting just below each new root system.

MAINTAINING A HERB WHEEL

The herb wheel (*shown left*) can be kept in productive condition by planning for renewal and replacement. Clockwise from the top, renew herbs as follows:

Origanum vulgare 'Compactum' (Compact marjoram). Hardy perennial. Divide and replant after two seasons.

Coriandrum sativum (Coriander). Annual. Renew from seed in spring and again in summer.

Mentha spicata (Spearmint). Hardy perennial. Divide and replant each spring.

Anthriscus cerefolium (Chervil). Annual. Renew from seed in spring and again in summer.

Allium schoenoprasum (Chives). Hardy perennial. Divide and replant after two growing seasons.

Petroselinum crispum (Parsley). Hardy annual/biennial. Renew from seed each spring and autumn.

Artemisia dracunculus (Tarragon). Hardy perennial. Divide and replant after two growing seasons.

Salvia officinalis (Sage). Evergreen shrub. Take cuttings in the third summer to replant the following spring.

Rosmarinus officinalis (Rosemary). Evergreen shrub. Take cuttings in the third summer to replant the following spring.

Thymus species and cultivars (Thyme). Take cuttings in the third summer to replant the following spring.

Anethum graveolens (Dill). Annual. Renew from seed in spring and again in summer.

HERBS IN CONTAINERS

Growing herbs in containers not only turns them into a decorative feature but is often the only choice for those without space for a herb garden. Containers are not only ornamental in themselves but can be positioned for maximum enjoyment and effect wherever is most convenient. Placed against a wall, or brought under cover in winter, herbs are cosseted against the elements, and enjoy relative freedom from some of their worst enemies – mudsplashing and slug

Propagation shortcuts ....
Rooting stem tip cuttings in water is a simple shortcut. Nothing roots as quickly as mint, but it is also worth trying marjoram, lemon balm, sage, tarragon, hyssop, bay and myrtle.

◄ Place a few stem tips in water, having removed any leaves that will be below water. When roots are 2.5–5cm (1–2in) long, carefully pot up each cutting separately.

attack. Propagate and replant the herbs regularly to keep containers looking good all season, or add different herbs for a change.

Containerized herbs must be fed and watered regularly, yet never allowed to become waterlogged. Water from the top and stand the pot in a saucer to increase water uptake if the compost becomes very dry. Then, feed the plants every week with a liquid fertilizer. If overcrowded, herbs dry out quickly, exhaust nutrients, and become prey to pests and diseases. You need to know the right kind and number of herbs to a pot and when to replace individual herbs.

All young herbs fit nicely into a 7.5cm (3-inch) pot, but rates of growth and eventual size differ greatly. It is best to treat a containerized herb as a short-term proposition. Replace annuals at least once a year, perennials after two seasons and shrubs after three years. The exceptions are bay, lemon verbena and myrtle, all of which can remain healthy in pots for many years.

• Check final height and spread, and whether a herb is an annual, biennial or perennial in order to determine how often it will need replacing.

• Do not overplant containers and ensure that they have a drainage hole and crocks at the bottom.

• Use loam-based (e.g. John Innes) compost for better moisture retention. It is also heavier, so containers are less likely to blow over.

• Add a top layer of grit for additional weight and to prevent mud-splashing.

• Use harvesting as an opportunity to prune and tidy herbs, and check their condition.

DIRECTORY OF
HERBS

Below are key tips on a selection of herbs that are particularly suitable for propagation. Unless otherwise specified, follow the detailed instructions given under the propagation section on pages 162–165.

Key

H	Height
S	Spread
HA	Hardy annual
HHA	Half-hardy annual
HB	Hardy biennial
HP	Hardy perennial
HSh	Hardy shrub
HHSh	Half-hardy shrub
TH	Time to harvest
✎	Division
🌱	Seed
⚘	Germination

Allium   Alliaceae

About 700 species of rhizomatous and bulbous perennials with onion-scented leaves *(see also Bulbs directory, pp.64–71 and Vegetables directory, pp.202–211)*. Two are used as herbs; they tolerate semi-shade.
A. schoenoprasum (Chives). Has deciduous, grass-like, mildly onion-flavoured leaves. May be forced for winter use. **'Forescate'** is larger, with pink flowers. HP. H 45cm (18in), S 30–45cm (12–18in)
A. tuberosum (Garlic chives, cuchay). Has flat, garlic-flavoured leaves, and white flowers in

late summer. HP. H 30–45cm (12–18in), 30cm (12in).

PROPAGATION
✎ autumn.
🌱 *in situ* in spring.
TH throughout growing season.

Aloysia   Verbenaceae

Some 37 shrubs with either deciduous or evergreen, aromatic leaves. Only *A. triphylla* is commonly grown.
A. triphylla syn. *Lippia citriodora* (Lemon verbena). This has deciduous, lemon-scented leaves and tiny, pale lilac flowers in summer. Needs shelter and is hardy to about -5°C (23°F). Frost-damaged plants usually survive, re-sprouting from the base in late spring or early summer. HHSh. H and S to 3m (10ft), but seldom exceeding 1.2m (4ft).

PROPAGATION
Heel cuttings – spring.
Softwood cuttings – early summer.
TH throughout the growing season.

Anethum   Apiaceae/Umbelliferae

A genus of only two species, one a biennial, one an annual. Both with very attractive, feathery, aniseed-scented leaves.

A. graveolens (Dill). Umbels of tiny yellow flowers above the leaves are followed by flat, oval seeds. Leaves and seeds have similar flavour but seeds are stronger. **'Dukat'** has luxuriant foliage. **'Mammoth'** has sparse foliage but large heads of seeds. Dill bolts if overcrowded or too dry, and self-seeds in good conditions, although seedlings do not transplant easily. Dill and fennel can cross-pollinate to produce a hybrid. HA.
H 60–90cm (2–3ft), S 15–30cm (6–12in).

PROPAGATION
🌱 *in situ*, spring and early summer. Sow at monthly intervals for a succession of young leaves. Alternatively, sow in pots or trays at 7–10°C (45–50°F) for cutting like mustard and cress.
TH leaves before flowering. Cut seed heads as they start to ripen and hang upside down in a paper bag.

Angelica   Umbelliferae

About 50 species of herbaceous biennials and perennials. One is grown as a herb.
A. archangelica (Angelica). Imposing specimen plant usually grown as a biennial with lush, aromatic foliage and large umbels of green-white flowers. Needs sun or semi-shade in fertile, moist soil. Self-sows prolifically, so remove unwanted seedheads before they ripen. HB. H 1.5–3m (5–10ft), S 1m (3ft).

PROPAGATION
🌱 *in situ* in autumn or spring. Home-grown seed must be sown in autumn, it loses viability within three months.

Anthriscus   Apiaceae/Umbelliferae

Some 12 species of annuals, biennials, and herbaceous perennials with small flowers in umbels and ferny leaves. Only chervil is usually grown for its anise-flavoured leaves.

Allium schoenoprasum

Angelica archangelica

166

Artemisia dracunculus

Borago officinalis

Chamaemelum nobile

A. cerefolium (Chervil). Chervil has fern-like, anise-flavoured leaves. Grow in sun or semi-shade in cool, moist soil; it bolts if overcrowded or too dry. Take off flower buds to prolong leaf production. HA/HB. H 30–45cm (12–18in), S 23–30cm (9–12in).

PROPAGATION

🌱 sow *in situ* at monthly intervals, in spring and summer, or at 7–10°C (45–50°F) under glass in early autumn for winter leaves. TH before flowering.

Armoracia   Brassicaceae/Cruciferae

Just three species of perennials with deep, woody or fleshy taproots, variable leaves and small flowers. Only horseradish is cultivated.
A. rusticana (Horseradish). Dock-like leaves grow from thick, pungent taproot, which can be difficult to eradicate once established. **'Variegata'** is less invasive, with cream-variegated leaves. Tolerates semi-shade. HP. H 60cm (24in), S indefinite.

PROPAGATION

✂ autumn or early spring. Take root cuttings when plants are dormant.
🌱 species only, *in situ*, in spring.
TH lift roots from summer to late autumn. Store in boxes of sand for winter use.

Artemisia   Asteraceae/Compositae

Around 300 species of evergreen or deciduous, annuals, perennials and shrubs, with usually aromatic, often grey or silvery leaves. Several are classed as herbs *(see also Herbaceous Perennials directory, p.35).*
A. abrotanum (Southernwood, Lad's love). Deciduous or semi-evergreen shrub grown for its feathery, grey-green, pungent leaves. It rarely flowers in cold climates. Leaves retain

their scent on drying and are used in pot-pourri and insect-repellent sachets. HSh. H 60–90cm (2–3ft), S 30-60cm (12–24in).
A. dracunculus (French tarragon). Deciduous subshrubby perennial with narrow, green, anise-flavoured leaves. **subsp. *dracunculoides*** (Russian tarragon) has an inferior flavour. Remove flower stems to prolong leaf production. May be forced for winter. HP/HHP. The subspecies is hardier than the species. H and S 45–60cm (18–24in).

PROPAGATION

✂ early spring.
Cuttings – *A. abrotanum*: semi-ripe, with a heel – late summer. *A. dracunculus*: basal – spring. TH throughout growing season.

Borago   Boriginaceae

Three species of annuals and perennials, of which only borage is usually grown.
B. officinalis (Borage). Borage has cucumber-flavoured leaves and edible, star-shaped blue flowers. Needs to be grown in moist but well-drained soil. Self-sows freely. HA. H 18–36in S 6–12in

PROPAGATION

🌱 *in situ* from spring to midsummer.

Carum   Apiaceae/Umbelliferae

Some 30 species of taprooted biennials and herbaceous perennials. Caraway is the only species generally in cultivation.
C. carvi (Caraway). Upright plant with carrot-like foliage and umbels of tiny white to pink-rayed flowers, then aromatic seeds. Seedlings do not transplant well. Seeds may not ripen from spring sowings in a cool summer. HB.
H 60–90cm (2–3ft), S 30cm (12in).

PROPAGATION

🌱 *in situ* in autumn or spring.
TH cut seed heads in summer–autumn, and hang upside down in paper bags.

Chamaemelum   Asteraceae/Compositae

Some four species of aromatic annuals and evergreen perennials with attractive feathery leaves and white daisy flowers.
C. nobile, syn. *Anthemis nobilis* (Roman chamomile). Mat-forming with bright green, apple-scented foliage and daisy-like flowers. Prefers well-drained soil in full sun. **'Flore Pleno'** has double white flowers. **'Treneague'** is non-flowering and recommended for chamomile lawns. The plants may become rather bare in very cold winters but usually recover. Handling chamomile may cause dermatitis. HP. H to 15cm (6in), S 45cm (18in).

PROPAGATION

🌱 *in situ* in spring.
✂ spring or autumn.
Cuttings – stem-tip cuttings of side-shoots – summer. Cultivars by cuttings only.

Coriandrum   Apiaceae/Umbelliferae

Two annual species with scented foliage and small flowers. Coriander is used in cooking.
C. sativum (Coriander, cilantro). Has strongly aromatic, lobed to divided leaves and umbels of white flowers, then round seeds. Leaves and seeds have different aromas and uses. Grow in sun if seeds are required; for leaf crops, grow in semi-shade. HA.
H 60cm (24in), S 30–45cm (12–18in).

PROPAGATION

🌱 *in situ* in spring for seed crops; at monthly intervals, from spring to summer for leaf crops. Leaves can also be produced

Foeniculum vulgare

Laurus nobilis

Lavandula angustifolia 'Hidcote'

at 10–13°C (50–55°F) under glass.
TH leaves before flowering. Cut seed heads
as they ripen in summer and autumn, and
hang upside down in paper bags.

Cuminum   Apiaceae/Umbelliferae

Only two species of annuals with very fine
foliage and umbels of white or pink flowers.
C. cyminum (Cumin). Cumin has dark green,
finely divided leaves and umbels of tiny white
flowers, followed by pungent, rather bitter
seeds. Needs a long, warm growing season
for seeds to ripen. HHA.
H 15–30cm (6–12in), S 8–10cm (3–4in).
PROPAGATION
🌱 *in situ* in late spring.
TH cut seed heads as they ripen in summer
and autumn and hang upside in paper bags.

Cymbopogon   Poaceae/Graminae

Some 56 aromatic grasses, usually evergreen.
They are aromatic and their narrow leaves
grow in tufted groups; their flowers are like
narrow, grassy seed heads. Lemon grass, the
only species cultivated, is used in cooking.
C. citratus (Lemon grass). Large, tropical grass
with thick stem bases and long, lemon-
scented leaves. The stem bases are used
whole, or finely chopped. The leaves are used
for herb tea. In cold areas, it is easily grown in
large pots of well-drained potting compost
on a sunny windowsill; it grows only to a
manageable size in pots, but is very much
larger grown outdoors in subtropical or
tropical gardens. Small plants are occasionally
offered for sale in the vegetable departments
of supermarkets. HP. It needs to be provided
with a minimum temperature of 7°C (45°F).
H 1–1.5m (3–5ft), S 1m (3ft).

PROPAGATION
🔧 spring.
TH cut off individual stems throughout the
growing season.

Foeniculum   Apiaceae/Umbelliferae

A single species of aromatic perennial. **F.
vulgare** (Fennel). An upright plant with
feathery, anise-scented foliage and umbels of
tiny yellow flowers, followed by aromatic
seeds. Not reliably hardy in heavy soil and
cold, wet winters. **'Purpureum'** (Bronze
Fennel) is hardier, with rich brown foliage. It
comes true from seed. HP.
H 1.8m (6ft), S 45cm (18in).
PROPAGATION
🌱 *in situ*, spring. Self-sows in light soils.
🔧 spring.
TH leaves before flowering. Cut seed heads
as they ripen in summer and autumn and
hang upside in paper bags.

Galium (Bedstraw)   Rubiaceae

Some 400 species of annuals and perennials,
usually with whorls of leaves and tubular
star-shaped, white, pink, or yellow flowers
G. odoratum is the only one grown.
G. odoratum (Sweet woodruff). This has
whorls of narrow, fresh bright green leaves
and in spring and early summer it bears
pretty heads of pure white, star-shaped
flowers. Needs shade or partial shade and
moist soil. The leaves have no apparent
aroma when fresh, but on drying, develop a
delicious scent of new-mown hay. HP.
H 15–25cm (6–10in), S indefinite.
PROPAGATION
🔧 autumn or spring.
TH when in flower.

Hyssopus (Hyssop)   Labiatae/Lamiaceae

Some five species of aromatic herbaceous
perennials and evergreen or semi-evergreen
shrubs with narrow leaves and spikes of
tubular flowers above the foliage.
H. officinalis (Hyssop). This is a semi-
evergreen shrub producing leaves with a
sage-mint flavour, and deep blue flowers in
summer. There are pink- and white-flowered
forms. **subsp. aristatus** (Rock hyssop) has a
dwarf habit, useful for edging and containers.
HSh. H and S 45–60cm (18–24in).
PROPAGATION
🌱 *in situ*, autumn or spring.
Softwood cuttings – summer.
TH throughout growing season.

Laurus   Lauraceae

Only two species of evergreen plants, one a
tree, the other, bay, a shrub or small tree.
L. nobilis (Bay). This has leathery, evergreen,
pointed leaves. An excellent plant for
containers, it thrives in a relatively small pot,
tolerates fluctuations in watering, and
responds well to clipping or growing as a
standard. Needs protection from frost and
wind in areas with hard winters. H/HHSh.
H 3–12m (10–40ft), S 3m (10ft); in containers,
H to 2m (6ft), S 90–120cm (3–4ft).
PROPAGATION
Semi-ripe cuttings –summer.
Suckers – detach in summer.
TH all year but best in summer for drying.

Lavandula (Lavender)   Lamiaceae/Labiatae

About 25 species of evergreen shrubs and
subshrubs with aromatic leaves and spikes of
fragrant tubular flowers often in shades of
blue or pink to purple, which are usually held

Mentha x *gracilis* 'Variegata'

Melissa officinalis

Monarda didyma 'Cambridge Scarlet'

on long stalks above the plant. They prefer a site that has well-drained soil and is sunny (*see also Shrubs directory, p.121*).
L. angustifolia (Common lavender, English lavender). Has downy, narrow leaves and spikes of purple flowers. HSh. H to 1m (3ft), S to 1.2m (4ft). '**Hidcote**' has dark purple flowers. HSh. H 60cm (24in), S 75cm (30in).
L. × *intermedia* (Lavandin). Variable, rounded, sometimes lax shrub with grey-green leaves, and long spikes of very fragrant flowers. HSh. H and S 45–90cm (18–36in). '**Grappenhall**' has lavender-blue flowers. HSh. H 1–1.2m (3–4ft), S 1.5m (5ft).

PROPAGATION
(See directions when grown as a shrub on p.121.) TH cut as the flowers begin to open.

Levisticum   Apiaceae/Umbelliferae
A single species of herbaceous perennial.
L. officinale (Lovage). Triangular to diamond-shaped leaves with a celery flavour. Provide moist fertile soil in sun or partial shade. HP. H 2m (6ft), S 1m (3ft).

PROPAGATION
🌱 sow *in situ* in autumn.
✂ spring.
TH throughout the growing season, but best before flowering.

Matricaria   Asteracae/Compositae
Some five annual herbs with divided leaves and daisy-like flowers.
M. recutita (German chamomile). Has finely divided aromatic leaves. HA. H 60cm (24in), S 15–30cm (6–12in).

PROPAGATION
🌱 *in situ*, autumn or spring.
TH when flowers first open.

Melissa (Balm)   Lamiaceae/Labiatae
Just three species of herbaceous perennials with leaves smelling strongly of lemon.
M. officinalis (Lemon balm). Has wrinkled, nettle-like leaves. '**Aurea**' has yellow-variegated leaves. Grow in sun or semi-shade in moist soil. Cut stems back after flowering to encourage new leaves. HP. H 60–75cm (24–75cm), S 30–45cm (12–18in).

PROPAGATION
🌱 species only, or divide in autumn or spring. TH before flowering.

Mentha (Mint)   Lamiaceae/Labiatae
Some 25 herbaceous perennials, most regarded as herbs, with fleshy, creeping roots and aromatic, serrated leaves. The flowers are small and tubular to bell-shaped. Grow mint in sun or semi-shade in moist soil. Mints are invasive, so plant in a large pot or sink an old container or heavy-duty plastic bag in the ground to control spread. HP. H 60–90cm (2–3ft), S indefinite.
M. × *gracilis* '**Variegata**' (Ginger mint). Mild, spicy spearmint flavour.
M. × *piperita* (Peppermint). Purple-flushed leaves with a strong peppermint flavour. '**Citrata**' (Eau-de-Cologne mint) has a lavender-mint aroma.
M. spicata (Spearmint). Bright green, sweetly scented leaves.
M. suaveolens (Applemint). Rounded, woolly leaves with a mild spearmint flavour. '**Variegata**' (**Pineapple mint**) is more ornamental, with cream-splashed leaves.
M. × *villosa* var. *alopecuroides* (Bowles' mint). variety of sterile hybrid between *M. Spicata* and *M suaveolens*. Large, woolly, spearmint-flavoured leaves.

PROPAGATION
✂ autumn or spring.
Stem tip cuttings of non-flowering shoots – spring or summer; root in compost or water. TH before flowering.

Monarda (Bergamot)   Lamiaceae/Labiatae
About 15 species of annuals and clump-forming rhizomatous perennials with aromatic leaves and whorls of tubular flowers, often with coloured bracts.
M. didyma. Has bright red flowers and leaves smelling like Earl Grey tea. Most plants in cultivation are hybrids like '**Cambridge Scarlet**' and '**Croftway Pink**'. Grow in sun in fertile, moist soil. HP. H 60–90cm (24-36in), S 30–60cm (12–24in).

PROPAGATION
✂ spring.
Softwood cuttings – early summer.
🌱 spring at 16–21°C (61-70°F).
TH leaves before flowering. Flowers as they open.

Myrrhis   Apiaceae/Umbelliferae
A single species of herbaceous perennial.
M. odorata (Sweet Cicely). Has fern-like, bright green leaves with a sweet, anise aroma, which can be used as a flavouring, and small star-shaped white flowers in summer. Grow in a sunny position or in shade in cool, moist, humus-rich soil. Self-seeds freely in good conditions. HP. H 90cm (36in), S 60–90cm (24–36in).

PROPAGATION
🌱 *in situ* in autumn or spring (often slow to germinate).
✂ autumn or spring.
TH throughout growing season.

Ocimum basilicum

Origanum vulgare

Petroselinum crispum

Myrtus (Myrtle) Myrtaceae

Two species of evergreen tree and shrubs.
M. communis (Common myrtle). A bushy
shrub with evergreen leaves, which have a
juniper-like aroma, and fragrant white flowers
in summer. **'Variegata'** has cream and grey-
green variegation. **subsp. *tarentina*** is dwarf,
compact, and free-flowering; it is good for
containers. Needs neutral to alkaline soil.
HHSh. It is hardy to about -5°C (23°F).
'Variegata' is less hardy. H and S to 2m (6ft),
in containers, H and S 60–90cm (2–3ft.)

PROPAGATION
at 16–21°C (61-70°F) in spring.
Semi-ripe cuttings – late summer.
TH throughout growing season.

Ocimum Lamiaceae/Labiatae

Some 35 species of annuals and evergreen
perennials which have aromatic leaves. Most
have culinary or medicinal uses. Basil is the
most commonly grown.
O. basilicum (Basil). Basil has bright green,
clove-scented leaves and small white flowers.
'African Blue' is a large-growing hybrid. H
90–120cm (3–4ft). It is propagated by
cuttings from overwintered plants. **'Anise'**
has purple-flushed foliage, pink flowers, and
an aniseed flavour. **var. *citriodorum*** has citrus-
scented leaves. **var. *crispum*** (Curly or
Lettuce-leaf basil) has large, wrinkled leaves.
'Dark Opal', syn. 'Purpureum', has purple-
black leaves. **var. *minimum*** (Bush basil) is
hardier, with small leaves and a compact
habit. H 15–30cm (6–12in). Grow in sun in
fertile, well-drained to dry soil.HA/HP.
Minimum temperature 13°C (55°F). Prone
to botrytis in cool, damp conditions.
H 60–90cm (24–36in), S 15–30cm (12–18in).

PROPAGATION
late spring, at 13–18°C (55–65°F).
TH throughout growing season.

Origanum Lamiaceae/Labiatae

About 20 species of often rhizomatous,
herbaceous perennials and evergreen or
deciduous subshrubs, mainly flowering in
summer and with aromatic leaves. Grow
origanum in well-drained to dry, neutral to
alkaline soil. Use leaves and flowering sprigs
in Italian, Greek and Mexican dishes. The
flavour is best when dried.
O. majorana (Sweet marjoram). This has
grey-green, strongly aromatic leaves and tiny
white flowers in bobble-like heads. Good for
growing in containers. HHSh, usually grown
as an annual. H 80cm (32in), S 45cm (18in).
O. onites (Pot marjoram). This has mildly
aromatic leaves and white or purple-flushed
flowers in summer and early autumn. HP.
H and S 60cm (24in).
O. vulgare (Oregano). Variable in aroma and
appearance, the flavour is more pungent in
hot, dry conditions. It bears purple-pink
flowers in summer. **'Aureum'** has bright
yellow-green leaves and mauve flowers and
is best in semi-shade to avoid scorching.
'Compactum' has a dense, rounded habit, to
15cm (6in) tall, and is good for edging and
containers. HP. H and S 45cm (18in).

PROPAGATION
species only, at 10–13°C (50-55°F) in
early spring, or *in situ* in late spring.
autumn or spring.
Basal cuttings – spring.
Tip cuttings – early summer.
TH leaves throughout the growing season;
flowering sprigs when flowers first open.

Petroselinum Apiaceae/Umbelliferae

Three species of biennials with toothed
divided leaves and taproots. Cultivars of
P. crispum are commonly grown. **P. crispum**
(Parsley). The true species has been
superseded by curly-leaved cultivars such as
'Moss Curled', **'Afro'**, and **'Clivi'**. Forms with
flat leaves are Italian or French parsley. They
are larger and more strongly flavoured. Grow
in sun or semi-shade in fertile, well-drained,
neutral to alkaline soil. Protect winter crops
under cloches or in a cold frame. HB/HA.
Italian and French parsley are hardier.
H 30–60cm (12–24in), S 30cm (12in).

PROPAGATION
in situ, at intervals from early spring to
late summer for a year-round supply. For
early crops, sow at 10–13°C (50-55°F)
under glass. Soak seed overnight in hot
water to speed germination, which otherwise takes 3–6 weeks.
TH throughout growing season in the first
year; before flowering in the second year.

Pimpinella Apiaceae/Umbelliferae

Some 150 species of annuals or herbaceous
perennials with hairy stems and umbels of
tiny star-shaped flowers, usually white or
yellow, followed by fruits.
P. anisum (Anise, Aniseed). Aromatic, divided
leaves and flat heads of tiny off-white flowers
followed by ribbed, aniseed-flavoured seeds.
HHA. H 30–50cm (12–20in), S 25–45cm
(10–18in).

PROPAGATION
sow *in situ* in spring.
TH leaves throughout the growing season.
Cut seed heads as they ripen and hang
upside down in paper bags.

Rosmarinus officinalis

Salvia officinalis 'Icterina'

Thymus x citriodorus 'Silver Queen'

Rosmarinus — Lamiaceae/Labiatae

Two species of aromatic evergreen shrubs with narrow leaves and whorls of flowers. *R. officinalis* (Rosemary). This shrub has spiky, resinous, highly aromatic foliage and pale blue flowers in spring. **'Miss Jessopp's Upright'** has a vigorous, erect habit. **'Sissinghurst Blue'** is free-flowering, upright, and relatively hardy. Grow in well-drained to dry, neutral to alkaline soil. HSh. Hardy to about -10°C (14°F), perhaps more with sharp drainage. H and S 1–2m (3–6ft).

PROPAGATION
🌰 spring, at 10°C (50°F), species only.
Semi-ripe cuttings – summer.
TH all year, but best in growing season.

Rumex — Polygonaceae

Some 200 annuals, biennials, or herbaceous perennials, often with taproots or rhizomes. The cultivated forms usually have basal leaves and flowers in clusters on erect stems. Needs sun or semi-shade, in moist soil. *R. acetosa* (Sorrel). Has acidic, spinach-like leaves. HP.
H 30–45cm (12–18in), S 25–45cm (10–18in).
R. scutatus (French sorrel, Buckler-leaf sorrel). Smaller, less acidic leaves than *R. acetosa* and a mat-forming, invasive habit. HP.
H 15–23cm (6–9in), S 1.2m (4ft).

PROPAGATION
🌰 in situ in spring.
🔧 autumn or spring.

Salvia (Sage) — Lamiaceae/Labiatae

About 900 species of annuals, biennials, herbaceous and evergreen perennials, and shrubs *(see also Herbaceous Perennials directory, pp.34–45).*

S. officinalis. Velvety, evergreen leaves with a scent of camphor, and purple-blue to pink or white flowers. **'Icterina'** has yellow-variegated leaves. **Purpurascens Group** (Red sage, Purple sage) has purple-grey leaves. Grow in well-drained to dry, neutral to alkaline soil. Replace plants every 3–4 years when they become woody. HSh. Less hardy in heavy soils and in cold, wet winters.
H 60–80cm (24–32in), S 60–90cm (24–36in).

PROPAGATION
🌰 spring, at 13–18°C (55–65°F); species only. Purple-leaved forms produce variable offspring from seed.
Softwood cuttings – in summer.
TH all year but best before flowering.

Satureja (Savory) — Lamiaceae/Labiatae

Some 30 species of annuals, herbaceous perennials, and subshrubs with aromatic leaves and spikes of flowers. The two listed are most commonly grown. Needs sun in well-drained to dry, neutral to alkaline soil. *S. hortensis* (Summer savory). Small, narrow, leaves taste peppery. Tiny lilac to white flowers. HA. H 25cm (10in), S 30cm (12in).
S. montana (Winter savory). Evergreen, with a less pleasant flavour than *S. hortensis*. HSh. H 40cm (16in), S 20cm (8in).

PROPAGATION
🌰 in situ in spring.
Softwood cuttings – spring, for *S. montana*.
TH summer.

Thymus (Thyme) — Lamiaceae/Labiatae

Some 350 species of evergreen perennials, shrubs and subshrubs, with aromatic leaves and clusters of tubular flowers. Many are cultivated as herbs or as ornamentals. Grow in well-drained to dry, neutral to alkaline soil. HSh. Less hardy in heavy soils or especially cold wet winters.
T. x citriodorus (Lemon thyme). Lilac flowers and a lemon flavour. **'Silver Queen'** has variegated leaves.
H 10–12cm (4–5in), S 60cm (24in).
T. herba-barona (Caraway thyme). Creeping stems and minute, spicy, dark green leaves.
H 5–10cm (2–4in), S 60cm (24in).
T. serpyllum (Wild thyme). Prostrate with pink-mauve flowers. Aroma like *T. vulgaris*.
H 5–8cm (2–3in), S 30–90cm (12–36in).
T. vulgaris (Common thyme). Variable, with dark green to grey-green, strongly aromatic leaves and mauve to white flowers.
H 30–45cm (12–18in), S 60cm (24in).

PROPAGATION
🌰 spring, at 10°C (50°F), or in a cold frame; species only.
Softwood cuttings – early summer.
Semi-ripe cuttings – midsummer.
🔧 creeping thymes. Spring or late summer.
TH summer.

Zingiber (Ginger) — Zingiberaceae

Some 100 herbaceous perennials with aromatic rhizomes and reed-like leaves. *Z. officinale* (Common ginger). The ginger root used in cooking. Needs fertile, well-drained, neutral to alkaline soil, in sun or semi-shade, with warmth and high humidity. It grows well in pots although it will not crop heavily in the greenhouse in cool areas. HP.
H 1–1.2m (3–4ft), S indefinite.

PROPAGATION
🔧 divide and plant rhizomes at 24°C (75°F) in early spring.
TH autumn.

$\mathcal{F}$RUIT

The fruit garden can be an idyllic place, alive with bees and other pollinating insects in spring and providing a feast for the eye and the table as the fruits develop and ripen from summer to autumn.

Most fruit sold in groceries and supermarkets has been bred for disease resistance, heavy cropping and long shelf life; flavour is a lower priority for commercial growers. However, in your own fruit garden, where you are growing for pleasure and not profit, you can concentrate on the taste and genuine quality of the produce.

Such is the range of fruit plants that a wide variety of propagation techniques must be used to ensure the continued life of the plants.

◄ *Keeping a well-stocked fruit garden involves a range of propagating techniques: some needed annually and others, like grafting, perhaps required only once in the life of the garden.*

WHY PROPAGATE
FRUIT?

The flavour of home-grown fruit, fully ripened on the plant, is infinitely superior to anything that can be bought in a shop, yet it is probably the easiest of the kitchen garden crops to produce. All you need is well-prepared ground and healthy plants, many of which are simple to propagate yourself using a variety of straightforward techniques.

Propagation is an important and integral part of fruit growing. Young plants often produce better quality fruits. Many soft fruits, particularly strawberries, are short-lived and need replacing regularly, and most fruit-bearing trees, though long-lived, need replacing as they age, or if they are damaged and become less productive.

Nearly all fruit plants are hybrid cultivars selected especially for their fruit quality and heavy cropping. Because of this, seed is seldom used except to produce new hybrids, and clonal methods are most common.

Apples

Raspberries

BETTER STRAWBERRY CROPS
Propagation by runner is used for strawberries, which are short-lived herbaceous perennials best replaced after three years or less. Regular propagation helps maintain virus-free stock and, if fresh plants are established in late summer, good crops will be assured in the next year.

TIP LAYERING
This method can be used for cane fruits that produce a quantity of flexible stems from their base. This is the way that blackberries spread naturally in the wild and the technique is virtually foolproof.

A VERSATILE TECHNIQUE
Propagation by cuttings is a straightforward method for a number of fruit plants. Hardwood cuttings taken in autumn are the easiest and can be used for a number of subjects including currants, gooseberries, figs and vines. Softwood cuttings can be used for blueberries and vines, among others, and are quicker to root but require bottom heat and high humidity for the best results.

The methods of leaf-bud and three-bud cuttings maximize the use of available cuttings material, but are slower to develop than conventional cuttings.

Blackberries

Red currants

The techniques for propagating fruit range from the simplest pegging down of strawberry runners to sophisticated forms of grafting that need skill and practice to perfect.

Strawberries

MAKING USE OF SUCKERS
Naturally suckering plants, such as raspberries and cobnuts, can generally be effectively increased by severing the suckers. This also benefits the parent on the whole, which could otherwise become congested, less productive and more prone to disease. This method should only be used on disease-free stock.

THE ATTRACTION OF GRAFTING

Top fruits are usually propagated by grafting onto a rootstock. Cuttings are seldom successful, since many are highly bred plants that have lost vigour in the selection process. The rootstock chosen can also promote improved disease resistance and affect the rate of growth. Using a dwarfing rootstock, for instance, enables you to grow, in a small space, trees that would otherwise be too big. It is also quite possible to graft material from several different varieties onto one rootstock to make a 'family' tree (*see box*).

The main methods are chip- or T-budding, in late summer, and whip-and-tongue grafting from late winter to spring. Using both methods on any tree to be propagated increases your chance of success without losing growing time since, if the former is not successful, the latter can be tried the following spring.

Family Trees

Very few apples are self-fertile, and so do not self-pollinate reliably or consistently. The standard advice is that more than one apple has to be planted to ensure cross-pollination and fruiting. In small gardens, where space is limited, this may not be possible. One answer to this is to plant a 'family', or 'several-in-one', tree. A family tree is one in which the branches of an established popular cultivar have been grafted with one or two other cultivars that are compatible pollinators. This also gives a choice of fruits in a limited space, and ensures that there is seldom a glut of one variety. On dwarfing rootstocks they can even be grown in a tub.

A family tree grafted with two different mutually-compatible cultivars of apple.

 Apples
Almost invariably grown as grafted plants, apples are exceptionally long-lived and seldom need re-propagating. They do not come true and take many years to fruit if they are grown from seed.

 Raspberries
These fruit can be increased by suckers, but only take suckers if the parent plant is healthy and virus free. Diseased stock should be replaced by certified virus-free stock from a garden centre.

 Blackberries
These and other related cane fruits increase naturally by tip layers and this is by far the easiest means of propagation. Propagation by leaf-bud cuttings is useful where greater numbers are required.

Red currants
Along with black and white currants, red currants are among the fruiting shrubs that can be increased simply by hardwood cuttings but are only likely to need replacement after 10–20 years.

 Strawberries
Strawberries are best propagated every second or third year as the best crops are obtained from young plants. Regular propagation also reduces the risks of virus infection.

PROPAGATING TECHNIQUES
FRUIT

The methods that one can employ for the propagation of fruit are as numerous and diverse as the species to which they apply. However, very few techniques will present problems or require much in the way of special equipment. Whichever of the many following methods you opt for, the result should always be the same: better-quality fruit.

SOFT FRUIT

Soft fruits are mainly those that are grown on bushes or canes, like currants, raspberries and blackberries, as opposed to top-fruits, such as apples and pears, that are borne on trees.

Propagation of strawberries by runners

Unique among the soft fruits, strawberries (*Fragaria* × *ananassa*) are herbaceous perennials. They are prone to soil-borne viruses and to fungi-like strawberry red core, and should be grown in rotation, that is, new plantings should be made in clean ground that has not grown strawberries before. Strawberries should not be grown in the same ground for more than three years and a supply of fresh plants should be maintained by regular propagation. Ideally, where space permits, one-, two- and three-year-old plants should be grown and harvested successively, so that the oldest three-year-old plants can be discarded after fruiting and burned.

Strawberry runners . . . .

The crown buds of strawberry plants develop stems that spread horizontally over the ground. These runners readily root at the leaf nodes to form new plants.

► Runners will be produced from mid- to late summer. Peg these down using U-shaped lengths of wire either onto the open ground or (preferably, to keep the new plants free from soil-borne diseases) into a 7.5cm (3in) pot filled with sterile, loam-based compost (John Innes No. 2) plunged into the ground with the compost surface level with the soil. When the runners are well rooted, usually by late summer, they can be severed from the parent plant.

When first planting a strawberry bed, it is essential to obtain certified virus-free stocks. When propagating from established plants, only use healthy material. Strawberries can be affected by several viruses, usually spread by aphids and other sap-sucking insects, which cause a range of symptoms, including stunting, spotting, yellowing or puckering of the leaves.

Although runners can be taken from fruiting plants, it is best to set aside a few plants specifically for runner production and grow them in a separate bed well away from fruits grown for cropping. A propagating bed can be expected to be productive for two years. Plant them 1m (3ft) apart in a nursery bed and remove any flowers so that all their energy goes into runner production. Runners will be ready to peg down between mid- and late summer. Keep the soil moist to encourage the runners to root. Once well rooted, usually by late summer, young plants can be set out in their cropping site to crop in the following season. In areas with very cold winters, it is advisable to delay planting out young plants until spring, but in this case it is best to remove the flowers in the first season to allow them to build up into strong plants before cropping.

Tip layering

Blackberries (*Rubus fruticosus*) and a number of other hybrid berries that have arching canes can be propagated by this simple method. A limited number of fresh plants can be made, since only well-placed stems can be used, each producing one new plant. Where larger numbers of plants are required leaf-bud cuttings or three-bud cuttings can be used (*see p.179*).

From late summer to early autumn, select strong, healthy canes, preferably towards the edge of the plant. Bring the tips down to soil level and, at the point where

Tip layering ....

This method of propagation is invaluable with various members of the *Rubus* family because their stem tips when buried will swell, develop roots and form new plants.

◄ Cultivate the ground thoroughly before digging a hole for the stem tip. This hole should be 10–15cm (4–6in) deep and have vertical sides on all but one side, which should be angled towards the parent plant.

they meet the ground, dig a hole 10–15cm (4–6in) deep. On heavy soils, work in a little grit or sharp sand to improve drainage. Bury the stem tips, securing them with wires bent into U-shapes if necessary.

Keep the soil moist. The tip should root within three to four weeks and a new shoot will develop from it. The following spring, sever the rooted tip from the parent plant, retaining about 23cm (9in) of the stem, and plant it out in a new position.

Hardwood cuttings

Soft fruits such as currants (black, red and white) and gooseberries, figs and vines can be increased by hardwood cuttings. Where the root pest *Phylloxera vastratrix* is present, vines must be grafted onto a *Phylloxera*-resistant rootstock.

Most cuttings root best if taken in early autumn, at or just before leaf fall, before they are fully dormant. This enables some root initials to form before the onset of winter, allowing rapid root growth the following spring. In cold climates, figs and vines need to be rooted under glass or in a closed cold frame.

Currants (red and white) and gooseberries: Red and white currants and gooseberries are usually grown as open-centred bushes, cordons or fans.

Take cuttings 30–38cm (12–15in) long, cutting with an angled cut just above a bud. Trim the base of the cuttings with a straight cut just below a bud. Remove the tips of the cuttings if they are very soft. On gooseberries, trim off large thorns for ease of handling.

On red and white currants, remove the lower buds to prevent suckers arising from below ground level, leaving four good buds at the top. Gooseberries do not root as easily, so, to promote root initiation retain all of the buds on the stem and the top two leaves, and dip the base of the cutting in hormone rooting powder.

Prepare a slit or straight-backed trench 15–22cm (6–9in) deep. On heavy soils run sharp sand into the bottom to aid drainage. Insert the cuttings to half their length, 15cm (6in) apart, and firm them in. In cold climates, lay a 1m (3ft) wide strip of black polythene along the nursery bed, burying about 15cm (6in) on either side. This prevents the soil surface from freezing and also retains moisture and discourages weed

Hardwood cuttings ....

The length of a hardwood cutting and how it is prepared depends on how readily a particular type of fruit develops roots – a longer cutting is needed for more reluctant types.

► The gooseberry cutting (*centre*) is similar in length to a red currant one (*left*), but also has two leaves at the tip to assist in root production. All but four buds are removed on red and white currants, to prevent suckers forming below ground, whereas the buds on the black currant cutting (*right*) are left intact.

germination. Make holes of the appropriate depth and insert the cuttings through the polythene into the soil.

Transplant the cuttings to their final positions the following autumn if they have made good growth. After lifting, rub off any buds below ground level to discourage suckering. If the cuttings are undeveloped, prune them lightly and transplant to a nursery bed or pot them up and grow on for another season.

Black currants: Select well-ripened shoots of pencil thickness from the current season's growth. Take cuttings 20–25cm (8–10in) in length, cutting just above a bud at the base. Trim the bases just below a bud and remove any soft wood at the tip, cutting just above a bud. Strip off any leaves, but retain all the buds.

Raspberry suckers . . . .

Any raspberry plant that shows signs of disease should not be used as propagation material, even if its suckers are apparently healthy. If at all uncertain, dig up and discard the plant.

◄ In spring and summer allow suckers to grow up away from the main row. In the autumn, lift them carefully, taking care not to damage the root system. Shorten the canes to about 23cm (9in) and plant them out in their final positions in the garden.

Prepare a trench as for red and white currants. Insert the cuttings 15cm (6in) apart, with the second bud from the top of the cutting level with the soil surface. Firm them in. Transplant the rooted cuttings to their final positions the following autumn.

Vines: Vines root easily from hardwood cuttings taken in midwinter when the plant is dormant. The sap bleeds if stems are cut while in active growth. Select stout stems of ripe wood, just above pencil thickness, from the current season's growth and cut into 60–90cm (2–3ft) lengths. Remove soft material from the tips. If you cannot make cuttings immediately, heel them in a cold frame in a sheltered site to two-thirds of their length; they can be stored for up to six weeks.

To root directly in a cold frame, dig in sharp sand at the base to improve drainage. Cut sections from the stems, each with three buds (i.e. three-bud cuttings). Trim the cuttings with a cut just below the lowest bud and a sloping cut just above the topmost one. Insert them to two-thirds of their length, 15cm (6in) apart. For a greater quantity of new plants, root two-bud cuttings inserted to half their length in 7.5cm (3in) pots of propagating medium and place these in a greenhouse.

Where there is less material available, or if more plants are required, single-bud cuttings, known as 'vine eyes', can be used. Make a cut above a bud and another 5cm (2in) below and insert these into a mix of equal parts peat and sharp sand with the bud just resting on the surface. For the best results, place the cuttings in a closed propagator with bottom heat of 18°C (64°F).

For optimum growth, pot the cuttings on in stages once rooted and grow them on under glass for a year. Keep them under cover for the second winter and plant them out the following spring, if sufficiently developed.

Leaf-bud cuttings

These are suitable for producing large numbers of plants from blackberries and hybrid berries.

Prepare a cuttings compost of equal parts peat and sand in 7.5cm (3in) pots or fill a cold frame to a depth of 7.5cm (3in) with the same mixture.

From mid- to late summer, take cuttings 30–45cm (12–18in) long from healthy canes. Shorten the tips to remove any soft, immature buds. Cut the stems into sections about 2.5cm (1in) long, each with a bud halfway along. Insert the cuttings into the cuttings medium so that the bud is just touching the soil surface. Keep them humid until rooted, usually within six to eight weeks, either by tenting the pots in polythene or by keeping the cold frame closed. Harden them off and overwinter in a cold frame. The following spring, plant out 30cm (1ft) apart in rows or pot them on and grow them on for a year before setting out.

Softwood cuttings

Softwood cuttings can be used for blueberries, vines, blackberries and hybrid berries.

Take cuttings 10–15cm (4–6in) long of the current season's growth in midsummer, cutting just above a bud. Trim the cutting just below a bud and remove the lower leaves, leaving the top three or four. Immerse them in a fungicidal solution. Dip the base in hormone rooting powder and insert into a mixture of equal parts sharp sand and peat in 7.5cm (3in) pots. Root in a closed propagator at 18–20°C (64–68°F), out of direct sunlight. They should root in four to six weeks. Check the plants regularly for fungal infection, remove any affected cuttings, and spray the remainder with fungicidal solution.

Once new topgrowth emerges, pot the cuttings up individually (blueberries must be potted up into lime-free compost). Gradually harden the cuttings off in a cold frame, keeping them shaded from hot sun. Apply a high-potash liquid fertilizer every ten days until late summer. Grow on for a year before planting them out into their final positions.

Suckers

The fruit plants most commonly increased this way are raspberries, cobnuts and filberts. Unless required for propagation, remove suckers as they appear, since they divert the parent plant's energies from fruit production.

Raspberries: Raspberries are very susceptible to virus infection and any plants that show signs of disease should not be used as propagation material, even if the suckers are apparently healthy. Symptoms to watch out for include mottled or crinkled leaves, stunted growth, small crumbly fruit, and reduced yield.

Cobnuts and filberts: Remove most of the suckers that appear, leaving the strongest to develop naturally, preferably those furthest from the tree. In autumn, after leaf fall, dig around the sucker, check that it has a good root system, and sever it from the parent below ground. Plant out in a nursery bed 45cm (18in) apart or pot them up and grow on for a year. The following autumn, transplant them to their final positions.

Pineapples: These can also be increased by suckers or slips: that is, suckers that appear in the leaf axils, or at the base of the fruit or stem. The crown shoot that appears at the top of the fruit can also be used as propagating material. Pineapples are tropical fruits that need high humidity and a temperature of 18–30°C (64–80°F) to produce fruit. They are grown outdoors only in tropical regions; elsewhere they need a warm greenhouse and full light.

TOP-FRUIT

Most top-fruits are propagated by grafting onto rootstocks of a closely related species or genus, a technique that has been used for thousands of years. There are good reasons why they are propagated in this way.

They do not come true from seed; every seedling is distinct and many are of inferior quality. They are slow to crop when grown from seed: apples may take seven to ten years; peaches four to five years. Nor, with some exceptions, do they strike easily from cuttings.

Apple rootstocks are derived from cultivated apples or other *Malus* species. Pears are commonly grafted onto quince (*Cydonia oblonga*), producing compact trees which are early to crop; pear rootstocks themselves are

Pineapples ....

A pineapple plant can be increased from cuttings, 'slips' (which arise from immediately beneath the fruit), or suckers (which occur on the stem and at the base of the stem).

▲ **Propagation by cuttings**
1 Carefully cut out the complete crown shoot. Dip in fungicide, then allow to dry for a few days.

▲ 2 Fill a pot with cuttings compost and insert the pineapple cutting. Set at 18°C (64°F) while the roots develop.

▲ **Propagation by 'slips'**
Sever the 'slip' from immediately under the fruit. Remove the lower leaves, then treat as for a cutting.

▲ **Propagation by suckers**
Using a sharp knife, cut off each sucker close to the stem. Then treat, as above, for a cutting.

Rootstocks ....

Most fruit trees are grafted onto rootstocks of a different cultivar to control their height and fruiting vigour.

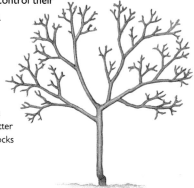

▶ When buying a fruit tree, always check the type of rootstock onto which a tree is grafted and the type of soil that rootstock requires. For a small garden it is generally better to select the dwarfing rootstocks M27 and M9 than one of the larger, more vigorous ones.

Tree forms ....

Trees can, from an early age, be trained into a variety of shapes to increase their flowering and fruiting potential, to confine their growth to fit a particular area, or to make them more accessible for picking. In a small garden, it is particularly useful to grow a fruit tree against a wall or fence, in a cordon, espalier or fan, which can look highly attractive.

1 The cordon is an excellent tree form in a small garden, where its main stem can be trained obliquely, thereby saving space and height. The most popular rootstock for an apple cordon in a very confined area, or one with very fertile soil is M9; elsewhere, use M26 or MM106. For pears, choose Quince C or A.

2 Cordons may also be trained with two or more stems. Obliquely trained double cordons tend to be more fruitful and less vigorous than those trained vertically.

3 Dwarf pyramid apple trees are generally grown on M9 and M26 rootstock and pears on Quince C or A. Planted closely together, they make compact trees, 1.8–2.1m (6–7ft) in height, which are easy to crop.

4 Espaliers have one or more pairs of opposite stems trained at right angles to a vertical main stem. Such a tree form makes very economical use of space. Espalier apples are generally grafted on MM106 or MM111 rootstock, and pears on Quince A.

5 This goblet-shaped tree with its open centre is best suited to gardens where space is relatively unrestricted. This tree form is grown on M9 to MM111 apple rootstock and Quince C and A pear stocks.

6 A spindlebush tree is cone shaped and has its central leader removed at an early age. Thereafter most branches are trained almost horizontally by tying them to pegs in the ground to encourage fruit production. Spindlebush apples are grown on M9, M26 and MM106 rootstocks and pears on Quince C and A.

7 The fan is best trained against a wall or fence, where it will not only make excellent use of space but also be easy to pick from. Apple fans are generally grown on MM106 rootstocks, and pears on Quince A.

difficult to propagate and not sufficiently dwarfing for most gardens. Cherries are grafted onto rootstocks of related *Prunus* species. Peaches, nectarines, apricots and almonds are commonly grafted onto plum rootstocks.

Some cultivars are not compatible with all rootstocks. For example, not all pears can be grafted directly onto quince and an interstock of a compatible cultivar must be used, such as 'Beurré Hardy' or 'Doyenné du Comice'. Peaches, nectarines and apricots are not directly compatible with the dwarfing rootstock 'Pixy', but 'Pixy' can be used with an interstock of the compatible rootstock St Julien A.

The most common rootstocks, in order of ascending vigour, are:

Apples	M27	M9	M26	MM106	MM111
Pears			Quince C	Quince A	
Plums			'Pixy'	St Julien A	
Peaches/			(with 'Pixy'	St Julien A	
Nectarines/			interstock)		
Apricots					
Cherries		'Edebritz'		'Colt'	F12/1
		('Tabel')			

The choice of rootstock will control the size of the tree grafted onto it and the various rootstocks have been selected to provide good anchorage, disease resistance and early cropping. Rootstocks are propagated by layering, stooling or, in some cases, by cuttings.

TECHNIQUES OF GRAFTING

Grafting unites two plants so that they form a strong union and grow together. The plant to be propagated is the scion; the plant onto which it is grafted is the rootstock. For any graft to be successful there are three main criteria that must be met. The timing must be correct and the material for stock and scion must be compatible, of similar size and in good condition. There must be good contact between the cambium layers of rootstock and scion. In addition, all cuts made for grafting must be made with a sharp knife. Although grafting is ·a relatively advanced technique, attention to detail and practice will eventually lead to success.

The most common and successful methods for top-fruit are bud grafting (by chip-budding and T-budding) and whip-and-tongue grafting.

Your choice of method is dictated to some extent by the type of plant you are trying to propagate. Budding is done from mid- to late summer; whip-and-tongue grafting in late winter or early spring.

Preparing the rootstocks

Buy good-quality rootstocks and plant them out 45cm (18in) apart, in rows 1m (3ft) apart, in a nursery bed until you are ready to start propagating. For the best results, ensure that the rootstocks are well established before budding or grafting. Rootstocks planted in the dormant season will be ready for budding in mid- to late summer and for whip-and-tongue grafting late the following winter.

On planting, remove any side shoots from the bottom 30cm (1ft) of trunk. During the growing season, rub out any side shoots that develop below 30cm (1ft). Water the rootstocks well during the summer, so that they are growing actively and so that the rind will lift easily (this is especially important for T-budding).

It is vital to select good-quality material for the rootstock, and for the parent plant to be propagated. With few exceptions, viruses in top-fruit are graft-transmitted so it is always best to propagate from guaranteed virus-free stock for both rootstock and scion to ensure that the resulting plant is virus free. However, for older and rare varieties, guaranteed virus-free stock may not be available. In this case, propagate from the healthiest-looking material available.

Bud grafting

Bud grafting, which includes chip-budding and T-budding, is economical with material, since only a single bud of the scion is needed for each new plant. More importantly, it produces high-quality trees with strong graft unions.

Chip-budding is generally more successful than T-budding, because it provides better cambial contact between the scion and rootstock, and there is less risk of infection by the canker *Nectria galligena* and other pathogens that can enter through wounded tissue. With T-budding, the bud is enclosed beneath the rind of the rootstock, and so the spores of any pathogens will be trapped in a good position to infect the wound.

It is important to lose as little time as possible between cutting the scion and carrying out grafting, since any loss of moisture will militate against a good union taking place.

In late summer, cut well-ripened stems from the sunny side of the tree. These bud sticks must be vigorous, of pencil thickness and with dark green leaves and well-developed buds. They should just be turning woody at the base. Strip the stems of leaves immediately to prevent water loss by transpiration, but leave the petioles (leaf stalks) intact; remove any stipulary leaves (small leaves near the base of the petiole). Wrap the stems in a damp cloth and bud graft straight away.

It is always preferable to bud graft immediately after collecting the scions but, if necessary, you can store the stems for a few days – at the most – in a dry polythene bag in a refrigerator.

Chip budding ....

Always take scion material from a vigorous, healthy stem of the current season's growth and with well-developed buds. Clear this bud stick of any leaves and trim off the soft tip.

► 1 About 2cm (¾in) below the bud make a 5mm (¼in) downward-angled cut at about 45° into the scion. Next, make a shallow cut starting 2cm (¾in) above the bud and bring the blade down to meet the first cut.

► 2 Locate a smooth area of stem on the rootstock (free from any buds) about 23cm (9in) from the base, preferably on the shady side (where the cuts are less likely to dry out). Make a concave cut corresponding to the bud.

► 3 Put the bud in place. Ideally it should fit exactly, but if, as is likely, the rootstock is broader than the bud, place the bud to one side so that there is cambial contact between the stock and bud chip on one side.

► 4 Tie the stock and bud chip firmly with grafting tape but not so tightly as to constrict the bud. After 4–6 weeks, callus tissue should form around the bud, indicating that the union has 'taken'. Remove the tape carefully.

Chip-budding

Chip-budding is carried out at a height of 15–30cm (6–12in) on the rootstock, with 23cm (9in) being the preferred height.

Remove any hard wood at the bottom of the scion and any immature wood at the top. Working from the bottom of the scion, locate healthy buds, avoiding any buds with multiple leaves, which may be fruit buds. Shorten the petioles to about 5mm (¼in).

To remove a bud, first make a downward-angled cut at 45°, 5mm (¼in) deep, at about 2cm (¾in) below the bud. Make the second cut about 4cm (1½in) above the first cut and about 2cm (¾in) above the bud so that it slopes downward to meet the first cut. Take care not to damage the bud when making this cut. Remove the bud chip, handling it by the bud in order to avoid contaminating the cambium layer.

On the rootstock, select a smooth, clean piece of stem, free of any buds, at about 23cm (9in) high. Make a shallow, slightly concave cut corresponding in shape to that of the bud chip and put the bud chip in place. Ideally, the cuts should match, but if the cut on the rootstock is larger than the bud, as is often the case with a thick rootstock, place the bud to one side so that there is cambial contact between rootstock and scion on one side only.

Tie the graft firmly with grafting tape. Trap the end of the tape below the bud and wrap the bud with only a slight overlap, tying off just above the bud with a half-hitch. The tie should be firm but not constricting. It is essential to pay careful attention to detail at this stage, since more grafts fail from poor tying than from poor grafting technique. Keep the grafting tape in place until callus tissue forms around the bud. This usually takes four to six weeks. Remove the tape by cutting the tie behind the bud and unwrapping it carefully.

If the bud has taken successfully, the bud will appear healthy, and the petiole will remain plump and healthy until autumn, when it will drop off with the other leaves on the rootstock. If budding has failed, the petiole will shrivel but remain attached.

The following spring, head back the rootstock with a backward-sloping cut just above the grafted bud. A strong shoot should develop from the bud. For the benefit of the plant, remove any flowers that form but take care not to damage the shoots behind them. If the new leading shoot does not grow straight, encourage it to do so by attaching it to a vertical cane inserted close to the stem with soft twine.

Allow any side shoots that emerge on the rootstock below the bud to develop until they are 5–7.5cm (2–3in) long (they help feed the plant), then remove them. By the following autumn, the new tree should be ready to plant in position, ready for further pruning and training depending on the tree form required.

T-budding

The preparation of the rootstock and collection of scion material is the same as for chip-budding, but the budding technique is slightly different. To ensure success with T-budding, it is most important that the rootstock is growing well so that the rind (or bark) will lift easily for insertion of the scion bud. If there is prolonged dry weather during the two weeks before budding, keep the rootstocks well irrigated.

Collect the bud sticks and prepare them as described for chip-budding, but trim the petiole to 12mm (½in) instead of 5mm (¼in). Starting from the top of the bud stick, locate a healthy bud and make a shallow cut beginning 2cm (¾in) below the bud. Draw the knife upwards and then lift it so that the bud is removed with a long tail of bark.

Choose a smooth piece of stem on the rootstock at around 23cm (9in) above soil level, and make a horizontal cut by pressing firmly with a clean sharp knife. Next, make a vertical cut, 2.5cm (1in) long, that joins up with the centre of the horizontal cut. Gently lift the bark using the spatula end of a budding knife or the flat of a knife blade. Insert the bud into the T-shaped cut and slide it down into position, using the petiole as a 'handle'. Trim off the excess tail of bark level with the horizontal bar of the T, then trim off the petiole. Wrap the graft with grafting tape as described for chip-budding, but do not enclose the bud. Put a spot of petroleum jelly on the bud to protect it from the red bud-borer (*Resseliella oculiperda*).

The rootstock should be headed back the following spring by cutting back with a sloping cut just above the grafted bud. Aftercare is the same for chip-budding, and by the following autumn the young tree will be ready to plant out into position to begin training into the required form.

T-budding

The secret of success for T-budding is to ensure that the rootstock is kept well watered so that its bark can be lifted without damage before the bud is inserted.

▶ **1** Collect and prepare the material as for chip-budding but leave a length of 1cm (½in) of the petioles on the scion. To remove a bud, make a shallow, upward cut starting 2cm (¾in) below the bud and ending 2.5cm (1in) above it. Lift off the bud, together with a long 'tail' of bark at the top. This is to help you handle the bud.

◀ **2** Find a smooth area on the rootstock about 23cm (9in) from ground level and make a horizontal cut. Next make a 2.5cm (1in) long vertical cut up to and joining the centre of the first cut, in a T-shape.

▶ **3** Gently lift the rind using the end of the budding knife or the back of the blade. Insert the bud and slide it down to fit snugly, using the tail of bark as a handle. Very carefully trim off the excess tail so that it is level with the horizontal cut on the rootstock.

▶ **4** Bind around the budded area with grafting tape but leave the bud exposed. Trim the petiole.

Aftercare
Aftercare is as for chip-budding (*see p. 182*).

Bud grafting generally produces better trees than whip-and-tongue grafting, but if budding fails, whip-and-tongue grafting can be carried out in the following spring and a tree will be produced at the same time as one budded the previous season.

Whip-and-tongue grafting ....

If the rootstock is thicker than the scion, move it to one side until there is good contact between the cambial layers. This will encourage a quick union between the two parts.

◄ 1 At the base of the scion, make a sloping cut 3.5cm (1½in) long through to the other side of the stem. Then cut a 'tongue', 1cm (½in) deep, two-thirds of the way up the previous cut. Prepare the scion by shortening it to 3 or 4 buds (including the stock bud).

▲ 2 Starting just opposite to and below the bud, make matching cuts on the scion (i.e. with a groove to receive the tongue).

▼ 3 Fit the scion groove into the rootstock tongue, aligning the cambial layers carefully.

► 4 Bind the graft with grafting tape. Seal any exposed cut surfaces with grafting wax. The graft should take in 4–6 weeks and fresh growth should emerge from the union. Then, cut the tie behind the stock bud and carefully unwrap it.

Whip-and-tongue grafting

This is the most common and reliable method of grafting rootstocks using dormant scions. It should be carried out in late winter to early spring when the sap is beginning to rise in the rootstocks and its buds are just starting to swell.

Scions are collected while fully dormant in mid-winter. Choose healthy, well-ripened stems from the previous year's growth and take cuttings about 23cm (9in) long, cutting just above a bud. Keep them cool by burying them, in bundles of five or six, to three-quarters of their length in a sheltered part of the garden, or put them in a sealed, dry polythene bag and store them in the bottom of a refrigerator.

As the buds start to break on the rootstocks, cut the stem tip back with a sloping cut just above a clear smooth part of the stem about 23cm (9in) from the base. Trim off any side shoots. At the top of the rootstock, make an upward-sloping cut, 3.5cm (1½in) long. Make a second downward cut, about one-third of the way down the first cut, to create a slit about 1cm (½in) deep. This forms the 'tongue' which will hold the scion. At all stages, avoid touching the cambium to avoid contamination.

Prepare the scion by removing any soft wood at the tip. Make a 3.5cm (1½in) sloping cut behind the bud (the stock bud) and cut a 'tongue' two-thirds of the way up the first cut, about 1cm (½in) long. Trim the scion to three to four buds including the stock bud.

Unite the rootstock and scion by slotting the scion carefully into the tongue at the top of the rootstock, ensuring that the cut cambial surfaces are matched as nearly as possible. Wrap with grafting tape as described for chip-budding, and seal any exposed surfaces with grafting wax. The graft union should form within four to six weeks, after which time the grafting tape should be carefully removed by cutting its tie and unwrapping gently.

In spring, the buds on the scion will begin to shoot. Select the strongest shoot (usually from the topmost bud) and allow only this one to develop. Pinch the remainder back to about 7.5cm (3in).

Any side shoots on the rootstock should also be removed once they are about 7.5cm (3in) long. If necessary, tie the leading shoot to a cane to encourage upright growth. Transplant the new tree to its final position the following autumn, or leave it in place while pruning and training it to the desired form.

Grafting over

This is a technique that may be used to introduce a new pollinating cultivar to the orchard or simply to replace old cultivars with new and more productive cultivars. It is mainly used in commercial orchards to graft new scions on to established apple or pear trees, having the advantage that the new cultivar fruits relatively quickly, because it involves grafting onto a well-established root-and-branch system. For the amateur propagator, the easiest way of doing this is by bark grafting.

Bark or rind grafting

Before bark grafting, it is important to pollard all but two of the main branches on the rootstock to within 60–75 cm (24–30in) of the main branch framework, in early spring.

◄ **1** Make one or more vertical cuts, 2.5cm (1in) long, into the bark at the top of the pollarded tree, depending on how many scions are to be grafted. With the back of the knife, ease the bark away from the cambial layer.

► **2** Prepare each scion by reducing it to three buds, making an angled cut at the top, just above a bud, and a more tapering one, 2.5cm (1in) long, at the base. Insert each scion into a bark slit, facing its cut edge inwards.

◄ **3** When all the scions have been inserted, bind them in place with soft twine. Then seal all the exposed surfaces with grafting wax.

The receiving tree is prepared by cutting back most of the main framework branches in early spring to within 60cm (24in) of the trunk, leaving one or two central branches to continue to draw the sap upwards. This reduces the number of shoots that would otherwise proliferate from around the wounds. Alternatively, the main branches may be left intact and one or two cut back to receive scions.

Prepare the scions by taking cuttings of the well-ripened wood of the previous season's growth. Trim them down to three buds, with a slanting top-cut just above a bud and a sloping cut at the base, about 2.5cm (1in) long.

Prepare the rootstock branches by making a vertical slit, 2.5cm (1in) long, through the bark at the top of the branch. Slide the scion into the slit with the sloping cut facing inwards to make cambial contact with the rootstock. Insert two or three scions at even spacings around the branch. Bind with soft twine and seal the exposed surfaces with grafting wax. Once the graft union has formed, remove the binding. Select the strongest of the scions and remove the remainder. If more than one shoot grows from the scion, retain the most vigorous and shorten the remainder to about 7.5cm (3in). The new shoot should begin to fruit within three to four years.

Double-working

Double-working is a modification of grafting used mainly for pears, some of which are not directly compatible with quince, which is commonly used as a pear rootstock. It involves using an 'interstock' of a cultivar such as 'Beurré Hardy' that is mutually compatible with the rootstock and the intended fruiting scion. The most frequently used technique is double chip-budding, although double grafting using a whip-and-tongue graft is also used.

In the first year, the interstock is chip-budded onto one side of the quince rootstock and allowed to grow away. In the second year, the interstock receives a bud chip of the fruiting scion. This is inserted on the opposite side to the first bud chip and about 5cm (2in) above it. This gives a stronger union and ultimately a straighter stem than would develop if the bud chips were inserted on the same side.

Once the scion takes and begins to grow away, the interstock is cut back just above the new bud. Any shoots that arise on the interstock should be rubbed off as soon as they are seen.

Double working

Some pears' cultivars are incompatible with quince rootstocks, so that the rootstock is grafted with a mutually compatible interstock, and the interstock is then grafted with the cultivar.

◄ **Double budding**
This method involves chip-budding an interstock onto a quince rootstock. The following year the selected cultivar is chip-budded onto the opposite side of the interstock.

► **Double grafting**
This is similar to double budding except that the interstock is whip-and-tongue grafted onto the rootstock and scion of the selected cultivar.

DIRECTORY OF
FRUIT

*Below are key tips on a selection of fruits that are particularly suitable
for propagation. Unless otherwise specified, follow the detailed instructions given
under the propagation section on pages 176–185.*

Key

CR   Chilling requirement

🌰   Seed

Actinidia   Actinidiaceae

Some 40 mainly deciduous climbers.
A. deliciosa, syn. *A. chinensis* (Kiwi fruit).
Deciduous, trailing climber grown for its
soft, green-fleshed fruit and as an
ornamental. It grows best in areas with mild
winters and warm springs and summers,
and it needs fertile, well-drained soil, shelter,
and sun. It is hardy but young growth can be
damaged by spring frosts. In cool temperate
areas, it is best grown in a cool greenhouse
if fruit is required. Mostly dioecious, both
male and female plants are required for
pollination, at a ratio of one male plant to
five females. Hermaphrodite cultivars include
'Jenny'. CR 400 hours below 7°C (45°F).
H 10m (30ft).

PROPAGATION

Hardwood cuttings – late summer.
Softwood cuttings – in spring.
T-budding or whip-and-tongue grafting
can be used but do not always take well as
Actinidia tends to 'bleed' and this interferes
with the union of the grafted material.

Ananas (Pineapple)   Bromeliaceae

About six tender, evergreen perennials,
grown as ornamentals and for their fruits.
A. comosus. Has spiky, dark leaves and
bears edible pineapples. Needs full sun,
temperatures of 18–30°C (64–86°F), and
humidity at 60–80 per cent to grow and fruit
well. In temperate regions, it needs a warm
greenhouse or a special frame to produce
edible fruit. H 1m (3ft), S 50cm (20in).

PROPAGATION

Suckers – from the leaf axils or slips which
arise from the fruit stem or fruit crowns.
Remove with a sharp knife, treat with
fungicide and allow to dry for a few days
then insert into sandy, well-drained compost.
Scooping – scoop out the crown shoot with
a knife, taking care not to damage the shoot
base. Remove any flesh and the lower leaves,
treat with fungicide and allow to dry for
2–3 days before potting up as above.
Root all in a propagator or under plastic
to maintain humidity. Rooting takes 4 weeks.

Citrus   Rutaceae

Some 16 subtropical, evergreen shrubs and
trees with fragrant flowers and edible fruits.
Most, including **C. limon** (Lemon) and

C. sinensis (Sweet orange) need optimum
temperatures of 15–30°C (58–86°F) to
grow and fruit well. In temperate areas, grow
under glass during the cooler months and
stand outdoors in summer. Plant in fertile,
well-drained, slightly acid soil. The most
usual tree forms are bush and standard (an
attractive form for a pot). Citrus are self-
fertile but may need hand-pollination.

PROPAGATION

🌰 as soon as ripe. Most citrus are
polyembryonic, and offspring are very similar
to the parent. They take 7–10 years to fruit.
Inverted T-budding, onto a seedling rootstock
(use a similar seedling to the cultivar that is
being budded).

Corylus (Hazel)   Betulaceae

Up to 15 hardy, deciduous trees and shrubs.
C. avellana (Cobnut) and **C. maxima** (Filbert)
produce edible nuts. They grow and crop
best in cool, moist summers. Plant in slightly
acid, moist but well-drained, not-too-fertile
soil, in a sheltered site in dappled shade. They
are best grown as open-centred bushes on a
short leg of about 60cm (24in). They are
wind-pollinated and, although self-fertile, they
benefit from pollinators as male and female
flowers on the same tree do not always
mature at the same time. The cultivar
'Cosford' is an excellent pollinator.
CR 800–1200 hours below 7°C (45°F).

PROPAGATION

Suckers – winter.
Simple layering – autumn.

Cydonia (Quince)   Rosaceae

A single species of small deciduous tree,
C. oblonga, grown for its edible fruit.
C. oblonga. Has white to pink flowers
followed by pear-shaped fruit. It grows best
in areas with mild winters and hot summers.

Actinidia deliciosa

Citrus sinensis

Corylus avellana

Cydonia oblonga 'Bereczki'

Fragaria 'Pegasus'

Grow in moist but well-drained, slightly acid soil. It can be grown as a bush tree in the open in warm areas; in colder areas, fan-train against a sheltered sunny wall. It is self-fertile, but fruits better with a pollinator. CR 100–450 hours below 7°C (45°F). H and S 5m (15ft).

PROPAGATION
Chip- or T-budding or whip-and-tongue grafting onto 'Quince C' or 'Quince A' (see **Pyrus**, pear, p. 188).
Hardwood cuttings – late autumn. Less satisfactory than grafting; the resulting tree will be vigorous and prone to suckering.

Diospyros   Ebenaceae
Some 450 evergreen or deciduous trees and shrubs, all of which produce edible fruit.
D. kaki (Persimmon). This can be grown as an ornamental for its glossy leaves with good autumn colours, but to set and ripen fruit it needs a lot of warmth and sunshine (1400 hours). It will grow well with a minimum of 10°C (50°F), but requires 16–22°C (61–72°F) in autumn for adequate ripening. Grow in well-drained, fertile soil. It can be grown as a bush or spindlebush tree under glass and is suitable for pots. Persimmons are dioecious; some are self-fertile (producing seedless fruits) and others need pollinators. It may be seed-raised, but can take 5–10 years to produce fruit of dubious quality. It must be propagated vegetatively for good quality fruit. CR 100–200 hours below 7°C (45°F). H to 10m (30ft), S 6m (20ft).

PROPAGATION
Chip- or T-budding, or whip-and-tongue grafting onto seedling rootstocks of *D. kaki* or *D. virginiana*. It can also be propagated by

softwood cuttings but these need heat and high humidity (preferably under mist) to root.

Ficus (Fig)   Moraceae
Genus of 800 often ornamental, tender and hardy, mainly evergreen shrubs, trees and climbers. *F. carica* is grown for its fruit.
F. carica. Deciduous tree or large shrub with lobed leaves and brown or purple fruit near the tips of the previous year's shoots. It is best in climates with mild winters and long, hot summers, where it may be grown as a bush tree. In cooler areas, fan-train against a warm, sunny wall. Plant in humus-rich, well-drained soil. It needs root restriction to control vigour, and is ideal for a container, although it then needs to be brought into a frost-free place over winter. No pollinator is needed. CR 100–300 hours below 7°C (45°F). H 3m (10ft), S 4m (12ft).

PROPAGATION
Hardwood cuttings – early autumn.

Fragaria (Strawberry)   Rosaceae
About 12 hardy herbaceous perennials. Most species are grown for their edible fruits.
F. x ananassa cultivars. These low-growing, spreading perennials tolerate a range of climates. Most fruit according to day length, but some day-neutral cultivars grow and fruit according to temperature and suit warmer regions. In cool climates, day-neutral types behave as perpetual cultivars. They thrive in fertile, well-drained soils, but not on shallow chalk. Most strawberries are self-fertile.

PROPAGATION
Runners – mid- to late summer. Some perpetual cultivars produce few runners; propagate by division.

🛈 Alpine strawberries do not produce runners; sow seed in autumn or spring.

Juglans (Walnut)   Juglandaceae
Some 15 species of deciduous trees producing pinnate leaves and edible nuts.
J. regia (English walnut, Persian walnut). This grows and fruits best in areas with warm springs and hot summers. In cooler climates the young growth can be damaged by late spring frosts, and fruit may not ripen fully in short, relatively cool summers. Even in Britain, however, the young unripe fruit can be excellent for pickling. Grow in fertile, moist but well-drained, near-neutral soil. Walnuts are monoecious and self-fertile but are wind-pollinated, and male flowers often release their pollen before the females are ready to receive it. Two or more cultivars should be grown to ensure pollination; the cultivar 'Franquette' is a good pollinator. CR 500–1,000 hours below 7°C (45°F). H 12–18m (40–60ft), S 15m (45ft).

PROPAGATION
Chip-budding, or whip-and-tongue grafting onto seedling rootstocks of *J. regia*.

Malus (Apple, Crab apple)   Rosaceae
Genus of 35 hardy, deciduous trees and shrubs, grown for their flowers which mainly appear in the spring; some are also grown for their fruit.
Malus sylvestris var. *domestica*. This is the basic species from which apples of all kinds have been developed. Apples are hardy over a wide climatic range but cultivars must be selected to suit your climate, and sizes to fit the space available. Apples are tolerant of most well-drained soils, but to crop well need

Malus 'Discovery'

Passiflora caerulea

Persea americana

a sheltered site in sun. Apples are trained in many forms, each using a different rootstock:
M27: very dwarfing; for dwarf bush, spindle-bush, dwarf pyramid, and horizontal cordon.
M9: dwarfing; for dwarf bush, spindlebush, dwarf pyramid, and cordon.
M26: semi-dwarfing; for bush, spindlebush, pyramid, cordon, and pot-cultivation.
MM106: semi-vigorous; for bush, spindlebush, pyramid and espalier.
MM111: semi-vigorous; for bush, half-standard and espalier.
Most are not self-fertile and need cross-pollination by other cultivars flowering at the same time. Most are compatible, but some closely related cultivars are incompatible, e.g. 'Cox's Orange Pippin' with 'Holstein'. Triploid cultivars (with 3, not 2, sets of chromosomes) are ineffective pollinators and must be grown with 2 diploid pollinators. The following are arranged in compatible pollination groups; cultivars can be pollinated by those in the same or adjacent groups.
T = Triploid   B = Biennial bearing
Group 1: **'Gravenstein'** (T), **'Lord Suffield'**, **'Stark Earliest'**, **'Vista-Bella'** (B).
Group 2: **'Adam's Pearmain'**, **'Beauty of Bath'**, 'Bismarck', **'Bolero'**, **'Cheddar Cross'**, **'Egremont Russet'**, **'George Cave'**, **'Idared'**, **'Irish Peach'**, **'Keswick Codling'**, **'Lord Lambourne'**, **'McIntosh Red'**, **'Melba'**, **'Norfolk Beauty'**, **'Reverend W Wilks'** (B), **'Ribston Pippin'** (T), **'St Edmund's Pippin'**, **'Warner's King'**.
Group 3: **'Allington Pippin'**, **'Belle de Boskoop'** (T), **'Blenheim Orange'** (T, B), **'Bountiful'**, **'Bramley's Seedling'** (T), **'Charles Ross'**, **'Cox's Orange Pippin'**, **'Crispin'**, **'Discovery'**, **'Elstar'**, **'Emneth Early'**, syn.

'Early Victoria', 'Epicure', 'Falstaff', 'Fiesta', 'Fortune', 'Granny Smith', 'Grenadier', 'Holstein', 'James Grieve', 'Jonagold' (T), 'Jonathan', 'Katy', 'Lane's Prince Albert', 'Lord Grosvenor', 'Merton Knave', 'Merton Worcester', 'Peasgood's Nonsuch', 'Spartan', 'Sturmer Pippin', 'Sunset', 'Worcester Pearmain'.
Group 4: 'Autumn Pearmain', 'Cox's Pomona', 'Delicious', 'Duke of Devonshire', 'Dumelow's Seedling', 'Ellison's Orange', 'Gala', 'Gloster '69','Golden Delicious', 'Jester', 'Lord Derby', 'Monarch' (B), 'Orleans Reinette', 'Superb', syn. 'Laxton's Superb' (B).
Group 5: 'Gascoyne's Scarlet', 'King of the Pippins' (B), 'Merton Beauty', 'Newton Wonder', 'Royal Jubilee', 'Suntan' (T), 'William Crump'.
Group 6: 'Ben's Red/Bess Pool', 'Court Pendu Plat', 'Edward VII'.
Group 7: 'Crawley Beauty'.
CR 900 hours min. below 7°C (45°F).

PROPAGATION
Chip- or T-budding or whip-and-tongue grafting. It is also possible to graft new cultivars onto healthy mature trees by grafting over (see p. 184).

Mespilus (Medlar)   Rosaceae
A single species of hardy, deciduous tree.
M. germanica. Has white flowers, apple-like fruit, and attractive autumn foliage. It grows and fruits best with warm summers. In colder areas, provide a sunny, sheltered site and moist, well-drained soil. Can be grown as a standard; bush and half-standards also cultivated. Self-fertile. CR 100–450 hours below 7°C (45°F). H 6m (20ft), S 8m (25ft).

PROPAGATION
Chip- or T-budding, or whip-and-tongue grafting onto either *Cydonia oblonga* or *Crataegus* rootstocks.

Morus (Mulberry)   Moraceae
Some 12 hardy, deciduous trees, grown for their edible raspberry-like fruits and their foliage, which colours well in autumn.
M. nigra (Black mulberry). Has dark purple fruit. Grows best in a sheltered, sunny site, in moist but well-drained, preferably slightly acid soil. Usually grown as bush or standard trees. Self-fertile. CR 800–1200 hours below 7°C (45°F). H to 12m (40ft), S 15m (50ft).

PROPAGATION
Heeled softwood cuttings – early summer. Heeled hardwood cuttings – autumn. Mulberry is not as easy to root from hardwood cuttings as is often supposed. Simple layering – autumn or spring.

Passiflora (Passion flower)   Passifloraceae
Genus of 500 evergreen or semi-evergreen climbing plants, grown for their flowers and edible fruit (passion fruit). Many also have attractive lobed leaves.
P. edulis. Has white flowers and purple fruit; f. *flavicarpa* has yellow fruit. These are relatives of the commonly-grown ornamental *P. caerulea*. Both are frost-tender and need minimum winter temperatures of 7–10°C (45–50°F). Greenhouse cultivation is necessary in temperate regions. Grow in fertile, but not too nitrogen-rich, well-drained soil in full sun. As climbers, they need to be trained on wires, with 2 leaders per plant. They are self-fertile but hand-pollination is necessary. H 5m (15ft).

Prunus armeniaca

Prunus avium 'Bigarreau Napoléon'

Prunus domestica 'Victoria'

PROPAGATION

🌱 named cultivars are seldom available in temperate areas. Seed is extracted from ripe fruit and fermented for 3–4 days. Sow in pots or trays, at 20°C (68°F). Transplant seedlings to permanent pots when they are 25cm (10in) tall.

Softwood cuttings – early summer.

Persea   Lauraceae

Genus of 150 frost-tender evergreen trees. *P. americana* is grown for its edible fruits.

P. americana (Avocado pear). Has large, pear-shaped fruit with leathery skin and soft, oily, green flesh. It needs high humidity and temperatures of 20–28°C (68–82°F) to flower and fruit. In temperate areas it must be grown under glass in a warm greenhouse and even there may not fruit freely. Needs fertile, well-drained soil and full sun. It is best pot-grown as a bush and requires little pruning or training. Self-fertile but fruits better if more than one cultivar, with over-lapping flowering times, is grown. H to 20m.

PROPAGATION

🌱 in temperate areas, seed is usually the only practicable means of propagation since clonal material – cultivars that have been bred and selected for good fruiting – is seldom available. (If clonal material can be obtained it can be grafted onto seedling rootstocks using a side-wedge graft.) Select seed from ripe fruit and soak in hot (not boiling) water for about 30 minutes. Remove the top 1cm (½in) from the pointed end of the seed and dip the wound in fungicide. Place the seed in a pot of well-drained compost with the cut top just above soil level. It should germinate in 3–4 weeks.

Prunus   Rosaceae

Genus of 430 hardy flowering trees and shrubs, some of which are grown for their edible fruit. Most are deciduous; a few are evergreen. Height depends on the rootstock.

P. armeniaca (Apricot). Flowers early in spring; in cold areas is best fan-trained on a sunny wall or grown in a cold greenhouse to protect from frost. Grow in deep, fertile, slightly alkaline loam. They can be grown in the same tree forms as plums. They are self-fertile. Hand-pollinate flowers with a soft brush. CR 350–900 hours below 7°C (45°F).

PROPAGATION

Chip- or T-budding, or whip-and-tongue grafting, onto 'St Julien A'. If grown on the dwarfing rootstock 'Pixy', use an interstock of 'St Julien A'.

P. avium (Sweet cherry). Bears fruit at base of previous year's wood and on spurs on older wood. Grow in well-drained soil, in shelter, as fans or bush trees. Most are self-sterile and only cross-compatible with certain cultivars. The following are compatible groups:

Group 1: **'Early Rivers'**, **'Noir de Guben'**.
Group 2: **'Merton Favourite'**, **'Merton Glory'**.
Group 3: **'Merchant'**, **'Roundel'**, **'Starkrimson'**, **'Van'** (SF).
Group 4: **'Governor Wood'**, 'Lapins' (SF), **'Bigarreau Napoléon'**, **'Stella'** (SF), **'Sunburst'** (SF).
Group 5: **'Bigarreau Gaucher'**, **'Bradbourne Black'**.
CR 800–1200 hours below 7°C (45°F).

PROPAGATION

Chip- or T-budding or whip-and-tongue grafting. The most reliable rootstock is the semi-vigorous **'Colt'**; newer dwarfing rootstocks include **'Edebritz'**, syn. **'Tabel'**.

P. cerasus (Acid cherry). Fruits on previous year's wood; best grown as a fan or pyramid. Thrives on a shady wall, in deep, fertile, well-drained soil. Most are self-fertile; **'Morello'** is one of the most reliable; **'Nabella'** and **'Montmorency'** are also recommended. CR 800–1200 hours below 7°C (45°F).

PROPAGATION

Chip- or T- budding, or whip-and-tongue grafting. The most suitable rootstock to use for propagation is 'Colt'.

P. domestica (Plum and Gage), *P. institia* (Bullace and Damson) and *P. cerasifera* (Cherry plum). All are grown in the same way. They are hardy but flower early and so fruit best with warm springs. They should be grown as pyramids, which are less prone to branch breakage. They can also be fan-trained against a warm wall and, using the dwarfing rootstock 'Pixy', as cordons. Some, including most bullaces and damsons and all cherry plums, are self-fertile, but benefit from cross-pollination. Pollination groups follow.

Group 1: **'Angelina Burdett'**, **'Blue Rock'**, **'Heron'**, **'Jefferson'**, **'Mallard'**, **'Monarch'** (SF), **'Utility'**.
Group 2: **'Ariel'**, **'Avalon'**, **'Brahy's Greengage'** (SF), **'Coe's Golden Drop'**, **'Denniston's Superb'** (SF), **'President'**, **'Warwickshire Drooper'** (SF).
Group 3: **'Allgrove's Superb'**, **'Bountiful'** (SF), **'Bryanston Gage'**, **'Czar'** (SF), **'Early Laxton'**, **'Early Rivers'**, **'Edwards'** (SF), **'Golden Transparent'** (SF), **'Goldfinch'**, **'Herman'** (SF), **'Late Orange'**, **'Laxton's Cropper'** (SF),

Prunus persica

Pyrus 'Conference'

Ribes sativum

'Laxton's Gage' (SF), 'Merryweather Damson' (SF), 'Merton Gem', 'Opal' (SF), 'Pershore' (SF), 'Purple Pershore' (SF), 'Reine Claude Violette', 'Severn Cross' (SF), 'Sanctus Hubertus', 'Thames Cross', 'Victoria' (SF), 'Washington'.
Group 4: 'Blaisdon Red' (SF), 'Bradley's King Damson' (SF), 'Cambridge Gage', 'Count Althann's Gage', 'Early Transparent Gage' (SF), 'Farleigh Damson', 'Giant Prune' (SF), 'Kirke's Ontario' (SF), 'Oullins Golden Gage' (SF), 'Wyedale'.
Group 5: 'Belle de Louvain' (SF), 'Blue Tit' (SF), 'Excalibur', 'Late Transparent Gage', 'Marjorie's Seedling' (SF), 'Old Greengage', 'Pond's Seedling', 'Prune Damson' (SF).
There are three incompatibility groups:
Group 1: 'Allgrove's Superb', 'Coe's Golden Drop', 'Coe's Violet Gage', 'Crimson Drop', 'Jefferson'.
Group 2: 'Cambridge Gage', 'Late Orange', 'Old Greengage', 'President'.
Group 3: 'Blue Rock', 'Early Rivers'.
CR 700–1000 hours below 7°C (45°F).

PROPAGATION
Chip- or T-budding, or whip-and-tongue grafting onto 'St Julien A', or onto the dwarfing rootstock 'Pixy' for cordons.
P. dulcis (Almond). Very ornamental in flower; flowers are produced on the bare shoots in spring. It flowers early in spring, and only crops well in areas with warm springs and hot summers. Grow in neutral to slightly acid, well-drained fertile soil in a sheltered, sunny site. Usually grown as bush or half-standard trees. Usually self-fertile, but crop better if 2 cultivars are grown for pollination.
CR 300–500 hours below 7°C (45°F).

PROPAGATION
Chip- or T-budding or whip-and-tongue grafting. The best rootstock is 'St Julien A', but peach and almond seedlings are also used.
P. persica (Peach) and var. *nectarina* (Nectarine). These are both hardy, but grow and fruit best in areas with warm springs and hot, dry summers. They flower early, needing frost protection when flowering, and often require hand-pollination. Grow in a sheltered, sunny site, in deep, fertile, slightly acid soil. In cool temperate areas, they are best fan-trained against a warm, sunny wall, or grown in a cold greenhouse. In warmer areas, they can be cultivated as bush trees. With few exceptions, they are self-fertile.
CR 600–900 hours below 7°C (45°F).

PROPAGATION
Chip- or T-budding or whip-and-tongue grafting, onto 'St Julien A'. They may be double-worked onto 'Pixy' using an interstock of 'St Julien A'.

Pyrus (Pear)   Rosaceae
Genus of about 30 species of hardy, deciduous trees, some grown for their fruit.
P. communis var. *sativa* (Common pear). This is the basic species from which all pears have developed. Best in areas with warm springs and hot summers. In cooler areas, select late-flowering cultivars; flowers may escape frost damage. Grow in fertile, well-drained soil in full sun. There are 2 main rootstocks: 'Quince C' is semi-dwarfing and suitable for cordons, bush and pyramid forms; 'Quince A' is semi-vigorous and used for bush, half-standard, pyramid and espalier forms.
Most are not self-fertile and need cross-pollination. Most cultivars flowering at the

same time are compatible. Triploid cultivars are ineffective as pollinators and must be grown with at least 2 diploid cultivars. Pollination groups follow.
Group 1: 'Brockworth Park', 'Maréchal de la Cour' (T), 'Précoce de Trévoux'.
Group 2: 'Doyenné d'Eté', 'Duchesse d'Angoulême', 'Emile d'Heyst', 'Louise Bonne of Jersey', 'Packham's Triumph', 'Passe Crassanne', 'Seckle'.
Group 3: 'Beurré Hardy', 'Beurré Superfin', 'Black Worcester', 'Concorde', 'Conference', 'Dr Jules Guyot', 'Durondeau', 'Fondante d'Automne', 'Hessle', 'Jargonelle' (T), 'Joséphine de Malines', 'Merton Pride' (T), 'Souvenir du Congress', 'Thompson's', 'Williams' Bon Chrétien'.
Group 4: 'Beth', 'Beurré Bedford' (MS), 'Bristol Cross', 'Catillac' (T), 'Clapp's Favourite', 'Doyenné du Comice', 'Glou Morceau', 'Gorham', 'Nouveau Poiteau', 'Onward', 'Pitmaston Duchess' (T), 'Winter Nelis'.
There are also two incompatibility groups:
Group 1: 'Fondant d'Automne', 'Laxton's Progress', 'Louise Bonne of Jersey', 'Précoce de Trévoux', 'Seckle', 'Williams' Bon Chrétien'.
Group 2: 'Beurré d'Amanlis', 'Conference'.
CR 600–900 hours below 7°C (45°F).

PROPAGATION
Chip- or T-budding, or whip-and-tongue grafting. Some are not compatible with quince rootstock and are double-worked using a mutually compatible interstock, such as 'Beurré Hardy' or 'Doyenné du Comice'. Graft the interstock in spring, and bud the required cultivar the same or next summer.

Rubus fruticosus 'Oregon Thornless'

Rubus idaeus 'Autumn Bliss'

Vitis 'Richtenstein'

Ribes (Currant and Gooseberry)
Grossulariaceae

Some 150 hardy, deciduous or evergreen shrubs, some grown for their fruit.

R. nigrum (Black currant), *R. sativum* (Red and White currants). Black currants fruit on the previous year's wood and are grown as stooled bushes, pruned on a replacement system. Red and white currants fruit on base of previous year's wood and on older wood; grown as bushes, standards, cordons and fans. Hardy; grow best in damp, cool temperate climates. Grow in sun, in well-cultivated soil. All are self-fertile. H and S 1–1.5m (3–5ft).

PROPAGATION

Hardwood cuttings – late autumn. For black currants, 20–25cm (8–10in) long, inserted with two buds above ground level. For red and white currants, 30cm (12in) long, remove lower buds, leaving top 4; insert to half their depth.

R. uva-crispa (Gooseberry). Fruit is produced at the base of the previous year's wood and on older wood. Best in cool, moist climates. Grow in sun, in fertile, well-cultivated soil. Grown as bushes, standards, cordons and fans. Self-fertile. H and S 1–1.5m (3–5ft).

PROPAGATION

Hardwood cuttings – early to late autumn. Leave top 2 leaves and all buds, and insert to half their depth. To produce standards, chip-budding or whip-and-tongue grafting are used; graft onto *R. odoratum* or *R. divaricatum* at 90–120cm (3–4ft) high.

Rubus (Blackberry, Bramble) Rosaceae

Genus of 250 species that include woody-stemmed, scrambling climbers grown for their edible fruits. Blackberries are hardy and crop reliably; many blackberry cultivars are hybrids with other *Rubus* species. Hybrid berries include the raspberry x blackberry hybrids – loganberry and tayberry – as well as boysenberry and king's acre berry. They produce good-quality fruit, but not all are as hardy as the blackberry and they are less suited to cultivation in cold, exposed areas. The boysenberry is best in warmer, drier conditions. All fruit in late summer or early autumn, on canes made the previous year, and all are self-fertile. Grow in sun or part-shade in fertile soil. They are trained in various ways, including fanning, weaving and roping; all involve separating fruiting canes from those that will fruit the following year.

PROPAGATION

Tip layering – summer.

Leaf-bud cuttings, or 3-bud cuttings can be used where greater numbers are required.

R. idaeus (Raspberry) Hardy and grows best in cool, damp climates. Plant in moderately fertile soil in sun. Raspberries fall into two groups: summer-fruiting cultivars, which fruit on the previous year's canes in early to midsummer, e.g. **'Glen Moy'** and **'Leo'**; and autumn-fruiting, or primocane, cultivars, which fruit from late summer to autumn on the current year's growth, e.g. **'Autumn Bliss'** and **'Heritage'**. Autumn-fruiting raspberries are unsuitable for more northerly locations as the fruit seldom ripens satisfactorily. Raspberries are self-fertile.

PROPAGATION

Suckers – late autumn, when dormant. Ensure that parent plants are healthy. Root cuttings – winter.

Vaccinium Ericaceae

Some 450 species of shrubs, small trees or vines, some with edible fruit. American blueberries are produced by high-bush blueberry hybrids of *V. corymbosum* and *V. australe.* They are very hardy, thriving in cool moist climates. Need sun and moist but well-drained acid soil, with a pH 4–5.5. They can be grown in tubs of ericaceous compost. Blueberries are grown as stooled bushes, and fruit on 2–3-year-old wood. Once established, some of the oldest wood is cut out to the base annually in winter. Blueberries are only partially self-fertile and crop best if more than one cultivar is grown. CR 700–1200 hours below 7°C (45°F).

PROPAGATION

Softwood cuttings – early to midsummer.

Vitis (Vine) Vitaceae

About 65 deciduous, mostly climbing species, some producing edible fruit. Grape vines grow best in warm temperate climates with long, hot, dry summers. In cooler climates provide very sheltered sites, or grow by a sunny wall. In even colder areas grow in a cool greenhouse. They prefer well-drained, humus-rich soil. Vines are self-fertile. They can be trained in many ways on permanent frameworks or using the Guyot system, which is widely used in vineyards.

PROPAGATION

Hardwood cuttings – winter, 20cm (8in) long. Also by vine-eye cuttings, or three-bud cuttings.

Softwood cuttings – early summer.

In countries where the pest *Phylloxera* is present, vines are whip-and-tongue grafted on to resistant rootstocks.

VEGETABLES

There is enormous satisfaction to be gained from growing your own produce to eat and share, and vegetables from your own garden will be far superior in quality and taste to any you can buy in the shops. Whereas commercial growers aim for yield and uniformity, you can grow for freshness and flavour and do not need to restrict yourself to cultivars that have a long shelf life.

Regular propagation ensures the best of all types of vegetable, from simple hardy crops, such as cabbages and carrots, to tender aubergines and the like that need warmth to germinate and a long growing season. Propagating will help you plan sowing, planting, and harvesting times to get the best from your garden all year round.

◄ *The succession of vegetable seeds, sets and tubers that were sown during spring and early summer will begin to yield harvests from midsummer onwards.*

WHY PROPAGATE
VEGETABLES?

To grow your own vegetables is one of the most satisfying experiences a gardener can have. Not only does produce cooked fresh from the kitchen garden taste wonderful, it is also packed full of vitamins and minerals. Self-sufficiency may be beyond most people's means these days, but we can all find space for a few choice crops.

Nearly all vegetables are increased by seed but success depends on timing of sowing and using appropriate techniques.

Most vegetables are started every year from seed, tubers or bulbs. Plantlets are usually available from garden centres, but raising them yourself is not difficult and gives a much better choice of cultivars. It also lessens the risk of introducing soil-borne diseases such as clubroot to the garden. Some vegetables are perennials and others are biennials or can be grown as such, sown one year for harvesting the next. Time your sowings so that you have early crops from overwintered seedlings, mid-season crops from seed sown early in the year in warmth, and later crops from seed sown *in situ*.

THE ADVANTAGE OF SEED

Propagation by seed ensures healthy crops and allows you to experiment with different varieties. Try several cultivars of the same vegetable, for instance, and assess which gives the heaviest crops, provides the best eating and is easiest to grow in the conditions that prevail in your garden. Most gardeners quickly find out which is their favourite tomato, for instance, basing their judgement on taste, yield and ease of cultivation, but you should always be ready to experiment with new varieties that may turn out to be superior.

Specific cultivars have been developed for harvesting at certain times of year. Winter cabbage cultivars, for example, are hardier than summer ones. Cultivars may also mature at different times. Early cultivars mature more quickly, and thus can be useful both for early crops and for areas with short summers.

F1 hybrid cultivars give more vigorous, uniform plants of reliable quality. However, crops tend to be ready for harvest

Cabbage
All cabbages are treated as annuals and grown from seed, but different cultivars are bred to crop at different times of the year and so sowing dates vary according to cropping season.

Ruby chard
Chards are hardy and vigorous biennials, that, from spring sowings, will crop until the spring following. To ensure continuity of supply, sow successionally in spring, midsummer and late summer.

Onions
Onions need a long season to crop well. Choose between seed or sets; seed is inexpensive but slow; sets are quicker and easier but the available cultivar range is more restricted.

Carrots
Although truly biennial, carrots are grown as annuals. Early ones are sown as soon as soil warms up in spring; maincrop carrots are sown between late spring and early summer.

at the same time, which can be a problem unless they store well. Quick-growing vegetables such as radishes can be sown in succession for continuity of cropping.

BULBS AND TUBERS

Shallots and onions are usually grown from bulbs, as is garlic. Bulbs, or sets, are robust and easy to handle and generally give good yields. Onion sets in particular mature earlier and give higher yields than seeds sown *in situ*. However there is a more limited choice of cultivars available and plants are more likely to run to seed. Potatoes are nearly always grown from seed tubers bought in fresh each year.

PERENNIAL VEGETABLES

Globe artichokes and rhubarb are usually propagated by divisions or offsets of mature plants. As with all vegetative methods, this guarantees the resulting plants

Cut-and-come-again Crops
Many leafy vegetables re-grow after they have first been cut, giving two or more cuts from one sowing. One advantage of cut-and-come-again cropping is that harvesting takes place when the plants are immature – sometimes even at seedling stage – giving very quick crops. Most can be spaced closely (with seedlings, only 2–2.5cm [¾–1in] apart), so make good use of space. Those that can be cropped as immature plants include salad-bowl lettuce and curly kale. Seedling crops include salad rocket, cress and chicory. In cold

areas, cloches will protect early sowings from frost.

Rucola sativa (rocket) is a good example of a vegetable that will re-grow after cropping.

are true to type, although they can also be grown quite successfully from seed. Asparagus, which is a long-lived perennial, can be grown from seed or crowns.

⑤
Curly kale
Kale is among the hardiest of brassicas and may be grown as an annual or biennial; sow crops for summer in early spring, sow in late spring for winter and spring harvest.

⑥
Broad beans
For very early crops, sow hardy cultivars in a sheltered site, in autumn or late winter with cloche protection. Sow early and late crops in an open site, between spring and early summer.

⑦
Runner beans
Frost-tender perennial climbers grown as annuals. Sow *in situ* when danger of frost has passed and the soil is warm, but for good crops in cold areas, sow earlier under glass.

195

PROPAGATING TECHNIQUES
VEGETABLES

In the majority of cases vegetables should be propagated from good-quality annual seed, but seed can deteriorate if kept for any length of time and some plants do not give of their best when raised in this way. In these instances, vegetative methods can be deployed instead. Rhubarb, for example, is commonly propagated by division.

Most vegetables are easy to propagate and can be produced with the minimum of equipment. Some form of crop protection will widen your options as well as lengthening the growing season. Every crop has a minimum germination temperature, and higher temperatures usually speed both germination and growth. However, for some crops (such as lettuce), germination is inhibited above an upper temperature limit. Minimum germination temperatures and upper temperature limits where these are low enough to be encountered, are given in the plant directory (*see pp. 200–209*).

Some crops (such as beetroot) should not be sown too early where late frosts are likely, as exposing young plants to cold can cause premature bolting. Others, such as Chinese cabbage, are sensitive to day-length and grow best if sown after midsummer.

Vegetable cloches ....
When planning a vegetable garden, you need to consider your local climate and soil conditions as well as whether you wish to extend the natural seasons by using cloches.

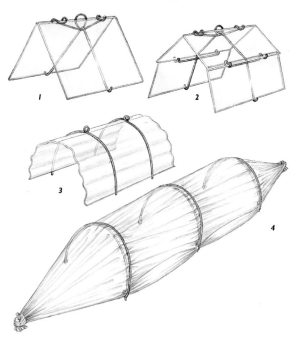

1 A tent cloche made from glass is inexpensive and easy to erect.
2 The extra height of a barn cloche is useful for tall plants.
3 A corrugated plastic cloche is cheap but becomes brittle with age.
4 A plastic-covered tunnel cloche completely covers the plants.

Protected cropping
Various techniques can be used to extend the growing season for vegetable crops. Crop covers can raise soil and air temperatures and protect young plants from wind and frost. A combination of methods can extend the growing season at both ends of the year, and may enable tender vegetables to be grown in colder areas.

Clear plastic sheeting: A most effective way of raising soil temperatures early in the year. Place it over the seedbed a few days before sowing, and replace after sowing to maintain temperatures. Remove after germination.

Black plastic: Is less efficient in raising soil temperatures significantly, but suppresses weed growth and keeps a seedbed moist and clean ready for sowing.

White plastic: This reflects heat and light and prevents soil warming – useful where summer soil temperatures are too high for heat-sensitive crops like lettuce.

Floating mulches: These films lie on the crop to give it protection. They are permeable to light, air and water and lightweight enough to be supported by the plants. They warm the soil and air around the plants and filter strong winds. There are several types. Perforated polythene film warms soil rapidly, but offers little protection from frost and does not let in much rain. It is useful for speeding germination and protecting young crops early in the year, but, later on, can create undesirable heat and humidity. Horticultural fleece is much softer, more permeable to light, air and water, and gives several degrees of frost protection. It is useful for early-and late-sown hardy crops and can, if necessary, be left on until harvest or over winter. It gives significant protection from flying pests like aphids and carrot fly.

Cloches and tunnels: These give good frost protection, and can be used to cover a seedbed, or seedlings in trays or modules. They are useful for tender vegetables like tomatoes and French beans, and early- and late-season hardy crops. Various designs are available (*see below left*).

SEED

Most vegetables are raised from seed annually. Since nearly all are cultivars, many do not come true from garden-collected seed. Buy fresh seed each year and, if it is not sown at once, keep it cool and dry. All seed deteriorates with age, especially in a warm, moist atmosphere, so check the dates on seed packets.

Pelleted seeds: These have a protective coating to make them easy to place; this disintegrates if the soil is kept moist. Pelleted seeds are useful for crops with small seed sown *in situ*, and helps avoid wasteful thinning later.

Chitted seed: This is seed that has started to germinate, each seed showing a tiny root. It is a useful way of starting off vegetables that are difficult to germinate. You can also chit or pre-germinate seed yourself.

Primed seed: This is seed brought to the point of germination, then dried and packeted. It is useful for crops such as carrots and parsley that germinate slowly.

Treated seed: Seed of certain crops is sometimes dressed with chemicals to help combat diseases.

Sowing *in situ*

This is the main method for hardy, closely spaced crops like carrots that do not transplant easily. Before sowing, you must create a suitable 'tilth' – a crumbly structure

Sowing seeds in a narrow drill ....

Seeds should be covered in their own depth of soil, so ensure any drill is only twice the seed depth. If they are planted too deep, successful germination will be delayed or reduced.

◀ **1** Mark the position of the row with a line held taut between two pegs, and make a drill along the line using the corner of a draw hoe or spade. Alternatively, press the narrow edge of a plank into the ground. Either space seeds thinly and evenly along the row, or put three or four seeds at each point where a plant is needed and thin the seedlings that emerge.

▶ **2** After sowing, cover the drill by gently pushing back the soil with a rake, a hoe or your fingers.

free of clods and stones. The finer the seed, the finer the tilth required, so that the seed makes good contact with the soil to take up moisture.

To improve soil structure, mulch with organic matter the autumn before sowing. The following spring, remove the surplus from the surface. On heavy clay, dig the soil over roughly before winter, leaving large clods to be broken down by frost.

Just before sowing, rake the topmost layer of soil to create a level, fine-crumbed surface. Keep cultivation to the minimum, however, as overworking the soil can damage the structure. Never try to rake out a seedbed when the soil is excessively wet or dry.

Water dry ground thoroughly the evening before sowing. If ground is wet and rain is forecast, put cloches over the area a few days before to help it dry out.

Sowing in narrow drills

The usual method of sowing *in situ* is in narrow drills. The depth of the drill depends on the size of the seed. Small seeds need shallower drills. About 1–2cm (½–¾in) is ideal for lettuce, for example, the deeper limit being

Sowing seeds in a broad drill ....

Broad drills are suitable for such crops as early carrots and peas, which are grown closely together in an intensive manner and cropped before they are fully mature.

► **1** Use pegs and string to mark out parallel drills, 23cm (9in) wide. The exact distance between drills depends on the crop being sown. Then, with a draw hoe or narrow spade, create flat-based drills to the required depth.

◄ **2** 'Station-sow' the seeds in three parallel rows within the drills by placing large seeds individually or by sowing three or four smaller seeds together at each point and thinning the seedlings later. Then cover the seeds with their own depth of soil, using a draw hoe.

best for light soils. Large seeds can be sown much deeper (about 2.5–4.0cm (1–1½in) for peas, for example). (*For the sowing depths of other vegetables, see the plant directory, pp.200–209.*) Make sure the depth is uniform along the drill, or germination will be uneven.

Sowing in broad drills

Flat-bottomed drills, usually 8-15cm (3-6in) across, are useful where a wide, dense row is required – for peas, early carrots, spring onions, and cut-and-come-again crops, for example.

If the soil at the base of the drill is dry, water just along the bottom. Sow the seed and cover with dry soil. If the soil is still wet when you come to sow, make the drills as described, but at the maximum recommended depth, then line with spent seed or potting compost, and cover the seed with the same mixture.

Broadcasting seed: Broadcasting, where seed is scattered over the surface and raked in, is a method sometimes used for quick, closely spaced crops, but is only

advisable on relatively weed-free soil, since it may not be immediately apparent whether the emerging seedlings are of the germinating crop or of alien weeds.

Sowing in a seedbed

To save space, slow-growing hardy vegetables such as Brussels sprouts and leeks can be sown in a seedbed and transplanted later to their final positions. The ground they will eventually occupy can meanwhile be used for another crop. Only a small area needs to be prepared as a seedbed, and this is easier to protect from the weather and pests. Choose an open, unshaded site for the seedbed, otherwise the seedlings will become drawn as they develop. Cultivating the soil to create a friable tilth will minimize root damage when transplanting. A seedbed protected by a cold frame gives the ideal conditions for early sowings.

Prepare the seedbed and make drills as for sowing *in situ.* Rows can be closely spaced: about 10–13cm (4–5in) apart for leeks and about 20–23cm (8–9in) for brassicas. Sow seed thinly and evenly along the rows and cover with soil.

Aftercare: Whether seed has been sown *in situ* or in a seedbed, it must not be allowed to dry out. If you have

Transplanting leeks ....

Leeks need a long growing season so should be started early, either in modular trays, 3–4 seeds to a cell, or else in a seedbed in the garden. Transplant at the three-leaf stage.

► Leeks respond well when multi-sown, so those started in modular trays should be retained in their modular clumps when transplanted into the garden. Plant them 22cm (9in) apart and very slightly deeper than they were in the module, aligning them against some string.

► Leeks that have been sown singly, in a seedbed, should be transplanted into dibbled holes, 15–20cm (6–8in) deep, and 10–15cm (4–6in) apart, against a guide line. Water the hole gently, allowing the soil to fall in around the seedling.

to water before the seedlings emerge, keep the soil surface continuously moist to prevent it forming a hard cap. Covering with polythene can help avoid this. Thin in stages, starting when the seedlings are large enough to handle, and ending with the final spacing.

Transplanting: Plants sown in a seedbed for later transplanting should be thinned to about 7.5cm (3in) apart so that their roots do not intertwine. Most seedlings are ready for transplanting when they have formed three or four true leaves, four to five weeks after sowing.

Water the seedlings before lifting and, if the planting site is dry, water that too. Handling them only by their leaves, transfer them to a hole slightly bigger than the root ball and plant them with the lowest leaves just above the soil surface. Firm them in, then water in thoroughly. Shade them from hot sun until well established. (*For transplanting leeks, see opposite, below.*)

Chitting

Sometimes it is advantageous to germinate seed before you sow it (chitting), for instance when the temperature outside is too low for germination. It also acts as a check on the viability of the seed, so that valuable space in the garden is not wasted.

Sprinkle the seed evenly on moist absorbent paper at the bottom of a plastic, lidded box. Put the lid on the box, and keep it warm. (*For temperatures required for individual vegetables, see the plant directory, pp. 200–209.*) When a tiny rootlet emerges, after a few days in some cases, the seed can be sown in the normal way.

Large, chitted seed can be picked out when ready and sown individually. Handle them carefully, using tweezers if necessary. Smaller seeds can be fluid-sown, since this minimizes damage to their rootlets and helps to ensure even spacing.

Sowing in containers

Sowing seeds in containers under glass or in a heated propagator rather than directly in the ground is useful in cold areas for vegetables that are not fully hardy and/or need a long growing season. This method can also be used for early crops of hardy vegetables. As you are creating a controlled environment for germination, it is also appropriate for seed that is scarce or expensive.

Fluid-sowing ....

This technique is sometimes used for sowing small, chitted seed, because it is an easy way to sow large numbers of seeds and it also protects the rootlets on the pre-germinated seeds.

When more than 50 per cent of small, chitted seeds have germinated, wash them off the paper into a sieve. Mix the seeds with a special gel or a fungicide-free wallpaper paste to protect the rootlets. Then put the mixture in a plastic bag. Cut off a small corner, and pipe the mixture into the drill. Cover over with soil in the usual way.

Seed can be sown in pots or seed trays and then 'pricked out' and potted on. Sow the seed thinly and evenly in a container of moist seed compost and,

Sowing in modular trays ....

Each cell is filled individually with proprietary seed compost to within 1cm (½in) of the top. Holes are then made in the centre of each cell using the blocking tool.

▲ **1** Sow seed individually into each cell and cover it as for sowing and pricking out. (If you expect germination to be poor, sow several seeds per cell, or block and nip out any excess seedlings that emerge.) For certain crops, however, you can sow several seeds per cell and allow all the seedlings to grow on.

◄ **2** When the seedlings are ready to be transplanted, water them well. Then press them out from underneath the modular tray, using the blocking tool. Plant the seedlings out as one unit, but at a wider spacing than for individual plants. Despite the uneven spacing, each plant will develop normally.

except for very fine seed, cover with a thin layer of sieved compost. Put a sheet of glass or polythene over the container to prevent it drying out, and keep it in a warm place. (*For temperatures, see the plant directory, pp.200–209.*)

Remove the cover as soon as the seedlings have germinated. When they are large enough to handle, prick them out into pots or trays of potting compost and gradually harden them off (*see below*).

Sowing in modules or compost blocks: Raising seedlings in modules or compost blocks saves time on pricking out. It also keeps root disturbance to the seedlings to a minimum, and it is useful for crops that normally resent transplanting, such as carrots and Chinese cabbage.

Modules are typically moulded plastic or polystyrene trays consisting of a number of cells that vary in size according to the crop. They often come with moulded pressers that are used to push out the seedlings and rootball when they are ready for transplanting. Compost blocks can be made with a proprietary 'blocking compost' and blocking tools of various sizes that compress loose compost into cubes.

Aftercare and hardening off: For optimum development, seedlings must be kept in warm, light conditions. Transplant or pot them on as soon as the roots fill the containers, and do not allow overcrowding or they will be starved of nutrients and may not crop well.

Seedlings that are raised in a greenhouse need to be acclimatized to the harsher conditions outside ('hardened off') before they can be planted out. Move the containers outdoors into a cold frame or under cloches, and increase ventilation gradually for an increasingly longer period each day. Alternatively, stand the plants outside, first for a few hours in good weather, and gradually for longer. The hardening-off period should ideally be about ten to fourteen days.

Transplanting: Ideally, choose a dull, still day for transplanting. Water plants in a seedbed, then loosen the ground with a fork and lift them out gently, aiming to keep root damage to the minimum. If necessary, shade the newly transplanted vegetables from the sun with fleece or newspaper when they are first planted out. Conditions are less critical for seedlings in pots and

Planting out asparagus crowns ·················

Good drainage is vitally important for asparagus, so always choose a well-drained site and create a bed with a raised ridge of soil along its centre.

► With guide lines, mark out trenches 30cm (12in) wide for each row of the asparagus bed, allowing 30cm (12in) between rows. Dig each trench, 20cm (8in) deep, between the guides, and create a raised central mound. Set the crowns, 38cm (15in) apart, on the raised mound with their roots spread widely and evenly around the crowns and into the bottom of each trench.

modules, because these suffer less root damage. Keep all plants well watered until they are established and growing away well. Thereafter, most will need extra water only during periods of very dry weather.

VEGETATIVE METHODS

There are a few perennial vegetables that may be increased by seed, but which are more commonly propagated by vegetative means.

Rhubarb is usually propagated by division, since seed-raised plants are so variable in quality. In autumn, after the leaves have died down, lift the crown and cut off sections of the rhizome (sets), each with at least one growing point or bud. Return the parent to the ground and plant the sets with the bud just below ground level (light soils) or just above (heavy soils).

Globe artichokes can be lifted in spring and divided like a herbaceous perennial.

Garlic can be increased by detaching and growing on individual cloves from a parent bulb but should only be grown from disease-free stock. Lift the bulbs in autumn and separate the cloves. Those with a diameter of at least 1cm (½in) produce the best plants. Plant them to twice their depth about 18cm (7in) apart. In cold areas, plant them in modules kept in a sheltered place through the winter. Plant them out the following spring, preferably into pre-warmed soil.

Asparagus can be raised cheaply from seed sown *in situ* in spring, but choose an all-male F1 hybrid seed strain, since these are higher yielding. For quicker cropping, buy year-old crowns for spring planting.

Asparagus can be productive for many years, but the gardener must be patient in the early years. Only a few spears should be cut in the first year after planting crowns. In the second year, the bed can be cropped for up to six weeks. In the third and subsequent seasons, spears may be cut for a period of about two months.

Special techniques

Some plants need special treatments after sowing and planting out to produce attractive and well-flavoured crops. Rhubarb, for example, produces sweeter more tender stems earlier in the season if forced, that is, grown under a light-excluding cover such as a forcing pot. The stems of leeks and bulb-like stems of Florence fennel are both blanched by excluding light, in this case by earthing up. Self-blanching cultivars of celery are available, but even these are sweeter if light is excluded from the stems by packing with straw. Trench celery can be blanched (*see instructions on right*).

Chicory and endive are blanched because otherwise the green leaves have a distinctive, rather bitter flavour that is too strong for most palates. The blanching technique differs slightly for the cut or curled leaved and the broad leaf types (*see instructions below right*).

Blanching chicory ....

Chicory leaves tend to be somewhat bitter for most palates, but their blanched, leafy shoots, or 'chicons', are a popular vegetable. These are obtained by digging up mature chicory plants in autumn and forcing their roots by potting them up and blanching them.

▲ **1** Dig up one or more mature chicory plants in autumn and trim off all leaves to within 2.5cm (1in) of the crown. Remove the root tips and any side roots. Fill a pot with moist potting compost and then insert the prepared roots vertically, so that their crowns are just visible above the surface.

▲ **2** Take another pot of equal size and line it with aluminium foil. Position this over the roots in the first pot so that all light is excluded. Leave in a warm (15°C/59°C) environment until the chicons are ready for harvesting; this is generally in 3–4 weeks' time.

Blanching celery ....

Much celery is now self-blanching, but trench celery still needs to be blanched artifically. This relatively easy process is started when the celery plant is 30cm (12in) tall.

◀ **Blanching celery on the flat**
In well-prepared, flattened soil, plant celery plants *in situ*, after all risk of frost has passed. Once the stems reach 30cm (12in) high, wrap a light-excluding paper collar around them, keeping it in place with raffia or soft twine, and allowing the leaves to emerge from the top. Wrap a second collar around the plant as more stem develops.

◀ **Blanching celery in a trench**
Prepare the soil very well and then make a trench 30cm (12in) deep and 38cm (15in) wide. Fill the trench with copious organic matter and then level it before planting. Plant the celery seedlings. As they develop, tie their stems with twine or raffia and keep earthing up the plants to just below the leaves. Ensure that no soil falls between the stems.

Blanching endive ....

Endive leaves can be sweetened by blanching, either partially or totally, but cover only a few leaves at a time as they tend to deteriorate rapidly after such treatment.

▶ **Partial blanching**
Select a nearly mature plant and, when dry, cover the central rosette with a large, domed plate. Harvest the leaves after 10 days.

▶ **Total blanching**
When the leaves are dry, loosely wrap a mature endive in soft twine or raffia and cover it beneath a bucket that excludes all light. Leave until the foliage has turned almost white and is ready for harvesting.

DIRECTORY OF
VEGETABLES

Below are key tips on on a selection of vegetables that are particularly suitable for propagation. Unless otherwise specified, follow the detailed instructions given under the propagation section on pages 196–201.

Key

Sp   Spacing
TH   Time to harvest
🌱   By seed

Allium cepa (Onion)   Alliaceae

A staple crop grown for its bulb, used fresh and from store. Onions are grown from seed or 'sets' (small individual bulbs) and need a long growing season. Most cultivars are started in spring for summer use and winter storage. Some are planted in autumn, to give an early crop the next year.

PROPAGATION

Sets – push sets into the ground, with their tips just protruding. Plant maincrop late winter to mid-spring (or in late spring if heat-treated); overwintering sets, early to late autumn.
🌱 at minimum 7°C (45°F), maximum 24°C (75°F). Multi-sow in modules, 6 per cell, or in a seed tray for pricking out. Sow maincrop in late winter to early spring under glass; plant out mid- to late spring. For sowing *in situ* sow in drills, 1–2cm (½–¾in) deep. Sow maincrop in early to mid-spring, under polythene film or cloches. Sow overwintering onions in late summer. The exact timing of sowing for overwintering crops is critical and depends on the locality; plants should reach a height of 15–20cm (6–8in) to overwinter successfully. Delay thinning until spring.
Sp – multi-sown modules, 25–30cm (10–12in) apart each way. Single plants or maincrop sets, 5–10cm (2–4in) apart, in rows 25cm (10in) apart, or 15cm (6in) apart each way. Overwintering sets: 10cm (4in) apart, in rows 30cm (12in) apart.
TH 5–6 months for maincrop onions.

Allium cepa (Spring onion)   Alliaceae

Spring, or salad, onions can be used fresh from mid- spring to mid-autumn with successional sowing. They are usually sown *in situ*, but sowing in modules can be useful for early spring and midsummer sowings.

PROPAGATION

🌱 in succession, early spring to early summer, at minimum 7°C (45°F), maximum 24°C (75°F). Multi-sow in modules with up to 10 seeds per cell. Sow thinly in drills, 1–2cm (½–¾in) deep, 10cm (4in) wide. Sow hardy cultivars in mid- to late summer to achieve an early spring crop.

Sp – multi-sown modules, 15cm (6in) apart each way. Seeds 2–3cm (¾–1¼in) apart. TH 8–12 weeks for summer crops.

Allium esculentum (Shallot)   Alliaceae

Shallots are grown for their bulbs, usually stored for winter use. Traditionally, they are raised from sets, which multiply into a cluster of bulbs by the end of the season. A few cultivars, however, can be grown from seed.

PROPAGATION

Sets – mid-spring. Choose sets 2cm (¾in) in diameter for planting. Put them in shallow drills or push into the soil, so that only their tips are showing. Firm the soil around them.
Sp – 15cm (6in) apart, in rows 23cm (9in) apart, or 18cm (7in) apart each way.
🌱 mid-spring. Sow in a drill, about 1cm (½in) deep and 10cm (4in) wide.
Sp – about 1–2cm (½–¾in) apart to get single bulbs; larger spacings encourage clusters of 2 or 3 bulbs to develop.
TH 5 months.

Allium porrum (Leek)   Alliaceae

A very hardy vegetable grown for its white stems, cropping from early autumn to spring of the following year depending on cultivar. Leeks need a long growing season. Those used as mini-vegetables can be sown *in situ*.

PROPAGATION

🌱 germinate at a minimum of 7°C (45°F). Sow in a seed tray and prick out into deep boxes, or in modules with 3–4 per cell. Sow early cultivars, in gentle heat, late winter to early spring; later cultivars early to late spring. Alternatively, sow in drills, 2.5cm (1in) deep, early to late spring. Protect with frames, cloches or crop covers. When 20cm (8in) tall, transplant into individual dibbled holes, 15–20cm (6–8in) deep. Water in and allow the hole to fill naturally with soil.

Allium cepa 'Ailsa Craig'   *Allium cepa*

Allium sativum

Apium graveolens var. rapaceum

Beta vulgaris

Sp – multi-sown modules, 23cm (9in) apart each way. Single transplants, 7.5–15cm (3–6in) apart, in rows 30cm (12in) apart, or 10–15cm (4–6in) apart each way. Mini-leeks, 1cm (1.2in) apart, in rows 15cm (6in) apart. TH 7–9 months for mature crops. 13 weeks for mini-leeks.

Allium sativum (Garlic)   Alliaceae

Garlic is grown for its strong-flavoured bulb but the leafy shoots can also be eaten. It is very hardy. The individual cloves, split from the parent bulb, are used for propagation. Best planted in autumn, as it benefits from a cold period and long growing season; spring-planted garlic may not mature satisfactorily.

PROPAGATION

Cloves – late autumn or early spring, *in situ*, 5–10cm (2–4in) deep, pointed end up. For best results, cloves should be at least 1cm (½in) across. Alternatively, plant in modules, one clove per cell, in late autumn, and overwinter in a cold frame. Plant out when sprouted in mid- to late spring.
Sp – 18cm (7in) apart each way.
TH 7–9 months.

Apium graveolens var. dulce (Celery)   Umbelliferae

Celery is grown for its crisp stems. Both trench celery and self-blanching celery are propagated in the same way. Trench celery is hardier but more difficult to grow.

PROPAGATION

🌱 late winter to early spring, at 13–16°C (55–60°F), and no higher than 19°C (66°F), in seed trays or modules. Do not cover seed, it needs light to germinate. Grow on in deep boxes, or singly in pots and plant out

in early summer. Temperatures below 10°C (50°F) cause bolting later: do not plant out too early, and use crop covers if necessary.
Sp – self-blanching celery 15–27cm (6–11in) each way, closer spacing gives more slender stems. Plant trench celery about 30–45cm (12–18in) apart.
TH 8 months

Apium graveolens var. rapaceum (Celeriac)   Umbelliferae

A winter vegetable grown for its knobbly, swollen root. It needs a long growing season.

PROPAGATION

🌱 late winter to early spring, at 13–16°C (55–60°F), or in a cold frame in mid-spring, in seed trays or modules; germination can be slow and erratic. Grow on in deep boxes or singly in pots and plant out in early summer. Exposure to temperatures below 10°C (50°F) can cause bolting later so do not plant out too early, and use crop covers if necessary.
Sp – 30–38cm (12–15in) each way.
TH 8 months

Asparagus officinalis (Asparagus)   Liliaceae

A perennial grown for its young shoots in late spring and early summer. One-year-old crowns are widely available. Asparagus can also be grown from seed. Modern F1 hybrids are most productive. Traditionally sown in a seedbed outdoors, module-sowing under glass is a good method of raising small numbers of F1 hybrids.

PROPAGATION

🌱 early spring, pre-soak overnight and sow at 13–16°C (55–60°F), singly in modules,

or in a seed tray and prick out into pots. Germination can be slow and erratic. Plant out early to midsummer, in holes 10–12cm (4–5in) deep; fill in the holes in the autumn. In a seedbed, sow in drills, 2.5cm (1in) deep, in mid-spring; thin to 7.5cm (3in) apart; transplant the largest crowns in mid-spring the following year.
Sp – 30–45cm (12–18in) apart, in rows 75cm (30in) apart, or in beds of 2–3 rows 38cm (15in) apart.
TH cut a few spears the first spring after planting modules, or year-old crowns of F1 hybrids. Leave other cultivars for another year. Next season, cut spears over about 4 weeks; in subsequent seasons, increase to 6 weeks.

Beta vulgaris (Beetroot) Chenopodiaceae

A summer root crop with either round or cylindrical roots; the leaves are also good to eat. Usually has seed in clusters; monogerm cultivars have single seeds. Exposing young plants to cold can cause bolting later, so use bolt-resistant cultivars for early sowings.

PROPAGATION

🌱 germinate at a minimum of 7°C (45°F). Multi-sow in modules, 3 seed clusters per cell, from early spring to midsummer. Thin to 4 or 5 seedlings. Alternatively, sow in drills, 1–2cm (½–¾in) deep. For small beet to be used fresh, sow in early spring to midsummer, using cloches for early crops. For maincrop for winter storage, sow in late spring or early summer.
Sp – multi-sown modules, 23cm (9in) each way. Small young beet 2.5cm (1in) apart, in rows 20cm (8in) apart, or 5cm (2in) each way; to encourage early cropping use maincrop spacing. Maincrop 7.5cm (3in)

203

Beta vulgaris subsp. *cicla*

Brassica oleracea Acephala group

Brassica oleracea Botrytis group

apart, in rows 20cm (8in) apart, or 13–15cm (5–6in) apart each way.
TH 9–11 weeks for small young beet; 12 weeks for maincrops.

Beta vulgaris subsp. *cicla*

(Spinach beet)   Chenopodiaceae

A biennial with more drought tolerance than true spinach (*Spinacia oleracea*). It is winter-hardy, and will not run to seed until the spring after sowing. It will grow in light shade.

PROPAGATION

germinate at minimum 7°C (45°F). Sow singly in modules, or in drills, 2cm (¾in) deep, in mid- to late spring. Do not sow or plant out too early, as exposing young plants to cold can cause bolting. For an extra winter crop, sow in mid- to late summer.
Sp – 25cm (10in) apart, in rows 38cm (15in) apart, or 30cm (12in) apart each way.
TH 10–12 weeks; can be harvested until late autumn, during mild winters, and until late spring the following year.

Beta vulgaris var. *flavescens*

(Swiss chard)   Chenopodiaceae

Swiss chard is a type of spinach beet with thick white midribs and stems. The stems and leaves can be used as separate vegetables. It is less hardy than leaf beet, and usually needs protection from cloches to overwinter.
Propagation – as for Spinach beet (*above*).

Brassica napus Napobrassica group

(Swede)   Cruciferae

A brassica grown for its relatively hardy winter root. Normally sown *in situ*, but can be sown in modules if outdoor sowing conditions are poor. Roots can be used from

the ground, but early cultivars are best lifted and stored in early winter.

PROPAGATION

germinates at minimum 5°C (41°F). Sow thinly or station-sow in drills 2cm (¾in) deep, in late spring or early summer. It is essential to thin seedlings early for good roots to develop.
Sp – 23–30cm (9–12in) apart, in rows 38–45cm (15–18in) apart, or 30–35cm (12–14in) apart each way.
TH 18–20 weeks.

Brassica napus Rapifera group

(Turnip)   Cruciferae

Turnips are a quick-growing root crop; the tops are also useful for eating as spring greens. Successional sowings of suitable cultivars will give crops for summer harvest and winter storage. They are nearly always sown *in situ*.

PROPAGATION

germinates at a minimum of 5°C (41°F). Sow in drills 2cm (¾in) deep; early thinning is essential for good roots to develop. Make the first sowings of summer turnips in early spring with protection, followed by outdoor sowings every 3–4 weeks from mid-spring to late summer. Summer sowings may bolt quickly in hot and dry conditions. Sow hardy cultivars, for use in winter, from mid- to late summer.
Sp – for summer crops, 10–15cm (4–6in) apart, in rows 23cm (9in) apart, or 15cm (6in) apart each way. For storage, 25–30cm (10–12in) apart, in rows 30cm (12in) apart, or 25cm (10in) apart each way.
TH 6–8 weeks for summer cultivars, and 10–12 weeks for winter cultivars.

Brassica oleracea Acephala group

(Kale)   Cruciferae

A hardy winter brassica used for leaves in autumn and winter, and young shoots in spring. There are curly and broad-leaved types. Traditionally grown in a seedbed for transplanting, but can be sown in modules; dwarf cultivars can be sown *in situ*. Some curly kales are also used for mini-vegetables and as a seedling crop.

PROPAGATION

germinates at minimum 5°C (41°F). Sow singly in modules from mid- to late spring. Plant out early to midsummer. Or, sow in drills, 2–2.5cm (¾–1in) deep, for transplanting in midsummer; thin to 7.5cm (3in).
Sp – 30–75cm (12–30in) apart each way, the closer spacing for dwarf cultivars. 15–20cm (6–8in) each way for mini-vegetables.
TH 7 months for leaves from mature plants. 18 weeks for mini-vegetables.

Brassica oleracea Botrytis group

(Cauliflower)   Cruciferae

Cauliflowers are grown for their large 'curds', or heads, which are usually white, although purple and green types are available. They are grouped according to the season that the heads form. With successional sowing they can be harvested from early spring to early winter in most regions, and all year in mild areas. They are mostly large and slow-growing, and are sown in a seedbed or in containers for transplanting. Some cultivars can be closely spaced to produce a quick crop of mini-cauliflowers for sowing *in situ*.

PROPAGATION

germinates at minimum 5°C (41°F). Sow in a seed tray for pricking out, or singly

Brassica oleracea Capitata group 'Firensa'

Brassica oleracea Gemmifera group

Brassica oleracea Gongylodes group

in modules. Or sow in drills 2–2.5cm (¾–1in) deep, thinning to 7.5cm (3in) apart. Transplant when still young (after about 6 weeks), in order to minimize the likelihood of transplanting shock.

Early-summer cauliflowers
Sow in early autumn with protection and overwinter under cloches or frames. Alternatively, sow in containers under glass at 16°C (61°F) in late winter; plant out early to mid-spring.
Sp – 45cm (18in) apart, in rows 60cm (24in) apart, or 50cm (20in) apart each way. TH 5–7 months.

Summer and autumn cauliflowers
Sow in mid-spring to early summer, planting out in early to late summer.
Sp – 45–60cm (18–24in) apart, in rows 60–70cm (24–28in) apart, depending on cultivar, or 50–65cm (20–25in) apart each way. For mini-cauliflowers, 12–15cm (5–6in) apart each way.
TH conventional crop, 5–6 months. For mini-cauliflowers, 12–16 weeks.

Winter-/spring-heading cauliflowers
Sow in early summer, planting out in late summer.
Sp – 60–70cm (24–30in) apart each way. TH 10 months.

Brassica oleracea Capitata group
(Cabbage)   Cruciferae
Leafy brassicas, usually forming dense heads, cabbages are grouped roughly according to their season of maturity; cultivars can be selected to harvest fresh all the year round. They are usually transplanted from containers, or from a seedbed. The spacing greatly affects the size of the heads – the

recommended spacing giving moderate-sized heads and a good yield for the particular cultivar. For smaller heads, use closer spacings.

PROPAGATION
🌱 germinates at minimum 5°C (41°F). Sow singly in modules, or in a seed tray for pricking out. Alternatively, sow in drills 2–2.5cm (¾–1in) deep, thinning to 7.5cm (3in) apart.

Spring cabbage
Sow in midsummer in cool areas, or in late summer in mild areas, and plant out in early to mid-autumn.
Sp: 30cm (12in) apart each way; or 10cm (4in) apart, in rows 30cm (12in) apart. Use two out of every three plants as 'spring greens' before they heart up.
TH 8–9 months.

Summer and autumn cabbage
There are early and later maturing cultivars, and two or more sowings are needed for a continual supply. Red cabbage is included in this group. For a first crop, sow an early cultivar in gentle heat in early spring, for planting out in mid- to late spring. Sow in mid- to late spring in the open, for planting out late spring to midsummer.
Sp – 35–45cm (14–18in) apart each way. TH 14–20 weeks.

Winter cabbage
There are several types, varying in hardiness. Dutch white 'coleslaw' cabbages are included in this group. Sow in the open in late spring, plant out mid- to late summer.
Sp – 50cm (20in) apart each way.
TH 4–5 months; most types will stand *in situ* for several months, but Dutch white cabbages should be lifted and stored before the first hard frosts.

Brassica oleracea Gemmifera group
(Brussels sprout)   Cruciferae
A hardy winter vegetable grown for the buttons (swollen buds) on the stem. There are early, mid-season, and late-maturing cultivars. The traditional method of sowing is in a seedbed for transplanting, but plants can also be raised in modules.

PROPAGATION
🌱 germinates at a minimum of 5°C (41°F). Sow singly in modules, in early to late spring depending on cultivar. Plant out deeply, otherwise plants raised in this way may keel over at a later stage. Alternatively, sow in a seedbed, 2–2.5cm (¾–1in) deep and thin to 7.5cm (3in) apart. Sow early cultivars in early spring, protected by a cold frame or cloches; plant out in late spring. Later cultivars can be sown in mid- to late spring outdoors, planting out in early summer.
Sp – dwarf cultivars 60–75cm (24–30in) apart each way; tall cultivars 90cm (36in). TH: 8–10 months; most cultivars crop for 2–3 months.

Brassica oleracea Gongylodes group
(Kohlrabi)   Cruciferae
A quick-maturing brassica grown for its swollen stem, although the leaves can also be eaten. Successional sowings are needed for crops throughout summer and autumn. Use green cultivars (which are quicker to mature) for early sowings and hardier purple cultivars for autumn use. Modern cultivars stand for longer in good condition.

PROPAGATION
🌱 germinates at minimum 5°C (41°F), but exposing young plants to cold, below 10°C (50°F), can cause bolting. Sow singly in

Brassica oleracea Italica group

Brassica rapa Pekinensis group

Capsicum annuum 'Apache'

modules in late winter or early spring, in gentle heat; plant out under cloches. Alternatively, sow in drills 1cm (½in) deep, mid-spring to late summer.
Sp – 10–15cm (4–6in) apart, in rows 30cm (12in) apart, or 23cm (9in) apart each way. Use closer spacings for tender mini-roots.
TH: 9–12 weeks

Brassica oleracea Italica group
(Calabrese)   Cruciferae

A quick-maturing type of broccoli producing large, green heads and smaller side shoots. It is not very hardy. Some cultivars mature more quickly, but successional sowing is necessary for continual cropping from mid-summer to mid-autumn. Calabrese does not transplant well, so sow *in situ* or in modules.

PROPAGATION
 germinates at a minimum of 5°C (41°F). Sow singly in modules in early spring to midsummer, under glass, and plant out under cloches for earliest crops. Alternatively, sow in drills 2–2.5cm (¾–1in) deep, mid-spring to midsummer.
Sp – 15cm (6in) apart, in rows 30cm (12in) apart, or 23cm (9in) apart each way. Closer spacing will suppress side shoots.
TH 11–14 weeks, depending on cultivar.

Brassica oleracea Italica group
(Sprouting broccoli)   Cruciferae

A hardy, overwintering brassica grown for its white, or purple flowering shoots in spring. Purple types are the hardiest. The plants are large and widely spaced. They are usually transplanted from a seedbed, but can be grown in modules. There are early and late maturing types. (*See also* Calabrese, *above*.)

PROPAGATION
at min. 5°C (41°F). Sow in drills 2–2.5cm (¾–1in) deep, thinning to 7.5cm (3in) apart, or sow singly in modules, in mid- to late spring. Plant out in early to midsummer.
Sp – 60cm (2ft) apart each way.
TH 11 months; individual plants usually crop for 6–8 weeks.

Brassica rapa Pekinensis group
(Chinese cabbage)   Cruciferae

Quick-growing leafy brassicas for late-summer or early-autumn use. They are only marginally frost-tolerant. Some modern cultivars are less prone to bolting. All dislike transplanting, so sow in modules or *in situ*.

PROPAGATION
germinates at minimum 10°C (50°F), but see below. For early crops, sow bolt-resistant cultivars singly in modules, in late spring or early summer, maintaining a minimum temperature of 18°C (64°F) for the first 3 weeks after germination to reduce the risk of premature bolting. Plant out under cloches or crop covers. Make main sowings without heat in early to late summer, and at the end of summer for transplanting under cover for a cut-and-come-again crop. Station-sow in drills 2–2.5cm (¾–1in) deep, early to late summer.
Sp – for mature heads, 30–35cm (12–14in) apart each way.
TH 9–10 weeks.

Capsicum annuum
(Pepper, Sweet and Chilli)   Solanaceae

Frost-tender plants grown for their fruits, which come in a variety of shapes and colours. In cool temperate areas, peppers

are raised under glass with some heat, and are best cropped in a greenhouse or polytunnel, or under cloches. Dwarf cultivars grow well in pots.

PROPAGATION
sow singly in small pots or modules, or in a seed tray for pricking out, in early spring, at 21°C (70°F). Pot on successively, into the final pot at 10cm (4in) high. Do not plant outside until danger of frost is past.
Sp – 30cm (12in) apart for dwarf cultivars, 38–45cm (15–18in) for standard cultivars.
TH 5–6 months.

Cichorium endivia (Endive)   Compositae

A slightly bitter salad plant sometimes blanched to make it sweeter. The period of cropping depends on the cultivar: the frilly types are generally more suited to summer cropping, and the hardier, broad-leaved types to autumn and protected winter cropping. Endive can also be grown as a seedling crop. It is often sown *in situ*, but sowing in modules is useful for early and midsummer sowings.

PROPAGATION
in drills 1–2cm (½–¾in) deep, or singly in modules, in early spring to late summer, giving protection to early and late crops.
Sp – 25–38cm (10–15in) apart each way, depending on cultivar.
TH 12–16 weeks.

Cichorium intybus (Chicory)
                                         Compositae

Chicories are grown for their leaves, which are mainly used as salad crops from late summer to spring. There are three common types; all are sown singly in modules, or *in situ*, in drills 1–2cm (½–¾in) deep.

Cichorium endivia

Cucumis sativus

Cucurbita pepo 'Hundredweight'

Red chicory

Most red chicories are for late-summer or autumn cropping, but some cultivars are hardy and will overwinter under cloches or in a greenhouse. They can be treated as cut-and-come-again crops.

PROPAGATION

❦ sow early cultivars in late spring to mid-summer. Sow hardy cultivars in mid- to late summer for a protected winter crop.
Sp – 20–35cm (8–14in) apart each way.
TH 12–14 weeks.

Sugar-loaf chicory

Forms dense, conical heads when mature, usually in late summer and autumn. Fairly hardy. Can also be grown as a cut-and-come-again crop, or as a leafy seedling crop sown from spring to early autumn.

PROPAGATION

❦ in early to midsummer; cover late sowings to protect from frost.
Sp – 25–30cm (10–12in) apart each way for mature heads.
TH 12–14 weeks.

Whitloof chicory

The roots of Whitloof chicory, produced in summer, are forced in darkness in winter and early spring to produce tight, white heads.

PROPAGATION

❦ in early to midsummer; cover late sowings to protect from frost.
Sp – Plant 23cm (9in) apart, in rows 30cm (12in) apart.
TH Lift roots for forcing from late winter to early spring, or, on light soils, force *in situ*. Cut off the leaves and cover stumps with 15cm (6in) of soil.

Courgette, see *Cucurbita pepo* (Marrow).

Cucumis sativus (Cucumber)
Cucurbitaceae

Tender, summer-fruiting plants, most of which trail or climb. Greenhouse cucumbers have long, slender, smooth fruits, and need warm conditions to flourish; modern all-female cultivars are easier to cultivate, needing no cross-pollination by hand. Ridge cucumbers are grown outside or in frames, as for marrows (*see below*).

PROPAGATION

❦ sow singly 1cm (½in) deep, in pots, at 24°C (75°F) in late spring for growing on in a frost-free greenhouse. Grow on at 19°C (66°F). Plant in permanent position at 30cm (12in) high.
Sp – 45cm (18in) apart, trained on string or netting.
TH 10–12 weeks.

Cucurbita pepo (Marrow, courgette and summer squash)
Cucurbitaceae

Frost-tender crops grown for their fruits in summer. Marrows traditionally have green, cylindrical fruits; other types are called 'summer squashes'. There are both bush and trailing cultivars. Courgettes are the small immature fruits of some bush types of marrow; and many F1 hybrid cultivars have been bred specifically for courgette production. All dislike root disturbance and are best sown in pots or *in situ*. Some initial protection is usually necessary.

PROPAGATION

❦ sow singly in small pots, 13°C (55°F) in late spring, about 4 weeks before the last expected frost. Sow seeds on their edge with their flat sides vertical. Transplant when risk of frost has passed, protecting with cloches or crop covers at first. Alternatively, station-sow 1cm (½in) deep, in late spring or early summer, and cover each station with a jam jar or cloche.
Sp – Bush types, 90cm (3ft) apart each way; trailing types, at least 1.2m (4ft) apart if allowed to sprawl, or 45cm (18in) if trained up trellis or netting.
TH 8–10 weeks for courgettes; a few weeks longer for large marrows.

Cucurbita pepo, *C. maxima* (Pumpkin and winter squash)
Cucurbitaceae

Frost-tender plants grown for their late summer fruits, stored for winter use. The large orange Hallowe'en pumpkins are the most familiar in the UK, but there are many other types. Most plants are trailing, but there are a few bush cultivars.

PROPAGATION

❦ germination and sowing: as for marrows (*see left*).
Sp – 1.2m (4ft) up 1.8m (6ft) for very vigorous types.
TH about 16–20 weeks; harvest before first frosts. Fruit can be stored for up to 6 months.

Cynara scolymus (Globe artichoke)
Compositae

A large perennial plant, grown for its immature flower buds in summer. Plants can be started off from seed, or from offsets (rooted suckers) of mature plants. Seed-raised plants will be variable in quality.

PROPAGATION

Offsets – spring or autumn. In spring, slice suckers away from the parent plant with a sharp knife, and plant out immediately, about 5cm (2in) deep, in their final positions.

Cynara scolymus

Daucus carota 'Nantes'

Foeniculum vulgare var. *azoricum*

Alternatively, take offsets in autumn and overwinter them in pots in a greenhouse. ☙ under glass, singly, in small pots or in a seed tray for pricking out. Sow in early spring for planting out in early summer. Alternatively, sow in a seedbed, in drills, about 2.5cm (1in) deep, in mid-spring, for transplanting in early- to midsummer. Sp – 90–120cm (3–4ft) apart each way. TH plants grown from seed or offsets usually crop in late summer of their first year. Mature plants produce their main heads in early summer.

Daucus carota (Carrot)   Umbelliferae

Moderately hardy root crop used from the ground throughout summer and autumn, and usually stored for winter. Early cultivars have relatively short (sometimes round) roots and are mostly used fresh; maincrop cultivars are larger and longer, and are the best for storage. Carrots are generally sown *in situ*, but some early cultivars can be sown in modules. Pre-germination and protection with cloches or crop covers can help early sowings; horticultural fleeces left in place until harvest also protects against carrotfly.

PROPAGATION

☙ at a minimum of 7°C (44°F); slow to germinate. Multi-sow round, early cultivars in modules, 4 seeds per cell, under glass in late winter; plant out with protection. Or, sow in drills 1–2cm (½–¾in) deep. Sow early cultivars in early spring with protection, and in the open from mid-spring to midsummer for a continual cropping. Sow maincrop cultivars from late spring to midsummer.
Sp – multi-sown modules, 7.5–10cm (3–4in)

apart each way. Early protected crops can be sown in 7.5–10cm (3–4in) bands, with seeds 2cm (¾in) apart; wider spacings encourage quicker growth. In drills; 15cm (6in) apart with plants 4–5cm (1½–2in) apart.
TH early cultivars 10–12 weeks. Maincrop cultivars 5–6 months.

Foeniculum vulgare var. *azoricum*

(Florence fennel)   Umbelliferae

Annual summer vegetable grown for its bulbous stem base. The leaves can be used like those of herb fennel. The plants tend to bolt in lengthening days, or if checked by cold or dry conditions, so crops maturing in late summer are often more successful. Modern cultivars are less prone to bolting. Young plants dislike root disturbance, so sow *in situ* or in modules.

PROPAGATION

☙ in succession, from late spring to late summer, in drills 1–2cm (½–¾in) deep. Use bolt-resistant cultivars if sowing before midsummer, and protect late-sown plants with cloches.
Sp – 30cm (12in) each way.
TH 3–4 months.

Helianthus tuberosus

(Jerusalem artichoke)   Compositae

This is a hardy, easy-to-grow vegetable producing knobbly, edible tubers. The tubers will continue to grow if left in the ground from year to year, but they need to be lifted and replanted in order to produce good crops.

PROPAGATION

Tubers – plant from late winter to mid-spring, 10–15cm (4–6in) deep, in sun or

partial shade. Small, smooth tubers the size of hens' eggs are best for planting. These can generally be saved from the previous year's crop without risk of carrying disease.
Sp – about 30cm (12in) apart, in single rows; 18in (45cm) each way for block planting.
TH 7–8 months; can be harvested from the ground throughout winter.

Lactuca sativa (Lettuce)   Compositae

This popular salad crop can be grown nearly all the year round, provided the right cultivars are used and winter crops are protected from the cold. Soft **Butterhead lettuces** mature quickly but also run to seed rapidly in hot weather. **Crisphead lettuces** are slower to mature and to bolt, and are good for summer use. **Cos lettuces** are generally the hardiest and some cultivars can be sown for winter as well as spring and summer use. Loose-leaf, salad-bowl lettuces, used as a cut-and-come-again crop, are very versatile all year round. All types of lettuce can be sown *in situ*, in a seedbed, in seed trays, or in compost blocks or modules. Modules or blocks are useful for early and midsummer sowings. Transplanting from a seedbed is not advisable in midsummer. Lettuce can also be grown as a seedling crop.

PROPAGATION

☙ germinates well at low temperatures, but not above 25°C (77°F) for Butterheads, or 85°F (29°C) for Crispheads. Sow in a seed tray for pricking out, or singly in modules or compost blocks. Sow from early spring to late summer; use gentle heat for the first sowings and transplant under cloches to obtain an early crop. Sow from late summer to mid-autumn for winter cultivars in green-

Lactuca sativa 'Lakeland'

Lycopersicon esculentum 'Gardener's Delight'

Phaseolus coccineus 'Pole Star'

houses. Outdoors, sow in a seedbed for transplanting, or *in situ*, in drills 1–2cm (½–¾in) deep, from mid-spring to midsummer. In hot conditions, sowings are best made in containers or *in situ*; using soil-cooling film. Alternatively, sow in the late afternoon so that the heat-sensitive period of germination occurs in the evening.
Sp – varies according to cultivar, from 15cm (6in) apart each way for small Cos cultivars; 25cm (10in) each way for standard Butterheads; 38cm (15in) each way for large Crispheads.
TH 8–16 weeks for headed lettuces, depending on the season; loose-leaf varieties can be harvested a few weeks earlier, before they are mature.

Lycopersicon esculentum (Tomato)
Solanaceae

One of the most versatile of the summer fruiting vegetables. There are both bush and tall types. Suitable cultivars can be grown in a warm, sheltered spot outdoors in most regions, but greenhouse, polythene tunnel, or cloche protection gives earlier crops and higher yields.

PROPAGATION
🌱 sowing in containers: Sow singly in modules or small pots, or in a seed tray for pricking out, at 20°C (68°F). Sow from late winter to early spring for greenhouse crops, early to mid-spring for outdoor crops. Grow at 10°C (50°F), potting on as necessary. Plant out after about 8 weeks, but wait until there is no risk of frost. Alternatively, sow pre-germinated seed of bush tomatoes *in situ* in late spring, under cloches, 2.5cm (1in) deep, and cover with seed compost.

Sp – plant tall cultivars 38–45cm (15–18in) apart; dwarf types 25–30cm (10–12in) apart; bush types 45–60cm (18–36in) apart.
TH 5–6 months.

Pastinaca sativa (Parsnip)   Umbelliferae

A hardy winter root crop, which needs a long growing season to produce large roots. Normally sown *in situ*, but can be sown in modules. Seed deteriorates rapidly in storage, so use fresh seed every year.

PROPAGATION
🌱 at a minimum of 7°C (45°F), germination is very slow. Sow singly in modules, from late winter to late spring; plant out seedlings before the tap root starts to develop. Alternatively, station-sow in drills 1–2 cm (½–¾in) deep, in early to late spring.
Sp – depends on cultivar and size of root required. For small roots, 5cm (2in) apart, in rows 20cm (8in) apart, or 10cm (5in) apart each way. For long roots, 20cm (8in) apart, in rows 30cm (12in) apart, or 25cm (10in) each way.
TH 6–8 months.

Phaseolus coccineus (Runner bean)
Leguminosae

Frost-tender bean grown for its long, flat pods, from midsummer to early autumn. Most are climbing, but there are some dwarf cultivars which give earlier crops but lower yields. Runner beans may be sown *in situ*, but sowing in containers is useful in cold areas.

PROPAGATION
🌱 germinate at a minimum of 10°C (50°F). Sow in deep boxes or large modules under glass, in mid-spring, and plant out after last frosts. Alternatively, station-sow, 5–7.5cm

(2–3in) deep, from mid- to late spring. Protect with cloches initially (this is easier with dwarf cultivars).
Sp – 15cm (6in) apart, in double rows 30–38cm (12–15in) apart for climbing types; 23cm (9in) apart each way for dwarf types.
TH 8–12 weeks.

Phaseolus vulgaris (French bean)
Leguminosae

Frost-tender bean usually grown for its pods, in early summer to early autumn. The shelled beans can also be eaten, fresh or dried. There are climbing and dwarf types, the pods varying in colour and shape according to cultivar. Dwarf types crop earlier but give lower yields, and two successional sowings are usually needed for continual cropping. All types can be sown *in situ*, but sowing in containers is useful for early sowings and in cool areas.

PROPAGATION
🌱 germinate at minimum 10°C (50°F). Sow singly in large modules or in a deep seed tray; dwarf cultivars, early to mid-spring under glass for planting out under cloches; other cultivars in mid- to late spring. Alternatively, station-sow 4–5cm (1½–2in) deep, in mid-spring under cloches or late spring to early summer in the open. Sow dwarf cultivars in midsummer for late crop.
Sp – 23cm (9in) apart each way for dwarf cultivars; 15cm (6in) apart, in double rows 30–38cm (12–15in) apart, for climbing types.
TH 8–10 weeks.

Pisum sativum (Peas)   Leguminosae
Ordinary garden peas are grown for the peas inside the pod; petit pois produce very small,

Pisum sativum 'Oregon Sugar Pod'

Raphanus sativa 'Crystal Ball'

Rheum rhaponticum

sweet peas. In the flat-podded mangetout and succulent round-podded sugar peas, the whole pod is edible. There are tall and dwarf cultivars of all types. All peas are hardy; round-seeded peas will overwinter in mild areas to give an early crop. The summer harvest can be extended by sowing early, second-early and maincrop cultivars at the same time. Sow successionally for continual cropping of all dwarf peas throughout summer. Peas are usually sown *in situ*. Pre-germination and sowing under cloches or crop covers are useful for the production of earlier crops.

PROPAGATION

🌱 germinate at a minimum of 7°C (45°F). Sow 2.5–4cm (1–1½in) deep, in 15cm (6in) wide drills. Sow earlies in early spring with protection; in open ground, sow from mid-spring to midsummer. Midsummer sowings of dwarf cultivars may give a late crop in good seasons. In mild areas, sow hardy types in mid- to late autumn for overwintering.
Sp – 5–7.5cm (2–3in) apart, in wide drills, 60–120cm (2–4ft) apart, depending on the height of the cultivar. Grow dwarf, leafless cultivars in blocks, at spacings about 12cm (5in) apart.
TH earlies, dwarf mangetout and sugar peas 11–12 weeks; maincrops 13–14 weeks.

Raphanus sativa (Radish) Cruciferae

Radishes are cultivated mainly for their roots, although they are also grown for their seed pods or as a leafy seedling crop. The three main types are: small, quick-growing radishes for salad use, large oriental types, and hardy winter radishes. They are usually sown *in situ*, but oriental types can be sown in modules.

PROPAGATION

🌱 germinates at a minimum of 6°C (43°F). Sow salad radishes in drills, 1cm (½in) deep, from late winter to early autumn. Protect early and late sowings from the cold, and make summer sowings in light shade. Thin seedlings when they are still small.
Sp – 2–2.5cm (¾–1in) apart, in drills 10–15cm (4–6in) apart.
TH 3–5 weeks; crops run to seed quickly.

Oriental radishes

🌱 sow singly in modules, and transplant before tap roots start to develop. Or, sow in drills, 1–2cm (½–¾in) deep. Sow from late spring to late summer, depending on the cultivar. Use bolt-resistant cultivars for sowings before midsummer.
Sp – 10cm (4in) apart, in rows about 25cm (10in) apart.
TH 7–8 weeks.

Winter radish

🌱 station-sow in drills 1–2cm (½–¾in) deep, in mid- to late summer. Protect or lift in late autumn for winter storage.
Sp – 20cm (8in) apart, in drills about 30cm (12in) apart.
TH 12 weeks.

Rheum rhaponticum (Rhubarb) Polygonaceae

A perennial plant grown for its leaf stalks, picked from early spring to midsummer, depending on the cultivar. A few cultivars can be raised from seed, but rhubarb is normally grown from sets which are taken from established plants.

PROPAGATION

Sets – late autumn to early spring. Lift the parent plant and divide into pieces 10cm

(4in) across, each with at least one bud.
🌱 early to mid-spring, in a seed tray. Prick out into small pots and plant out in early summer. Sow *in situ* in mid-spring, in drills 2.5cm (1in) deep, 30cm (12in) apart, thinning to 15cm (6in) apart. Transplant in autumn or the following spring.
Sp – 75–90cm (30–36in) apart.
TH pull stems sparingly in the second growing season after planting. In subsequent years, harvest from spring to midsummer.

Scorzonera hispanica (Scorzonera) Compositae

This is a perennial vegetable that is grown for its long, black-skinned roots, which are similar in flavour to those of salsify. It is propagated from seed, but any roots that are not big enough to use in the first winter can be left in the ground to allow another year's growth in order to thicken up. Sowing, spacing, and harvesting, as for *Tragopogon porrifolius* (Salsify) (see *opposite page*).

Solanum melongena
(Aubergine, Egg plant) Solanaceae

Tender plants, most with long, shiny, purple fruits. Closely related to tomatoes and peppers, but needing slightly higher temperatures to crop and grow well. In cool temperate climates, they are grown under glass or cloches.

PROPAGATION

🌱 sow singly in small pots or modules, or in a seed tray for pricking out, in early spring, at 21°C (70°F). Pot on sucessionally, into final pots when 10cm (4in) high.
Sp – 38–45cm (15–18in).
TH 5–6 months.

Solanum melongena

Solanum tuberosum

Vicia faba 'Bonny Lad'

Solanum tuberosum (Potato) Solanaceae

Frost-tender crop grown for its tubers, used fresh in summer, or from store. Cultivars are grouped into earlies, second-earlies, and maincrop, according to the time they take to mature. All are grown from seed tubers, preferably certified as virus-free stock, which are chitted (allowed to sprout) in a cool, light, frost-free place for 6–8 weeks before planting; the shoots should then be about 2–2.5cm (¾–1in) long.

PROPAGATION

Seed tubers – earlies, from early to mid-spring. Protect young leaves from late frost by earthing up or covering with straw. Grow under cloches or crop covers for an extra early crop. Plant later cultivars in mid- to late spring. Place seed tubers in a drill 10–15cm (4–6in) deep, or in individual planting holes made with a trowel, 5cm (2in) below the soil surface.

Sp – early potatoes 30cm (12in) apart, in rows 38–50cm (15–20in) apart; others 38cm (15in) apart, in rows 75cm (30) apart. TH 15 weeks to maturity for earlies, 17 weeks for second-earlies, 18–20 weeks for maincrop.

Spinacia oleracea (Spinach)
Chenopodiaceae

True spinach is a quick-growing, leafy annual. It is moderately hardy and grows best in cool spring and autumn days, tending to bolt in hot weather. It can also be grown as a seedling crop. Traditionally, round-seeded types were used for summer crops and prickly-seeded types for autumn crops. Modern cultivars are generally suitable for all sowings. Normally sown *in situ*.

PROPAGATION

🌱 in drills 2cm (¾in) deep, in early spring under protection in a warm site. Continue successional sowings in the open as required, making any early-summer sowings in light shade. Sow in late summer to early autumn for a winter crop.

Sp – 15cm (6in) apart, in rows 30cm (12in) apart, or 23cm (9in) each way. TH 6–10 weeks, depending on the season.

Tragopogon porrifolius (Salsify)
Compositae

A hardy biennial usually grown for its thin winter roots; the flower buds and blanched shoots can also be eaten the following spring.

PROPAGATION

🌱 sow *in situ*. Sow thinly or station-sow in drills, 2.5cm (1in) deep, from mid- to late spring. Germination can be erratic.

Sp – 10–15cm (4–6in) apart, in rows 30cm (12in) apart, or 18–23cm (7–9in) apart each way. TH 7–9 months.

Vicia faba (Broad bean) Leguminosae

A hardy crop, usually grown for the green or white beans inside the pods, although very young pods can be eaten whole. The pods can be picked throughout the summer from successional sowings. Sowing in boxes for transplanting in warmer weather is useful for early crops in cold areas.

PROPAGATION

🌱 germinates at minimum 5°C (41°F). Sow in deep boxes in early winter for early spring planting; late winter for mid-spring planting. Alternatively, station-sow, *in situ*,

4–5cm (1½–2in) deep. For an early summer crop, sow hardier cultivars in mid-autumn or early winter; protect with cloches during the coldest months. In cold areas, sow quick-maturing cultivars in early spring. Sow mid- to late spring for a later crop.

Sp – in double rows, 23cm (9in) apart with 45–60cm (18in–24in) between rows, or in blocks, 22–30cm (9–12in) apart each way. TH 7–8 months from autumn sowings; 12–16 weeks for spring sown plants.

Zea mays (Sweet corn) Gramineae

Tall, frost-tender plant grown for its sweet cobs formed in late summer. 'Supersweet' cultivars produce sweeter corn but the plants are less vigorous and not so hardy. There are also cultivars for producing 'mini' sweetcorn. These are cobs that are picked when they are only a few inches long and eaten whole, raw or cooked. Sweetcorn does not transplant well, so sow *in situ* or use modules. In cool areas, use fast-maturing cultivars and start the plants off under glass with heat.

PROPAGATION

🌱 sow singly in modules in mid-spring, at 10°C (50°F). Plant out after the risk of frost has passed. Protect with cloches or crop covers at first. Alternatively, station-sow, 2.5cm (1in) deep, in late spring, providing protection from the cold, or in early summer in the open.

Sp – 30cm (12ft) each way for short cultivars, 30–45cm (15–18in) each way for tall cultivars. Plant in blocks to assist pollination. For mini-corn, 15cm (6in) apart; in single rows; pollination is not necessary. TH 16–20 weeks.

211

SEED BOTANY AND HYBRIDIZING

SEED BOTANY

The seeds of all plants share the same basic structure, consisting of an embryo and a food reserve, protected by a seed-coat or testa. The embryo is the growing point, from which develops the roots, stem and leaves. The food reserve is often stored within the seed leaves, and these also serve to cushion the embryo from physical damage, including excessive heat and cold.

Flowering plants are classified as Monocotyledons or Dicotyledons, based on whether the seeds have one or two seed leaves. When a seed germinates, it is often the seed leaves which appear above ground first, the true leaves following later. This is called epigeal germination. However, in plants like sweet peas the seed leaves remain below the ground – hypogeal germination.

Commercial seed is stored in a partially dehydrated state and may remain viable for months or even years, until the right conditions are present to stimulate germination. Not surprisingly, the necessary conditions vary depending on the species, and especially on its native habitat. Seeds of tropical natives usually require higher temperatures than those from temperate zones.

A further complication is the dormancy shown by the seeds of some species. In these, even in the presence of suitable warmth and moisture, germination will not occur until dormancy is 'broken'. This may require exposure to darkness or to light, a period of low temperatures, alternation of low and high temperatures or the gradual decay of the seed coat in which germination-inhibiting chemicals reside. Gardeners have developed various techniques to overcome seed dormancy in a controlled and predictable way.

Seed dormancy is a survival aid for the plant. It prevents the seed from germinating when conditions would be unfavourable for the subsequent survival of the seedling.

HYBRIDIZING

Gardeners often assume that cultivars and hybrids are the same thing, but this is not true. Cultivars are selected variants within a plant, and may be chance seedlings, mutations ('sports'), simple or complex hybrids. They seldom breed true to type, because the development of a seed involves a recombination of the parent's genetic material. Hybrids have two generally diverse parents, so there is even more scope for genetic variation in their offspring.

Plants are hybridized in the hope of combining desirable characteristics – for example, flower colour, growth habit, or disease resistance – from each parent. The plant breeder chooses the parent plants with such qualities in mind.

To create a hybrid, the grower transfers pollen from the stamens of one plant to the stigma of the seed-parent. To prevent the risk of the seed-parent being fertilized by its own pollen, its stamens are removed before they mature. There is still a possibility of pollen from a plant other than the intended parent arriving, perhaps wind-borne, or via a visiting insect. Enclosing the flower in a muslin bag before and after pollination helps to prevent this.

Hybrid plants are often more expensive, for various reasons. Firstly, the element of chance, even in planned hybridization, means that the desired flower colour, or disease resistance may or may not appear among the progeny and, in woody plants, it may be several years before this can be assessed.

The breeding of highly-developed plants, such as roses or rhododendrons, involves the sowing of thousands of hybrid seeds, growing them on for some years, and perhaps grafting them to accelerate maturity, perhaps only to find that the particular crossing has not achieved the desired result. It is understandable, therefore, that such plants can be quite expensive.

Among hybrids, F1 hybrids are often encountered. The term indicates the 'first filial generation', that is, the direct progeny of the act of hybridization. Subsequent generations may show a decline in the desirable qualities of the F1 plants. This is avoided only by repeating the original crossing for each generation, hence the high cost of such seeds.

PROPAGATING MEDIUMS

POTTING AND PROPAGATION MEDIUMS

Garden soil does not make a good growing or sowing medium for plants in containers. It is prone to compaction, thus depriving the roots of oxygen and impeding good drainage. It is also likely to contain legion pests and diseases. Always use a good quality, purpose-made medium that is designed to have a durable physical structure, with free drainage and air movement as well as being able to retain moisture. The ingredients used to make up the mix will be free of pest, diseases and weeds. The level of nutrients added to the mix will depend on its use.

LOAM-BASED AND SOILLESS COMPOSTS

Loam-based mediums are the more traditional potting and propagation mixes. Clay loam from pasture land has an ideal structure and texture, combined with a pH between 6.0 and 6.5. Peat and grit are used to provide drainage and aeration.

Because of the difficulty in obtaining the correct type of loam, in recent years, loam-based mixes have been superseded by peat-based ones. Peat is lightweight with good aeration, drainage and water retention, but many peat bogs have been over-exploited to such an extent that its universal use can no longer be considered sustainable.

Alternatives to peat include coir (coconut fibre) and granulated, composted softwood bark. Both have slightly different drainage characteristics and such mixes need more careful attention to watering than more traditional types.

To aid re-wetting and aeration, coarse sand may be added to all types of mix. Perlite and vermiculite can be used instead of coarse sand; both are lightweight and sterile. Perlite absorbs and holds large quantities of air and moisture. Vermiculite has similar properties, but also retains plant nutrients.

Proprietary mixes of both types are easily obtained from your local garden centre. Potting mixes contain a balanced level of fertilizers to sustain growth for 4-6 weeks. After this period, extra nutrients can be applied as a liquid fertilizer when watering. Propagating mixes contain low nutrient levels, because high levels damage the developing roots of seedlings and cuttings.

For gardeners who wish to prepare their own mixes there are a number of tried and tested formulae:

LOAM-BASED MEDIUMS

Seed Sowing Mix
2 parts by volume sterilized loam
1 part by volume sphagnum moss peat
1 part by volume lime-free, coarse sand or grit
To each cubic metre add a base dressing thus: (kg/m³)
Ground chalk or limestone, 0.6 kg
Superphosphate, 1.2kg

Cutting Mix
1 part by volume sterilized loam
1 part by volume moss peat
1 part by volume lime-free coarse sand or grit
To each cubic metre add a base dressing thus: (kg/m³)
Superphosphate 1.2kg
Ground chalk or limestone 0.6 kg

SOILLESS MIXES

Seed Sowing Mix
5 parts by volume sphagnum moss peat
1 part by volume vermiculite
To each cubic metre add a base dressing thus: (kg/m³)
Potassium nitrate 0.4 kg
Superphosphate 0.75 kg
Ground chalk or limestone 3.0 kg

Cutting Mix
4 parts by volume sphagnum moss peat
1 part by volume coarse sand or Perlite
To each cubic metre add a base dressing thus: (kg/m³)
Superphosphate 1.2kg
Ground chalk or limestone 0.6 kg

Once prepared, all mixes are ready for immediate use, and should only be stored for a short period. In storage, nitrogenous fertilizers break down to release ammonia which damages the roots of young seedlings and cuttings. Mixes should be kept in sealed bags in a cool, dry atmosphere.

PROPAGATION
BY SEASON

MID- TO LATE WINTER

Now completely dormant, selected cultivars of *Betula* can be grafted, followed by the softer-wooded Rhododendrons in the New Year; these in turn are followed by the harder-wooded varieties into early spring.

Conifers to side-veneer graft onto understock include *Abies*, *Cedrus* and *Picea*.

Some plants that are raised from seed annually, including fibrous-rooted and tuberous begonias and bedding Pelargoniums, need relatively high temperatures and a long growing season. Begin sowing 6–8 weeks into the New Year.

Early sowing also applies to shrubby plants that need to be large enough to survive the following winter; rhododendrons and other ericaceous plants sown in late winter will be sturdy seedlings by the autumn.

EARLY SPRING

Layering of shrubs, if not carried out in the autumn, can be done in early spring: the flowing sap makes branches as pliable as they would have been then. These include: *Abelia, Clematis, Cotinus, Hamamelis, Kolkwitzia, Magnolia, Paeonia, Rhododendron, Wisteria.*

Some house plants can be divided now: *Achimenes, Aspidistra, Chlorophytum,* and seed sown of others, *Agave, Aloe, Philodendron, Pittosporum,* and *Sinningia.*

Cuttings of *Achimenes,* small-leaved begonias and *Euphorbia pulcherrima* (Poinsettia) can be rooted now.

The bulk of summer bedding should be sown at this time leaving those that mature quickly until late spring.

EARLY TO MID-SPRING

The first of the basal cuttings will be large enough now , including the Belladonna and Elatum groups of Delphiniums (normally the earliest) followed by chrysanthemum (*Dendranthema*) then the tuberous-rooted Dahlias.

When the soil has warmed and become workable Onion sets, Shallots and Potatoes can be planted with the first sowings of hardy vegetables and herbs.

On heavy soil, mid-spring is the best time to divide herbaceous perennials, including *Achillea, Aster* x *novi-belgii, Geum, Helenium* and many others. On light, sandy soils, division during autumn is usually more successful.

Conifer seed, of *Abies, Calocedrus, Cedrus, Larix, Pinus,* can be sown outside in prepared beds now. Some form of frost protection should be at hand, because this seed can germinate quickly and will be damaged by frost.

MID- TO LATE SPRING

The first seedlings and plants propagated in early spring can be grown cooler to harden them off, making room to sow more tender plants for the vegetable garden, Peppers and Chillis Marrows, Pumpkins etc. and Tomato.

Many of the herbaceous perennials will have made sufficient growth to be propagated from basal cuttings: *Achillea, Anaphalis, Anthemis, Aster, Echinacea, Erigeron, Nepeta, Rudbeckia.*

Hardy annuals can be sown outside in shallow drill or broadcast, including *Calendula, Centaurea, Clarkia, Helianthus* and *Linaria,* are plants that can be grown this way. Most ferns divide readily at this time, there are some exceptions which are more difficult to propagate, but for the majority this is the easiest way.

Some of the water plants, in particular the marginals like *Acorus, Butomus, Calla, Menyanthes, Peltandra, Pontederia, Sagittaria, Saururus,* and *Sparganium,* can be divided as the water warms up.

EARLY SUMMER

Softwood cuttings of deciduous shrubs and climbers now become available through to mid-summer, including *Abelia, Ace*r, *Actinidia, Chimonanthus,* Knaphill azaleas , *Kolkwitzia,* and *Wisteria.*

Some of the deciduous fruiting plants that root from softwood cuttings include *Actinidia deliciosa, Morus, Vitis,* and *Passiflora.*

The spring flowering *Cattleya* species are propagated by division, and stem bulbils are removed from *Ceropegia* to be potted up.

Stem tip cuttings offer another method of propagation. With the coming of good light at this time of the year, other houseplants can be propagated either by stem cuttings or leaf cuttings.

Now the pond has warmed, aquatic water plants are increased by division or cuttings, including *Ceratophyllum, Egeria, Elodea, Glyceria, Myriophyllum* and *Nymphaea*.

MID-SUMMER

Some of the bulbs are ready for division or separation of offsets now, including *Amaryllis belladonna, Anemone, Colchicum*; with *Leucojum* after flowering.

Strawberry runners offer a way of increasing stock for growing in pots or renewing old plants.

Rubus including blackberries and hybrid berries will readily produce a plant from tip-layering now.

Bud-grafting, either by chip- or T- budding, of fruit trees and ornamentals should begin now and carry on through to early autumn.

Selected cultivars of *Acer japonicum* and *A. palmatum* are side-veneer grafted onto seedling understocks.

Plants grown as biennials and used for spring bedding can be sown outside now and planted in the flowering sites later, including *Bellis, Erysimun*, and *Myosotis*. Give attention to the alpines from now on. Many that do produce seed in cultivation will germinate more readily if the seed is sown as soon as ripe, including *Aethionema, Androsace, Campanula, Cyclamen, Dryas*, and *Pulsatilla*. Others can be grown from soft cuttings taken now: *Aubrieta, Aurinia, Campanula, Dianthus, Edraianthus*.

Herbaceous perennials that could be killed by a hard winter, such as penstemons should also be propagated by stem cuttings to insure your stock.

Iris (rhizomatous) can be increased after flowering, by sectioning the rhizome with a fan of leaves attached.

Ericas, the heaths, root well through this season, including *E. arborea, E. carnea, E. × darleyensis* and *E. vagans*.

MID- TO LATE SUMMER

Semi-ripe cuttings of many plants will be ready from now and on through to the autumn, starting with: *Abelia, Cornus, Cotoneaster, Cytisus, Elaeagnus, Escallonia, Garrya, Hypericum, Ilex, Lavandula*, and *Mahonia* as well as the heathers, the many *Calluna* cultivars and *Daboecia*.

Hamamelis cultivars are grafted on to seedling understocks.

From now on lilies can be propagated from bulb scales.

EARLY AUTUMN

More semi-ripe cuttings to take from shrubs and conifers, including *Aucuba*, evergreen *Berberis, Buxus, Cotoneaster*, and *Mahonia*.

The conifers include *Chamaecyparis, Cryptomeria, Cupressus, Juniperus, Podocarpus, Prumnopitys, Taxus, Thuja* and *Tsuga*.

Among the bulbous plants, *Allium, Chionodoxa, Muscari* and *Scilla* can be lifted, divided and then replanted.

MID-AUTUMN

Stock of half-hardy tubers and herbaceous perennials

for producing basal cuttings in the spring, should be made safe in a frost free area.

On light, sandy soils, division of herbaceous perennials will be successful now; they have the chance to make good root growth while the soil still retains the warmth of summer.

LATE AUTUMN

Hardwood cuttings can be inserted just after leaf fall in a sheltered border outside, or in a frame.

Evergreen shrubs can be layered now, or left until spring.

EARLY WINTER

The season for taking root cuttings begins now. Root cuttings are taken when weather conditions are right for the lifting of the stock plant (not too wet or cold, and not too dry).

Begin taking root cuttings of *Anemone, Papaver orientale* and the cultivars of *Phlox maculata* and *P. paniculata* to produce plants free of stem eelworm.

MID-WINTER

Root cutting of herbaceous perennials to propagate now include: *Acanthus, Echinops, Eryngium* and *Paeonia*.

Aesculus parviflora, Embothrium, Romneya and *Yucca*, can also be propagated in this way, provided that soil conditions are suitable for lifting roots. A similar technique can be used with *Bergenia* by sectioning rhizomes.

Fruiting and ornamental *Vitis* can either be grown from single buds (vine-eyes) or from hardwood cuttings.

215

PESTS AND DISEASES

PESTS

Aphids

Most plants are susceptible. Aphids of various species are green, black, yellow or pink. They suck sap, cause distorted growth and transmit virus diseases. Infested plants become sticky with aphid excrement (honeydew) which allows sooty moulds to develop. Control by spraying with a specific aphicide that will not harm bees and other beneficial insects, including natural predators introduced to combat other greenhouse pests.

Black vine weevil

Most plants are susceptible. The adult beetles are 7-9mm (¼–⅜in) long and have dull black, pear-shaped bodies. They are active between spring and autumn and eat irregular notches in leaf margins. Although unsightly, this is generally something the plants can tolerate. It is the grubs in the soil that kill plants by eating roots, corms and tubers. The grubs are up to 10mm (½in) long with plump, creamy white, legless bodies and brown heads. Plants grown in pots or other containers are more at risk than those in the open ground. Plant losses caused by the grubs occur between early autumn and spring. Control is difficult as both adult weevils and grubs are tolerant of insecticides sold to amateur gardeners. Search for and destroy adult weevils at night during the summer. Control the grubs

by watering pathogenic nematodes, such as *Heterorhabditis megidis* or *Steinernema carpocapsae,* into the compost during late summer.

Flea beetles

Brassicas, turnip, swede and some outdoor annuals and herbaceous perennials are susceptible. Beetles, 2-3 mm (¹⁄₁₆–⅛in) long, eat rounded holes in the foliage and can kill seedlings. The beetles are black, sometimes with a yellow stripe along the wing cases, or they are metallic blue or green. Limit the numbers of overwintering adults by clearing away plant debris. Keep seedlings watered to speed their growth through this vulnerable stage. Chemical sprays or dusts are available if necessary.

Fungus gnats or sciarid flies

Seedlings and soft cuttings under glass are susceptible. Grey-brown flies, 3-4mm (⅛in) long, run over the compost or fly up when disturbed. Small white maggots with black heads feed on seedling roots and bore into the base of cuttings. Suspend yellow sticky traps over seed trays to capture adult flies. Introduce the predatory mite, *Hypoaspis miles* to the compost. Chemical controls are available but may damage young seedlings.

Red Spider Mite

Most plants are susceptible. Yellow-green, eight-legged mites, less than 1mm (¹⁄₁₆in) long, live on the

underside of leaves, causing a fine pale mottling of the upper surface. Chemical controls are available but pesticide-resistant strains are widespread. Treat with the predatory mite *Phytoseiulus persimilis.*

Slugs and snails

Most seedlings and cuttings are susceptible. These pests feed mainly at night, causing irregular holes in leaves and stems. A silvery slime trail is sometimes left on the plants. Use slug pellets with care; they can be harmful to children, pets and slug-eating wildlife such as frogs, birds and hedgehogs. Alternatively use the pathogenic nematode, *Phasmarhabditis hermaphrodita.* Good hygiene and tidiness in greenhouses will remove slugs and their daytime hiding places.

Whitefly

Most plants are susceptible, especially house- and greenhouse plants. White-winged insects, 2mm (¹⁄₁₆in) long, and flat, oval, pale green nymphs suck sap from the lower leaf surface. Infested plants become sticky with excreted honeydew on which sooty moulds thrive. Chemical controls are available but pesticide resistance is common. The parasitic wasp, *Encarsia formosa,* kills the nymphs, causing them to turn black. With practice, adult numbers can be reduced by first disturbing them into flight, and then sucking them up with a vacuum cleaner.

DISEASES

Many plant diseases can be controlled by chemical treatments, but prevention, as far as possible, is a far better option both in terms of expense, and in reducing the chemical load on the environment. This is especially true in the case of edible crop plants.

The risk of disease attack and subsequent development is much reduced by maintaining a high standard of hygiene during propagation, as well as providing your plants with optimal growing conditions to keep them vigorous and healthy.

When selecting material for any form of vegetative propagation, whether it be bulbs, corms, tubers or cuttings, it is vital to ensure that the material is healthy and free from any disease. All forms of vegetative increase carry the risk of passing on any diseases to the resulting young plants.

Botrytis (Grey mould)

This fungal disease frequently causes problems on protected plants under glass. In humid conditions, masses of spores develop which can be transported by air currents to infect other plant material. Grey mould can be prevented to a large degree by avoiding conditions favourable to its development; general good hygiene is important as well as avoiding overcrowding of plants. Good ventilation in frames and greenhouses, together with avoiding condensation or water splash on the leaf surfaces will reduce attacks.

Remove any affected material as soon as seen and spray the remaining plant material with an appropriate fungicide.

Crown gall

Crown galls are knobbly swellings caused by a soil-borne bacterium and are found on roots, at the junction of roots and stems and occasionally on the stems. On herbaceous material, they can provide a site of infection for rotting organisms that then penetrate the crown. Aerial galls are frequently found on roses and *Daphne* spp. and provided that they are not widespread can be cut out.

The disease is more prevalent on wet soils. No chemical control is available. Infection usually occurs when the bacteria penetrate small wounds. Try to avoid any damage to the roots or stems when transplanting or planting out and avoid planting in sites known to be affected.

Damping-off

This is a common disease of seedlings both under glass and outdoors, especially on rapidly growing annual bedding plants. It is caused by a number of different fungi. Plants are attacked at or just above soil level before they fall over and die. This disease can largely be prevented by using sterilized compost, avoiding overwatering and ensuring good hygiene of all equipment and growing areas. Good ventilation and drenching with a copper-based fungicide will help to control disease attack.

Most seedlings are susceptible, especially if they are weak, overcrowded, or growing poorly.

Downy mildew

This fungus can attack young plants and seedlings, causing yellowing of leaves in patches, followed by wilting and death. On the undersides of affected leaves they produce an off-white or purplish mould. Downy mildews are generally host specific in any genus. Remove affected plants or leaves and control with an appropriate fungicide.

Leafy Gall

Infection by this bacterium results in a mass of stunted and often distorted, thickened shoots. Sweet peas, dahlias, chrysanthemum and pelargoniums are commonly affected as well as on bedding plants causing blindness. Destroy diseased propagation stock plants.

Powdery mildew

These fungi are among the most common air-borne plant diseases. A grey-white powdery coating develops on leaves, stems and other plant parts, distorting their growth. Plants are most susceptible when the soil is dry and development of the disease is promoted by humid, stagnant air around the foliage. It can be treated with fungicide, but repeat applications at two week intervals throughout summer are likely to be necessary.

Viruses

Viruses induce a wide range of symptoms, including stunting, spotting, mottling or blotching. There are no chemical controls. Avoid the use of propagating material from affected plants and control the aphid vectors.

GLOSSARY

Acid (of soil) Having a pH level of less than 7; lime-free or almost so. .

Alkaline (of soil) having a pH level above 7; limy.

Alpine 1. A plant native to mountains, usually above the tree line. 2. A small plant grown in a rock garden.

Annual A plant that completes its lifecycle from germination to shedding seed in a single growing season.

Basal cutting A cutting taken from the base of a plant, usually a herbaceous plant, as growth begins in spring.

Biennial A plant that completes its lifecycle in two seasons., producing leaf growth in its first year to flowers, set seed and die in the second.

Bleed To lose sap from a wound, usually one made during pruning or when taking cuttings.

Bolt To produce flowers and seedheads prematurely.

Broadcasting To scatter seed evenly over a seed bed.

Bromeliad A member of the family Bromeliaceae.

Bud-grafting A grafting technique that involves uniting a single bud from the *scion* with a *rootstock*; a general term that includes chip budding and T-budding.

Bulb A storage organ formed from tightly packed, fleshy scales. Also used generally for other underground storage organs including *corms* and *tubers.*

Callus Protective tissue that forms over a cut or wounded surface.

Cambium The layer of actively dividing cells just beneath the bark or *rind* of a plant.

Chilling requirement A period of time needed by a dormant plant below a given temperature to initiate the next season's flowers.

Cloche A temporary and moveable structure of glass or plastic used to protect young plants and/or to warm the soil.

Cold frame A low structure consisting of a timber, brick or concrete frame with the top and sometimes the sides glazed with glass or clear plastic.

Corm A solid underground storage organ developed from a swollen stem base. New corms are produced annually from buds on the parent corm.

Crown The part of a plant at, or immediately below soil level from which leaves and shoots develop.

Cultivar A cultivated variety; a named selection of a species with distinctive characteristics that are retained when a plant is propagated by sexual or vegetative means.

Cuttage A generic term for bulb propagation techniques that involve cutting into the bulb, e.g. scooping, scoring or sectioning.

Cutting A piece a plant detached from a parent plant which forms roots and develops into a new plant that is usually identical to the parent plant.

Division A propagating technique that involves dividing a parent plant into smaller sections, each with roots and growth buds.

Dormancy The temporary cessation of growth and slowing down of metabolic processes, usually as a mechanism to permit survival in adverse conditions.

Drill A straight, shallow furrow made for the sowing of seed.

Earthing up The process of drawing soil up around a plant's stem for blanching, or to encourage roots to grow from the stem.

Epicormic shoot A vigorous shoot that develops on or from the trunk. They arise from latent buds beneath the bark, often in response to wounding or pruning. Also known as a water shoot.

Eye 1. A dormant growth bud, such as those found on dahlia tubers. 2. A dormant bud in the leaf axils (see leaf-bud cutting).

F1 hybrid Plants produced by crossing two selected, pure-breeding parents to produce vigorous, floriferous and uniform offspring.

F2 hybrid A plant which results from crossing selected F1 parents.

Frond The 'leaf' of a fern.

Fungicide A manufactured or naturally occurring chemical that controls or kills fungi.

Grafting A propagating technique whereby a *scion* from one plant is artificially united with the *rootstock* of another.

Graft union The point at which the *scion* and *rootstock* are united.

Half-hardy A plant that will not tolerate temperatures below freezing point, 0°C (32°F).

Hardy A frost-tolerant plant that survives outside year round without the need for special protection.

Hardening off The gradual

acclimatization to the open garden of plants raised in a protected environment.

Hardwood cutting A cutting made from the fully ripened tissue of a woody plant.

Heel cutting A cutting taken with a heel or sliver of older wood at its base.

Hybrid The progeny that results from crossing genetically distinct parents which belong to a different species or genus.

Internodal cutting A cutting made with the basal cut between the *nodes*.

Internode The section of a stem between two *nodes*.

Layering A propagating technique whereby a stem is induced to root while attached to the parent plant.

Leaf cutting A cutting made from the whole or part of a leaf.

Leaf bud cutting A cutting made of a short length of stem with a bud or pair of buds at the *node*.

Mallet cutting A cutting made from a side shoot with a plug of older wood at its base.

Medium A mixture or substrate in which plants are grown or propagated. Also known as compost.

Mutation A genetic change which results in the production of tissues that are atypical; for example, when green-leaved plants produce coloured or variegated shoots.

Neutral Of soils; with a pH of 7.

Nodal cutting A cutting made with the basal cut at or just below a node.

Node The point on a plant stem at which leaves shoots branches or flowers emerge.

Offset A young plant that arises at the base of its parent.

Perlite An expanded volcanic mineral that is granulated for use in propagating or other *mediums*.

Petiole A leaf stalk.

pH A scale of measurement of alkalinity and acidity, from 1–14, with pH 7 being the neutral point.

Potting on Transferring a plant from a smaller to a larger sized pot.

Potting up Transferring a seedling from its germinating medium to an individual pot.

Pricking out Transferring a seedling from its germinating medium to a bed, tray, or pot to give them more space to grow.

Reversion The process whereby a *sport* or *mutation* returns to its original form.

Rhizome An underground stem, modified as a storage organ, which produces aerial growth at it tip and from buds along its length.

Ripewood cutting Alternative term for hardwood cutting (q.v) often applied to evergreens.

Rooting hormone A natural or manufactured chemical used to encourage root initiation.

Rootstock A plant that provides the root system for a grafted plant.

Runner A stem that creeps above ground and roots where its nodes touch the soil.

Scarification The process of nicking or abrading a hard seed coat so that water is imbibed and germination can proceed

Scion The bud or shoot that is grafted onto the rootstock of another.

Semi-ripe cutting A cutting made of the current season's growth just as it begins to harden at the base, usually in midsummer.

Spore The reproductive structure of non-flowering plants like fungi, ferns or mosses.

Sport An alternative term for *mutation*.

Stem cutting A general term for a cutting made from any part of a plant stem.

Stem tip cutting A cutting taken from a shoot tip, usually herbaceous, but also used for softwood cuttings of woody plants.

Stock plant A plant used as propagating material.

Stolon A spreading stem, usually above ground, that roots at its tip (cf. *runner*).

Softwood cutting A cutting made from the current season's immature growth.

Sport See *mutation*.

Stratification Chilling or occasionally warming of seed to overcome dormancy.

Sucker 1. A shoot that arises from below the soil surface from the stem or roots. 2. A shoot that arises from below the *graft union* of a grafted plant.

Top-dressing A dressing applied to the soil surface around a plant's roots. Refers to fertilizers, new soil or compost, decorative or weed-suppressing materials.

Tuber A swollen, underground food storage organ derived from the root or stem base.

Turion A detached, fleshy overwintering bud produced by some water plants.

Variety A naturally occurring variant of a wild species; abbr. var.

Vegetative propagation The propagation of plants by asexual methods, that is, by methods other than seed, resulting in genetically identical offspring.

Widger A spatula-like tool used for transplanting and pricking out seedlings.

INDEX

ACKNOWLEDGEMENTS

The publishers would like to thank the following organizations and individuals for their kind permission to reproduce the photographs in this book:

Key: ALP: Andrew Lawson Photography; CNP: Clive Nichols Photography; GPL: Garden Picture Library; HSC: Harry Smith Collection; MaP: Mise au Point; PH: Photos Horticultural.

Back jacket: Jerry Harpur (Barnsley House); *Front jacket:* ALP; 1 GPL (Mayer Le Scanff); 2 GPL (Gary Rogers); 4 GPL (J S Sira); 5 Jerry Harpur (Beth Chatto); 6–7 Jerry Harpur (Bank House, Borwick); 8–9 GPL (Lamontagne); 10 John Glover; 11 PH; 16 *bottom left* GPL (Ron Evans); 16 *bottom right* HSC; 17 *right* ALP; 17 *left* PH; 17 *centre* HSC; 18 *left* ALP; 18 *centre* PH; 18 *right* HSC; 19 *left* PH; 19 *centre* HSC; 19 *right* HSC; 20 *centre* GPL (Vaughan Fleming); 20 *left* GPL (Howard Rice); 20 *right* PH; 21 *centre* GPL (Brian Carter); 21 *right* ALP; 21 *centre* HSC; 22 *centre* John Fielding; 22 *right* PH; 22 *left* PH; 23 *left* Jerry Harpur (Nick and Pam Coote); 23 *right* ALP; 23 *centre* HSC; 24–5 GPL (Sunniva Harte); 24–5 CNP (Red Gables, Worcs); 26 CNP; 27 *top* GPL (Sunniva Harte); 34 *left* Hugh Palmer (RHS Wisley); 34 *right* PH; 35 *left* John Glover; 35 *centre* ALP; 35 *right* PH; 36 *left* PH; 36 *right* PH; 36 *centre* HSC; 37 *centre* Eric Crichton; 37 *right* GPL (Cambridge Botanic Garden); 37 *left* ALP; 38 *right* Eric Crichton; 38 *centre* John Fielding; 38 *left* John Glover; 39 *left* Eric Crichton; 39 *centre* GPL (J S Sira); 39 *right* Hugh Palmer (RHS Wisley); 40 *centre* GPL (J S Sira); 40 *right* PH; 40 *left* PH; 41 *right* John Glover; 41 *left* HSC; 41 *centre* HSC; 42 *left* Eric Crichton; 42 *centre* PH; 42 *right* PH; 43 *left* GPL (J S Sira); 43 *centre* ALP; 43 *right* PH; 44 *right* Eric Crichton; 44 *left* ALP; 44 *centre* HSC; 45 *right* Eric Crichton; 45 *centre* John Fielding; 45 *left* GPL (Neil Holmes); 46–7 GPL (Jerry Pavia); 48 Eric Crichton; 49 GPL (J S Sira); 52 *left* Eric Crichton; 52 *right* John Glover; 53 *centre* Eric Crichton; 53 *right* John Fielding; 53 *left* PH; 54–5 CNP (Mrs Frank's garden, Steeple Aston, Oxon); 56 Eric Crichton; 57 PH; 64 *right* John Fielding; 64 *left* HSC; 65 *left* GPL; 65 *centre* GPL (J S Sira); 65 *right* ALP; 66 *centre* John Fielding; 66 *right* PH; 66 *left* HSC; 67 *left* John Glover; 67 *centre* CNP (Beth Chatto Gardens, Essex); 67 *right* HSC; 68 *centre* GPL (Philippe Bonduel); 68 *right* GPL (Philippe Bonduel); 68 *left* PH; 69 *right* GPL (John Glover); 69 *left* PH; 69 *centre* PH; 70 *centre* GPL (John Glover); 70 *right* ALP; 70 *left* HSC; 71 *centre* ALP; 71 *left* CNP; 71 *right* PH; 72–3 ALP; 74 Jerry Harpur; 75 PH; 80 *left* GPL (Roger Hyam); 80 *right* HSC; 81 *right* CNP (Coates Manor Garden, Sussex); 81 *left* PH; 81 Centre PH; 82 *left* PH; 82 *centre* HSC; 82 *right* HSC; 83 *centre* John Glover; 83 *left* PH; 83 *right* PH; 84 *centre* John Fielding; 84 *right* GPL (Juliette Wade); 84 *left* PH; 85 *centre* John Fielding; 85 *right* PH; 85 *left* HSC; 86–7 GPL (Ron Evans); 88 Eric Crichton; 89 HSC; 94 *left* PH; 94 *right* HSC; 95 *left* Eric Crichton; 95 *centre* GPL (Brian Carter); 95 *right* GPL (Jerry Pavia); 96 *centre* John Glover (RHS Wisley); 96 *left* HSC; 96 *right* HSC; 97 *centre* GPL (Brian Carter); 97 *left* CNP; 97 *right* PH; 98 *centre* PH; 98 *right* PH; 98 *left* PH; 99 *left* John Glover; 99 *right* HSC; 99 *centre* HSC; 100–1 GPL (Steven Wooster); 102 PH (Jane Sterndale-Bennett); 103 GPL (Howard Rice); 114 *right* John Glover; 114 *left* HSC; 115 *centre* John Glover; 115 *left* HSC; 115 *right* HSC; 116 *left* John Fielding; 116 *right* CNP; 116 *centre* HSC; 117 *left* John Fielding; 117 *right* John Glover; 117 *centre* PH; 118 *centre* GPL (Clive Nicholls); 118 *right* PH; 118 *left* PH; 119 *centre* CNP; 119 *right* PH; 119 *left* PH; 120 *right* Eric Crichton; 120 *centre* PH; 120 *left* PH; 121 *centre* ALP; 121 *left* CNP; 121 *right* PH; 122 *left* John Fielding; 122 *right* John Fielding; 122 *centre* PH; 123 *centre* John Fielding; 123 *right* HSC; 123 *left* HSC; 124 *right* Eric Crichton; 124 *centre* GPL (Jerry Pavia); 124 *left* GPL (Jerry Pavia); 125 *left* GPL (David Askham); 125 *right* PH; 125 *centre* PH; 126 *right* ALP; 126 *left* PH; 126 *centre* PH; 127 *centre* John Glover; 127 *right* PH; 127 *left* HSC; 128–9 John Fielding; 130 GPL (John Ferro Sims); 131 GPL (Steven Wooster); 138 bottom *left* GPL (Bob Challinor); 138 bottom *centre* PH; 139 top *centre* PH; 139 top *right* PH; 139 top *left* PH; 140 *centre* GPL (Brian Carter); 140 *right* John Glover; 140 *left* HSC; 141 *right* John Fielding; 141 *centre* GPL (Densey Clyne); 141 *left* GPL (John Glover); 142 *left* John Fielding; 142 *centre* GPL (John Glover); 142 *right* ALP; 143 *centre* Eric Crichton; 143 *right* GPL (Brian Carter); 143 *left* PH; 144 *right* ALP; 144 *left* PH; 144 *centre* HSC; 145 *centre* John Fielding; 145 *right* John Glover; 145 *left* ALP; 146–7 Jerry Harpur (Mirabel Osler); 148 Neil Campbell-Sharp; 149 GPL (John Glover); 152 *centre* Eric Crichton; 152 *left* GPL (Ron Sutherland); 153 *centre* GPL (Densey Clyne); 153 *right* Hugh Palmer (RHS Wisley); 153 *right* PH; 154 *right* Eric Crichton; 154 *left* GPL (Howard Rice); 154 *centre* GPL (J S Sira); 155 *right* GPL (J S Sira); 155 *centre* ALP; 155 *left* HSC; 156 *centre* Eric Crichton; 156 *right* PH; 156 *right* HSC; 157 *right* PH; 157 *centre* PH; 157 *left* PH; 158–159 ALP; 160 John Glover; 161 GPL (Lynne Brotchie); 166 *centre* GPL (Bob Challinor); 166 *left* CNP (Cerney House Garden, Glos); 167 *centre* John Fielding; 167 *left* PH; 167 *right* PH; 168 *right* John Glover; 168 *left* Jerry Harpur; 168 *centre* PH; 169 *left* ALP; 169 *centre* CNP; 169 *right* PH; 170 *centre* GPL (John Miller); 170 *left* GPL (John Neubauer); 170 *right* PH; 171 *right* John Glover; 171 *left* Jerry Harpur; 171 *centre* PH; 174–5 MaP (Arnaud Descat); 186 *left* GPL (David Russell); 186 *centre* GPL (Michel Viard); 187 *right* PH; 187 *left* PH; 187 *centre* PH; 188 *right* GPL (Philippe Bonduel); 188 *centre* GPL (Neil Holmes); 188 *left* PH; 189 *centre* ALP; 189 *left* ALP; 189 *right* PH; 190 *centre* GPL (Neil Holmes); 190 *left* PH; 191 *right* GPL (Michael Howes); 191 *left* ALP; 191 *centre* PH; 194–5 GPL (Mayer/Le Scanff); 196 GPL (Ron Sutherland); 197 GPL (John Miller); 202 *centre* John Fielding; 202 *left* HSC; 203 *left* John Fielding; 203 *centre* John Fielding; 203 *right* John Fielding; 204 *centre* HSC; 204 *right* HSC; 204 *left* HSC; 205 *left* John Fielding; 205 *right* John Glover; 205 *centre* PH; 206 *right* John Fielding; 206 *left* HSC; 206 *centre* HSC; 207 *left* CNP; 207 *right* PH; 207 *centre* PH; 208 *left* John Fielding; 208 *right* PH; 208 *centre* HSC; 209 *left* GPL (John Glover); 209 *centre* John Glover; 209 *right* PH; 210 *centre* John Fielding; 210 *right* PH; 210 *left* PH; 211 *left* Eric Crichton; 211 *right* PH; 211 *centre* HSC.

The publishers would also like to thank the following individuals: David Ashby; Peter Barnes; Caroline Bingham; Joanna Chisholm; Richard Dawes; Andrew Halstead; Andrew Jackson; Jodie Jones; Nicholas Morgan; Maggie O'Hanlon; Jane Royston; Sheila Seacroft; Jo Weeks; Sarah Widdicombe.

CL825356